Hellenic and Christian
Studies

Professor A. H. Armstrong

A. H. Armstrong

Hellenic and Christian
Studies

VARIORUM

British Library CIP Data

Armstrong A. H. (Arthur Hilary)
Hellenic and Christian Studies
(Collected Studies Series 324)
1. Greek philosophy, ancient period.
2. Christianity.
Influence of Greek philosophy, ancient
period
I. Title. II. Series
180

ISBN 0-86078-273-5

Copyright © 1990 by

Variorum

Published by

Variorum
Gower Publishing Group
Gower House, Croft Road, Aldershot
Hampshire GU11 3HR
Great Britain

Gower Publishing Company
Old Post Road
Brookfield
Vermont 05036
USA

Printed in Great Britain by

Galliard (Printers) Ltd
Great Yarmouth, Norfolk

COLLECTED STUDIES 324

CONTENTS

Introduction

I   Some Advantages of Polytheism   181–188

Dionysius V.
Halifax, Nova Scotia, 1981

II   Iamblichus and Egypt   179–188

Les Etudes Philosophiques 2–3/1987.
Paris, 1987

III   The Negative Theology of *Nous*
in Later Neoplatonism   31–37

Platonismus und Christentum: Festschrift
für Heinrich Dörrie, ed. H.-D. Blume &
F. Mann (Jahrbuch für Antike und Christentum,
Ergänzungsband 10. Münster/Westfalen:
Aschendorffsche Verlagsbuchhandlung, 1983

IV   The Divine Enhancement of Earthly Beauties:
The Hellenic and Platonic Tradition   49–81

Eranos 53: Lectures given at the Eranos
Conference in Ascona, 22–30 August 1984.
Frankfurt am Main: Insel Verlag, 1986

V   The Hidden and the Open in Hellenic Thought   81–117

Eranos 54: Lectures given at the Eranos
Conference in Ascona, 21–29 August 1985.
Frankfurt am Main: Insel Verlag, 1987

VI   Platonic Mirrors   147–181

Eranos 55: Lectures given at the Eranos
Conference in Ascona, 20–28 August 1986.
Frankfurt am Main: Insel Verlag, 1988

VII Negative Theology, Myth and Incarnation   47–62

Néoplatonisme: Mélanges offerts à
Jean Trouillard (Cahiers de Fontenay 19/22).
Fontenay-aux-Roses, 1981

VIII The Self-Definition of Christianity   74–99
in Relation to Later Platonism   228–234

Jewish and Christian Self-Definition, I:
The Shaping of Christianity in the Second
and Third Centuries, ed. E.P. Sanders.
London: SCM Press, 1980

IX Pagan and Christian Traditionalism
in the First Three Centuries A.D.   414–431

Studia Patristica XV: Papers presented to
the Seventh International Conference on
Patristic Studies, Oxford 1975, part I,
ed. Elizabeth A. Livingstone (Texte und Unter-
suchungen, Bb 128).
Berlin: Akademie-Verlag, 1984

X Philosophy, Theology and Interpretation:
The Interpretation of Interpreters   7–14

Eriugena, Studien zu seinen Quellen:
Vorträge des III. Internationalen
Eriugena-Colloquiums, Freiburg im Breisgau,
27–30 August 1979, ed. W. Beierwaltes.
Heidelberg: Carl Winter — Universitäts-
verlag, 1980

XI Two Views of Freedom: A Christian Objection in
Plotinus, *Enneads* VI 8. [39]7, 11-15?   397–406

Studia Patristica XVII: Papers presented
to the Eighth International Conference
on Patristic Studies, Oxford 1979,
ed. Elizabeth A. Livingstone, part 1.
Oxford & New York: Pergamon Press, 1982

XII Dualism, Platonic, Gnostic and Christian   29–52

Plotinus amid Gnostics and Christians:
Papers presented to the Plotinus Symposium,
Free University, Amsterdam, 25 January 1984.
Amsterdam: Free University Press, 1984

XIII   The Way and the Ways: Religious Tolerance and
       Intolerance in the Fourth Century A.D.   1–17

       Vigiliae Christianae 38.
       Leiden, 1984

XIV   Itineraries in Late Antiquity   105–131

       Eranos 56: Lectures given at the Eranos
       Conference in Ascona, 19–27 August 1987.
       Frankfurt am Main: Insel Verlag, 1989

XV   On Not Knowing too Much About God   129–145

       Philosophy, supplement 25: Philosophy
       in Christianity.
       Cambridge, 1989

Index   1–7

This volume contains xii + 317 pages.

PUBLISHER'S NOTE

The articles in this volume, as in all others in the Collected Studies Series, have not been given a new, continuous pagination. In order to avoid confusion, and to facilitate their use where these same studies have been referred to elsewhere, the original pagination has been maintained wherever possible.

Each article has been given a Roman number in order of appearance, as listed in the Contents. This number is repeated on each page and quoted in the index entries.

INTRODUCTION

An aged man is but a paltry thing,
A tattered coat upon a stick, unless
Soul clap its hands and sing, and louder sing
For every tatter in its mortal dress.
(W.B. Yeats, Sailing to Byzantium)

My first volume of collected papers (*Plotinian and Christian Studies*, Variorum 1979) contained all the papers which I thought worth preserving in this form published between 1936 and my seventieth birthday in 1979. The present volume contains papers published, and for the most part written, between 1979 and my eightieth birthday in 1989. The slight change of title to *Hellenic and Christian Studies* is intended to indicate two things. One is that though my main concern and interest has continued to be Plotinus, I have become more and more interested in setting him in his world, not only the world of later Greek philosophy, our understanding of which has been so greatly increased by the work of many scholars in the last decade, but the whole world of Hellenic culture, centred on the ancient cults and ways of thinking about the divine, which already in the time of Plotinus, Platonic philosophers were beginning to think it was their duty to defend against the growing attack of Christianity. The other is that I have become more and more interested in the great debate and struggle between Hellenism and Christianity itself, many of the consequences of which I see as continuing into our own time and having a good deal of relevance to contemporary debates and struggles. "Hellene" (and its derivatives) should be taken, both in the title and in the papers themselves, in the sense in which it was understood by both sides in the great debate itself, as meaning some one who holds to the old ways of worshipping and thinking about the Divine, in more or less conscious opposition to Christianity.

A volume containing papers for the most part written within ten years will obviously need less in the way of introductory explanation than a volume of papers published over forty years. The papers are arranged in two groups, the first concerned exclusively or predominantly with Hellenism, the second with Hellenism and Christianity: there is inevitably a good deal of overlapping between the groups in the subject-matter of particular papers. The order within the groups is generally chronological, but not strictly so: papers on related themes are placed together. My understanding of

Plotinus has not changed fundamentally from that expressed in the last nine
papers of the previous volume (XVI onwards). But it may be worth drawing
attention to a certain one-sidedness in that understanding of which I have
become more conscious myself lately: this appears clearly in this volume
in "Platonic Mirrors" (VI). It may be described as a fascination with the
"elements in the thought of Plotinus at variance with classical
intellectualism" (the title of *Plotinian and Christian Studies* XVI). E.R.
Dodds, in whose honour this paper was written, remarked to me when
he read it that he thought that this aspect of Plotinus was really there, but
was peripheral. With this judgement, from the point of view of a sober
historian of religious philosophy, I do not disagree and have never disagreed.
But in some times and circumstances what is peripheral may become
centrally important, and I am inclined to think, as I have indicated in
"Platonic Mirrors" that at the present time those wild characteristics of
the thought of Plotinus in which I am interested, and which have been noted
with disapproval by a number of serious and superior persons from
Iamblichus to conservative Christians in my own time, may help quite a
number of people who find traditional systematic metaphysics and theology
meaningless, incredible, or downright repulsive, to recover the awareness
of spiritual and eternal reality present in but transcending the world of our
ordinary experience which they so badly need. At least they can, and I
think should, test the truth of this by reading Plotinus, which I have spent
most of my serious working life trying to make it easier for them to do
(the last two volumes of the Loeb Plotinus, containing my translation of
the *Enneads*, were published in 1988).

As the four papers delivered at the Eranos conferences at Ascona from
1984 to 1987 occupy a large part of this volume it may be as well, for
the benefit of those who have not had the privilege of attending these
meetings, to say something about them. At Eranos one is addressing a highly
intelligent but non-specialist audience on the theme prescribed for the year
from the point of view of one's own discipline and special field of interest,
in company with colleagues from many parts of the world, each of whom
represents a different area of science or scholarship. This in itself tends
to produce a certain freedom and expansiveness. But there is something
a good deal more about the experience of Eranos than this, something hard
to describe which goes back to its foundation, under the inspiration of Otto
and Jung, by Olga Froebe-Kapteyn, and has been maintained and developed
by Rudolph and Catherine Ritsema. There seems to be a presence there
of gods too real for theology which generates a sort of freedom and
seriousness (not necessarily solemnity) not far from the spirit of Plotinus
as I understand him, and tends to make an Eranos lecture rather different
from a normal scholarly paper.

The first paper in this section on Hellenism and Christianity, "Negative

Theology, Myth and Incarnation" (VII) contains one paragraph (pp.53–54) which seems to me now rather dated, and might, taken by itself, give too negative an impression of my attitude to the Christian religion and my expectations for its future. It certainly makes too sharp and exclusive distinctions between history and myth and between Hellenic and Biblical elements in our Inherited Conglomerate. My views have since developed on lines better suggested by the next paragraph (pp.54–55) and, for those who have read the book referred to and other works by the same author, by the *Additional Note*. Meijering has been a great help to me in enabling me to accept some contemporary liberal forms of Christianity as authentic and viable to a greater extent than I was quite yet prepared to do when I wrote the paper. These, in so far as I find them acceptable, are of course a development of the liberal Christianity which I encountered at Cambridge in the late 1920's, which for me was exemplified by that great, though now forgotten, Christian Platonist Alexander Nairne, a former Regius Professor of Divinity who was in my time a Fellow of my college. A liberal Christian Platonism, including much which I learnt from my father, a more conservative clergyman whose favourite theologian was Bishop Gore, was in fact my true personal tradition or *paradosis*, what was handed down to me. But in what I now regard as immature and exaggerated reaction against both its defects and its virtues I abandoned it for a more conservative form of Christianity, and have only recently fully and consciously returned to it. Consequently, when I wrote "Negative Theology, Myth and Incarnation", I wrote it as a deeply dissident Roman Catholic, with something of the bitterness and exaggeration usual in that unhappy religious condition. I write this introduction as a worshipping member of the church of my baptism and confirmation, the Church of England, generally strongly on the liberal side in its contemporary debates, though not perhaps an extremist by contemporary theological standards: at least I still have what Louis XVI regarded as the minimum necessary qualification for appointment as Archbishop of Paris. I believe in God. This personal change of attitude may not be clearly apparent in the later papers included in this volume, as they are concerned not with modern developments but with the Christianity of the Fathers, that is, of the Roman Empire in the century or so before and the century or two after the conversion of Constantine; and in the conflicts and controversies of that period, whose outcome determined our future religious direction, my sympathies are fairly obviously on the Hellenic side. It is more apparent in "Plotinus and Christianity", a paper to be published in a belated *Festschrift* in honour of Edouard des Places, and perhaps here and there in a small work recently published separately "Expectations of Immortality in Late Antiquity" (Aquinas Lecture 51, Marquette University Press, Milwaukee 1987). When I permit myself to consider some modern Christians and their presentation of the teaching of Christ my tone becomes kinder and my judgments more positive than when I am concentrating my attention on the great bishops of the Empire and their flocks.

My obligations to other scholars and thinkers continue to be many. It is encouraging for the future of our studies that so many of those to whom I feel a strong gratitude are younger, often considerably younger, people. The quotations and references in V, VI and XIV indicate two, John Kenney and Peter Manchester, to whom I feel myself particularly indebted, but there are others, notably Kevin Corrigan, whose recent work on Plotinus is outstanding. One contact which has meant a great deal to me is indicated by the reference in the *Concluding Note* of the Introduction to *Plotinian and Christian Studies* to the joint article by Dr Ravindra and myself "Buddhi in the Bhagavad-Gita and Psyche in Plotinus" (*Religious Studies* 15, September 1979, pp.327–342: reprinted in *Neoplatonism and Indian Thought* ed. R. Baine Harris, International Society for Neoplatonic Studies, Norfolk, Virginia, 1982, pp. 63–86). My conversations with Ravi Ravindra have greatly enlarged my mind and given me some understanding of Indian religious thought and its close kinship and resemblances, in some important ways, to Neoplatonic thought and to Hellenic religious thought in general (though I remain somewhat sceptical about actual historical influences of one on the other). This is apparent in several places in the *Eranos* papers: it came naturally to mind at Ascona.

The permission of the original publishers of these papers to reproduce them is gratefully acknowledged. I am most grateful to my daughter Teresa for her work in compiling the Index, and to the typists, Denise Matthews and Sandra Bargh who, especially since my retirement from Dalhousie University in 1982, have done so much to help me get the papers into print.

A.H. ARMSTRONG

Ludlow, Shropshire
March 1990

I

Some Advantages of Polytheism

All (or nearly all) of us in our post-Christian civilisation are inclined to be rather complacent and unreflective about monotheism.[1] This is true of both those of Protestant and strictly Biblical tendency and those of Catholic tendency, and both of believers and unbelievers. Even those who think that the question "God or no God?" has been settled decisively in favour of the latter alternative, or that it has no practical importance and is unprofitable to discuss, are generally disposed to think that the question "God or the gods?" was settled long ago in favour of the monotheist supposition, and, even today, many of us are still inclined to think of it as an "either-or" question. Either you worship one God or you worship a lot of idols. (The way in which Catholics and Orthodox still talk about the idolatry of the heathen is sometimes quite embarrassing to a historically minded person of Catholic tendency.)

This sort of monotheist complacency is becoming more and more difficult to maintain as we become more and more vividly aware of other religious traditions than the Judaeo-Christian-Islamic, notably that of India. But there is enough of it around still to be worth disturbing, and I propose here to attempt to disturb it. I shall do so by considering one or two points about the most powerful polytheism within our own tradition, the Hellenic, which has influenced that tradition in many important ways. The Greeks in the end found it perfectly possible to combine this with monotheism, to believe in God without ceasing to believe in the gods. If I am to be taken as recommending anything in this essay, it is something like this that I am recommending, not a futile nostalgia for temples, idols and sacrifices. I have sometimes been sufficiently irritated by the way Christians talk about Greek heathenism to think about setting up in my garden a statue of Priapus or of Diana of the Ephesians (you can still buy quite good ones of her at Ephesus). But I have never actually done so. I shall begin with a look at pre-philosophical Greek polytheism, of the sort which we can know and understand best from the Greek

---

1. William James was a notable exception. See the conclusion of his *Postscript* to *The Varieties of Religious Experience* (pp. 499-500 in the Fontana edition). His argument in *A Pluralistic Universe* leaves room for polytheism as a serious possibility, as he himself clearly recognizes (p. 140 of the Harvard edition).

Dionysius, Vol. V, Dec. 1981, pp. 181-188

poets: though when we read them we should always remember what we are so often truly told, that this was a religion of worship, not of belief. Cult was primary, myth was secondary, and one could interpret cult and myth as one pleased. Plato and other philosophers criticised the poets' stories severely, and we have been inclined to repeat their criticisms rather uncritically, and without noticing how much the philosophers took over from the old religion, and how they simply assumed that polytheistic cult would continue to provide the religious environment of the ordinary man, as it did down to the end of antiquity, and beyond, in more or less Christianized forms. But for some time now classical scholars have been pointing out forcibly that, despite the philosophers' criticism, there was a great deal in the old poetic religion worth seriously considering. So let us take a brief look at it.

It was a religion which recognised many divine powers in one divine universe. The unity of the divine is often very much in the background, but it is always there. The universe is something given, for gods as well as men, not the product of a divine creation. The old stories of its beginnings are stories of birth, not making. The actions of the many powers within the one universe are various and often unexpected. They can clash and conflict and do not appear to serve any great obvious overriding purpose. The powers do not seem necessarily friendly to man, though people often felt that, especially, their local gods and the gods of their personal devotion were kindly disposed towards them, and one could love as well as fear the gods. Any moral concerns which the gods may have appear at best spasmodically and are not always of a sort very comfortable to man: they visit the sins of the fathers on the children in strange and terrible ways, and they punish more certainly than they reward. The world of the old gods is a hard and dangerous world apprehended unflinchingly by their worshippers in all its hardness and danger. But it is not a bad world and the gods are not evil, but beautiful and delightful to contemplate, as well as terrible. The ancient Greeks were not a gloomy people, oppressed by religious fear and depression. Nor in their hard world were they often quite as hard and cruel to each other as Mediaeval and Reformation Christians. Perhaps they were kept from gloomy and cruel fanaticism by the way they instinctively understood the time of their divine world. Under all the changes and chances of divinity lies the rhythm which is the expression of the unity of the divine cosmos, the rhythm of the seasons, of day and night, of birth and death. Those who have this rhythm in them as the Greeks had it are not optimists or pessimists: they can always look at things either way up. How sad that winter follows

Fall! But how wonderful that spring follows winter! How sad that I
must die! But how happy that my grandchildren have been born!
The city is destroyed and the fruit-trees cut down. How terrible!
But new cities will be built and new trees planted, of course to be
destroyed in their turn; and so it will go on.

The philosophers, from Plato onwards, with some important
exceptions, wanted to see in the world a more unified order and a
more explicitly good divine purpose. This led them into a good
deal of rather unconvincing and decidedly anthropocentric
teleological explanation, which took its most exaggerated forms in
the thought of the Stoics. Aristotle does not seem to have gone this
way. His universe has the unity of a great machine, with all
biological processes dependent on the movements of the heavenly
spheres. But the teleology in which he and his successor
Theophrastus seem to have been interested was the kind of limited
teleology modern biologists admit, the appearance of purpose-
built design within a particular species tending to the ends of that
species. And it is interesting for our present purposes to note that
the Epicureans, whose conviction of the meaninglessness of reality
has been so attractive to many moderns, were the most explicit and
conscious polytheists of antiquity. There is no one divinity behind
the many gods in whom they firmly believed: and the idea of
divine purpose is for them a terrifying delusion. But even the
mainstream Stoics and Platonists who insist most strongly on the
unity of the divine and the one good divine purpose make room for
divine plurality in the unity. They did not repudiate the gods for
the sake of God (as early Christian writers noted frequently and
indignantly). The explication of divine intelligence which they see
as the order of this world is a harmony of clash and conflict, an
endless tension between warring opposites. And the world-order
moves with the old seasonal, alternating rhythm, the rhythm of a
dance rather than a march to a goal. The greatest of ancient
theodicies, the treatise of Plotinus *On Providence*[2] remains
surprisingly close in its vision of the world to the spirit of the great
tragedians. Plotinus is by no means anthropocentric in his outlook.
He displays the beauty and terror of our world magnificently. And,
though he considers carefully several solutions to the problem of
evil, he seems in the end by no means convinced that he has solved
it.

What are we to make of this ancient Hellenic religious view of
the world now-a-days? We must begin, if we are honest, by
admitting its extraordinary clear-sightedness. It is a vision of the

---

2. III 2-3,[47-48].

world which is true to our day-to-day experience of it, and at least less difficult to reconcile with the discoveries of modern science about it than a simple-minded monotheism. Even if we retain any sense of a divine presence in the world, we have to admit that it manifests itself in innumerably various, apparently clashing and conflicting, often inscrutably odd and horrifying ways. Divine unity, not divine plurality, requires an effort of reflection and faith to attain it; and, when attained, it does not necessarily exclude plurality. As for whether we can or should have a sense of divine presence in the world, I cannot argue convincingly against those who say we cannot and should not: perhaps nobody has ever been able to. I can only say that awareness of God in the natural world is the heart and foundation of any religion I have, and that more and more people, including many who are not in any way formally religious, seem to be coming to the same awareness (there have always been a good many): it is to them that I am speaking: everybody cannot speak acceptably and understandably to everybody. Those of us who have this awareness should recognise that the old polytheisms, and, for most of us, especially the Hellenic, can convey the sense of the universal divine presence and the holiness of the world with incomparable poetic force. As Plotinus says, expanding what Sophocles said about his beloved native village, Colonus, to apply to the whole universe: —

"All the place is holy, and there is nothing which is without a share of soul."[3]

And this recognition may bring with it a content with the Hellenic awareness of the movement of the universe as rhythmic, as a dance, which is so close to what seems to be the basic time — experience of all living things, that of the alternation of light and dark: and a discontent with and disbelief in the alternative linear understanding of it as the march of one purpose irresistibly onward to a glorious or horrifying future, which, if it could in any way be demonstrated, would perhaps provide some support for intransigent Judaeo-Christian monotheism and the anthropocentrism which usually accompanies it: though it seems to survive and flourish very well in completely secularized forms. Some of us are beginning to see this as not only probably false but dangerous, in so far as it invites us to sacrifice not only our own past and present, but that of our planet, to an increasingly dubious future. Nobody

---

3. Sophocles, *Oedipus at Colonus* 54cp. 16. Plotinus *On What Are and Whence Come Evils*, I 8 [51] 14, 36-37: my translation from the Loeb *Plotinus*, Vol. I, p. 313.

I

has shown this danger better than Hans Jonas in his great work of moral philosophy *Das Prinzip Verantwortung*[4]. The austere argument of this book does not start from or require any metaphysical or religious presuppositions: and it is concerned with secular, not religious versions of eschatological hope, particularly, though not exclusively, with E. Bloch's *Das Prinzip Hoffnung*. But, perhaps for these very reasons, it provides an excellent foundation for a critique of theologies of hope.

In developing the theme which has begun to appear of the importance of a polytheistic element in religion for personal piety, I shall start from the other end of the Hellenic religious tradition, with a look at the polytheistic element in the monotheism of the great Neoplatonists. This took two successive forms. The first is to be found in the great third-century Neoplatonist, Plotinus, and his pupils. Plotinus sees the multiplicity of the gods appearing in the eternal outgoing of divine life into multiplicity from the One, the self-diffusion of the Good first into Divine Intellect and then into universal Soul. The following passages give a very clear idea of how he interpreted traditional polytheism, and the last, from his treatise *Against the Gnostics*, shows how vigorously he was prepared to maintain it against an intransigent and exclusive monotheism. He says of *Nous*, the Divine Intellect "For he encompasses in himself all things immortal, every intellect, every god, every soul ..."[5] and he prays "May he come, bringing his own universe with him, with all the gods within him, he who is one and all, and each god is all the gods coming together into one: they are different in their powers, but by that one manifold power they are all one: or rather the one god is all: for he does not fail if all become what he is ..."[6] And in his great challenge to the other kind of monotheism he says:

> "It is not contracting the divine into one but showing it in that multiplicity in which God himself has shown it which is proper to those who know the power of God, inasmuch as, abiding who he is, he makes many gods, all depending upon himself and existing through him and from him."[7]

The later Neoplatonists who maintained an intellectual opposition to Christianity from the age of Constantine to the age of

---

4. Frankfurt, Insel Verlag, 1979.
5. *On the Three Primary Hypostases*, V1 [10], 4, 10-11.
6. *On the Intelligible Beauty*, V8 [31] 9, 14-19.
7. *Against the Gnostics*, II 9 [33] 9, 37-39: all translations from Plotinus are my own.

I

Justinian were not satisfied with Plotinus' placing of the gods. No doubt with some anti-Christian intent, they wanted to place the many gods whom they devoutly worshipped (not only the gods of the Hellenes, but the gods of all mankind as far as they knew them) more nearly on the level of God, the First Principle, the One or Good Himself. So there evolved in the fifth-century Platonic school of Athens the remarkable doctrine of the Henads. As our concern here is with the religious driving-force behind the evolution of the doctrine rather than with the details of late Neoplatonic theology, I shall not illustrate or discuss the appalling complexities of the doctrine as it appears in the voluminous works of the great fifth century Athenian philosopher Proclus. I shall quote a simple statement of it from the sixth century commentator Simplicius, and add the most penetrating comment I know on its importance for the personal piety of these last Hellenes. Simplicius in his commentary on the Enchiridion of Epictetus says, "The Good is source and principle of all beings. For that which all things desire, and to which all things reach up, this is the principle and the goal of all things. And the Good brings forth all things from himself, the first and the middle and the last. But the first, the beings close to himself, he brings forth like himself: one goodness, he brings forth many goodnesses: and one Simplicity, and the Henad (or Unity) above all henads, he brings forth many henads: and one principle, many principles."[8] My comment comes from A. J. Festugière, one of the great French Catholic scholars who have done so much to increase our understanding of these last anti-Christian thinkers of antiquity. He says, speaking of the religion of Proclus: "The same religious soul who aspires to this Unknown God aspires also to a more immediate contact with more accessible, less separate forms of the Divine. From this comes the tender devotion of many Christian mystics to the Virgin. And I explain to myself in the same way, in the case of Proclus, his tender devotion to Athena. There is nothing there, I repeat, which surprises me: or rather, this piety seems natural to me, as the necessary complement of intellective contemplation."[9] Perhaps in his last words Festugière suggests an inappropriately sharp disjunction between affective piety and intellectual contemplation.

---

8. *Commentarius in Epicteti Enchiridion*, p. 5, 4-11 Dubner: my own translation.
9. "Proclus et la réligion traditionelle" in *Mélanges Piganiol* Paris 1966. rp. in *Études de Philosophie grecque*, Paris 1971, pp. 575-584: Quoted in the introduction to Proclus *Théologie Platonicienne* III ed. Saffrey-Westerink, Paris 1970, p. LXXII: my own translation from the French.

There is plenty of hard dry thinking in the theology of the henads, and a deep and passionate affective piety drives on the search for the Unknowable One. But on the whole this seems very just, and an excellent example of the right way to talk about other peoples' religion. These last Hellenes wanted to find the divine presences that they and their ancestors and all mankind had known and loved in their cities and villages, their trees and springs and rivers and mountains, all together yet still distinct with the One, to meet the Unknowable in the likeness of many familiar friends.

There are, perhaps, more people in our own time than in any age since the fourth century A.D. who can understand and respond to the message of this defence of polytheism by the last Hellenic monotheists. As one of them, I should like to end by reflecting on what it might say to us in our present circumstances. There is much in it, as Festugière recognised, which has survived in the simple piety of Catholic and Orthodox people, and much that can be grounded in a perfectly traditional theology of the universal activity of the Logos: and we should not let any of this go. But we may have to expand our belief in Divine plurality and make it less church-bounded and man-centred.[10] We need to understand that if we are to think of God as "having descended" (as we inadequately and inaccurately say) into history, as being present and somehow deeply involved in our contingent changes and chances and joys and pains, we must think of him as "descended" everywhere and at all times. This he can only be, while still being God, if unbounded plurality as well as unity is somehow grounded in his transcendent and eternal nature, which is beyond the opposition of one and many, as it is beyond all such dialectical oppositions and therefore unknowable. Our time has been one of enormous development in our critical understanding of history, of the problematic character of much historical evidence, of historical difference and distance, of the historical limitation and relativity of our own thoughts and beliefs. Many Christians, including some who talk glibly about "history", do not seem to have seen the real implications of this. But to those of us who have, it seems that if God "descended" once for all, in one particular time and place, into history, he would be limited by history and alienated from us by history, and his descent would become, not a ground of faith but an everlastingly disputed historical problem.

---

10. A most convincing and well documented account of how Catholic piety in the West moved away from the forms and spirit of the old religion to become church-bounded and man-centred is Peter Brown's *The Cult of The Saints* (Chicago and London 1981).

Another characteristic of our time, of course, has been the enormous increase in our knowledge of the universe and our power to damage it. We know now how little room man occupies in cosmic space and time, how comparatively insignificant the duration of our species has been even compared with the history of life on earth: and we know that Western man occupies a much more modest place in human history than we used to think. But we also know that we may now have power, in whatever remnant of our short span may be left to us, to do irreparable harm at least to our own small planet. This knowledge and this power seem to require a new degree of awareness of the holiness of all things, of divine presences quite outside man and his history, as well as of God's epiphanies in the gods of other men. We may perhaps be being called more urgently than ever before to a very difficult sort of humility, which, if we ever attained to a decent measure of it, might establish our unique spiritual greatness among the beings we know by our very capacity of denial of that unique greatness. This is the humility of putting ourselves out of the centre of the picture, of no longer supposing that all the lives of earth and all the galaxies and all God's purposes converge on our culture or our religion or our species or our future. This is difficult to do properly. It is easier to proclaim that we are nothings before God or miserable sinners before God, often in a way which enhances our own importance, than to accept quietly that in the divine sight we may be insignificant somethings in a very small corner of space and time.

I am not recommending a return to Hellenic polytheism, even of the late Platonic kind, in the manner of that great and good, but rather cranky, man, the Emperor Julian. That sort of archaizing and nostalgic attempt to return to the past, Christian or pagan, is always futile and unreal. But, if we find, as I have done, that the polytheists have a good deal to say to us which is relevant to the contemporary needs of which I have just been speaking; then we shall do well to keep their theology and their gods in our thoughts and in our prayers, in the way which seems appropriate to each of us. It is not by one path only that so great a mystery can be approached.

II

IAMBLICHUS AND EGYPT*

The imposing *persona* of the high-ranking Egyptian priest Abammon, adopted by Iamblichus,[1] justifies the title *Les Mystères d'Egypte* given to his work on theurgy. This *persona* was of course made appropriate for him by the fact that he was replying in the *De Mysteriis* to the critique of theurgy which Porphyry had addressed to the Egyptian priest Anebo.[2] But this title would otherwise be somewhat difficult to justify from the text. If the work had come down to us without the first chapter or any external indications of its "Egyptian" setting it is unlikely that modern editors would have adopted it. Consideration of distinctively Egyptian rites and teachings occupies only a small part of it, 18 pages out of 178 of the Budé text.[3] A great deal of the attention throughout is directed to the traditional observances of Hellenic public worship. This is particularly true of Book V, the most theologically important part of the work, which deals with sacrifice and prayer. And of the "Oriental" and esoteric elements in the content, the "Chaldaean" or "Assyrian" is more important than the Egyptian.[4] And of course if one turns one's attention to the principal theurgic scriptures, the *Chaldaean Oracles*[5] themselves one soon

* On trouvera une traduction française, due à Luc Brisson, de cet article dans le n° 4/1987 *(N.d.l.r.)*.
   1. The attribution to Iamblichus is now generally accepted. See the excellent summary discussion by E. des Places in his edition (Jamblique, *Les Mystères d'Egypte*, Paris, Les Belles-Lettres, 1966, Notice, pp. 5-8). I am much indebted throughout this article to this edition of the *De Mysteriis*. References to the text will be given in the form adopted by des Places, i.e. his own lines within Parthey's pages.
   2. On Porphyry's *Letter to Anebo* (ed. and tr. A. R. Sodano, Naples, 1964) see J. Bidez, *Vie de Porphyre* (Gand, 1913, repr. Hildesheim, Olms, 1964), chap. 8.
   3. Pp. 186-202 (VI 5-end of VIII, 245.11-272.15).
   4. In VI 7 (249.4-8) which deals with the ticklish question of menaces addressed to the gods, Chaldaean practice is explicitly preferred to Egyptian.
   5. What remains of these is now generally accessible in another admirable edition by E. des Places, *Oracles Chaldaïques, avec un choix de commentaires anciens*, Paris, Les Belles-Lettres 1971.

discovers that their theological content is mostly derived from popular Stoic-Platonic philosophy of the immediately pre-Neoplatonic period. The *De Mysteriis*, in fact, conforms to the normal pattern of Greek philosophical consideration of the wisdom of the East and of Egypt. This wisdom was generally highly respected. But Greek knowledge of the real content of the sacred writings and teachings of the great older civilizations whose superior knowledge of the divine they reverenced was for the most part minimal: and what they did know they interpreted very firmly in accordance with their own ways of thinking. The account of Egyptian religion given in the *De Mysteriis* illustrates this excellently. Iamblichus' principal exposition of Egyptian theology in Book VIII[6] is simply an exposition of his own distinctive form of Neoplatonism, which he easily discovers in a selection of Egyptian myths by the bold exegetical methods general in his period. In this article, therefore, I shall make no attempt to discover an authentically qnd distinctively Egyptian metaphysics or philosophical theology in the *De Mysteriis*, but shall concentrate on the philosophically interesting aspects of ancient theurgy, as expounded by Iamblichus, and of recent judgements of it.

A remarkable change in the attitude of many Neoplatonic scholars to theurgy has taken place in the last decade or so. Before the beginning of the 1970s it was generally dismissed with contempt and hostility as a phenomenon of intellectual and spiritual decadence. This was sometimes especially evident among those scholars (including myself) who by no means dismissed Neoplatonism as a whole and had come to honour, and even love, Plotinus as a true Hellenic philosopher, and one of the greatest. The general attitude was well summed up by that great Neoplatonic scholar E. R. Dodds, whose edition of the *Elements of Theology* of Proclus[7] (whom he disliked) will always remain one of the foundations of the scholarly study of later Neoplatonism. In the appendix "Theurgy" to his *Greeks and the Irrational* he writes : "As vulgar magic is commonly the last resort of the personally desperate, of those whom God and man have alike failed, so theurgy became the refuge of a despairing intelligentsia which had already felt *la fascination de l'abime*."[8] But from the early 1970s onwards clear evidence began to appear that the increasingly close and sympathetic study of the later Neoplatonists was producing some revision of this sweeping condemnation. A leader in this, as in all recent advances

6. VIII 1-3 (260.3-265.10). The rest of the book is occupied by a brief account of Hermetic astrology (which had some genuinely Egyptian elements) followed by an entirely Hellenic discussion of astrological fatalism.

7. *Proclus, The Elements of Theology*, a Revised Text with Translation, Introduction and Commentary by E. R. Dodds, Oxford, Clarendon Press, 2nd Edition 1963.

8. *The Greeks and the Irrational*, Berkeley, University of California Press, 1968, Appendix II, p. 288.

9. See especially the *Conclusion* : *La Theurgie* of his *L'Un et l'Ame selon Proclos*, Paris, Les Belles-Lettres, 1972.

in our understanding of Neoplatonism, was Jean Trouillard[9]. In English scholarship the first important sign of change is A. C. Lloyd's assessment of the theurgy of Iamblichus in the *Cambridge History of Later Greek and Early Mediaeval Philosophy*[10]. My own remarks on theurgy in a paper read at the congress held in Rome to celebrate the seventeen-hundredth anniversary of the death of Plotinus in 1970 were largely inspired by Lloyd's revaluation.[11] The first full scholarly consideration in English of theurgy which illustrates the revised point of view is that of A. Smith in the second part of his book on Porphyry.[12] This tendency to take a more favourable view of theurgy has, on the whole, continued among scholars working in this field, powerfully assisted by the later work of Trouillard;[13] and it has continued on more solid scholarly foundations because of the increasing availability of good critical editions of the writings of the later Neoplatonists, among which the Budé edition of the *Théologie Platonicienne* of Proclus by H. D. Saffrey and L. G. Westerink must take pride of place both because of the importance of the text and the outstanding excellence of the edition.[14]

The reasons for this change of attitude are worth considering. They can tell us something about our own recent intellectual and religious history. The most solid and important is one common to most fields of study: that a more careful reading of more easily accessible texts has shown us that our earlier judgements were ill founded. We have discovered that Iamblichus and his successors, when they are writing on theurgy, have a good deal more to offer us than dubious apologetic justifications for what remains in essence vulgar magic. They give strong and carefully worked out arguments for the importance of sacred rites and ceremonies and the use of material symbols in our approach to the Divine and the Divine's approach to us. And the principles upon which they base these arguments are by no means always non-Hellenic or altogether incompatible with the thought of Plotinus, or even of Plato. Once one understands what Iamblichus is trying to do, it becomes possible to see, for example, that a justification for ritual religion (the necessity of which for the great mass of mankind Plato always maintained) not dissimilar to that in the *De Mysteriis* could be developed from the following two texts in the *Laws*, legitimately and with full regard to their context,

10. A. C. Lloyd, Theory and Practice according to Porphyry and Iamblichus, Chapter 18C, Part IV of *The Cambridge History of Later Greek and Early Mediaeval Philosophy*, Ed. A. H. Armstrong, Cambridge, University Press, 1970, pp. 295-7.

11. A. H. Armstrong, Tradition, Reason and Experience in the Thought of Plotinus, in *Plotino e il Neoplatonismo in Oriente e in Occidente*, Roma, Accademia dei Lincei, 1974, pp. 185-7 = *Plotinian and Christian Studies*, London, Variorum, 1979, XVII.

12. A. Smith, *Porphyry's Place in the Neoplatonic Tradition*, The Hague, Nijhoff, 1974.

13. Notably his Mystagogie de Proclos, Paris, Les Belles-Lettres, 1982.

14. Proclus, *Théologie platonicienne*, texte établi et traduit par H. D. Saffrey and L. G. Westerink, Paris, Les Belles-Lettres, 1968 sq. Four volumes have been published and the edition will be completed within the next few years.

in both cases the regulation of that sacred music and dance which is our highest duty and supreme solace:

ATH. Why, I mean we should keep our seriousness for serious things, and not waste it on trifles, and that, while God is the real goal of all beneficient serious endeavour, man, as we said before, has been constructed as a toy for God, and this the finest thing about him.... MEG. I must say, sir you have but a poor estimate of our race. ATH. Do not be amazed by that, Megillus; bear with me. I had God before my mind's eye, and felt myself to be what I have just said. However, if you will have it so, man shall be something not so insignificant but more serious (VII 803C 1–5: 804 B5–C1).

But the gods, in their compassion for the hardships incident to our human lot, have appointed the cycle of their festivals to provide relief from this fatigue, besides giving us the Muses, their leader Apollo, and Dionysus to share these festivals with us and keep them right, with all the spiritual sustenance these deities bring to the feast (II 653 D, 1–7: tr. A.E. Taylor)

As regards the relationship of Iamblichean theurgy to the Platonism of Plotinus, I have remarked elsewhere[15] that it would be possible to develop a theory of theurgy from one side of the thought of Plotinus, starting from statements about the union with the One which is beyond rational knowledge (e.g.: VI 9 [11]4) or the great chapter (V 5 [32]12) in which Plotinus sets that perpetual presence of the Good to us which is quite independent of our awareness of it against the troubling incursions of Intelligible Beauty into our consciousness:

But the Good, since it was there long before to arouse an innate desire, is present even to those asleep and does not astonish those who at any time see it, because it is always there and there is never recollection of it; but people do not see it, because it is present to them in their sleep. (loc.cit, 11–14 tr. A.H. Armstrong.)

but that in order to want to do so one must have a vivid experience of the presence of the divine in rites and ceremonies, which Plotinus did not have. But we can perhaps draw Plotinus and the theurgists a little closer together if we consider more carefully than has always been done the celebrated story of his answer to Amelius. Porphyry tells us in his *Life of Plotinus* (10, 33-37) that when Amelius, who had come to set great store by the external observances of traditional religion, invited Plotinus to go round the temples with him on some feast-day, Plotinus replied : "They ought to come to me, not I to them." What he meant by this remark need not concern us here: none of his circle ever dared to enquire, and modern interpretations have been various.[16] What is important for our present

---

15. « Tradition, Reason and Experience in the Thought of Plotinus » (see n. 11), p. 187.
16. An interesting (at least to the participants) stage in the discussion, not irrelevant to the general theme of magic and theurgy in Neoplatonism, is represented by P. Merlan, Plotinus and Magic, in *Isis*, 44 (Dec. 1953), pp. 341-8, and A. H. Armstrong, Was Plotinus a Magician ?, in *Phronesis*, I (1955), pp. 73-9 = *Plotinian and Christian Studies* (see n. 11), III.

purposes is to bring together what we are told here about the decidedly
"theurgic" disposition of Amelius with what the *Life* tells us elsewhere
about the position of Amelius in the Plotinian circle. Porphyry makes it
perfectly clear that Amelius was, and was generally regarded as, the senior
member of the circle, the closest to Plotinus and his trusted intellectual
and spiritual collaborator. The religion of Plotinus, to which he remained
consistently faithful, was entirely inward, intellectual and spiritual. But
the fact that the religion of Amelius was more like that of Iamblichus
does not seem in any way to have diminished the master's respect for and
confidence in him. Even so, of course, the gap between the religious
standpoints of Plotinus and of Iamblichus remains considerable. Iamblichus and the theurgists would by no means have been satisfied with
the kind of recognition Plotinus was prepared to accord to the sacred
rites and those who believed in and practised them. I shall return to this:
but at present it is necessary to complete the case for theurgy as it has
been presented in recent years by observing that the by no means altogether un-Hellenic or un-Platonic principles of the theurgists were not
only applied to the defence of exotic and esoteric rites practised in their
own little coteries but to justify the whole tradition of Hellenic public
worship. That devout Iamblichean the Emperor Julian did not wish to
impose Chaldaean rites on the whole Empire but to restore to their
pristine splendour the temples and sacrifices and all the traditional religious observances of the Graeco-Roman *oecumene*. Proclus wished to be
"the hierophant of the universe" and his deepest personal devotion seems
to have been to that most Hellenic of deities, Athena.[17] Further, the range
of possible application of theurgic theology has been shown by recent
studies to be considerably wider. Much of what Iamblichus in the *De
Mysteriis* and other theurgists say must play its part (in this or later forms)
in any attempt to justify a way to God through rites and sacraments and
material symbols which are in some sense God-given. A reading of what
is said in the *De Mysteriis* about the necessity of material cult and about
prayer will illustrate this excellently.[18]

     This revaluation of theurgy has been, to a great extent, simply a
matter of sound scholarship and fair-mindedness: and these are, or should
be, quite independent of the scholar's own philosophical or religious
convictions. A. C. Lloyd, who has no belief in (and perhaps little liking
for) this kind (or any kind) of religion, has set us all a good example here.
We should of course, precisely in so far as it is based on solid and disin-
terested scholarship, be a little cautious in drawing any conclusions about
it as a phenomenon of the developing religious or irreligious consciousness of our own times. Negatively, room has been made for it by the

17. Marinus, *Life of Proclus*, 19, 9 and 30 (this last chapter contains the moving story of
how Athena came to dwell with Proclus when she was turned out of the Parthenon).
18. V 15-9, 219-26 (material cult and human needs) : 26, 237.8-240 (prayer).

decline of the influence of the Church and of reverence for the Fathers and Doctors of the Church, which is equally evident in much recent work on patristic and mediaeval Christian theology. Few of us nowadays are likely to be much affected, even unconsciously, by the torrent of Christian vituperation directed at the theurgists from their first public appearance in the fourth century to the time of the Patriarch Photius, and later. But on the positive side we should beware of taking the revaluation of theurgy too seriously as evidence for the revival of any kind of religious belief or sensibility. (The scholars who have been responsible for the rehabilitation of theurgy have not on the whole been greatly affected by its popularity in modern occultist or theosophical circles: and, though the growing esteem for the religious thought of India has certainly played some part in the revaluation of Neoplatonism in general, this has not affected the esteem for theurgy in particular, but rather that for the more spiritual, Plotinian, side of the tradition.) What we very often encounter (especially, perhaps in the English speaking world) in studies of theurgy, and of later Neoplatonism in general, as in some studies of patristic and mediaeval theology, is a detached scholarly interest inspired by the fascinating philosophical oddity of the doctrines being studied. Iamblichus presents us with a cabinet of choice logical curiosities. This is perfectly compatible with a full awareness of the historical importance of these doctrines because of their influence, direct or indirect, on the thought of later centuries: especially if this awareness of historical importance in the past is combined with the conviction, so widespread among modern historians, of the remoteness from us, the strangeness, the alien quality of all that past. The spirit which inspires much modern study of ancient philosophy and theology is not very different from that which has impelled great scholars, often with little taste or feeling for poetry, to devote their lives to the study of the few great poets and many second-rate versifiers of antiquity, regarding both impartially and equally as an inexhaustible source of textual and philological problems. I salute in some of my colleagues working in the field of later Neoplatonism that detached but intense scholarly passion which Browning celebrated in all its genuine, if sometimes slightly absurd, grandeur in *A Grammarian's Funeral*:

> So, with the throttling hands of death at strife,
> Ground he at grammar;
> Still, thro' the rattle, parts of speech were rife:
> While he could stammer
> He settled *Hotis* business-let it be!-
> Properly based *Oun*-
> Gave us the doctrine of the enclitic *De*,
> Dead from the waist down.

The development of interest in theurgy is no more necessarily a sign of the rebuilding of the temple than that in the logical peculiarities of the theology of the Trinity. It may rather indicate the opening of a new wing of the museum of the mind to accomodate the collections of Hellenic and Christian theology, in which Plotinus and Iamblichus, Augustine and Thomas Aquinas, exellently displayed in their appropriate glass cases, will be objects of the same sort of historical and scholarly interest which, in other parts of the museum, is given to T'ang ceramic horses or the mummified cats of Bubastis. But for those of us who retain some sympathy for, or even belief in, forms of religion in which rites and sacraments and holy images are important there is a strong subsidiary reason for welcoming and assisting in the serious reconsideration of theurgy. This is that we have come to see that it is particularly unjust for us not to recognise in the theurgic Neoplatonists much that we value in our own religious tradition. This awareness has been most impressively apparent in the work of the two French Dominican scholars, A. J. Festugière and H. D. Saffrey, to whom we owe so great an increase in our understanding of the spirituality of late antiquity. And, if we are sometimes tempted to return to a less fair-minded and more patristic view of theurgy, we have a stinging reminder ready to hand in the remark of A. C. Lloyd : "It is pointless for the historian to call these beliefs and rituals superstitious. In such a context superstition usually means other peoples' religion."[19]

None the less, when all this has been said, there remain serious reasons for wondering whether the reaction in favour of theurgy has not gone rather too far. I myself have approved of it from the beginning, and perhaps done something to assist its progress in the English-speaking world. But recently I have been more and more inclined to think that there is, after all, a good deal that can be said in favour of the attitude of Dodds to theurgic rites and some aspects of the theology of the theurgic Neoplatonists. A distinction must be made here. The return to a more critical and even hostile view of the esoteric rites performed by the theurgists, and their theological justifications for them, does not involve a return to any sort of wholesale condemnation of the personal religion or the philosophical theology of the later Neoplatonists. As we have seen, they were concerned to maintain and defend the whole Hellenic tradition of thought about and worship of the Divine: and much of what they say has an even wider application. I do not feel spiritually remote from Iamblichus when I light my candle at Chartres or Einsiedeln. This, combined with an awareness that a good deal of what has to be said in criticism of theurgic theology can be applied to some utterances of Christian theologians, Protestant as well as Catholic or Eastern Orthodox, should safeguard us against any return to a patristic (that is to say sectarian and fanatical) judgement of theurgy. But even if one remembers all this, a reading of the *De Mysteriis* can be rather

---

19. A. C. Lloyd in the *Cambridge History of Later Greek and Early Mediaeval Philosophy* (see n. 10), chap. 17, p. 279.

disconcerting: one begins to see all too clearly what Dodds was getting at. The main objects of the theurgic rites seem to have been the evocation of visible manifestations of the divine, apparitions or the animation of statues, which have not in the great spiritual traditions been generally considered the highest or the most secure means of communion with the divinity; or divination, admittedly not simply in the vulgar sense of fortune-telling or forecasting, but with a considerable element of that in it. And the long account of the sort of apparitions of the higher powers which the theurgists can call forth, in Book II,[20] does not exactly inspire confidence. Nor does there seem to be much evidence that the true theurgic divination described in such exalted language and so carefully distinguished from its counterfeits in Book III was ever of much spiritual or practical use to theurgists, or anybody else. And the anxious indignation with which Iamblichus distinguishes between the results of true theurgy and those of the operations of vulgar magicians, conjurors and impostors,[21] arouses, like so much of this kind of apologetic, the suspicion that the difference in practice might not have been so great after all. And this suspicion is confirmed when we turn from the De Mysteriis (which is, perhaps deliberately, vague about the details of theurgic rituals) to the rather scanty, but as far as it goes more precise, information about theurgy available elsewhere. This has been carefully collected and accurately reported[22] by Dodds, who was after all one of the greatest scholars of our time, with a special expertise in the field of late Neoplatonism and a lifelong interest in occult or supernormal phenomena, to which his attitude was by no means crudely rationalist or altogether unsympathetic. What we can discover about theurgic procedures and attitudes from our sources, not always hostile, from Eunapius to Psellus, does make the theurgists look remarkably like superstitious magicians after all: nor are the modern parallels which Dodds produces of a sort to be reassuring to most of us. He had some solid reasons for his hostile judgement of theurgy.

But there is a deeper, and more properly theological, reason why anyone who is to any extent influenced by the older Hellenic philosophical tradition, especially in the intensely religious form which it took in Plotinus, may feel profoundly uneasy about theurgy after a reading of the De Mysteriis; and one may continue to feel this uneasiness even if, like many Platonists, one is prepared to grant more importance to material symbols, rites and sacraments on the way to God than the pure intellectualism of Plotinus, or Porphyry in his more Plotinian phase, will allow. This is the extreme supernaturalism of Iamblichus, which pervades the De Mysteriis from beginning to end. A word which recurs constantly

20. II 3-11 (70.9-99.10).
21. II 10 (93.10-95.14) : III 28-30 (167.9-175.4).
22. « Theurgy » (see p. 180, n. 8) : see also his Supernormal Phenomena in Classical Antiquity, in The Ancient Concept of Progress, Oxford, University Press, 1973, pp. 200-10.

when Iamblichus is speaking of the gods and the sacred rites is *huperphues*, which Des Places translates "surnaturel", clearly to be understood in a fairly strict theological sense. This is (as one would of course expect) a perfectly correct rendering of the sense of the Greek word in Iamblichus; though in all earlier non-Christian Greek it means simply "extraordinary", "prodigious", "larger than life", whether in a good or a bad sense, and there does not seem to be an instance of it, in the precise sense of "supernatural", even in Christian Greek which is earlier than Iamblichus (the *De Mysteriis* cannot be dated much later than 300 A.D.). The gods in Iamblichus are external to and far above the natural universe and the human *psyche*. Their true world is not our world, and our thoughts cannot reach them. They intervene from above, and select the material means by which they deign to lead us to them in ways beyond our understanding. This is why Iamblichus, from the first pages of his work, insists that theurgy must be exempt from philosophical discussion and criticism. The theurgic way to God must be exalted above the philosophical, and we must submit to be led in it uncritically by the *magisterium* of the theurgists, who have been exalted to some participation in the divine supernaturality. We should not mistake what is at issue here (and in analogous later claims). What is being said is not simply that it is inappropriate to apply in these sacred matters the methods of ordinary logical analysis or the procedures of empirical science. Plotinus and Porphyry were, after all, hardly rationalists in the modern sense or scientific materialists. What is being excluded as illegitimate is the whole range of independent activities of critical discernment of the free human spirit, from those prompted by something like the "inner light" of the Quakers to that *raison* which Molière's Chrysale opposes to the *raisonnement* which inspires the remarkable domestic proceedings of the ladies of his household:

> Raisonner est l'emploi de toute ma maison
> Et le raisonnement en bannit la raison[23].

This kind of supernaturalism sets the divine in a kind of "metaphysical space"[24] separate from and not accessible in or through the world of our inner and outer experience. This inaccessible divine is most strongly affirmed to be the source and ruler of the world of experience, but can only be contacted through its own self-revelation to a privileged group of human beings whose sacred writings, teachings and hieratic practices are by the revelation exalted beyond the reach of normal human discernment, criticism and objection. This is profoundly objectionable to those,

---

23. Molière, *Les Femmes savantes*, Acte II, Scène VII.
24. I owe this phrase to Marie-Louise von Franz. See *The Golden Ass*, revised edition Dallas, Spring Publications, 1980, p. 167. In speaking of Iamblichus or of Christian theologians it must of course be used metaphorically. They are very well aware that the divine is not in space or time.

including many Christians, who have continued to hold to the older tradition of Hellenic theology, still so finely exemplified in Plotinus and his circle. And if we look back to that circle we may find it possible to give a properly honourable place to ritual and sacramental religion without accepting an Iamblichean or any other kind of supernaturalism which would lift its scriptures, teaching and ruling authorities, and practices beyond the reach of continual critical discussion. We do not have to set the purely intellectual and spiritual religion of Plotinus and Porphyry against the theurgic religion of Iamblichus and his successors as if they were two different religions: The later Hellenic Neoplatonists certainly did not do so. We should remember Amelius, the "lover of sacrifices" *(philothutès)*[25] — an epithet which would suit Iamblichus or his disciple the Emperor Julian admirably—whose recognised position in the circle was so high that that acute observer and courteous opponent Longinus couples his name with that of Plotinus,[26] and who seems always to have remained on quite friendly terms with Porphyry. If we do so (taking into account of course what Amelius may have thought of Plotinus as well as what Plotinus may have thought of Amelius, and not necessarily feeling bound to observe the group from the religious standpoint of Porphyry), we can find here a mutual recognition of those two ways to God, without domination or exclusion of either, which conforms well to Indian teaching about and practice of the Yogas,[27] and is by no means incongruous with the teaching and practice of many Christians in our own time, and some throughout the Christian centuries.

25. Porphyry, *Life of Plotinus*, 10, 33.
26. *Op. cit.* (n. 25), 20, 32-3 and 71.
27. A. H. Armstrong and R. Ravindra, *Buddhi* in the Bhagavadgītā and *Psyché* in Plotinus, in *Neoplatonism and Indian Thought* (Ed. R. Baine Harris, Norfolk, Virginia, International Society for Neoplatonic Studies 1982, p. 63-86, especially pp. 71 and 82-3. [Reprinted from *Religious Studies*, 15 (September 1979), pp. 327-42.]

III

THE NEGATIVE THEOLOGY OF NOUS IN LATER NEOPLATONISM

Dr. HEINRICH DÖRRIE, whose birthday we are celebrating, is justly renowned for his work in one of the most lively and growing fields of contemporary scholarship, that of the study of later Greek philosophy and its intricate relationships with Christian thought. It is therefore most appropriate that we should honour him with a volume whose theme is »Platonism and Christianity«. For my own contribution I offer a discussion of a late Platonic way of thinking which perhaps helped to make easier the acceptance by so many Christian thinkers, especially »Dionysius« and those influenced by him down to Cusanus[1], of the negative or apophatic theology of Plotinus and his successors. Its importance in this context is only secondary. The main reasons why Christian thinkers found it possible to accept Neoplatonic apophatic theology so whole-heartedly are to be found in the Judaeo-Christian tradition itself (which I do not propose to discuss) and in some aspects of Neoplatonic thought about the First Hypostasis, the One or Good. Nevertheless a way of thinking about the Second Hypostasis, Divine Intellect or Being, which can be called apophatic did exist, and does not always, perhaps, receive due attention.

It has been solidly established by recent studies of the relationship of Christian to Hellenic Neoplatonist thought that one of its most striking features is the way in which the Christians bring together and apply to God what is said by the Hellenic Neoplatonists about the first two hypostases (or, in terms of the traditional interpretation of the Parmenides, the first two hypotheses): or, to be more precise, apply some of what is said about Nous to God along with what is said about the One and use other statements about Nous, especially those in which its multiplicity and derivation are stressed, in constructing their account of the angelic world, which they sometimes refer to as the χόσμος νοητός[2]. And, since HADOT's rediscovery of the metaphysics of Porphyry[3], we can see this Christian development as in some way related to a movement of thought within Hellenic Neoplatonism

---

[1] I have not the competence to discuss what happened to the negative theology after Cusanus. But there is a remark of WERNER BEIERWALTES in the chapter on Hegel in his Identität and Differenz which I find particularly interesting and stimulating. He says, in distinguishing the aim of Hegel's religious philosophy from that of the conjectural philosophy of Cusanus and the negative dialectic of Neoplatonism: »Die Überzeugung von der Durchschaubarkeit und Formulierbarkeit der Sache selbst bleibt das Trennende, wenn Hegel durch Denken das Mysterium lichten zu können meint.« (Identität u. Differenz = Philosophische Abhandlungen B. 49 Frankfurt 1980, p. 249). This leads me to wonder how far the revolts, not only against traditional metaphysics but against any form of theistic belief, which have played such a notable part in the intellectual life of our times, are to some extent due to the neglect and eventually virtual disappearance of the negative theology. Are they, at least in part, reac-

tions to claims to know too much about God?
[2] This development is one of the main themes of STEPHEN GERSH's excellent and comprehensive study of the relationship of Christian to Hellenic Neoplatonism, From Iamblichus to Eriugena (Leiden 1978): see also W. BEIERWALTES Identität in der Differenz (in Identität und Differenz, Frankfurt 1980 pp. 24–56). For accounts of the angelic world in terms of the Neoplatonic χόσμος νοητός see Basil of Caesarea Hex. 1, 5, (PG 29, 13A), Gregory of Nyssa In Cant. 6 (PG 44, 893A–B) Augustine Confessions 12, 11–15 and De Gen. ad litt. 1, 1 (with my Spiritual or Intelligible Matter in Plotinus and St. Augustine, Plotinian and Christian Studies [London 1979] 7).
[3] P. HADOT, La Métaphysique de Porphyre in Porphyre = Entretiens sur L'Antiquité Classique T. 12, Vandœuvres–Genève 1966, pp.127–157 and Porphyre et Victorinus (2 vols. Paris 1968).

itself. (I am aware that some very difficult and intricate questions arise here, both about the relationship of the fourth-century Commentary on the Parmenides to the thought of Porphyry himself and about the, perhaps never precisely determinable, degrees of influence on this development of Christian tradition, the survival of Middle Platonist ways of thinking, and Porphyrian metaphysics. But it seems now established that the bringing together of the hypostases in this way is a development which did in fact occur within Hellenic Neoplatonism without Christian influence.)

The survival of the negative theology, with undiminished vigour, in this uniting of the One beyond being and the One-Being is explained primarily, on the Neoplatonic side, by the fact that the assimilation of the hypostases took place, to parody with pious intent the Athanasian Creed, »not by the conversion of the One into the One-Being, but by the taking of the One-Being into the One«. HADOT's rediscovery of Porphyry, and the attention which this has focussed on the Turin palimpsest Commentary on the Parmenides, a master-work of Neoplatonic negative theology, have enabled students of Plotinus to understand better the full significance of the strongly positive and affirmative statements which he sometimes makes about the One and to see Porphyry's metaphysics as a legitimate development of one side at least of the thought of his master. If we read 6 8 [39], where the theology is more kataphatic than anywhere else in the Enneads, closely, as we should, with its neighbour in both the Enneadic and chronological order 6 7 [38], and pay proper attention to the Plotinian οἷον, we can see its strongly positive affirmations about the One, which seem to point forward almost inevitably to Porphyry's assimilation of the First and Second Hypostases, as part of the exercise of the most radical negative theology, that of the *negatio negationis*[4], so well exemplified in the Parmenides commentary. They are part of the dialectic which leads the mind exercising it, not to total negativity or super-affirmation or higher synthesis, but to fruitful and illuminating silence before that for which the mind is not big enough, that which is absolutely beyond us. It is first and foremost this ultimate radicalism of Neoplatonic thought which could make possible the application of the affirmations of the Second Hypothesis to God without weakening the negative theology. It explains why »Dionysius« and his followers, though rather »Porphyrian« in their positive statements about God, can be »Proclan« or even »Damascian« in the radicalism of their negations.

But there is a secondary, but still important, reason for this. There runs through Neoplatonic thought about the Second Hypostasis a profound doubt of the adequacy, or even the applicability, of the discursive, analytic, defining thought and language which belong to ἐπιστήμη here below to the unity-in-diversity of the One-Being, the eternal life of the Intellect which is the World of Forms. The foundation-text in Plato for this is the philosophical digression in the Seventh Platonic Letter (341A–344D). It is clearly apparent in Plotinus, where it has been very fully and carefully studied by KLAUS WURM[5]. But the generally informal and unsystematic character of his thought and writing make it somewhat less noticeable than it is in his more systematic successors, and sufficient attention has not always been paid to it. It is considerably more striking when it appears in Proclus,

---

[4] The *negatio negationis* is not often explicit in Plotinus. But it is clearly stated at 6 8, 9, 39–41: ἀλλ᾽ ἔστι τῷ ἰδόντι οὐδὲ τὸ οὕτως εἰπεῖν δύνασθαι οὐδ᾽ αὖ τὸ μὴ οὕτως· τί γὰρ ἂν εἴποις αὐτὸ τῶν ὄντων, ἐφ᾽ ὧν τὸ οὕτως.

[5] KLAUS WURM, Substanz und Qualität (Berlin–New York 1973). See also A. SMITH, Potentiality and the Problem of Plurality in the Intelligible World in Neoplatonism and Early Christian Thought, London 1981, pp. 99–107.

who is generally, and rightly, regarded as the most rigorously systematic of Neoplatonic thinkers, one who pushes defining logical discourse far further than on his own assumptions it should go, even above the intelligible level to the Henads. Yet there are several passages in his works where he states, clearly as common and accepted doctrine, the inadequacy of discursive ἐπιστήμη to apprehend or express the intelligible[6], and one in particular where he develops this theme with such vigour as to give good grounds for speaking of a »negative theology of Nous«.

The passage in question is from the exposition of the doctrine of the Demiurge in the Commentary on the Timaeus[7]. The text being commented is Timaeus 28C. The Demiurge in Proclus ranks comparatively low in the hierarchy of divine intelligences; he is noeric, not noetic[8]. This makes the language used here about our attainment of him and the utter inadequacy of our thought and speech to attain to him particularly remarkable.

The first part of the passage is a comment on »It is a hard task to find the maker and father of this universe«. Proclus strongly and repeatedly insists that this is not a task which can be performed by epistemic reason: and the language he uses is strikingly close to the language which Plotinus uses about vision of and union with the One, though it is made clear that we are dealing with a reality of the order of Intellect. »For this is the finding, encountering him, being made one with him, keeping company alone with him alone, encountering his immediate self-revelation, snatching itself away from all other activity; when the soul has done this it will think that epistemic reasonings are just stories, when it is in company with the Father and feasts with him on the truth of being and »in a pure light«, purely, »is initiated to the beholding of complete and changeless visions« (302, 1–8). »... for after the wandering of coming to birth and the purification and the epistemic light the intelligent activity shines out, and the intellect in us, which brings the soul to harbour in the Father and settles it unpolluted in the demiurgic intellections, and joins light to light, not like the light of epistemic reason, but more beautiful and more intelligible and more like the One: this is the Father's haven, the finding of the Father, the unpolluted union with him« (302, 17–25)[9]. Though the hierarchy is formally preserved, and the passage is not at all »Porphyrian«, the assimilation upwards of the vision of and union with the Demiurge to vision of and union with the One is very noticeable, and appears to be deliberate. And it is made very clear, and becomes clearer still in the continuation of the passage, that this union is not epistemically thinkable and is not properly expressible in any sort of language. The remark »When the soul has done this it will think that epistemic reasonings are just stories«[10] should be noted. Some implicit reference is perhaps intended to the passage in which Plotinus speaks of the inadequacy of both myths and discursive reasonings to express eternal reality because of their separative and divisive character[11]. And these passages of Plotinus and Proclus seem to make clear that the Neoplatonists' awareness of the inadequacy of philosophical discourse did not lead them to give any preference to the language of myth and symbol as more suited for expressing the nature of eternal realities. They may often seem to modern philosophers to be using »the

---

[6] Platonic Theology 2, 10 (2 64, 7 SAFFREY–WESTERINK): In Alcibiadem 245–249 CREUZER (113–115 WESTERINK): In Parmenidem 1015, 33–40 COUSIN.
[7] In Timaeum 2 92C–93A (1, 301, 23–303, 25 DIEHL).
[8] On the place of the Demiurge in the hierarchy see DODDS's commentary on Proposition 167 of the Elements of Theology (E. R. DODDS Proclus, The Ele-

ments of Theology[2], Oxford 1963, pp. 285–287).
[9] All translations of Proclus are my own.
[10] ὅτε καὶ τοὺς ἐπιστημονικοὺς λόγους μύθους ἡγήσεται ... 302. 4–5.
[11] 3 5 [50] 9, 24–29: for the discursive inadequacy of λόγος cp. 6 7 [38] 35, 27–30.

language of poetry and religion«[12] rather than of philosophy. But this does not mean that they regard language of this kind as in any way privileged in comparison with the abstract logical discourse which they all, including Plotinus, use most of the time. When the inadequacy of language is most clearly perceived, it is the inadequacy of all language, not of logical discourse as compared with poetic symbolism. This, of course, leaves open the possibility that both kinds of language, though inadequate, can be helpful in bringing us to the point where we can see[13].

The second part of the passage is devoted to the exegesis of »and having found him it would be impossible to declare him to all mankind«. Here the Seventh Letter is brought into play and the scepticism about language becomes radical: though this does not prevent Proclus from continuing at considerable length thereafter his epistemic discourse on the theology of the Demiurge. »For the finding did not belong to a speaking soul, but to one keeping holy silence and lying open to the divine light; it did not belong to a soul moving with its own motion but to one which keeps a kind of silence: for since the soul is not naturally adapted to grasp the substances of the other things by a name or a limiting definition or epistemic reasoning, but only by a direct intelligence, as he says himself in his Letters, how could it find the substance of the Demiurge in another way than by immediate intelligence? But how, when it has found in this way, could it express its vision by nouns and verbs? For discourse which moves in composition is unable to present the simple nature which is like the One?« »Well then«, someone might say, »do we not say a great deal about the Demiurge and the other gods and the One itself? We do indeed speak about them, but we do not speak each one's real self, and we can speak epistemically, but not intelligently: for this is finding, as we said before. But if finding belongs to the silent soul, how could the talk which flows through the mouth suffice to bring to light what we have found?« (303, 5–23). This is one of the most powerful developments to be found in the writings of the Neoplatonists of the great Neoplatonic theme of silence; and the incurable discursivity and separativeness of *all* speech and its consequent complete inability to express *any* eternal reality could hardly be more strongly stated. A gap has opened between the object of philosophy and philosophical discourse which Proclus seems to find disconcertingly wide, as he certainly should in view of his normal practice, but which he recognises none the less. And it is this sense of the gap which is common to, and is the driving force of, all forms of Neoplatonic negative theology.

The passage from the Platonic Theology which states the same doctrine[14] is a simple, though very strongly worded statement that every kind of knowledge will destroy itself[15] if applied to an object which does not concern it. The passages from the Commentaries on the Alcibiades[16] and the Parmenides[17] which are related to the passage under discussion stress the inadequacy of epistemic reasoning less strongly and give an account of why, in spite of its incapacity to attain the intelligible, the philosopher must continue to use it,

---

[12] A. C. LLOYD in The Cambridge History of Later Greek and Early Mediaeval Philosophy (Cambridge 1970) 4 The Later Neoplatonists, Epilogue p. 324.

[13] In 5 8 [31] 6 Plotinus does suggest that hieroglyphic picture-writing is helpful to the understanding of noetic non-discursiveness: but this is by no means equivalent to saying that poetry, pictures or music express the intelligible better than philosophical discourse.

[14] 2, 10 (2 64, 5–9 SAFFREY–WESTERINK).

[15] ἑαυτὴν ἀναιρήσει: the language becomes even more violent when the level of the One is reached: ὥστε καὶ εἰ λόγος εἴη τοῦ ἀρρήτου, περὶ ἑαυτῷ καταβαλλόμενος οὐδὲν παύεται καὶ πρὸς ἑαυτὸν διαμάχεται.

[16] In Alcibiadem 245–249 CREUZER (113–115 WESTERINK). Festugière notes the resemblance in Commentaire sur le Timée 2 (Paris 1967), p. 154 note 4.

[17] In Parmenidem 1015, 33–40 Cousin.

which is worth some consideration. They present it as a γυμνασία, an exercise, and a fine sentence in the Parmenides commentary extends this to the whole life of the philosopher. »All our life is a training-ground for that vision [of intelligible truth] and our wandering through dialectic hastens to that haven«[18]. This belongs to that way of looking at philosophy which was so important to the ancients and which has been excellently expounded by HADOT[19], philosophy as »spiritual exercise«. Ancient philosophers hardly ever regarded their philosophy as simply the theoretical pursuit of conclusions by a process of abstract reasoning. It was rather a process of training and exercise aiming at total self-transformation, at final enlightenment and liberation. (This brings our own ancient traditions much closer to the thought of India than is always realised by those who seek from Hindu or Buddhist masters what they may indeed find there, but might find in a less exotic and more easily assimilable form nearer home.) It is a way of thinking which still deserves serious consideration, especially perhaps by those of us who continue to wish to call ourselves Platonists, because the commoner alternative way in which the Neoplatonists consider and pursue normal philosophical activity does not seem to be altogether coherent or satisfactory.

Their normal way of proceeding is, while making a very sharp distinction between νόησις and διάνοια and insisting sometimes, as we have seen, on the inability of the latter to grasp or express noetic reality, to continue reasoning about the intelligible realm in a manner which may be sharply distinguished as higher Platonic dialectic from lower Aristotelian logic[20], but seems in practice to be attempting to operate discursively within quite ordinary logical rules. The supreme examples of this are the Elements of Theology of Proclus and the Periphyseon of Eriugena. But this way of proceeding has very considerable difficulties. It is extremely difficult to see how there can be any kind of thought about an eternal reality which is not only one but discrete and diversified, with very complex internal relationships, which is not so incurably discursive that attempts to raise it to the level of its subject can only result in paradox and incoherence. As A. C. LLOYD says »It is very difficult, though it has to be done in Neoplatonism, to call the ›single-mindedness‹ attributed to Intellect intellectual«[21]. A courteously-worded judgement on Eriugena by a scholar who looks at the Periphyseon from the point of view of modern Cambridge philosophy may help to make what I am trying to say clearer. »The conclusion to be drawn from these remarks is not that Eriugena was not a philosopher, but that he was not the creator of a *philosophical* system. The thought of the Periphyseon does form a system, but one which could be called ›philosophical‹ only in an unhelpfully broad sense of the word. It is a system which does not attempt to provide an explanation of reality by means of reason, but rather to make an imaginative whole of ideas, arguments and dogmas taken from a variety of sources, including Holy Scripture«[22]. It does not seem that the application of logic or dialectic to intelligible or spiritual reality produces results which are very satisfac-

[18] Πᾶσα τοίνυν ἡμῶν ἡ ζωὴ γυμνάσιόν ἐστι πρὸς ἐκείνην τὴν θέαν, καὶ ἡ διὰ τῆς διαλεκτικῆς πλάνη πρὸς τὸν ὁρμον ἐκεῖνον ἐπείγεται (1015, 39–40).

[19] P. HADOT, Exercices Spirituels (Annuaire de l'École Pratique des Hautes Études, 5ᵉ Section 84, 25–70) = Exercices Spirituels et Philosophie Antique, Paris 1981, 13–58.

[20] Plotinus On Dialectic 1 3 [20] 5.

[21] The Cambridge History of Later Greek and Early Mediaeval Philosophy (Cambridge 1970) 4 The Later Neoplatonists, Epilogue p. 324. For a fuller discussion see A. C. LLOYD, Non-Discursive Thought – An Enigma of Greek Philosophy in Proc. of the Aristotelian Society 1970, p. 261–274.

[22] J. MARENBON, John Scottus and the Categoriae Decem in Eriugena: Studien zu seinen Quellen ed. W. BEIERWALTES (Heidelberg 1980), p. 131.

tory or convincing to logicians: unless of course they have been trained to accept this way of proceeding rather uncritically for extra-logical reasons.

This in itself should be enough to make reasonably open-minded adherents of traditional philosophy rather uneasy and dubious about presenting our metaphysics as the total, certainly and universally true, explanation of reality by means of reason. But even if we are less sensitive than we should be to contemporary criticism, there are reasons very deep in our tradition why we should pay serious attention to the very far-reaching doubts which, as we have seen, arise in the minds of ancient Platonists about the competence of epistemic reason to apprehend or express even the lower levels of eternal reality. An important reason why we should do so is that overmuch confidence in metaphysical or theological discourse, especially of a controversial or polemical kind, inevitably leads to the negative theology being pushed very much into the background, or even eliminated altogether. And without the negative theology our representation of reality loses all depth and becomes abstract, flat and unreal. We can detect in the later Hellenic Neoplatonists, who were quite as dogmatic and concerned to prove other people wrong as Christian theologians, a move very like that which MAURICE WILES has detected in Christian theology. In considering the move within Arianism from Arius's insistence on the incomprehensibility of God to Eunomius's insistence on his comprehensibility and definability WILES says: »The move to Eunomius's position would be one that follows a pattern not uncommon in the history of Christian theology – but none the less regrettable for that. If a theologian stresses the mystery of God, it is bound to be more difficult for him to show that his opponents' beliefs must be false. In his desire to exclude what he believes to be false teaching, he is likely to be tempted to claim greater precision (and therefore greater power of exclusion) for his formulations than the evidence warrants or even than he himself in his heart of hearts wants to claim«[23]. A proper consideration and development of the radical doubts which we have been examining in these same Hellenic Neoplatonists (and they continue in the Christian Neoplatonist tradition) may save us from making this regrettable move. And a similar study and development of their thought about ἐπιστήμη as γυμνασία, about reasoning as a training for vision and liberation, will give us very positive grounds for insisting on the continual necessity of reasoning for the most radical negative theologian, and may also help us to recover something of the ancient understanding of philosophy as not only a way of thinking but a way of life.

I conclude with two aphorisms which seem relevant from one of the few professed Christian Platonists of the Eastern Orthodox tradition, the late Mother Maria (Lydia Gysi), whose whole spiritual life was founded on the double negation, and who lived her philosophy to the ultimate point[24]. In a selection of her occasional writings and notes published by her community there appear the following:

»We will not accept a logical plane between Mystery and event upon which the super-logical Mystery would be projected down and the sub-logical event projected up.«

»When the mind is like an animal craving for food it will make a noise, but if it is fed and worked hard, it will gladly be quiet. Therefore ›down reason, down‹. But if this is

---

[23] From a paper given to a seminar at Oxford in the summer of 1980.
[24] This phrase is taken from the letter (November 1974) in which she told me that she was dying of cancer.
»Is it a grace, to be allowed to live, or try to live, or make it one's ›work‹ to live one's philosophy to the ultimate point? I take it as an infinite tenderness of God; although at times I have to take a deep breath not to yield to fearfulness.«
(Mother Maria, Her Life in Letters, edited by Sister Thekla, London 1979, p. 108).

enacted by asserting theological statement of paradox as the higher wisdom of God, there we would say that paradox is but a negative logic – a non-logic – which is however on the same plane as flat logic«[25].

---

[25] The Fool, Greek Orthodox Monastery of the Assumption, Normanby, Whitby, North Yorkshire, England, 1980, pp. 106 and 108. Though she knew nothing of Indian thought, her Platonist estimation of »mind« or »reason« here (and elsewhere) is strikingly like some Indian estimations of that tricky and unreliable constituent of our lower selves *manas*. (On *manas* and *buddhi* in the *Gita* see A. H. ARMSTRONG and R. RAVINDRA, The Dimensions of the Self in Religious Studies 15 [1979], pp. 329–330).

IV

THE DIVINE ENHANCEMENT OF EARTHLY BEAUTIES: THE HELLENIC AND PLATONIC TRADITION

This paper comes out of and is part of a lifetime's attempt to make present to our very different world the great Platonists of the first centuries of our era and the Hellenic tradition within which they imagined, thought and worshipped. This attempt has been increasingly inspired in more recent years by a sense of contemporary urgency. A very curious and distinctive feature of European culture is its double religious foundation in two different ways of thinking about the divine, the Hellenic and the Biblical. The full implications of this have not been realized till recently, when the manifest disintegration of our "inherited conglomerate", our complex and not altogether consistent spiritual and intellectual inheritance, has led both to the rapid advance of quite new kinds of materialism and rationalism and to the search for a new kind of spirituality, a new understanding and awareness of the divine. In this search the work of Jung and of Eranos has been of central importance. Many have tried to find this new understanding by a free interpretation of at least some of what is given in the developed Christian tradition with its strong Hellenic elements, or, if they identify the Hellenic inheritance too closely with its critical-rationalist side from which Enlightenment thought developed, by a reaction to what is considered a more primitive, "Biblical", sort of Christianity. But there has also been a strong tendency, apparent in the work of Eranos over the years, to look for it in the great spiritual traditions of the East, of which we have come to know so much more in this century, and in the archaic spiritualities of the Old and New Worlds. And in the last two or three decades the great increase in our knowledge and understand ing of the thought and piety of late Graeco-Roman antiquity, and especially of those last Hellenic Platonists whom we call Neo-platonists, has brought some of us to understand that we have here a vital link with Oriental spiritualities and archaic piety which is firmly present and of great influence and importance in our own complex tradition. The question of the relationship of the philosophy of Plotinus to the thought of India has been discussed since the publication of E. Bréhier's *La Philosophie de Plotin* in 1928, and I have been aware of it all my working life. But when I began to make my own, admittedly rather touristic and superficial, excursions of mind and spirit into the worlds of Indian thought[1] and of esoteric Islam I came to understand more clearly than ever before the value of the treasures which we have inherited from the philosophy and piety of late antiquity, because I came to see how many of them we hold in common with the East. This is a matter of great importance in our urgent search for a spirituality which will meet our present needs and be rooted in our ancient depths, as a spirituality must be if it is to live and grow. It will help our quest and increase the meaning of what we find if we understand that, when we venture into the great realms of Eastern spiritual experience, though the differences from the world we know are many and profound, we are not walking on altogether alien soil. The flowers we enjoy and the fruits we try to gather sometimes grow on plants and trees of which there are species native to, and to be found flourishing in, the soils and climates of our own tradition.

My subject is the way in which, in the Hellenic tradition, the beauties of earth and the beauties of the gods, or the divine, or

---

1 Here I have been very greatly helped by my friend and colleague at Dalhousie University, Professor Ravi Ravindra. An example of our close collaboration in the study of our respective traditions is "*Buddhi* in the *Bhagávadgita* and *Psyche* in Plotinus" in Religious Studies 15 (September 1979) pp. 327-342: also published in *Neoplatonism and Indian Thought* ed. R. Baine Harris (Norfolk, Virginia 1982) pp. 63-86.

God, are apprehended together, so that earthly beauties stimulate
and provide expression for awareness of divine presence, and, in
turn, the sense of divine presence enhances earthly beauties. I shall
begin by considering this in the old pre-philosophical and non-
philosophical awareness of divine beauty in the beauties of earth
which continued to surround and stimulate philosophical awareness of the divine down to the end of the ancient world. Then I
shall go on to show how in the Platonic, and particularly the late
Platonic, philosophical tradition the sense of divine enhancement
of earthly beauty persists and develops in a most powerful and
influential form.

The beauties with which we shall be concerned are primarily
natural beauties, including of course in an eminent degree the
beauties of human bodies. The beauties of works of art, though
sometimes highly esteemed, occupy generally a rather modest
place in Hellenic sensibility. One does not meet many aesthetes in
the ancient world, and ancient "philosophies of art" have to be
painstakingly constructed by moderns who have this sort of
concern from, generally rather incidental, observations in contexts
where the main interests of the philosophers do not lie in the
appreciation of works of art. The kind of beauty with which
philosophers are most concerned is of course not the beauty of
nature or of artefacts but moral and spiritual beauty, the beauty of
souls, not of bodies. This should always be borne in mind, but
should not be misunderstood. In the Hellenic tradition the
awareness of and appreciation of moral excellence and spiritual
majesty, in humans or gods, is not cut off from or apprehended as
something intrinsically different from awareness and appreciation
of the beauties of earth. Moral beauties for the philosophers
certainly rank higher in the scale of beauties than the beauties of
bodies. But it is a continuous scale and the beauties are all really
beauties. Moral and aesthetic philosophy are not separately
distinguishable, still less separable, in the Hellenic tradition. In
anachronistic modern terms one might say that Hellenic ethics are
a sort of moral aesthetics. And in the Platonic tradition the quest

for God is always driven on by the love which is the response to beauty, and only to beauty.

I

In considering what non-philosophical Greeks felt and thought about earthly beauty and its divine enhancement I shall be guided mainly by the poets. The ancient sacred sites, and the poor remnants which we have of the mass of works of visual art, sculptures and paintings, which adorned them, can tell us something, but not perhaps very much, about how the ancients responded to the beauties of earth: any general statements about this, based, as they would have to be, to a great extent on our own response to the sites in their present state and the works of art which we have, would be insecurely founded. But the poets can, if we read them carefully, help us to understand a good deal. At first reading it may seem that they do not tell us very much. They do not, as a rule, dilate on their own feelings or write pages of the sort of rich description which can sometimes be found in later European or in Eastern literatures. Hellenistic sensibility seems closer to other literary sensibilities here than classical. But in reading the greatest of Hellenistic poets and the one most successful at giving a vivid impression of the beauties of earth, Theocritus, one is struck by the economy of his vivid descriptions and the way in which they are firmly integrated into and support the story: one can perceive this very well, for instance, at the beginning of the *Thyrsis* (Idyll I) or the end of the *Thalysia* (Idyll VII) or the description of the spring in the *Hylas* (Idyll XIII 39-45). We may note particularly in this last that there is only one little phrase, though a marvellous one, about the beauty of the Nymphs who catch Hylas, *eär th' horoōsa Nycheia*, "Nycheia with her look of Spring". When Theocritus gives us some real lush gush about beauty it is about the artificial beauty of Queen Arsinoe's Adonis celebration, and it is put into the mouths of those silly chattering women Gorgo and Praxinoa and of the singer whose song suits their taste so admirably. (*Adoniazousae*, Idyll XV, 78-86 and 100-144.) I am not, of course, suggesting for a moment that Theocritus is intending to be rude or satirical about the show. A poet who desires royal patronage is not rude about religious entertainments put on by the Queen. At the most he is expecting his readers to be aware of a slight inflection of tone, or to observe him with their minds' eye raising his eyebrows slightly.

The character of the Greek poetic way of evoking earthly beauty can be particularly well appreciated when we turn to the sort of human or human-divine beauty which in other literatures gives occasion for rich and lavish description. We can see its quality very well in the most famous of evocations of the most famous beauty, the appearance of Helen on the walls of Troy (*Iliad* III 139-160). This was remembered and kept its power down through the centuries. Norman Baynes, following Psellos, recalls how it was remembered and used in eleventh-century Constantinople: "In the eleventh century when the beautiful Caucasian mistress of the Emperor first appeared by his side in a public procession to the hippodrome a courtier expressed his admiration in two words, *ou nemesis*, 'it were no shame...'. The lady saw the impression created by the quotation, but did not understand: she summoned the courtier to her side and asked for an explanation. But for the court of Byzantium those two words from Homer had sufficed to conjure up the picture of the old men on the walls of Troy who gazing at Helen in her radiance said, *ou nemesis*, 'It were no shame that men should fight for such as she'."[2] But when we read this most powerful of Greek celebrations of an earthly beauty we find that there is not a word of description in it of what that beauty looked like. Baynes' romantic "radiance" seems to come from the "shimmering garments" in which Helen wraps herself before setting out in line 141. And what the old men at the Skaian gates

2 Norman Baynes "The Hellenistic Civilisation and East Rome" (*Byzantine Studies* I, London, Athlone Press 1955) pp. 22-23, referring to Psellos, *Chronographia* VI 61.

said in their high chirping voices, and the Byzantine courtier alluded to, was simply

> Surely there is no blame on Trojans and strong-greaved Achaeans
> if for long time they suffer hardship for a woman like this one.
> Terrible is the likeness of her face to immortal goddesses.
> Still, though she be such, let her go away in the ships, lest
> she be left behind, a grief to us and our children.[3]

And if we turn from this to ancient descriptions of the theophanies of goddesses, in which they appear in their full beauty and glory, we do not get much nearer to knowing what they looked like. When Aphrodite manifests herself to Anchises after she has been to bed with him,[4] all we read is that she grew so tall that her head touched the roof and that the sort of beauty which Aphrodite has shone from her face. It is a description of the event according to the proper formula for theophanies, though not necessarily less powerful for that. We can perhaps feel the power of this standard description more in the two great theophanies of Demeter in the Eleusis hymn.[5] In both she grows taller and a light shines round her: in the second and more solemn, after she has commanded the institution of her cult at Eleusis, the light grows more intense, like lightning, and there is a fragrance about her: and, to show clearly that she has returned from her appearance as an old woman to the everlasting youth which belongs to the gods, we are told that her hair flows golden over her shoulders. The Eleusis hymn contains other good examples of this terse and powerful evocation of beauty, the picture of the daughters of Celeus running down the road to fetch the disguised goddess and the old lady in her long dark robe following them back (174-183) and Persephone among the flowers at the beginning (1-14). In this scene, which has inspired so many imaginations down the centuries, Persephone's beauty gets a couple of conventional epithets and of the great

3 *Iliad* III 156-160 tr. Richmond Lattimore.
4 Homeric Hymn V *To Aphrodite* 172-175.
5 Homeric Hymn II *To Demeter* 188-189 and 275-280.

narcissus which fatally attracts her we hear only about its size and that "the broad sky above and the whole earth and the salt wave of the sea laughed because of its fragrance" (14).

In all these passages what is evoked is a whole scene and its impact upon the participants. It is the power rather than the aesthetic enjoyability of beauty which is brought out: and this is particularly so where there is anything explicitly divine or godlike about the beauties evoked, as there generally is where they are experienced with some intensity. We can see very well how this works in the most powerful of all ancient evocations of the non-human beauties of earth, in the *Oedipus at Colonus* of Sophocles. When Antigone describes to her blind father the beauty of the sacred wood of Colonus, with its strong growth of laurel, olive and vine and its crowd of nightingales (16-18) and when the old men of the village elaborate her description in the first part of the most memorable of Sophoclean choruses (668-692), what is evoked is well summed up in the first words of Antigone's description *chōros d'hod' hiros*, "this place is holy" (16). When the beauties of earth are experienced intensely they are experienced as beauties with something divine in them. And of course the divine to the ancients, though always beautiful, is not just beautiful in a way to which the proper response is a comfortable sort of aesthetic enjoyment. Those who know the passages which I have just referred to in their contexts will understand very well that where there is divine manifestation there is at least a potency of terror. I shall return to this later.

We now need to consider something about this older awareness of the divine in the beauties of earth which will become important when we begin to think about the relationship to it of the Platonic understanding of the way in which the divine is present in them. This is that it is awareness of the divine in one single world, the only one there is, but awareness of it, not in a bland uniformity of presence but in an innumerable diversity. In the old way of thinking, feeling and imagining which is that of the Greeks and other Mediterranean peoples, as of all archaic cultures, there is only one world and it is divine. There is no question of the divine belonging to and intervening from a higher or different sphere or world. The gods are born in the world. They do not make it. The history of the generation of the world is the family history of the gods. The starting-point for awareness of divine enhancement of the world's beauties is a general awareness of divinity present everywhere and an apprehension of it as part of all experience. How, then, can we speak of a divine *enhancement* of earthly beauty when all earthly beauty is divine? We can, in a very real sense, because in the Greek, as in all archaic cultures, there is an intense awareness of the *poikilia* of the one divine world, of the continual variations in kind and degree of the divine manifestations in its beauty. So the awareness of the divine in the world is not vague or undifferentiated. It is apprehended specially, in varying ways and degrees of intensity, in innumerable theophanies, special moments, special signs, precise disclosure-places. It is these which continually enhance and intensify the sense of the divine beauty: all sorts of particular natural signs, from thunder on the mountains to a sudden flight of birds: a visit to a great holy place or, more often, to a little one, a local spring or a shrine at the end of one's own fields: the apprehension of the beauty of a particular person imaginatively intensified by memories of the manifestations of divine beauties in earlier poetry, of the sort which I spoke about in the preceding paragraphs. That light-hearted but also intensely devout poem of Sappho which begins *Poikilothron' athanat' Aphrodita* gives, I believe, an appropriate instance of this kind of little theophany in its opening verses:

> Aphrodite, undying in intricate splendour,
> Child of the Father, braider of snares, I beg you
> Do not, Our Lady, with torments and tribulations
> Crush me in spirit,
> But come! Come here, if ever in time beforehand
> Hearing my cries afar you attended, and leaving
> The golden house of your Father you came to me, yoking
> Birds to your chariot.
> Then the quick beautiful sparrows brought you, circling,

> Wings beating thick and fast, over the dark earth,
> Down from the sky through the bright air, and suddenly
> There they were with me.[6]

"There *they* were with me." It seems that what touched off Sappho's awareness of the presence of her goddess was a sudden flight of small birds into a bush or tree near her, which can be a numinous occurrence to those attuned to this sort of thing.

The divine powers who were experienced as present in and as intensifying the beauties of earth included many who were apprehended as especially wild, dark, and terrifying (there is always some degree of terror in the manifestations of the divine). The mountain, the high wild lands always very close to the farms and cities, had its own powers. There was Artemis, in her very ancient aspect as Lady of the wild beasts. There was Pan, a genial enough character in most of his manifestations, but master of his own special terror. And the many-sided Dionysus was master of the most terrible of mountain powers, the madness which drove out the women to the mountain – running and dancing of which the climax was the tearing of living flesh. The Greeks very well knew that divine beauty could send men mad. Aphrodite and Erōs had their own kind of maddening power, more universal than the mountain-madness of Dionysus, that prehistoric but vividly remembered and ritually re-enacted experience whose beauty and terror are so well conveyed to us by Euripides in the *Bacchae*. It is important to remember that the wild beauty of the mountain powers was never cut off from or opposed to the tamer world of farm and city. Artemis, sometimes, notably at Ephesus, in a very different but equally ancient and authentic aspect, could be a great city goddess. Pan demanded, and got, a cave-shrine under the Acropolis in the very middle of Athens, and seems to have been perfectly settled and happy there.[7] Dionysus lived on the best of terms with Apollo at Delphi, where the most powerful ritual re-enactment of the mountain running took place, and presided over

6 Sappho I (191 D. L. Page *Lyrica Graeca Selecta*) tr. A. H. A.
7 Herodotus VI 105-106.

the most sophisticated of city entertainments in his theatres and
the jolliest and most bawdy phallic revels on the farms.

Not only the terrifying powers of the wild but the powers of
darkness are included in the world-enhancing and beauty-enhancing divine presence of which the Greeks were aware. The powers
of darkness, the powers in the earth, were not of course for the
Greeks powers of evil. I need not at an Eranos meeting stress the
importance of this Hellenic awareness of divinity on the dark side
of things. We are probably all aware of the disadvantages of a
world-view which understands the cosmos and the things which
happen in it in terms of a battle between the good forces of light
and the evil forces of darkness. I shall speak briefly later about
what happens to this sense of the divinity of the dark in the
Platonic tradition. One of the best ways of coming to understand
what it meant in the older Hellenic world with which we are at
present concerned is a prolonged meditation on the *Eumenides* of
Aeschylus and the *Oedipus at Colonus* of Sophocles. In both plays
we are concerned with the most terrible of the dark powers in the
earth, the Eumenides who are also the Erinyes. In Aeschylus our
understanding of them progresses from the, perhaps somewhat
melodramatic, horror of the beginning to the splendour of the end
when they are conducted in the great procession to the shrine
which everyone in the audience knew, neither defeated nor
transformed but persuaded by Athenē to show to her people that
other aspect of which all their worshippers were aware. And,
going on to Colonus, we find that the beloved and beautiful sacred
wood of which I spoke earlier is pre-eminently the wood of the
Eumenides. We find that, for all the terror they inspire in the
villagers, the ritual for their propitiation which is described with
loving care by the Chorus has an austere beauty appropriate to
ancient powers of good and is no grotesque apotropaic ceremony
for averting the machinations of demons (466-492). And, from the
prayer of Oedipus (84-110) to the closing scene, we see them
working together with Apollo (to whom they are never reconciled
in Aeschylus' play) for that final consummation, in some way

good for Oedipus and for Athens, whose nature is best left to Sophocles to suggest.

Wild and tame, mad and sane, dark and light: in all these the divine is present, and where it is present there is an intensified beauty.

II

Before going on from the presence of the divine in the earthly beauties of the one world of the old Hellenic tradition to the Platonic awareness of the beauty-enhancing presence of a divine which is in some sense separate and transcendent, it will be desirable to say something about a way of thinking, feeling and imagining which has had a very powerful effect on the later thoughts and imaginations of Europeans. This is cosmic piety or religiosity. It is highly relevant to our theme that we should consider this and its consequences, and should distinguish it both from the older Greek experience of divinity in the beauties of the world and from what I believe to be authentic Platonism, more precisely than the ancients themselves always did and some moderns have done. Cosmic piety, like so much else in later ancient thought, does have its effective beginnings in Plato: and the early Stoics, with their passionate sense of the total unity of divine and world, developed it strongly. But the form in which it became lastingly powerful, which I propose to consider here, is that which it took as a result of a certain re-Platonizing and re-Aristotelianizing of Stoicism at some time not very long before the beginning of our era. This is the form which had such an immensely powerful influence on European thinking and imagining at least till the seventeenth century and still, I think, persists sometimes in many of our imaginations about the world and our selves. Its particular relevance at this point in this paper is that it carries in it a distinctive kind of pseudo-otherworldliness. There is for those who think and feel in this way only one world, the great divine material cosmos: though another spiritual and immaterial cosmos can be added outside and above the material one without any great disturbance of the structure of thought and feeling as long as it is thought of and imagined as outside and above. But the one cosmos is, as we shall see, very sharply and significantly divided into two, and the two parts are very differently valued.

The general picture of the world as it was seen by those who shared in the cosmic piety is familiar to anyone interested in the thought and imagination of late antiquity, the Middle Ages and the early Renaissance. But we should consider it rather carefully if we are to understand its consequences as they concern us here. Those who apprehended the world in this way still saw it as a great divine living organism, and thought of their own true rational selves as parts of the divine fire which animated and governed it. But that divine fire, whose animating and ordering presence on and around our earth was not of course denied, was thought of as predominantly concentrated in the Upper Cosmos, the region of the heavenly bodies, the intensely living and supremely intelligent visible gods, and it was there that men had to look if they were to see divinity in its true beauty and glory. These heavenly bodies were believed to be of vast size and to circle the earth in vast orbits, in accordance with the scientific astronomy of the Platonic and Aristotelian schools: we should never, of course, forget that a most important reason for the perdurance of the cosmic piety through so many centuries and its hold on men's intellects and imaginations was that it was in accord with the best available physical science. The earth lies in the centre of this vast celestial universe, a mere point in size compared with the great fiery bodies of the heavens, surrounded by its dark, damp, mistily impure lower atmosphere. Beyond this, and beginning with the sphere of the moon, the regions of intense and splendid fiery light, where the living and divine globes of moon and sun and stars circle in their everlasting dance, stretch out to the outermost sphere of heaven, the sphere of the fixed stars. We should appreciate the importance to this system of the stroke of intellectual and imaginative genius which disposed of the "fixed stars", in their potentially embarrassing number and variety, by setting them all in a single sphere. Was, perhaps, one of the most shatteringly revolutionary consequences of the new astronomy the dissolution of the *Primum Mobile*?

Let us now consider the consequences of this view of the cosmos in so far as they are relevant to our subject. Quite a good way of beginning will be to try to relate it to the three co-equal titles of our conference. There is certainly in it an intense devout concentration on the "Beauty of the World", if "World" is taken to mean the cosmos as a whole and the concentration is understood to be on those greatest parts of it which predominantly make the ordered beauty of that whole. There is a full appreciation of "Die Schönheit der Dinge" if "Dinge" is understood selectively. The heavenly bodies are undoubtedly Things quite overwhelming in their thingness. But when we turn to our French title "La Beauté sur la Terre" we find that cosmic piety was liable to lead to a radical devaluation of and disesteem for the beauty on earth, if by earth we understand this little globe which is our home here and now. It is, I hope, by now generally understood that though the ancient picture of the cosmos was in the astronomical sense geocentric, the piety which accompanied it was by no means geocentric in its scale of values. The central earth is not only insignificantly small in comparison with the least of the heavenly bodies. This central region below the moon in which it lies is low in every way and on every scale, and the earth is lowest in it. It is the darkest, dampest and dirtiest part of the universe, a kind of cosmic cesspit, full of corruption and decay. Divinity and beauty are not of course entirely absent from it: it is still part of the divine universe. But its beauties are dimmed and spoilt and its delights transitory and corrupting. We should lift up our hearts and minds from them to see true divine beauty in the glory of the great fiery spheres of heaven and their everlasting dance. (You will notice that I speak of the heavenly bodies as "fiery", and this is what the Stoics and Platonists believed they were. Aristotle's doctrine of the

Quintessence, the fifth celestial element different from the four here below, was not generally accepted by the devotees of the divine cosmos. But this made very little difference in practice, because they considered the heavenly fire to be so much purer and more authentic than fire here below that the difference in degree became almost a difference in kind.)

We can begin to see already what I meant by speaking of the "pseudo-otherworldliness" of cosmic piety. We shall see this even more clearly if we turn from its way of thinking about the macrocosm to its way of thinking about the microcosm. In my general account of cosmic piety I remarked that its adherents thought of their own true rational selves as being part of the divine fire of the heavens. This meant that the true life of those souls was thought of as being above in those visible heavens and that the spiritual journey was thought of in terms of an ascent to that true heavenly life, and the preparation for it by purging the soul of all the impurities of earth. Here below the soul was clogged and contaminated by the passions which belong to the dark impurities of this lowest region. We encounter here in a very strong form the ancient Greek opposition between the hot, bright, dry, active, male, good divine principle and the cold, dark, moist, passive, female, evil principle. (The characterization of the two principles as male and female should always be remembered. It has very deep roots and often produces very strange results in spiritualities affected by this way of thinking.) When we take into account this way of thinking and feeling about the soul and the spiritual life we can see very clearly how radically "other-worldly" cosmic piety is in the sense that it utterly despises and rejects the beauties and delights of earth. I am inclined to think that both in later antiquity and in the succeeding Christian centuries the rejection of earth and its beauties becomes particularly sharp, violent and harsh (and in Christians particularly anti-feminine) when this corporealist spirituality of the cosmic piety is somehow consciously or unconsciously at work: and it penetrated so deep into the religious outlook on the world that it can sometimes continue to work in feelings and imaginations, when the world-picture to which it properly belongs has been consciously rejected or abandoned.

There is another way in which it is possible that cosmic piety may have affected the sensibility to beauty of those influenced by it and led to a despising of the common beauties of earth. From the time when the scientific astronomy of the Academy became dominant the Upper Cosmos was thought of as pre-eminently the realm in which mathematical reason and order were dominant. (Pre-Socratic views of *ta meteora*, "the things up above" were often very different.) In the cosmic piety the noble purity of the spherical form of the visible gods and the grand regularity of their circular movements were powerful incentives to devotion. We should notice again the religious importance of the basic simplicity of this great vision of the world. The ancient scientific astronomers might well have been able to cope with a more complex picture of the heavens, at least a little closer to our own understanding of the vast intricacy and strangeness of what goes on up there. But this would have been destructive of cosmic piety. It was essential to it that the glorious manifestation of divine reason in the heavens should be apprehensible and expressible in simple terms – the sphere the perfect shape and the circle of the choral dance the perfect movement. Never have the rotund and the rotary been so religiously exalted. This devotion to simple and regular form and order may well have at least helped to intensify a tendency to despise the beauties of this earth with their endless variety of irregular shapes and unco-ordinated movements. Cosmic piety would tend to reinforce the "classicist" side of Hellenic sensibility, the preference for a beauty in which mathematical structure, symmetry and order can clearly be discerned, which was perhaps always in tension with that primaeval awareness of the *poikilia* of divine manifestation in the beauties of earth with which I began. I shall return to this subject when I come to speak of the thought of Plotinus.

III

The transition from the way in which the divine enhancement of earthly beauty was apprehended in the old Hellenic world to the way in which it was apprehended by the Platonists is generally presented as a transition from thinking of it in terms of one world to thinking of it in terms of two *cosmoi*, a material one and a spiritual or intelligible one: this is the true Platonic distinction, which needs to be carefully distinguished from that spatial distinction between Upper and Lower Cosmos which belongs to the cosmic piety we have just been considering: though the two often intermingle and even become somewhat confused in the thought of the ancients. The result of this Platonic way of thinking is that the divine enhancement of beauties by manifestation or theophany is interpreted in an "other-worldly" way as the appearance of a light and life from "beyond", from the incorporeal world only apprehensible by the intellect. There is of course a great deal of truth in this presentation. But if we simply leave it at that we shall be in danger of over-simplifying the Platonic understanding of the world and making too sharp a break between it and the old Hellenic awareness of divinity by which, to the end of antiquity, the Platonists were surrounded and in which they shared. This very simple fact that the context of Platonism was the old Hellenic piety needs to be continually remembered. The Platonists lived among the shrines and images of that older world: they practised its rites as a matter of course as members of Hellenic communities: and the greatest part of their education as children consisted in learning the poetry with which this paper began. This last observation was of course intended to recall Plato's own well-known hostility to that poetry. I do not propose in this paper to spend much time on the theme of the attitude of Plato and later Platonists to the arts. As I said at the beginning I am trying to concentrate our attention where the poets and philosophers concentrated theirs, on the beauty of nature and spirit. But something must be said at this point if the whole Platonic attitude to the beauties of earth is not to be misunderstood.[8] First of all, of course, we need to remember that by the time the Platonist understanding of theophany in the beauties of earth took its most powerful and influential form in the third century A.D. the old hostility to the poets and their piety had disappeared. Platonic and poetic religion had come together, and in the end it was the Neoplatonic philosophers of Athens who were the last defenders of the old Hellenic ways of recognizing and worshipping the Divine. They were well content that the Platonic imagination should be the old Hellenic imagination, as in fact it had never ceased to be.

On this point we should not over-simplify the attitude of Plato himself. In his treatments of the subject in the *Republic* and the *Laws* he is writing very much from the point of view of a Minister of Education who is also Prefect of the Congregation of Rites: he is considering, that is, what needs to be done about poetry in the interests of intelligent reform of education and public worship. (It is important in considering ancient thought about art to remember that, always in classical Greece and to a considerable extent still in Hellenistic and Roman times, it is considered as a public activity with which the public authorities must be concerned because it affects the well-being of the whole community.) Plato's lowly view of the ontological status of the work of art as the "representation of a semblance" (*phantasmatos mimēsis Republic* 598B) and his double-edged appreciations of poetic inspiration in the *Ion* and the *Phaedrus* fit in very well with his stance as reformer of faith and morals. But of course this position requires him to recognize fully the power of art and its consequent importance to the

8 In addition to the many well-known works on this well-worn subject (among which I have found Iris Murdoch's *The Fire and The Sun* [Oxford 1977] particularly helpful) I would like to draw attention to the thesis of my former pupil Astrid Brunner *The Metaphysical Relevance of Art: a study of contemporary aesthetic philosophy against the background of Platonic/Neo-Platonic metaphysics* (M.A. Thesis, Department of Classics, Dalhousie University, Halifax, Nova Scotia, Canada, Fall 1977). I have learnt a great deal from this and from our discussions in the course of its preparation.

community. He, like all other Greek philosophers, was well aware that true philosophers are very rare indeed – if they ever occur at all. He knew that the great mass of mankind would always, even in the most ideal society which he could conceive, have to find such awareness of divinity as they were capable of through their feelings and imaginations, in their apprehensions of the beauties of this material world stimulated by the right sort of art. And he knew that this was how even those who might later become true philosophers would have to start: they could not even begin the philosophic quest which might lead, after many years, to the vision of the Forms and of the Good, unless their feelings and imaginations were rightly trained by a right awareness of divine beauty in this world. This is splendidly expressed in the great passage on the proper function of poetry, music and the visual arts in the education of the future philosopher-rulers in the Republic (III 401B-402A). And when we look at Plato's ideal proposals for the ordering of religion (he was very well aware that the political and social orders which he proposed as ideals, or as the best theoretically possible, were unrealisable, or very unlikely to be realised, in practice) we find that, though liturgical texts are to be drastically censored and reformed, all the old divine rites and ceremonies and holy places which enhanced the beauty of earth for ordinary men are assumed as still there, part of the continuing background for ordinary men and philosophers alike.[9] Plato's apprehension of the divine in this world at the level of feeling and imagination was not after all so far from the old Hellenic way. He was more critical, as was appropriate to his time and place, of inherited religious traditions than his very traditionalist successors. But he might not have been so hostile to their rather wholesale and uncritical defence of all the old natural pieties of the Mediterranean world against alien barbarian attack as Christian

9 This is clearly implied in the statement that the religious ordering of the ideal *Politeia* is to be left to the Delphic Oracle (*Republic* IV 427B). *Laws* V 738B-E is a very strong affirmation of the necessity for the city to preserve all traditional shrines and observances.

apologists would have liked him to be. There is no suggestion anywhere in his writings that he wanted or would have approved a "new religion" in the sense in which Christianity was a "new religion".

In considering how the Platonists understand the divine enhancement of earthly beauties we need to think carefully about the way in which their two *cosmoi* are related. I shall say more about this when I come to discuss the thought of Plotinus, but some preliminary remarks are necessary here to avoid misunderstanding. One of the few uncontroversial (I hope) remarks which can be made about the Platonic Forms is that they are incorporeal and perceptible only by the intellect. It was Plotinus who most fully worked out the implications of this. But I think it would be true to say that already in Plato it means that the Forms should not be thought of as "separate" in the sense of being outside, beyond, or above the material world. What their separation means is that they are independent of the particular instantiations of them perceived by the senses and prior to them both in being and thought. The material world owes such existence as it has to the Forms; they do not owe their existence to it and could perfectly well exist without it. And we can only understand our sense-perceptible cosmos in terms of the Forms, not the other way round. But there is no spatial separation, because they are not in space at all. (They are not in time either, but some very difficult and controversial questions arise here about the meaning of eternity in Plato and the Platonists and the relation of eternity to time which it would not be relevant to pursue here.[10]) However, Plato did sometimes see them imaginatively and portray them mythically as "outside" and "above". He did this with special power in the enormously influential mythical part of the *Phaedrus*, where the Forms are

10 Some idea of the problems which arise here can be gained from J. Whittaker, *God Time Being (Symbolae Osloenses Fasc. Supplet* XXIII, Oslo 1971): A. H. Armstrong "Eternity, Life and Movement in Plotinus' accounts of *Nous*" (*Plotinian and Christian Studies*, London 1979, XV) and P. Manchester "Time and the Soul in Plotinus, III 7 [45] 11" in *Dionysius* II (1978) pp. 102-136.

IV

situated outside the heaven in the *huperouranios topos* (247C-E). This is very natural: the symbolism of light from above is very ancient and powerful. Do even those who have the most spiritual conception of God and the most intimate awareness of his presence here below always manage to avoid envisaging him as enthroned "above the sky"? But we must make the effort required to break away from this if we are to understand Platonic transcendence rightly.

This tendency to envisage the Forms as "up there" in spatial separation was reinforced, perhaps for Plato himself in his later years, and certainly for later Platonists, by that sharp emphasis on the spatially separate and transcendent divinity of the Upper Cosmos which was characteristic of the cosmic piety discussed earlier (pp. 59-63). And the tendency to make a very sharp separation between the intelligible and material worlds would also be reinforced by a literal interpretation of the *Timaeus* which set paradigm and copy apart with the Craftsman between them, and, later, by the Judaeo-Christian preference for a demiurgic or "artisan" understanding of creation.

An understanding of Platonic *erōs*, the passionate (in a modern, not the ancient sense[11]) drive towards beauty, is of course essential for any appreciation of Platonic thought about earthly beauties

11 It is most important in considering ancient thought about "the passions"' to remember how vividly aware the ancients remained that *pathos* and *passio* denote passivity. There is something feeble and soft about being dominated and marked by one's passions. The passionate person is not only pathetic but pathĕtic from the point of view of the ancient philosophers. Admittedly this is rather difficult to square with the Platonic doctrine of *erōs* which we are considering. William Blake brings out the difference between the ancient and the modern understanding of "passion" in a passage which, like so much in his writings, is consciously anti-Platonic in intention but deeply Platonic in feeling: "Men are admitted into Heaven not because they have curbed and governed their Passions or have no Passions but because they have cultivated their Understandings. The Treasures of Heaven are not Negations of Passion but Realities of Intellect, from which all the Passions Emanate Uncurbed in Their Eternal Glory. The Fool shall not enter into Heaven let him be never so Holy." (*Description of the Vision of the Last Judgement* p. 87 of *Additions to Blake's*

and their divine enhancement. Beauty for Platonists is what is lovable in a strong and vehement sense. And it seems that the *erōs* which drives the philosopher on to the vision of intelligible beauty is not different in kind from the commonest erotic *erōs*. This means that beauty at any level is always beauty because it always arouses *erōs*. The passage in the *Dialogues* on the ascent to the vision of absolute beauty which has most powerfully inspired later Platonists is of course Diotima's account of the final mysteries of *Erōs* in the *Symposium* (210A-212B). And if we read it carefully we shall find that it can tell us a good deal about the presence of absolute divine beauty in the beauties of earth.[12] The question which concerns us here is whether Plato intends to represent Diotima in her account of the ascent as recommending the kicking away of the steps at each stage, so that one is left at the end with a purely abstract contemplation of ultimate beauty which has no connexion with the particular beauties here below, and cannot enhance our awareness of them by a sense of its divine presence in them. I do not think that this is Plato's intention. To begin with, one has to start the ascent with a particular earthly beauty (210A, 4-8). This is in perfect accord with the *Phaedrus*: and I think that always in Plato a strong awareness of and a strong response to particular earthly beauties is the starting-point for the philosophical ascent. Plotinus expounds Plato's teaching excellently here in the first two chapters of his treatise *On Dialectic* (I 3 [20]). Then, at every stage from beginning to end, the universal and absolute beauty is present *in* particular beauties and is apprehended as what makes them beautiful (210 A8-B6 : 211 B2). Further, at each stage

---

Catalogue of Pictures etc. for 1810: p. 842 in *Poetry and Prose of William Blake* ed. Geoffrey Keynes, Nonesuch Press, 1927).

12 My exegesis of the *Symposium* is my own. But I have been greatly helped in it by the work which my former pupil, Elena Corrigan and I did on the dialogue in the course of the preparation of her thesis *The Structure of the Symposium* (M. A. Thesis, Department of Classics, Dalhousie University, Halifax, Nova Scotia, Fall 1979) which is a notable contribution to the understanding of the dialogue.

it is quite as important to expand horizontally as to ascend vertically: the move from particular to universal is at least as necessary as the move from lower to higher. To cling to one particular *epitēdeuma* is as petty and slavish as to cling to a particular human being (210D 1-2): and when one arrives at the vision it is as clear that absolute beauty is not a *logos* or an *epistēmē* as that it does not have hands or face (211A 5-7). I think that at the end all the steps are still there, and once one has the abiding vision of absolute beauty in one, one can go up and down them as one needs, and will then see lower beauties, even bodily and earthly ones, as enhanced by the divine presence in them of Beauty Itself.

There is another consideration about Platonic other-worldliness which needs to be borne in mind when we are assessing how far it is congruous with a strong sense of the divine enhancement of earthly beauties. What is the precise nature of the love and enjoyment of things here below which Plato and the Platonists urge their followers to overcome and escape from? This is something so commonplace to them, as to all great traditional moralists, Eastern and Western, that it is not always very much stressed, and this can lead to a misunderstanding of their true position. It is not stressed in the *Symposium*, but it is certainly there. In the passage which we are considering, the rather unexpected appearance of "gold and fine clothes" along with pretty boys among the things which Diotima says that one who has experienced the vision will no longer care about (211D 2-3), shows that the sort of attachment to earthly beauties which Plato, here as elsewhere, is most concerned to draw people away from, is the acquisitive and exploitative kind, with its endless fuss and worry about *possessing* and *using* the good things of this world. This is strongly confirmed by the portrayal of Socrates by Alcibiades as the best of all exemplars in the matter of *erōs* because he is so utterly unattached and unacquisitive (216D-219E). What the Platonic tradition, and with varying degrees of emphasis the other great Greek philosophical traditions and the older and more authentic Christian traditions, wish their followers to get rid of is the acquisitiveness which not only makes it impossible to start the ascent to the divine but breeds envy, hatred, and strife among mankind. They wish to eliminate desire for what Aristotle, following a lead given by Plato (*Phaedo* 66C 5-7) calls in a fine chapter of the *Nicomachean Ethics* (IX 8) the *perimachēta agatha* "the goods people fight about" (1168b 19 and 1169a 21). In Plato, Aristotle, and the older moral traditions generally the truly desirable goods of this world on which most emphasis is laid are those which belong to the possession and practice of moral virtue. Our best Western traditions are very close here to the commendation of non-attached action in the *Bhagávad Gitā* (III-V). The non-attached enjoyment of earthly beauties is always considered spiritually important, especially by those Christians influenced by the later Platonic tradition, but for its fullest and most splendid celebration we have to look, not to antiquity but to seventeenth-century England.

It is to be found in the *Centuries of Meditations* of my country neighbour Thomas Traherne, son of a shoemaker in the city of Hereford and for some years parish priest of the not otherwise very notable village of Credenhill. The *Meditations* were written for friends, and Traherne left his manuscript unsigned and made no attempt to publish it in his short lifetime.[13] They were only identified as his and published in the early years of this century. A few quotations will give an idea of the force of his celebration of the beauties of earth, his exhortation to see God in them, and his preaching of non-attachment.

> ... your Enjoyment of the World is never right, till you so Esteem it, that evry thing in it, is more your Treasure, then a Kings Exchequer full of Gold and Silver. And that Exchequer yours also in its Place and Service. Can you take too much joy in your fathers Works? He is Himself in evry Thing. Som Things are little on

13 Traherne lived from 1637 to 1674. Details of his life and works and of the rediscovery of the poems and *Meditations* are to be found in *Centuries, Poems and Thanksgivings* ed. H. M. Margoliouth, 2 vols (Oxford Clarendon Press 1958) and the more generally accessible *Poems, Centuries and Three Thanksgivings* ed. Anne Ridler, (London, Oxford University Press, 1966).

the outside, and Rough and Common: but I remember the Time, when the Dust of the Streets were as precious as Gold to my infant Eys, and now they are more precious to the Ey of Reason. (I. 25).

Wine by its moisture quencheth my Thirst, whether I consider it or no: but to see it flowing from his Lov who gav it unto Man, Quencheth the Thirst even of the Holy Angels. To consider it is to drink it Spiritualy. To Rejoice in its Diffusion is to be of a Publick Mind. And to take Pleasure in all the Benefits it doth to all is Heavenly, for so they do in Heaven. (I. 27).

You never Enjoy the World aright till the Sea itself floweth in your Veins, till you are Clothed with the Heavens, and Crowned with the Stars. (I. 29).

When I came into the Country, and being seated among silent Trees, had all my Time in my own Hands, I resolved to Spend it all, whatever it cost me, in Search of Happiness, and to Satiat that burning Thirst which Nature had Enkindled in me from my Youth. In which I was so resolut, that I chose rather to liv upon 10 pounds a year, and to go in Lether Clothes, and feed upon Bread and Water, so that I might hav all my time clearly to my self: then to keep many Thousands per Annums in an Estate of Life where my Time would be Devoured in Care and Labor. (III 46).

He thought also that no Poverty could befall him that enjoyd Paradice: for when all the Things are gone which Men can giv, A Man is still as Rich as Adam was in Eden: who was Naked there. A Naked Man is the Richest Creature in all Worlds: and can never be Happy, till he sees the Riches of his Nakedness. He is very Poor in Knowledge that thinks Adam poor in Eden. (IV 36).

Traherne shows particularly clearly that the ideal pursued, often very unsuccessfully, by Platonists and Christians who share his love of this world is to enjoy to the full the beauties of earth and to be intensely aware of the divine presence in them, while eliminating as far as possible all desire to possess them and exploit them for transitory and illusory satisfactions.

It was above all Plotinus, in the third century of our era, who gave Platonism the form in which it has helped most to make us vividly aware of the divine presence in the beauties of earth. There are several reasons for this in his presentation of what he believed to be the true teaching of Plato. We are not in considering any of them concerned with ideas which Plotinus simply originated. A long development of thought in the Platonic and other Greek philosophical traditions lies behind them. But it was his presentation of them which gave them the power which they have exercised in the following centuries. The first and most important is Plotinus' insistence that the first principle and source of beauty and all goodness, the One or Good, completely transcends the Divine Intellect which is the World of Forms. Not only do Forms and Intellect originate from that which is neither form nor intellect. They are only beautiful in the true Platonic sense, that is delightful and lovable, capable of arousing *erōs*, because of the light and life from the Good which eternally plays upon them (VI 7 [38] 21-22).[14] Formal perfection, in the full sense of the finite perfection of the World of Forms which contains all real being, is not enough. It needs, and of course eternally receives, a light and life from the Formless which alone is what the soul driven on by the *erōs* which is given by that Good truly seeks. And if we look at Plotinus' divine world the other way up, from the point of view of what lies below Intellect, we discover something else relevant to our present subject. This is that there is another way in which the self-enclosed, inturned perfection of the Intellect which is the Forms is not enough for Plotinus. Pierre Hadot brings this out very well in his exposition of Plotinus' interpretation of Plato's least favourite myth, the story in Hesiod about Ouranos, Kronos and Zeus, in his great anti-gnostic work.[15] What is of particular interest to us here is Hadot's comment on the remarkable text in which Plotinus says:

> The king there in the higher world does not rule over different, alien people, but has the most just, the natural sovereignty and the true kingdom: for he is king of truth and natural lord of all his own offspring and divine company, king of the king and of the kings, and more rightly than Zeus called the father of the gods; Zeus imitates him in this way also in that he is not satisfied with the

14 VI 7 [38] 21-22. See A. H. Armstrong "Beauty and the Discovery of Divinity in The Thought of Plotinus", *Plotinian and Christian Studies* XIX.

15 The great work is Cilento's *Paideia Antignostica* and the German *Großschrift*, the work which Porphyry split into four treatises placed in different Enneads III 8, V 8, V 5 and II 9. See P. Hadot "Ouranos, Kronos and Zeus In Plotinus' Treatise Against the Gnostics" in *Neoplatonism and Early Christian Thought*, London 1981 pp. 124-137.

IV

74

contemplation of his father but aspires to, we might say, the active power with
which his grandfather established reality in being (V 5 [32], 16-24; tr. A. H.
Armstrong).

The king here is of course the One or Good; the father of Zeus is
the Divine Intellect which is the World of Forms; and Zeus, the
grandson of the Good, is Soul. Hadot comments:

> There is a deep-seated affinity, so it appears, between the sovereignty of Zeus
> and the sovereignty of Ouranos, even though the sovereignty of Ouranos is
> wholly transcendent. Thus we discover in Plotinus' theory a hidden preference
> for the process of procession: the power characteristic of the One and of the
> Soul. ... the Beautiful is Beautiful above all for its own sake, for the sake of its
> conversion to itself; whereas the Good has no need to be Good for itself, because
> it has no need at all. The Good is Good only for things other than itself, in the
> movement of procession which it necessarily gives rise to. At root, it is this
> generosity of the Good which to Plotinus' way of thinking is the supreme value.
> Hence the principle, *bonum diffusivum sui*, the principle which, for Plotinus,
> explains and justifies the unfolding of the whole of reality.[16]

This primacy of generosity, of outgoing creativity, with its
accompanying sense that absolute perfection of being, the self-
enclosed, self-contemplating beauty of the World of Forms which
is Intellect is not enough, is a very striking development of
Platonism. When we bring it together in our minds, as I think we
should, with that unstructured light from the Good which alone
makes beauty truly beautiful, that is, lovable: (above, p. 73) that
light which is also life and belongs to the same kind of thought
which sees the first moment in the eternal procession of Divine
Intellect-Being from its source as an unstructured life which
becomes structured into the World of Forms in its checked return
in contemplation upon that source, the Good: then I think that we
can see the opportunities which Plotinian Platonism gives for
enjoying and valuing the imperfect and changing, but lively and
endlessly various beauties of this earth of ours: those beauties of
which Plotinus speaks so well in his great and austere late work
On Providence:

16 P. Hadot, art. cit. p. 136.

We must conclude that the universal order is for ever something of this kind from the evidence of what we see in the All, how this order extends to everything, even to the smallest, and the art is wonderful which appears, not only in the divine beings but also in the things which one might have supposed providence would have despised for their smallness, for example the workmanship which produces wonders in rich variety in ordinary animals and the beauty of appearance which extends to the fruits and even the leaves of plants, and their beauty of flower which comes so effortlessly, and their delicacy and variety, and that all this has not been made once and come to an end but is always being made as the powers above move in different ways over this world. (III 2 [47] 13, 17-27, tr. A. H. Armstrong).

We should not interpret what has just been said as meaning to imply that there is in the thought of Plotinus any devaluation of the World of Forms. He would be a very strange kind of Platonist indeed if there was. He is indeed very conscious, as we have seen, of the transcendent pre-eminence of its source, the Good, and of the light and life which flows from it. But his celebrations of the beauty and glory of the world of real being are unsurpassed in Platonic literature, and sometimes rather startling to those who are inclined to think of the Forms in text-book Platonist terms as some kind of hypostatized abstract universals composing a cosmos of static perfection. The light which is life predominates within it, as it transcends it and extends below it. Though its unity is incomparably more unified than that of our world here below, it is the unity of a plenitude in the richest variety. It contains absolutely everything in the material cosmos, even individuals wherever their individuality is more than merely numerical and is the result of a difference which must be considered one of form.[17] Everything is there, and everything there, even what is most irrational, lifeless and inert here below, is living thought which is formed and structured life at its most intense, united with and transparent to all else and so charged with unbounded glory. A

---

17 On Forms of individuals in Plotinus see A. H. Armstrong "Form, Individual and Person in Plotinus", *Plotinian and Christian Studies* XX: references to other important discussions are given in n. 1.

sentence from one of Plotinus' great visionary descriptions of the
World of Forms may give an idea of how he experienced it:

> They [the Forms in Intellect] all flow, in a way, from a single spring, not like one
> particular breath or one warmth, but as if there was one quality which held and
> kept intact all the qualities in itself, of sweetness along with fragrance, and was at
> once the quality of wine and the character of all tastes, the sights of colours and
> all the awarenesses of touch, and all that hearings hear, all tunes and every
> rhythm. (VI 7 [38] 12, 23-30. tr. A. H. Armstrong).

And this intelligible cosmos, which is our material cosmos with all
its beauties intensified and seen *sub specie aeternitatis*, is most
intimately an immediately present in our world here and now.
Plotinus is particularly concerned throughout the Enneads to
bring out to the full the implications of the incorporeality of the
intelligible, and, in spite of occasional slight distortions due to the
influence of the cosmic piety discussed above (pp. 59-63) succeeds
extremely well. One of the most important is that because the
intelligible, since it is incorporeal, is not in space or time, it is
immediately present as a whole at every point in space and every
moment of time. "For the sense-world is in one place, but the
intelligible world is everywhere" (V 9 [5]) 13-14 tr. A. H. A.). This
immediacy of presence is not affected by the intermediacy of Soul.
It is Soul, not Intellect, in Plotinus which forms, governs and
animates the material cosmos, imparting to it its proper degree of
divinity: but this does not make the intelligible cosmos more
remote from the sense-world,[18] any more than the intermediacy of
the two lower hypostases makes the Good any less immediately
present to us here and now. Hierarchical superiority in the
Neoplatonists does not mean greater remoteness.

One of Plotinus' most forcible ways of expressing this immediate presence is to insist that the material cosmos is a natural, not
an artificial image. Its relation to its archetype which is also its

---

18 See V 8 [31] 7, 12-16: the chapter is one of Plotinus' frequent powerful attacks
   on the "artisan" conception of divine creation required by a literal interpretation of the *Timaeus* and shared by many Middle Platonists and most Jews and
   Christians.

creator is more like that of a shadow or a reflection to its original than that of a statue or a painting.[19] This sense of the immediate presence of archetype to image and the total continuing dependence of image on archetype which it involves is one of Plotinus' grounds for objecting to the "artisan" concept of divine creation, which requires the material cosmos to be thought of as an artefact separable and distanceable from its divine maker. The other is his strong rejection of the idea that the Divine Intellect can properly be represented as planning its creative work: its thought is not in any way discursive and its contents are not at all like the concepts with which discursive reason necessarily operates. This understanding of the nature of divine intellect, which is common to all Neoplatonists,[20] also of course helps them to apprehend the divine archetype in its material image with the vividness and directness of sense-awareness at its most intense. This understanding of the material cosmos as an image which manifests and makes present its incorporeal divine archetype on the level of body and sense is the essential of the Platonic awareness of the divine presence in and enhancement of earthly beauties. As we have seen, it was developed and intensified with great power by Plotinus. But precisely because of the strength of his presentation we become particularly aware in reading the *Enneads* of an ambiguity intrinsic to the idea of "image" in the valuation of this world here below which runs through the whole Platonic tradition, an ambiguity, perhaps, very close to the ambiguity of the cosmos itself. The concept of "image" requires, and indeed demands, a sliding scale of valuation. At the lower end of the scale the emphasis is on the difference between image and archetype and the inferiority of the former to the latter. One says "How, poor, trivial and inadequate

---

19 See VI 4 [22] 10. VI 4 is the first part of the great work *On The Presence of Being, One and the Same, Everywhere as a Whole*, which is of central importance for understanding this aspect of Plotinus' thought.

20 For its powerful expression by Proclus see A. H. Armstrong "The Negative Theology of *Nous* in Later Neoplatonism" in *Platonismus und Christentum* ed. H.-D. Blume u. F. Mann [= this volume, study III], pp. 31-37.

a thing this mere image is compared with the original". At the higher end the emphasis is not only on the excellence of the image on its proper level, "this perceptible god, image of the intelligible, greatest and best, most beautiful and most perfect", as Plato calls it in the last sentence of the *Timaeus*. It is also, most strongly in Plotinus and later Platonism, on the presence in it of the divine archetype and the light which comes from beyond. Here one is moved to use *eikōn* not in its neutral or derogatory earlier Greek sense but in the strong and sacred sense which it has come to have in the Orthodox Church. One will say "How beautiful and venerable is this icon of the eternal not made with human hands. In it we encounter the presence and power of God". There are of course many intermediate stages on this scale of valuation: and lower and higher valuations can be held together in a Platonist's mind and applied to the world together at any one time, as is generally the case with Plotinus. But when the higher valuation predominates we can see coming together the basic Platonic and Christian faith in the goodness on its own level of the divinely made material world, the awareness of that light from the Good which reaches from its source beyond the real being of the intelligible down to the lowest limits of anything which can in any way exist, and the sense of the living presence of the archetype in its natural image, to give the late Platonic understanding of this world as the icon of the divine the enduring power which it has had in our tradition.

We have not, in the modern period of the scholarly study of ancient philosophy, been inclined to take the later Neoplatonists, Iamblichus and his successors, very seriously or to read very much of the voluminous surviving works of the great Athenian Proclus, until the last two decades or so. But the revival of interest in them which has led to the publication of admirable new critical editions and a closer and more comprehensive study of the increasingly accessible texts has recently led to a much better understanding and appreciation of some parts of their thought which were ignored, or rather contemptuously dismissed, by earlier generations. One which is of particular relevance to the subject of this paper is their final total rehabilitation of the dark, material, feminine principle. The history of this "dark other" in the Pythagorean-Platonic tradition is rather complex. I have attempted to sketch it elsewhere.[21] It is generally said to be *kakon* and the cause of *kaka* here below, and this means that it is regarded with hostility and suspicion, not least by Plotinus. But we always need to remember in considering this that the "dark other" which is *kakon* is one of the two absolutely indispensable constituents of a universe which is strongly affirmed to be good and beautiful, as indispensable to its very existence as the male principle of form and light. This makes it rather risky, and at times misleading, to translate *kakon* into modern languages by words which have sinister overtones from Christian demonology, as "evil" has in English. Platonic-Pythagorean dualism is never simply a conflict-dualism of the Iranian pattern, even in those Middle Platonists like Plutarch and Atticus who stand closest to this and were perhaps influenced by it. For the greatest part of its history it occupies a strange intermediate area between dualisms of Iranian type and those which are best symbolized by the Chinese Yang-Yin circle. What the last Hellenic Neoplatonists achieve is to bring it over firmly to the "Chinese" side by giving an account of the "dark other" and its relationship to the principle of light, form and order which is perfectly in accord with the Yang-Yin circle. They see the two principles as equal in honour, proceeding directly from the ineffable One/Good which is beyond all duality and difference. They are the father and mother of all that exists, of real being and the intelligible cosmos as well as of the material cosmos. And they see them in this way without denying that the "dark other" is really dark. They take full account of, and in their own way assent

21 In "Dualism, Platonic, Gnostic and Christian", *Plotinus Amid Gnostics and Christians* ed. David T. Runia (Amsterdam, Free University Press 1984) pp. 29 –52 [= this volume, study XII]. This will also be published in the proceedings of the International Neoplatonic Society's conference held at the University of Oklahoma in March 1984.

to, every thing which was said earlier in the tradition about her being responsible for the *kaka* in our necessarily imperfect world here below. But, none the less, they see in her darkness a divine and transcendent virtue.

This complete rehabilitation of the "dark other" appears fully developed in the venerated master of Proclus, Syrianus.[22] Proclus expounds it very fully and clearly in a number of passages.[23] His account in the *Timaeus* commentary brings out well how fully he takes into account all that was said by early Pythagoreans and Platonists in depreciation of the "dark other" (In Tim. I 175 Diehl, 54C 21-24).[24] And the fuller description of the two principles in the *Platonic Theology* shows particularly well the kind of divine virtue he discerns in her.

> All unity, wholeness and community of beings and all the divine measures depend in the Primal Limit, and all division and generative making (*gonimos poiēsis*) and procession to multiplicity come to be from the Supreme Un-Boundedness. (III 8, 19-23, p. 325 Saffrey-Westerink)

It is through this supreme principle, which, as Proclus notes in the *Timaeus* commentary, the ancients rightly called "darkness" and saw as the source of all the disorder and irrationality and irregularity of this world, that the creative generosity of the Good is mediated, that unbounded life-giving power which Hadot rightly saw as the supreme value for Plotinus (above, p. 74). And this generous creativity of the Unbounded extends to the lowest frontier of all the worlds, for the *hylē*, the "dark other" of the material cosmos, is her ultimate manifestation.

This recognition of the "dark other" as one of the highest divine

---

22 See Anne D. R. Sheppard "Monad and Dyad as Cosmic Principles in Syrianus", *Soul and the Structure of Being in Late Neoplatonism* ed. H. J. Blumenthal and A. C. Lloyd (Liverpool, University Press, 1982) pp. 1-17.

23 *Elements of Theology* prop. 89-92. *In Tim.* I 54 175-176 Diehl: *In Parm.* VI 1119,4-1123,21. *Platonic Theology* III 7-8. See J. Trouillard *La Mystagogie de Proclos* (Paris, Les Belles Lettres 1982) pp. 245-247.

24 The passage, characteristically, occurs in an allegorical exposition of the story of Atlantis.

principles can clearly do a great deal to remove the Platonic uneasiness, still apparent in Plotinus, about the beauties of the material world and their enjoyment, up to a point. The point is that at which cosmic optimism becomes altogether too roseate, and world-affirmation too easy-going and self-indulgent, and there is no longer any call to rise to the higher world of spirit. The doctrine of the Athenian Neoplatonists does not deny the evils of the material world: it is fully compatible with the austere morality of detachment from the "goods men fight about" of which I spoke earlier (pp. 70-72): and it still preserves something of the ambiguity of valuation inherent in the concept of "image" (above, pp. 76-78). But the image is now very much an icon. It becomes more necessary than ever before for the devout philosopher to be aware of the divine in and through material things and outward observances. The theory and practice of theurgy in the late Neoplatonists has recently received extensive reappraisal and is nowadays much more positively regarded by many students. In fact, though I have done what I could to help and encourage this from the beginning, I am now somewhat inclined to feel that the pendulum may have swung too far, and that we again need some of the vigorous good sense of E. R. Dodds to redress the balance.[25] But of course these last Neo-Platonists of Athens did not only practice and commend their own theurgic Chaldaean rites. They were champions of all the old Hellenic pieties and the traditional theophanies of all mankind in a world which had officially abandoned them. All the old neglected and ruinous shrines were still full of divine presences for them. Proclus heard Athena telling him that she was coming to live in his house when the Christians turned her out of the Parthenon.[26] He thought that a philosopher should be "the hierophant of the whole world".[27] So in the history of Hellenic and Platonic awareness of the divine in the beauties of earth the beginning was present in the end. The last defenders of the primaeval theophanies were Platonic philosophers.

25 See this volume, study II.
26 Marinus, *Life of Proclus* 30.
27 Ibid. 19.

V

THE HIDDEN AND THE OPEN
IN HELLENIC THOUGHT

Introduction

A "hidden course of events" or "Strom des Geschehens" must, if it is to concern us seriously at all, be not altogether hidden. We must be aware of it as flowing or going its way, and aware of it as not altogether disjoined from or without power over the course which we run in our ordinary, day-to-day experience, the common stream in which we swim or are ripples. People have always told stories about another world remote and detached from ours and reached, if at all, by hidden and difficult ways, the Land of the Hyperboreans, the Land of the Young. In Christian Europe this strange other world, which we inadequately call "Fairyland" came to be thought of as the world reached by the "third path" distinct from the two ways leading to Heaven and Hell,[1] and so

---

1 I take this image from the ballad of *Thomas the Rhymer*, stanzas 10-13 (*Oxford Book of Ballads* pp. 2-3).

> O see ye not yon narrow road
> So thick beset with thorns and briers?
> That is the Path of Righteousness,
> Though after it but few inquires.
>
> And see ye not yon braid, braid road
> That lies across the lily leven?
> That is the Path of Wickedness,
> Though some call it the Road to Heaven.
>
> And see ye not yon bonny road
> That winds about the fernie brae?
> That is the road to fair Elfland
> Where thou and I this night maun gae.

sharply distinguished from and set against the worlds dominated by the hidden power which most people most of the time thought of as ruling the course of events, the often terrifying and oppressive mystery of God.

It is of course possible to moralize and theologize Fairyland and so bring it back into the Christian world. This was done with much subtlety and imaginative power by George Macdonald in *At the Back of the North Wind* and more obviously by C. S. Lewis in his stories about Narnia. The modern English writer who has most fully and vividly presented Fairyland as an independent world outside the Christian scheme of things is Lord Dunsany. In *The Charwoman's Shadow* the Magician manages to get to the independent world just in time and so escape God's power and condemnation. In *The King of Elfland's Daughter* and *The Blessing of Pan* the other world takes over small places in this world. In the first, the representative of Christianity, the "Freer", with his chapel and a small group of the faithful, is left as a little island of ordinariness in the midst of the village which has passed into Elfland. In the second the official representative of the Church, the Vicar, after a long spiritual struggle, joins his parishioners at the stone circle, and, to their great relief and satisfaction, performs the sacrifice to Pan which inaugurates the passage of the community out of the common world. In both, the communities pass altogether out of the ordinary course of events over which the Christian God has power. In the Hellenic tradition, because the Divine is differently, more widely and variously, conceived, there cannot be this sort of sharp contrast. The gods take those of their human friends and relations whom they will to the Islands of the Blest, and the land of the Hyperboreans is Apollo's own special holy land.

But, though this kind of hidden world has its own sort of meaning and value, its powers are not usually taken very seriously. This is certainly true in Hellenic thought and imagination. The land of the Hyperboreans, the land at the back of the North Wind, and the Islands of the Blest, in their early unmoralized form in which they are something like a "fairyland," do not play an important part in it. That which is in some sense "hidden" about the stream of things is taken seriously and some knowledge of it, if such is possible, is desired, because it is conceived as power and truth not easily accessible, perhaps never fully accessible, which will help us here and now by enabling us to understand in some degree what is going on in the open world and to respond to it better. This is the kind of "hiddenness" whose place in Hellenic thought I shall try to explore.

The Hidden in non-philosophical Hellenic Thought

On the whole, the Hellenes had little belief in or respect for any hidden wisdom, any knowledge about or power to influence the stream of events, which was in the ordinary sense "esoteric" or "occult". (I take this "ordinary sense" to indicate a wisdom which is the secret possession of a group of spiritually privileged persons, who communicate it only to the select few whom they choose and initiate. Initiates into the mysteries of the ancient world did not form such an esoteric group possessed of an occult wisdom. What they had been initiated into were secret rites, which gave them a profound spiritual experience and a hope for a better lot in the next world not shared by non-initiates. They did not have secret doctrines.) I shall discuss real or supposed esotericism among the philosophers a little later: at this point I wish to concentrate on what ordinary thoughtful Hellenes thought about the hiddenness in the nature of things. One kind of hiddenness which certainly has something occult about it is the hidden power claimed by magicians. But, though the Greeks, like most other people, believed in magic, it was never of central importance in their society. The more primitive rituals of their religion certainly sometimes had a magical character. But in historical times they continued to be performed at least as much because that was the way things had always been done as with any expectation of producing a practical effect. And magicians were not respected or generally thought to possess any wonderful or desirable hidden wisdom. Even in the lightly Hellenized world of the Roman Empire, when fear of magic became very prevalent, it was fear, as usual accompanied by hatred, not veneration, which magicians provoked. They were particularly dangerous criminals. Those philosophers who rose above the fear of magic because they knew that the magicians' operations could touch nothing which deeply concerned them, but still believed in magic, explained it, as they explained the venerable rituals of divination, in an entirely open and generally accessible rational and naturalistic way as due to sympathies and correspondences in the great organism of the universe: the finest example of this kind of explanation is the concluding part of the main body of Plotinus' great work on the soul (IV 4 [28] 30-end: chapters 40-43 deal specifically with magic in the ordinary sense). The reason for the much greater prestige of astrology, which most people incline to consider nowadays an occult or superstitious activity more or less on the level of magic, was that within the framework of the ancient understanding of the organic universe the astrologers could easily present their discipline as intimately related to the most dignified form of natural philosophy, the study of the heavenly bodies. Astrology could be seen as a sort of applied astronomy. Not by any means all serious thinkers were prepared to take it so seriously. Plotinus engaged in vigorous polemic against some astrologers' claims in two treatises (III 1 [3] *On Destiny* and II 3 [52] *On Whether the Stars are Causes*). But A. A. Long has shown very well[2] how complex the debate was and how varied the positions of philosophers, and how competently and cleverly the great astronomer-astrologer Ptolemy could defend his science against philosophical objections.

2 A.A. Long "Astrology: arguments pro and contra" in *Science and Speculation: studies in Hellenistic theory and practice* ed. Jonathan Barnes and others, University Press, Cambridge and Editions de la Maison des Sciences de l'Homme, Paris 1982 pp. 165-192.

Though there was little occult hiddenness in the world of ordinary Hellenes, it was by no means all bright and clear and easily comprehensible. On the contrary, as anyone who has read their literature will know, it was full of darkness and mystery and the unexpected interventions of hidden powers. The dark and the wild always surround, and may invade, the small areas of clarity and order which we manage to establish for a time: and one never knows what is going to happen. The hidden powers which work in the world and determine the course of events in ways which we cannot understand or anticipate are the gods: and the gods in non-philosophical Greek religion are what straightforward experience and observation of the world would suggest that its hidden powers are, unaccountable, unpredictable and multifarious in their purposes, which are dark not in the sense of being evil but of being unpredictable. There was a fairly general belief in earlier times that the gods had a persistent tendency to resent and to bring down great power and prosperity. This was expressed as divine "jealousy" or "envy" (phthonos). It seems closely bound up with the Hellenic sense that *too much* of anything is dangerous: it carries people beyond the proper human limits, and the higher the rise, the harder the fall. This, after all, seems to have a good deal in our ordinary experience to commend it. When Solon in Herodotus says to Croesus "Though all the divine is envious and liable to cause trouble, you ask me about human affairs" (Herodotus I.32.1), the tone is not one of criticism or resentment, but of acknowledgement that this is the way things are, as the rest of the speech shows. But the operation of this "envy" is no more predictable than any other operation of divine power. In Solon's discourse *tuchē* or *sumphorē*, "chance" or "accident", quite naturally often replace *to theion*, "the divine". And in Hellenistic and Roman times the arbitrary, chancy aspect of the operation of divine power became detached and was worshipped in her own right as *Tychē* or *Fortuna*. M. P. Nilsson regards this development as evidence of the decay of genuine religion "ein Zeichen der Entgöttlichung der Welt". But it is most interesting to see in his, as

V

always, admirably precise and careful account of Tychē[3] how quickly she developed into a perfectly normal goddess with statues, temples and a regular cult. It was not so easy in the ancient world for even the irreligious or superficially religious to get away from the divine as it has proved to be in the officially Christian world.

In all Hellenic thought not deeply affected by philosophy, down to the end of antiquity, there is always plenty that is hidden and dark in the universe, plenty going on in the world of the gods, whose powers and proceedings only become perceptible to men dimly and fleetingly from time to time. But there is not a secret order, a hidden system of the cosmos – though it is certainly not conceived as an anarchy either. And there is no group of superior persons who are believed to have esoteric knowledge of the hidden course of things. This is a most important determinant of the course of Hellenic and of later European thought about the divine. The gods did indeed give signs and omens and oracles, and there were religious craftsmen with professional skills in interpreting them. But the interpretation of the signs was always considered to be a tricky business, and it was recognized that the interpreters, even if skilled and honest, might be wrong. Nor did the reputation of seers for honesty and faithfulness stand very high in real life. We can see this at least as early as the sixth century B. C. Onomacritus, the great Athenian oracle-specialist at the court of the sons of Pisistratus, must have acquired quite an aura of esoteric wisdom before he was found out. But we can read in Herodotus how he was remembered as a forger and unscrupulous manipulator of sacred texts (Herodotus VII 6).[4]

3 M.P.Nilsson *Geschichte der griechischen Religion*[5] (München 1950) II pp. 190-199. The remark quoted above is on p. 191.
4 This reputation persisted in later times. cp. Pausanias I. 22.7.

V

The Hidden and the Open in Philosophy

It is generally, and rightly, considered that philosophy for the Greeks was a very public and open activity. It seems to have developed from the endless uninhibited conversations about everything, in any public place where it is possible to stand or sit about, which are characteristic of the open-air life of Mediterranean males, and in which the Greeks have always indulged more freely and wide-rangingly than others, and with remarkably lasting effects. Of course we should not forget the presence in it, probably from the beginning, of a strong contemplative and at times introspective tendency. Heraclitus was certainly introspective, though not in a way which prevented him from looking outwards, for the Logos he encountered in himself was one and the same with the Logos he encountered in the world. And very intense meditation must have preceded the flash of intuition symbolically described in the Proemof Parmenides. Even before them, the Milesians must have spent a good deal of time in Aristotelian *Thauma*, gazing and wondering at the things up in the sky (*ta meteōra*) before they started talking and writing about them. Perhaps Thales never really fell into that well: but he and Anaximander and Anaximenes must have done a good deal of star-gazing – and, in the case of Thales, perhaps mud and mist-gazing by the Maeander, which would have seemed even odder to his fellow-citizens. But on the whole the object of Hellenic philosophers was not only to discover but to declare as clearly as possible the things that seemed to be hidden about the universe and the nature of man and the divine. We shall consider later what doubts and diffidences some philosophers had about their powers to do this and how in the end a mystery was apprehended before which philosophers must be silent. But first I propose to examine some cases of real or apparent esoteric discipline or procedure among philosophers.

Orphics and Pythagoreans

We must begin, of course, with the Pythagorean Brotherhood. But, before considering them directly it seems desirable to say something, very briefly, about those rather esoteric-looking people, the Orphics, whose beliefs clearly connect with one side of Pythagoreanism. I do not propose to spend long on them, as I agree with those scholars who do not think that there is sufficient evidence for supposing them to be as ancient, original, and important as has sometimes been claimed. The view of them which seems to me to fit the scanty and puzzling evidence best is that of Walter Burkert, very well and convincingly explained in a recent essay.[5] He shows that the only people who were clearly and certainly called "Orphics" were the wandering *telestai*, initiatory priest-magicians of whom we read in Plato (Republic II 364A-365A) and Theophrastus (*Characters XVI Of Superstition* 28). These went round in the Greek world offering to cure (for a consideration) the troubles of individuals and communities by performing for them the *telestai*, initiation-rites, contained in their voluminous sacred literature (which may have varied considerably from priest to priest: there was no Orphic canon of scripture). They certainly made esoteric claims as individuals to a superior hidden knowledge, revealed in the ancient poems which only they possessed, which enabled them to deal with the dark chances of life. But they did not form an esoteric brotherhood or society like the Pythagoreans, though some *telestai* may have gathered round them little *thiasoi*, small groups of disciples and devotees.

The Pythagorean Brotherhood in its earlier years had a very different sort of esoteric solidity. The *hetaireiai* founded by Pythagoras in Greek Italy, the organisation as well as the doctrines of which were probably due to his original genius, were unique

5 Walter Burkert "Craft versus Sect: the Problem of Orphics and Pythagoreans", in *Jewish and Christian Self-Definition III*, S.C.M. Press, London 1982, pp. 1-22.

and unparalleled in Greece, and perhaps in the whole history of esoteric movements. For a short time and in a limited space they actually exercised the political and social authority of which other occult groups have dreamed. It does seem to be true that their doctrine was secret, and that the secrecy was preserved by a strict discipline. And from the little we know about them it does seem likely that it was this doctrine of the great numerical-musical order of the cosmos, to which human beings must conform themselves and their communities, combining as it did concepts and precepts which we should separate out into religious, scientific and political, which inspired this powerful form of organisation (to whose power the secrecy must have contributed, though it may also have helped to provoke the final catastrophe) which brought about for a short time a reformed polity in Croton and elsewhere. Old Pythagoreanism, like the thought of Plato who was so much inspired by it, was eminently a practical philosophy. But this esoteric order broke up and finally disappeared in the course of the fifth and fourth centuries: some later Pythagorean groups (of which we know very little) may have imitated the original esotericism in their small and uninfluential conventicles, but the Pythagorean tradition which influenced Plato and, in its revival in the last centuries B.C. and first centuries A.D., the Neoplatonists, was a public philosophical tradition, transmitted by books and public teaching like other Hellenic philosophical traditions.

Plato and the Academy

The next instance of real or supposed esotericism which I propose to explore is that of Plato. The question of whether Plato taught an esoteric doctrine in the Academy different from, or going beyond, anything which we can find in the Dialogues has of course been interminably discussed and the literature on it is extensive. Here I shall simply give my own view, though I must acknowledge considerable help in forming it from an excellent article by Dr. Thomas Szlezak.[6] Our starting-points for this discussion in Plato's own writings are remarkably baffling and disconcerting: they must be, of course, the devastating observations on the inferiority of written to oral teaching in the *Phaedrus* (274C-276E) and the even more devastating reflections on the inadequacy of all language in the Seventh Letter (340B-344D).[7] The implications of the latter passage, to some extent worked out by the Neoplatonists, are very far-reaching indeed. But at this point we are only concerned with our present question of how Plato regarded his own written works, and their relation to his oral teaching in the Academy and how we are to relate what he says to the brief and baffling statements of Aristotle about that oral teaching. Did Plato really think, as a first reading of the *Phaedrus* suggests, that his dialogues were trivialities, of little philosophical worth? If so, why did he continue to expend so much time and trouble in writing them? A more careful consideration of the *Phaedrus*, especially of 276D-277A, in the light of the dialogue as a whole and of Plato's writings as a whole, suggests a less drastic conclusion, which it is not impossible to reconcile with Letter VII.

We need here, as always in studying Plato, to remember what for him is the end and object of all philosophical activity. It is that which is shown in the great ascent of the mind to absolute beauty in the *Symposium*: to develop a good and wise man who has attained to the highest well-being possible to mortals, who has the light of eternal reality in himself and no longer needs any outer guidance because he has seen (*Phaedrus* 277A: cp. Letter VII 341C-D, 344B-C). If we keep this fully and continually in mind it becomes easy to understand why Plato thought that this goal

6 T. Szlezak "Dialogform und Esoterik: Zur Deutung des Platonischen Dialogs 'Phaidros'" *Museum Helveticum* 35. Jahrgang pp. 18-32.

7 The genuineness of the letter is of course disputed. But it was part of the Platonic canon in antiquity, and had great authority for later Platonists, as we shall see. I myself find the philosophical digression here referred to an excellent piece of Platonism, not unworthy of Plato, whoever is the author.

could not be reached just by reading books. To attain this kind of enlightenment and liberation,[8] what he thought was needed was an intimate personal association, like that which he had had with Socrates, in which there was the sort of endless conversation and thinking together about great subjects of which he speaks in Letter VII (341C). In this much would inevitably be said or suggested which would not go into any written work. This may possibly be why he says in the passage just referred to that there is not and never will be any *sungramma* of his about the most important matters, the ones which he takes really seriously. This, however, remains difficult. Szlezak has shown[9] that there is no good ancient evidence for the common modern view that *sungramma*, here or elsewhere, can have the meaning of "formal treatise", in a sense which excludes or contrasts with "dialogue": any prose work can be called a *sungramma*. So the usual modern escape-route of supposing that Plato is not referring to dialogues here is blocked. The statement certainly accords well with the powerful demonstration of the inadequacy of all language, spoken as well as written, which follows (342-344). And I do not regard this as un-Platonic, or a reason for doubting the genuineness of the letter: though its full implications perhaps did not begin to be worked out before Plotinus. But this does not of course remove the difficulty of Plato's apparent denial of his own writings. All one can say is that, assuming the Letter to be genuine and the account of the circumstances of its writing which it gives correct, Plato was stung to an extreme and paradoxical negativity ("of course I didn't *really* write anything about the matters I take seriously") by the sort of transcendental chatter in which Dionysius had been indulging.

But, however inadequate Plato may have sometimes thought that any language was when the philosopher neared his goal, if we

---

8 I have deliberately used words here which are commonly employed in the West when speaking of Indian wisdom, to indicate my growing conviction that the Indian and Hellenic traditions have a great deal in common.

9 Szlezak, art. cit. pp. 25-6.

V

go back from the end of the philosophical way to the beginning, the *Phaedrus* seems to give us no reason to suppose that Plato did not think that the right kind of writing might be very helpful. The right kind would be that to which he himself devoted so much time and trouble: that which was an image of philosophical conversation designed to start the minds of its readers on the path of true dialectic. Writing for Plato is "play" (*Phaedrus* 276D), but play for him can be serious. The second part of the *Parmenides* is a *pragmateiōdēs paidia* (137B) – a very serious game indeed! And in the *Laws* the best thing about us trivial human creatures is that we are god's toys, and the most serious thing we can do is to play beautifully before him (VII 803C-D). The image of Socrates in these play-dialogues might, Plato seems to have thought, lead at least a few of the properly gifted and well disposed to what I believe was still a truly Socratic living, talking and thinking together in the Academy. We know too little of what went on there to be sure about anything. But a consideration of the evidence and of the persons involved suggests that it was something very different from the handing down by the Master of an esoteric dogmatic teaching to humbly receptive disciples. To say nothing of Aristotle, a collection of highly independent-minded and very diverse thinkers like Speusippus, Xenocrates, Eudoxus and Heracleides of Pontus would not have tolerated that sort of thing for long. Though I do not at all points agree with J.N. Findlay's interpretation of Plato, the following passage does seem to me to give a good idea of what Plato's teaching and relationship to his disciples in the Academy may have been like:

> The Platonic Dialogues are not, taken by themselves, the sort of works in which anyone's views on any matter could be clearly set forth: they point beyond themselves, and without going beyond them they are not to be understood . . . The historical sequence of the Dialogues . . . is also no clear document of the development of Plato's thought. It rather documents, on the view to which I come, Plato's ever-changing willingness to divulge parts of a long-held, profound programme, unclear as regards both goal and method, to which he felt ever varying attitudes of confidence and criticism, of impassioned defence and

despairing retreat, all inspired by the vivid controversies in the Academy of which we can have only the dimmest imagination.[10]

If this is anything like a true picture, we are not dealing here with anything like the esoteric doctrine and discipline of the Pythagoreans and other esoteric groups. Plato's oral discussions of the matters with which he was most seriously concerned were not, perhaps, usually accessible to those members of the general public who might wish to attend: though we need to take into account here Aristoxenus' account of Aristotle's anecdote about the lecture (or course of lectures) on the Good: the very unphilosophical people who attended this and were so disappointed by the absence of any instructions on body-building or money-making can hardly have been members of any sort of inner circle (Aristoxenus Harm. Elem. II 30). But even if we discount this or regard it as untypical, I do not think that we can discover in the Academy more than a well-developed example of the sort of selectivity and reserve common to nearly all Greek philosophical teaching, and indeed of a great deal of other teaching where the teachers have a reverence for their subject and a realistic estimation of the differences in human capacities for understanding. Even in a modern university one does not talk about everything to everybody. It seems to me rather confusing and misleading to speak of this sort of reserve and careful selection of one's hearers or partners in discussion as "esoteric", even when it is spoken of or commended in solemn language derived from the mystery-religions.[11] Aristotle's brief references to *exōterikoi logoi* (*esōterikos*, significantly, is a late and not very common word), if they are references to his own works

---

10 J. N. Findlay *Plato, The Written and Unwritten Doctrines*, Routledge and Kegan Paul, London 1974 pp. ix-x.

11 A recent article by Jean Pépin, who does not make the distinction between reserve and esotericism which I suggest here, gives a good account of the use of mystery-language by the Platonists ("L'Arcane Religieux et sa Transposition philosophique dans la Tradition platonicienne" in *La Storia della filosofia come sapere critico*, Franco Angeli, Milano 1984 pp. 18-35).

or philosophical activities at all,[12] seem to indicate the same sort of distinction between talks and discussions in a select group and works designed for a larger public.

The Pupils of Ammonius

I now move on to consider the most notable case of apparent esotericism in the Platonism of late antiquity. Porphyry in his *Life of Plotinus* (3 25-35) describes an agreement between three pupils of Ammonius Saccas, clearly those closest to him, Erennius, Origen and Plotinus, not to publish the teachings of their master. The real significance of this agreement has been very variously understood. Heinrich Dörrie,[13] who pictured Ammonius very much as a Pythagorean, saw it as springing from a Pythagorean esotericism which imposed on the group of his disciples the discipline of a mystery-religion. Richard Harder, on the other hand,[14] saw it as a simple and quite un-esoteric agreement between the three that none of them should publish under his own name material resulting from their common work with the master in the group. The agreement was soon broken, first by Erennius, then by Origen (the Hellenic Platonist, not the Christian). Finally Plotinus proceeded, though rather slowly and reluctantly, to publication. In assessing the nature of the agreement we need to take into account the fact that it was broken by all three, and especially that it was eventually broken by Plotinus, of whose high character and deep reverence for his master we know something. This seems to rule out any breaking of a sacred vow or oath like that of a mystery-initiate, or even of an obligation of honour not to publish common property as his own. Neither could really be excused, for

12 See the discussion of *Metaphysics* M. 1076a 28 in Ross's commentary (W. D. Ross *Aristotle's Metaphysics*, Clarendon Press, Oxford 1948, II pp. 408-410).
13 H. Dörrie "Ammonios, der Lehrer Plotins" in *Hermes* 83, 1955 pp. 439-77.
14 R. Harder *Plotins Schriften* V c. Felix Meiner, Hamburg 1958 pp. 86-87.

a man like Plotinus, by the fact that others had broken the agreement first. The most satisfactory account of the matter seems to me that given by Szlezak in another excellent essay, and adopted by H.-R. Schwyzer in the latest and best account of what is known and not known about Ammonius.[15] According to this interpretation of Porphyry's story Ammonius was a Platonist who took the Seventh Letter very seriously indeed (it remained a text of great authority down to the end of Neoplatonism). For this reason he wrote nothing himself (this is one of the very few things we know about him for certain), and did not wish his disciples to write anything though of course he had no objection, to their continuing the sort of oral teaching and discussion with carefully selected persons in which he had spent his life. The three disciples mentioned in the *Life* agreed to continue to follow their master in this, probably, as Schwyzer thinks, shortly after his death in Alexandria. But we can easily see that, after the other two had broken the agreement, Plotinus could have felt free to decide for himself how far he should continue to follow the practice of Ammonius. In the last section of his essay[16] Szlezak gives an account of the development of his thought and practice, faithful both to the relevant texts from the *Life* and the *Enneads* and to the spirit of Plotinus. He moved, it appears, at first rather slowly and hesitatingly, from the extreme reserve of Ammonius (to which Porphyry does manage to give a somewhat esoteric colour) to a willingness not only to give lectures to which all comers were admitted and to write, but to permit his writings to be prepared for general circulation, to a position, in fact, very much nearer the normal practice of Plato himself. And he did so because he had come to see that there was no need to take precautions to keep the final mystery inviolate, because it was inviolable. Szlezak con-

---

15 T. Szlezak "Plotin und die geheimen Lehren des Ammonios" in *Esoterik und Exoterik in der Philosophie* ed. Holzhey & Zimmerli, Schwabe, Basel/Stuttgart 1977, pp. 32-69. H.-R. Schwyzer *Ammonios Sakkas, der Lehrer Plotins*, Westdeutscher Verlag, Opladen 1983.

16 Szlezak, *l.c.* (n. 15) pp. 61-63.

cludes his essay with an observation which, as he says, has been made before, but which needs continual consideration if we are to understand at all what the Neoplatonists have to tell us about the hidden in and beyond the world:

> Die Untersuchung mündet ein in die paradoxe (nicht hier zum ersten Mal gemachte) Erfahrung, daß Plotin, der eindeutige Mystiker unter den Neuplatonikern, zugleich auch derjenige ist, der in allem – auch in der Frage der Esoterik – am eindeutigsten der Vernunft verpflichtet ist.

I shall try to explain the full significance of this a little later. But first it will be desirable to say something about the diffidence which generally accompanies the high confidence in reason of the Greek philosophers.

Philosophical Diffidence

Those Greek philosophers who were not Sceptics generally held the nature of reality to be understandable in principle. From the beginning they were trying to discover by observation and reasoning what things are and, at least in some senses of the question "why?", why things are. But for them "understandable in principle" did not mean easily understandable, or understandable by all. Their confidence in ultimate intelligibility was compatible with a great deal of diffidence about the difficulty for human intelligence of attaining to it. Xenophanes in most of the surviving fragments of his works appears remarkably confident in his dogmatism about the divine and well assured of his superiority to other people. But he is also the author of the earliest, and one of the best, expressions of this diffidence.

> No man knows, or ever will know, the truth about the gods and everything I speak of: for even if one chanced to say the complete truth, yet oneself knows it not: for seeming is wrought over all things.
>
> (Xenophanes fr. 34 DK tr. G. S. Kirk)

This diffidence recurs continually in later Greek philosophy, though all philosophers do not share it. It is of course much easier to maintain that clear and certain knowledge of everything can be attained, and that one has oneself attained it, if one thinks that there is only one cosmos, the world of our ordinary experience: and dogmatic self-confidence seems to have reached its highest point in the great one-world philosophical systems of the Hellenistic period. One should be careful, here as elsewhere, of generalizing too sweepingly about the Stoics: though the lack of dogmatic confidence about the nature of things in Marcus Aurelius is certainly not at all typical of Stoicism and marks his Stoicism as personal piety off rather sharply from the confident philosophical world-view of earlier Stoics. But there can be no doubt about the calm confidence of genuine Epicureans that they know everything and can explain everything about the world, which makes them so strikingly resemble later rationalist philosophers and Christian sectarians. When one comes to believe in some divine reality behind and beyond our world of sense-experience which is itself supremely intelligible and gives our immediate environment such intelligibility as it has, there is a good deal more room for diffidence, especially in the ancient form in which the wisdom which is the secure possession of the gods is contrasted with the human quest for wisdom: and there is plenty of this in Plato and Aristotle.[17] The works of Plato, even if one excludes the Seventh Letter, contain a good deal which can be, and has been, read as supporting a very considerable diffidence about the possibility of human knowledge of divine and ultimate reality. I would like here to discuss briefly one very odd passage which has not, I think, been much considered in this context. This is the description in the *Symposium* of the great *daimōn* or intermediary spirit Erōs (203B-

17 Two recent English books on Aristotle, *A History of Greek Philosophy* VI *Aristotle: an Encounter* by W.K.C.Guthrie (University Press, Cambridge 1981) and *Aristotle the Philosopher* by J.L.Ackrill (University Press, Oxford 1981), though approaching Aristotle in very different ways, are both rightly concerned to point out that Aristotle is by no means the rather complacent "Master of those who know" of older Aristotelian and anti-Aristotelian tradition, but a much more tentative, open-minded and self-critical philosopher.

E). He is clearly and explicitly presented as the spirit of philosophy, representing symbolically not only the power which drives us on to seek wisdom but that within us which seeks it. It is therefore not unreasonable to look at the passage in the hope of finding some indications of what Plato thought philosophy was like: but if we do, they seem rather disconcerting. They occur where Diotima is describing the paradoxical inheritance which Eros derives from his ill-assorted parents Beggary and the Entrepreneurial Spirit (*Penia* and *Poros*). She says:

> He philosophises all through his life – he's a terribly clever conjuror and drugger and sophist: he's not naturally immortal or mortal, but on one and the same day he's at one time alive and flourishing, when it's going well with him, at another he dies, and comes alive again by his father's nature, but what he acquires is always running away, so that Erōs is never without resources or rich, and is in the middle between wisdom and ignorance.
>
> (203D7-E5, tr. A.H.A.)

The only way in which I can make sense of this in its context is to take it as a description of the practice of philosophy, based on Plato's experience, which makes the contrast between divine wisdom and the human search which immediately follows (204A) very sharp indeed. The philosopher, it appears to be saying, will find again and again that the brilliant arguments which he thought so convincing are sophistic trickery, that he has been drugging and hallucinating himself and other people with words. The vitality and euphoria which he experiences when he thinks he has got it right and seen the truth will disappear very quickly. He will die many philosophical deaths, and what he thinks he has acquired will always be leaking away. But he will always, in the power of Erōs, begin and begin again.[18] And this seems to me something

18 The truest Christian Platonist whom I have known, the late Mother Maria Gysi, always insisted very strongly on this: in this life, she thought, the genuine philosopher must always be beginning again. The following, from a Socratic conversation with a bricklayer on death, may give an idea of how she understood Platonism:

Then B: "But we cannot be certain – not quite certain"; then I answered, would that could very well be thought and said, though not perhaps always or consistently, by the author of the Dialogues. It is certainly an understanding of philosophy, and a way of being a philosopher, which leaves plenty of room for the hidden.

But this should not be pressed too far. Plato and Aristotle may at times have had a stronger sense of human limitations and inadequacy than most Platonists and Aristotelians; but in general the high intellectualism of the Platonic-Aristotelian tradition aspired to know not only the cosmos but the higher realities on which it depends (though what it means by "knowledge" at this level is very different from what people in the West usually mean by "knowledge" now-a-days). This knowledge is indeed hidden from most men, but it is held to be attainable by philosophers, even if with great difficulty and perhaps only for brief periods. It is therefore the more impressive that it was this great intellectual tradition which, by its own processes and in its own way, came in the end to the recognition of a final mystery.

The Mystery in Later Platonism

Very soon after the revival of dogmatic Platonism, in the first two centuries of the Christian era, suggestions begin to appear that the first principle of reality is beyond speech or thought, because it is

it not be terribly sad if we *knew*? for that would mean that it would again be something as small as our minds and this life. And B. took it and said it was true, and there was a peace when people died which was nowhere else. The peace which passed understanding. And I said that at last we would reach our final beginning – not always begin and begin again, but BEGIN. I was amazed, and I shall never forget this . . . which gave me a sudden realization that Christian Platonism is that which minds, who think and can no longer take the everlasting assertions of the Church, need and love and which has a force of consolation which no assertion can ever convey. But can one put it forward? Is it teachable, other than as an answer to an endeavour; to an anguish and need?
(From a letter of 20 June, 1967, in *Mother Maria. Her Life in Letters,* ed. Sister Thekla, Darton Longman and Todd, London 1979, p. 120.)

"beyond being" that is, beyond the *ousia* which divine thought knows in secure possession and human thought strives to know. It is difficult to be sure when and where this conviction of the negative transcendence of the supreme divinity first appeared. It is found in these first centuries of our era among Gnostics as well as among Hellenic philosophers, and perhaps the best indication of the sort of thinkers among whom it may have originated is that it is expressed from its first appearances among the latter in a Pythagorean way. Platonized Pythagoreans or Pythagoreanizing Platonists, developing hints and suggestions in Plato himself and in his successor Speusippus, thought of the first principle as the absolute One from which all number, and so the multiplicity of beings, must proceed. This transcendental unitarianism, if it had not developed beyond its beginnings in Platonic-Pythagorean thought before Plotinus, might not have been of much more than historical interest. It was its powerful development by Plotinus which made it something very much more. For him and his Neoplatonic successors "One" is not an adequate name or description of God any more than the other preferred Platonic name "Good", or any other name or definition or concept. It simply points us on to the awareness that beyond the highest level to which philosophic intellect can attain, the realm of divine being which is divine intellect, there lies something beyond even divine thought, and so beyond any thought, attainable only in a union or encounter which is ineffable because it is incomparably more than what can be thought or imaged or spoken, though thoughts and words and images can lead us towards it.

We should notice at this point more carefully than has always been done (the Neoplatonists themselves can mislead us here) that according to this way of thinking we do not simply follow the path of discursive reasoning up to the very threshold of the mystery, the point where thought stops. To suppose this would be to misunderstand seriously not only Neoplatonism, but the whole tradition of Platonic-Aristotelian intellectualism. In reading Aristotle himself we need often to recall to our minds the conclusion of Stephen Clark's observations on Plotinus' critique of him:

Plotinus castigated Aristotle for retreating from his earlier suspicion that there was some yet more perfect thing than *nous*. In the *Peri Euches* (fr. 1 Ross) we are told that "the god is either *nous* or something beyond *nous*". Similarly in the *Eudemian Ethics*, "*logos* is not the source of *logos*, but something greater is, and what would be greater than knowledge or *nous* except God? (E. E. 1248a 27F). For the most part *nous* and the god are identical (cf. N. E I 1096a 21F); but this divine *nous* is not the same as *dianoia*, and is likely to be as far removed from ordinary thinking as Plotinus' One.[19]

And Plotinus and his successors make it clear that Divine Intellect does not reason and when we reach its level we must stop reasoning if we are not to get it hopelessly wrong. Proclus, who might at times be reasonably suspected of pushing discursive, defining[20] reasoning a good deal further than it will go, even to the Henads which are above Intellect, makes this point more than once with great force. He says in the *Platonic Theology*:

> Every knowledge applied to an object which has nothing to do with it destroys its own power: for if we speak of sensation as applying to the object of rational knowledge it will do away with itself, and the same is true of rational knowledge (epistēmē) if applied to the intelligible: so that if there could be a *logos* of the Ineffable, it never stops turning itself upside down and fights against itself.
> (*Platonic Theology* II 10. p. 109 Portus, II 64, 4-9 Saffrey-Westerink tr. A. H. A.)[21]

Jean Trouillard, whose death in November 1984 we lament, is the person who, in my lifetime, seems to me to have gone furthest in understanding and helping others to understand the full significance of this Neoplatonic awareness of final mystery and its relevance and helpfulness for our own thinking at the present time. I myself owe him a very great deal, not only for help in understanding the Neoplatonists but for the way in which his

---

19 Stephen R. L. Clark *Aristotle's Man* (Clarendon Press, Oxford 1975. reprinted 1983) pp. 174-5.

20 The German *definierendes Denken* is helpful in understanding what is at issue here.

21 See further A.H.Armstrong "The Negative Theology of *Nous* in Later Neoplatonism" in *Platonismus und Christentum,* ed. H. D. Blume and F. Mann [= this volume, study III].

writings both confirmed my faith in God and liberated my thought about him at a time of spiritual and intellectual crisis. In what follows I shall be treading in his footsteps, as I have been for some years: though of course I have also been interpreting and developing him, as he interpreted and developed the Neoplatonists. He was sometimes accused of reading more than was "really there" into the texts. This is, of course, a thoroughly Platonic thing to do, and something which anyone who is concerned to make an ancient way of thought alive and powerful in a later time must do. But, as a scholarly historian who at this point feels irresistibly impelled to go beyond the limits of scholarly history (which it is proper to conceive narrowly) I must admit that here the ancient texts will sometimes be read in a way in which it is unlikely that the ancients would have read them.

The part of Trouillard's interpretation which is particularly relevant to our main subject is that in which he shows how the Neoplatonists understood the inviolability of the final mystery, and what the consequences of this understanding must be for philosophy and theology. In one of a number of articles in which he explains this he says:

> Dès lors, la notion de "Dieu caché" change de sens. Le Dieu de saint Augustin et de Saint Thomas est caché parce que étant la plénitude infinie de l'intelligibilité, sa trop grande clarté nous éblouit, comme le soleil regardé en face offusque nos yeux. L'Un néoplatonicien est nocturne parce qu'il refuse tout contenu intelligible et toute pensée. Il est au déla de l'ordre de la conaissance. Il n'a donc pas de sécret, c'est à dire d'essence qui se déroberait au régard.[22]

What does this mean from the point of view of our enquiry into the hidden? It means that God, or the One, or the Good, the ultimate mystery, is in one sense totally hidden because he is totally undiscoverable by any intellect, human or divine. But in another sense this Unknowable is not hidden at all, and does not hide itself. There is no need of closed doors and passwords and

22 J. Trouillard "Théologie negative et autoconstitution psychique chez les néoplatoniciens" in *Savoir, faire, espérer: les limites de la raison* (Publications des Facultés universitaires Saint-Louis, Bruxelles 1976), p. 313.

initiation rites to protect the inviolable. There is no need for the mystery to surround itself with mist, like the gods in the Iliad. There is no need to dazzle the eyes of the intellect, which can see it no more than the eyes of the body. The hidden stands absolutely open, and is none the less absolutely hidden.

But what interest or relevance can this utterly Unknowable have for us? And why are the philosophers who are aware of it driven by their very awareness, not to abandon philosophy, but to pursue it more passionately than ever? Why does it intensify the Platonic *erōs*? Let us follow Trouillard a little further:

> Cela ne veut pas dire qu'il ne peut pas se communiquer et qu'il reste muré dans une transcendance inaccessible. Evitons encore un contresens qui serait un anachronisme. Chez les néoplatoniciens, la transcendance n'est pas exteriorité ni absence. Immanence et transcendance sont non en raison inverse, mais en raison directe. Le plus élevé est en chacun le plus fondamental: ce qui est déjà là, ce qu'on ne peut jamais précéder en soi-même. Le transcendant est moins le terme d'une visée qu'un *point de départ inépuisable.*[23]

What Trouillard says here about immanence and transcendence is essential for the proper understanding of all the great traditional religions, including Christianity (though some Christian language and thought about the Incarnation is difficult to reconcile with it). That which is utterly beyond us and cannot be expressed or thought is by its very transcendence of distance and difference most intimately present. The Neoplatonists express this with particular force: it was from them that Christianity and Islam learnt their understanding of the unity of transcendence and immanence. Plotinus, for instance, says:

> But the Good since it was there long before, to arouse an innate desire, is present even to those asleep and does not astonish those who at any time see it, because it is always there and there is never recollection of it; but people do not see it, because it is present to them in their sleep. . . . The Good is gentle and kindly and gracious, and present to anyone when he wishes.
>
> (V 5 [32] 12, 11-14 and 33-34 tr. A.H.A.)

And this most intimate and immediate of presences is, as Trouillard

23 Trouillard *l.c.*, n. 22. continued.

excellently puts it, the presence of an "inexhaustible starting-point": starting-point and source of our existence and life and all our activities, and so of that activity which, though it can never reach that starting-point, seeks to lead us back towards it, Platonic philosophy. When one speaks of philosophy like this one is already giving it a distinctive character which would seem to mark it off rather sharply from most modern understandings of the discipline, and is liable to cause it to be dismissed rather summarily as "religious" or "mystical". But Trouillard has gone deeper than this, and has discovered something else about Neoplatonism which is best expressed in the title of one of his most valuable articles, "Valeur critique de la mystique plotinienne".[24] What Trouillard draws our attention to here, and in many other places,[25] is something which was latent rather than apparent in the ancient Neoplatonists, though there are some signs of it in the last of the Platonis Successors at Athens, Damascius. In developing Trouillard's insight and trying to apply it in my own way I have sometimes felt that I was rather closer than the Neoplatonists would have approved to a very different kind of Platonism, that of the sceptical Academy. But without it, it is very difficult to understand, or to justify, that harmonious union in Plotinus of mystical experience of the highest order and a complete faith in philosophical discussion, as free and critical as any in the Hellenic tradition, as the way to that experience, which E. R. Dodds and Szlezak (see above p. 95) and others have noted.

In the article whose title I have just referred to Trouillard says:

> Mais alors surgit un autre problème. Au lieu du Plotin rationaliste qu'on nous présentait jadis, n'allons-nous pas avoir un Plotin infidèle à l'intellectualisme héllenique? Ne faut-il pas craindre une exténuation de la philosophie, si l'essentiel est acquis avant son intervention?
>
> La réponse est qu'il reste à la philosophie une function indispensable qui est essentiellement critique.

24 *Revue Philosophique de Louvain* 59 (août 1961) pp. 431-444.
25 A bibliography, selected by Trouillard, is to be found in *Néoplatonisme*: Mélanges offerts à Jean Trouillard (Cahiers de Fontenay 19-22) Fontenay-aux-Roses 1981, pp. 313-316.

He continues to develop this theme in a thoroughly Platonic way by showing how this critical function of philosophy is indispensable because it is a purification. And he shows later how radical the consequences of this purification are:

> Quelle qu'ait été l'intention de Platon, on voit à quoi tendent les néoplatoniciens: à une disjonction entre *l'order noétique et l'absolu*. C'est par une négation radicale que l'esprit se rapporte à la présence génératrice. En consequence, si l'analyse régressive remonte au Principe, jamais la dialectique ne parviendra à s'y accrocher. Car l'Inconditionné n'est aucunement intelligible. Il n'y a pas de première verité qui contienne nos raisons ni à quoi nous pouvions en suspendre la chaine. Dés lors la pensée demeurera hypothético-déductive et sans doute pluraliste.... Le caractère inintelligible de l'Un pourrait écraser l'esprit. En réalité, il garantit la rélativité de toute intelligibilité et de toute norme.[26]

The "sans doute pluraliste" should be noted. Trouillard here alludes briefly to the very close and intimate connection which those who follow this way soon discover to exist between the awareness of the universal presence of the open but inviolable mystery and the great Hellenic, Indian and Far Eastern conviction that there is not one path only to so great a mystery.[27] The liberating presence of that which is beyond speech and thought frees one from one's little local self and its ways of thinking, imagining and worshipping. Freedom does not mean abandonment, repudiation or contempt. One is still oneself, and these are the only ways in which that self has skill: and one must now think, imagine and above all worship more intensely than ever. The Neoplatonists have discovered that if one ceases to be active at any level – the mystery is present at all levels – including those of creative imagination and discursive reason, one may fall as far as one can (though never completely) below all ways into formless

26 *Loc. cit.* (see footnote 24) p. 442 and 443. Another article which adds some important points and makes clear the necessity of the continuing practice of philosophy for the Platonic mystic is "Raison et mystique chez Plotin" in *Revue des Études Augustiniennes* XX (1974) pp. 3-14.
27 This, and much else, is well expressed in the last two chapters of Stephen R.L. Clark's *From Athens to Jerusalem: The Love of Wisdom and the Love of God* (Clarendon Press, Oxford 1984).

and sterile fantasy or the mud of unawareness. So the ultimate silence must generate ever new critical discourse. But one will walk one's way in freedom, not taking oneself or it with absolute seriousness, playing before the mystery, and understanding in freedom that there are many other ways equal in honour, and eager to talk with and learn from those who walk them.

The Meaning of History

In considering how people understand what is hidden in the course of events it is desirable to ask at some stage how they understand the course of events itself. So I should like to conclude this paper with a few observations on how the Hellenes understood history. This is in itself a subject well worth returning to from time to time. The Greeks, after all, invented history as we know it in the West, and not only invented it but carried their practice of it to a very high degree of accomplishment. With all the immense and fruitful development of historical studies in modern times, it is still possible to read and honour Herodotus and Thucydides as very great historians, and to have a considerable respect for Polybius and Ammianus. It therefore seems very odd to classical scholars that some Christian thinkers, concerned to emphasize the importance of the Biblical and to play down the Hellenic element in our traditions, have for some time been addicted to saying that Greek thinkers lacked a "sense of history", that they were indifferent to or unconcerned about the significance and meaning of historical events. My "very odd" in the last sentence is in fact an example of the Greek rhetorical figure of *meiosis*. This Christian view tends to be regarded by ancient historians with such derision and contempt that I should hardly have dared to introduce it into a paper read before my professional colleagues, as the following quotation from the current *Classical Review* will show:

The broader context (some abstract nouns should carry a government health warning) seems to be the "widely agreed" idea that "for Graeco-Roman culture history is circular, repetitive, and therefore meaningless" whereas "for Judaeo-Christianity, history is linear, once and for all und therefore meaningful" (pp. 9F). Not surprisingly Press succeeds in showing the inadequacy of this notion: but it is revealing that he has to set up such a straw man in the first place.[28]

Nevertheless, in a gathering like the present where many different disciplines meet, there do seem to be good reasons for considering this Christian critique of the Hellenes, and to do so may help us to understand an important difference between two kinds of human experience of history. Let us reflect a little on the phrase "the meaning of history". What does "meaning" here mean? A good starting-point for our reflection will be an observation by Peter Manchester:

> Within any living historical experience, the past and the present and the future are woven together in mutual interaction; yet one or the other of the three can be dominant.[29]

This indicates very well that the Christian criticism of the Hellenes springs from a profound difference in the kind of experience of time and history that is being assumed. The Christian assumption is that the normative experience, the only one which can give historical events true significance, is the future-dominated or apocalyptic, in which the New Age, the World to Come, is experienced as at hand, pressing upon us here and now, and this experience is so overwhelming that the whole course of events can only be seen as significant in so far as it leads up to and prepares for the apocalypse. It is the end of this world, the Judgment and the inauguration of the Kingdom, which alone can give meaning to

28 T. P. Wiseman, review of G. A. Press *The Development of the Idea of History in Antiquity* in *The Classical Review*. N. S. 35.1. (1985), p. 108.

29 Peter Manchester "The Religious Experience of Time and Eternity" in *World Spirituality: an Encyclopaedic History of the Religious Quest*, Vol. 15 *Classical Mediterranean Spirituality*, Crossroad, New York 1986. I owe much in what follows to this article, and to Manchester's other writings on time and eternity in ancient thought.

all that has come before. This was certainly the experience of the early Christians: but like all apocalyptic experiences, it could only dominate a small group for a short time in its full and authentic religious intensity. None the less, it transmitted to the soberer Christian reflection on historical experience which inevitably succeeded it, when the Judgment did not occur and the Kingdom did not come, the conviction that it is only in the perspective of the end of the world that human life and history has meaning. This remains true even when later Christian reflection sees that is part of the primary Christian experience that the decisive moment, the beginning of the End, has already come in Christ, so that Christians live between his two comings in the last days which his first coming inaugurated, experiencing the presence of the Kingdom to come while they pray, work and hope for its consummation when he comes again. This future-dominated understanding of history continues very powerfully in secularized forms in the post-Christian world and sometimes passes back from them to reinforce the conviction of the Christians: so that it can be assumed without question that only in future-dominated experience can history have a meaning. But of course this is untrue, as an examination of the Hellenic awareness of meaning in history will show.[30]

In its beginnings Hellenic culture was an archaic peasant culture like others in its neighbourhood and throughout the world, and a great deal of its archaic quality persisted in it to the end. The historical experience of an archaic culture is past-dominated in the sense that the past in it is not remote but a powerful living presence now, to which those who share this experience are continually recalled by its regular re-presentation in the sacred rites which make that ancient time, that time in the beginning with its persons and events, present in all its living power here and now. In this kind of experience the present past is too powerfully dominant to

30 For a fuller account of Christian views of time and history see Professor Ulrich Mann's paper in this volume, *Verfallende Zeit und zersprühender Raum* pp. 1-46.

leave room for history, which requires a certain standing away from the past into which it enquires. It was only when the grip of the dominant archaic past had somewhat relaxed, at least for an educated minority of the Hellenes, and their experience became neither past- nor future- but present-dominated, that historical enquiry and writing could begin. The most powerful and satisfying form of Hellenic present-dominated historical experience is that which came to be fully understood by the Platonists, in which there is indeed a transcendent presence which gives meaning and significance to all that exists or happens in time and history, but it is the presence not of past or future but of eternity. But before turning to this we should consider something much simpler and a great deal more widespread both in ancient and in modern times.

This is the historical experience of the common historian. When some Hellenes had moved out of the archaic dominance of the present past sufficiently to look back from a conscious distance at the persons and events of years gone by, they soon began to enquire about them in that spirit of joyful curiosity in which they enquired into everything, which Aristotle in the first two chapters of the *Metaphysics* sees as the beginning of wisdom. The notable people and events of bygone time are among the most interesting things in the world. It is worth while to ensure that they are not forgotten, to enquire into them and record them, and so keep them in the consciousness of the community simply because they are what they are. They are part of ourselves, and to recollect them gives us depth and dignity. This is the historical spirit which animates, from its first words to the end, the first great history in our tradition, the enquiry of Herodotus into the Persian Wars and all that led up to them and all that had to be understood to understand them: and I think it still remains, or has again become, the dominant spirit among historians, in spite of the competition of future-dominated experience. If one is a serious-minded and politically and militarily active person like Thucydides, or wishes to commend one's historical work to such persons, one can of course add that history is not merely interesting and enjoyable but useful, because events and situations of more or less the same kind have a tendency to recur (Thucydides I.22.4). But historians have been, and are, by no means unanimous about the degree to which their works are useful as handbooks for statesmen or generals, and I think this has usually been a secondary motive for their pursuing their historical activities. This account of the historical experience of historians shows clearly that history for them has meaning. The meaningless is not interesting or enjoyable, and is most unlikely to be useful. But "meaning" has a different meaning here from that which it has in future-dominated experience. Events and persons and deeds and works do not derive their meaning from pointing forward to or preparing for the end or consummation of history. Their meaning lies in their being themselves as they are for us here and now. This understanding of meaningfulness is one which modern historians of the ancient world share, and know that they share, with the great Hellenic historians. This is why they become so extremely irritated when the Hellenes are accused of seeing no meaning or significance in history, from the point of view of a future-dominated historical experience which they do not share and are often inclined to think ill-founded in its assumptions and pernicious in its effects.

In the Platonic form of present-dominated historical experience it is the presence of eternity which gives meaning to all that exists or happens in time and history. This is continuous with and conformable to the historical experience of Hellenic historians in a most important way. To speak of the Platonic relationship of time and what is in time to eternity in terms of image and archetype is of course correct if rightly understood: but to speak of it in terms of sign and symbol can be seriously misleading, because it may lead us to forget that it is precisely by being themselves that temporal things image their eternal archetypes. When Platonists speak of this world as a world of signs and images of eternal reality they are sometimes thought to be carrying on the activity, to which they have admittedly been much addicted, of finding symbolic correspondences in the universe with such a degree of

V

seriousness as to lose all touch with and interest in the perceived natures of things here below. But in the intelligible heaven of Plotinus one does not meet spiritual realities of which the horse and the bull and the lion are symbols. One meets the Horse and the Bull and the Lion, with their hooves and horns and teeth and claws (VI 7 [38] 9-10). A serious Christian Platonist should see the pelican not, first and foremost, as a symbol of Christ's piety but as a symbol of Christ's pelicanity: that is, of that in the eternal Logos which can only be expressed in creation here below as a pelican. Platonists should have no quarrel with a poet or painter or musician who insists that his poem or painting or symphony means nothing else but itself, and is not symbolizing Sacred and Profane Love or the Virtue of Critical Circumspection, or telling a story which could just as well have been told in plain prose. The light of present eternity, which gives their full value and significance to the events and persons of history as we apprehend them here and now, shines in them because they are what they are. The deepest meaning of a person, a work, or a deed does not lie in their pointing forward to some future result but in the presence of the Good in them in their own place and time. What I am trying to say here has been splendidly expressed by a contemporary thinker who can certainly not be classified as a Platonist, Hans Jonas, in the concluding section of his great work of moral philosophy *Das Prinzip Verantwortung.*[31] I quote the following with particularly strong agreement because when I first read it I recalled over many years that I also had stood before that picture in Venice and shared that experience:

Als ich, ganz unerwartet, in der Sakristei von S. Zaccaria in Venedig vor Giovanni Bellini's Madonnen-Triptychon stand, überwältigte mich das Gefühl: Hier war ein Augenblick der Vollendung und ich darf ihn sehen, Aeonen hatten ihm vorgearbeitet, in Aeonen würde er, unergriffen, nicht wiederkehren – der Augenblick, wo im flüchtigen "Gleichgewicht ungeheurer Kräfte" das All einen

31 Hans Jonas *Das Prinzip Verantwortung* (Insel Verlag, Frankfurt am Main 1979) p. 381. The sixth chapter is devoted to a vigorous critique of Marxist Utopianism, and in particular of Ernst Bloch's *Das Prinzip Hoffnung.*

Herzschlag lang innezuhalten scheint, um eine höchste Versöhnung seiner Widersprüche in einem Menschenwerk zuzulassen. Und was dies Menschenwerk festhält, ist absolute *Gegenwart* an sich – keine Vergangenheit, keine Zukunft, kein Versprechen, keine Nachfolge, ob besser oder schlechter, nicht Vor-Schein von irgendetwas, sondern zeitloses Scheinen in sich.

"Absolute essential Present: no past, no future, no promise, no consequence, better or worse, no pre-appearing of anything whatever, but timeless Appearing in itself." That is what "meaning" means to anyone who in any way shares the Hellenic present-dominated experience of time and history. Of course for a Platonist the light of the eternal shining in the present can illuminate not only what things are but what they ought to be. It can show the imperfections in the instantiations of the eternal realities here below, and so may urge to action to make the eternal better and more effectively present in time and history. Platonic contemplation should always lead to action when the occasion and one's personal vocation requires it, because it is contemplation by assimilation to the creative and generous Good.[32] And the Platonist in action may well feel herself a free collaborator of that great artist-figure whom Plato chose as his preferred image of divine activity here below in the *Timaeus*,[33] helping to bring forth new works of divine art in the image-world of time and history: and may have as much hope as a reasonable person should that

32 In speaking of the gods, Proclus says "For it is the mark of goodness to bestow on all that can receive, and the highest is not that which has the form of goodness but which does good". *Elements of Theology* prop. 122, p. 108, 20-21 Dodds: (tr. E. R. Dodds). See further P. Hadot "Ouranos, Kronos and Zeus in Plotinus' Treatise Against the Gnostics" in *Neoplatonism and Early Christian Thought* Variorum London 1981 pp. 124-137 and A. H. Armstrong "The Divine Enhancement of Earthly Beauties. The Hellenic and Platonic Tradition", in *Eranos 53-1984,* [= this volume, study **IV**].

33 On the significance of the image of the Demiurge in the Timaeus see A.H. Armstrong "Dualism, Platonic, Gnostic and Christian" in *Plotinus Amid Gnostics and Christians,* ed. David T. Runia (Free University Press, Amsterdam 1984) pp33-4 [= this volume, study **XII**]. This sentence is to some extent an attempt at a Platonic consideration of a moderate version of the Christian view of history put forward by David Jenkins, Bishop of Durham, in a broadcast lecture this year.

under God her work may do something to help all God's creatures by bringing the course of events in that limited extent of space and time in which it can have effect closer to the eternal kingdom.

An apparently more precise form of the future-dominated accusation that history could have no meaning for the Hellenes is to say that this is so because it is for them cyclic, not linear, circling like a dance, not marching to a goal. A moment's thought will show that thinking of history as cyclic does not deprive it of meaning when historical experience is present-dominated. But the charge is worth a little closer examination. To begin with, we should enquire how well based it is on what we know about Hellenic thought. The assumption, at least implicit, which appears, very frequently, to be made by people who say this is that the strict doctrine of Eternal Recurrence was generally held in antiquity; that is, the doctrine that history repeats itself in an infinite series of Great Years and that the repetition is exact in every detail, or only admits of the smallest and least important variations. But in fact this is not the case. Aristotle's pupil, Eudemus of Rhodes reports that Eternal Recurrence was believed in by Pythagoreans.[34] It seems reasonably certain that it was held by the Old Stoics and the conservative Stoics of the period after Posidonius.[35] In its Stoic form, of course, it required belief in the *Ekpurosis* or Conflagration, the periodic re-absorption of all things into himself by the Divine Fire which is followed by the *Apokatastasis*, the restoration of the universe. It is therefore not at all likely that those Middle Stoics who denied the Conflagration,

---

34 Eudemus ap. Simplicius Phys. 732, 30 (DK 58. B34). "If one were to believe the Pythagoreans, that events recur in an arithmetical cycle, and that I shall be talking to you (muthologēso) again sitting as you are, with this pointer in my hand, and that everything will be just as it is now, then it is plausible to suppose that the time too will be the same time as now." (tr. J. E. Raven) This is generally accepted as reliable. But it seems to me to have an element of caricature: and in any case we cannot be sure how far back from the fourth century the doctrine goes, or how many Pythagoreans held it: it may possibly have been derived to some extent from Empedocles.

35 Nemesius *De nat. hom.* 38 p. 277 (SVFII625).

V

Boethus of Sidon, Diogenes of Babylon, and, most important of all, Panaetius,[36] and those who followed them, could have held it.

Outside these restricted circles, in so far as Hellenic thought about history was "cyclic" or "periodic", it was so in a much more natural and flexible way. The natural Hellenic experience of time is better described as rhythmic rather than cyclic. It moves in the alternating rhythms of day and night, of birth and death, and circles like the seasons as it goes on its way. This is a very natural kind of experience indeed, based on the alternation of light and dark which is the basis and origin of time-experience for all living things, and conforming to our deepest personal experiences of the course of events. On the foundation of this kind of experience Plato (*Timaeus* 22 C-D: *Laws* III 677) and Aristotle (*Metaphysics* XII 8.1074b) came to think of human history as periodic, each period terminating in a catastrophe which destroyed the greater part of the human race, leaving only a few survivors who had to start to build civilisation over again from the beginning. These catastrophes do not destroy the universe, which is everlasting. They are not all of the same kind, though fire and flood are predominant: and they were not necessarily thought of as occurring at absolutely fixed intervals of time. Nor is there any suggestion that each period is an exact repetition of previous periods. This kind of loose and open periodicity, based on natural rhythms, leaves plenty of room for change and variety in the course of events, for unique happenings and unique personal contributions to human destiny of lasting historical significance. One day is never exactly like another day, or one spring like another spring, and though the alternating rhythm of birth and death brings children to replace their parents, they are by no means exactly like them and do not do the same things. It is this kind of periodic recurrence, not the rigid Stoic doctrine, which the historian Polybius uses in his account of the cycle of constitutions (VI 5-9). Plotinus is willing to take the idea of world periods

36 Philo, *De Aeternitate Mundi* 76.

seriously (V 7 [18]) and the later Neoplatonists explicitly accept them (Proclus *Elements of Theology* props. 198-200). But, though they may have taken the idea immediately from the Stoics, their periods are Platonic rather than Stoic. They are, of course, periods in the endless history of an everlasting universe. No Platonist could accept the idea of the periodic destruction and restoration of all things. And there can be considerable variety in what happens in the periods, especially to human souls. Every soul which has a place in the material universe must descend into it at least once in every world-period. But most of them have to descend more than once, and their other descents depend on their free conduct of their lives in the body (Proclus *In Timaeum* III 275-279 Diehl). The noblest and best of human souls may even descend more often than they are obliged to, moved by love (*erōs*) to help those less perfect than themselves who are in need (Proclus *In Alcibiadem* 32, p. 14 Westerink).

There can, then, be considerable freedom and variety in Platonic world-periods, and individual lives and acts can have a great deal of significance: though this is not the main reason why time and history are full of meaning for Platonists: they are so first and foremost because they image present eternity. But it would be doing a grave injustice to the Stoics to suppose that their faith in Eternal Recurrence compelled them to experience history as without significance and pointless. To begin with, if in each Great Year the course of events repeats itself exactly in every detail, then from any point of view which is concerned with significance there is only one unique course of events, just as there is only one Jupiter Symphony, however often it is played. So every thing, every person, and every event can be seen as making its own unique contribution to the one history which circles endlessly.[37]

37 It can be objected here from the Christian point of view that the contributions of persons are not free contributions. Apart from the difficulties and inconsistencies into which the Stoics got themselves in trying to combine their strong belief as ethical philosophers in moral responsibility with the strict determinism which their physical theology required, this is an objection to Stoic determinism

What can be more satisfyingly significant than to take one's part in a great dance or play in a symphony? The point and meaning of such activities does not lie in their leading to anything or contributing to anything outside themselves and is not diminished by the number of times the performance is repeated. And the meaning becomes immeasurably deeper when, as in Stoic doctrine, God is the dance and all the dancers. The cyclic deployment of the universe is his perfect self-expression: he is altogether in his work and loves it. Further, we should remember that for the Stoics, as for most believers in Eternal Recurrence, we are now at a low point on the cosmic cycle: things are worse than they were, and are going to get considerably worse before the end. (This belief is of course perfectly compatible with a linear view of history and has very frequently been held by Christians. St. Cyprian expresses it as forcibly as any pagan philosopher or orator. (Cyprian *To Demetrian* 3: C.S.E.L.III.1.352-3.) The lines

> Hora novissima, tempora pessima sunt, vigilemus.
> Ecce minaciter imminet arbiter ille supremus.[38]

sum up a great deal of patristic and mediaeval writing and preaching about the present and future.).So the Conflagration was for the Stoics the great cleansing, when God burns away the accumulated evils of the old age of the world, and the *Apokata-stasis* was the spring of the universe, the return to the golden beginning of things. It would not last, of course, but who outside the shallower sort of fairy-tales can believe in "They lived happily ever after"? Absolute beginning, life without shadow of death, belongs to eternity, not to time and history: and in Stoic thought there is no eternity. If we consider all this, we can understand how

rather than to their cyclic view of history. It would certainly be very difficult to hold the doctrine of Eternal Recurrence without being a determinist, but determinism is perfectly compatible with a linear, Biblical view of history, as Christians and Muslims have shown.

38 The first lines of the poem of Bernardus Morlanensis on the Last Things (c. 1130-1140), to be found in most anthologies of mediaeval Latin verse.

for the Stoics human life and history could be full of significance, and why their belief in Eternal Recurrence filled them, as it has filled others who believe in it, not with boredom and depression but with intense joy.

VI

PLATONIC MIRRORS

I

A student of Plotinus will naturally and spontaneously welcome the theme of this year's gathering, "Human and Cosmic Mirroring." It will seem to him to be a theme which is in some way central in the Platonism of the great Platonic philosopher he studies: central, perhaps, in a manner and to a degree in which it is not in any other Western way of thinking about man and the cosmos. And when one begins to explore more precisely what "mirroring" means to Plotinus, and what his reflections upon mirror-reflections can tell us about the continuity of his thought with that of Plato himself and its differences from it, one soon discovers some interesting complexities and quite profound implications about the Platonic way of looking at the world. I propose to present my own exploration in this paper. To keep our minds focussed on the main theme of our discussions it will be necessary to return continually to a distinction which was important to Plotinus, that between the "natural" and the "artificial" image, so it will be as well to state this clearly here in his own words. The quotation is taken from the work *On the Presence of Being, One and the Same, Everywhere as a Whole* (VI 4-5 [22-3]: *On the Integral Omnipresence of the Authentic Existent*, MacKenna), in which Plotinus stresses particularly strongly the immediacy of the presence of the spiritual or intelligible to the world of sense-perception and the total dependence of the latter on the former for such reality as it has. He says:

> But if someone were to say that it is not necessary for the image to be dependent on anything in the original – for it is possible for a likeness to exist when the original is

VI

not there from which the likeness is taken and, when the fire has gone away, for the heat to exist in what has been heated – first of all, as regards the original and the likeness, if one is talking about the likeness made by the painter, we shall affirm that it is not the original which made the likeness but the painter, since even if some painter makes a self-portrait it is not a likeness of himself, for what made the painting was not the body of the painter or the bodily form which was represented: and it is not the painter, but this particular disposition of the colours which should be said to make this particular likeness. This is not in the strict and proper sense the making of likeness and image as it occurs in pools and mirrors, or in shadows – here the image has its existence in the strict and proper sense from the prior original, and comes to be from it, and it is not possible for what has come to be to exist cut off from it. (VI 4, 10, 1-15: tr. A.H.A.)

The idea of total dependence of image on original which we encounter here is of course a fundamental part of Plato's thought and of that of all later Platonists. The world perceived by the senses, with all the things in it, is totally dependent on the World of Forms or Ideas: everything here below has an existence which in some way is less authentic than that of its archetype and is derived from it. Plato himself expressed this total dependence in two ways, by talking about "participation," *methexis*, or "imitation," *mimēsis*. We do not need for our purposes here to enter into the vast and still continuing discussions about what precisely Plato meant by these terms, how he reconciled in his own mind whatever these two ways of talking about dependence on the Forms meant to him, and which, if either, he preferred to the other in the end. These are questions which, it seems to me, are very difficult, if not impossible, to answer if one takes a modern scholarly rather than a Neoplatonic view of the evidence at our disposal: if, that is, one has no confidence whatever that Plato at any stage in his life had in his mind a perfectly clear, coherent philosophical system precisely worked out in every detail, a Platonic Theology in the manner of Proclus, and that he took care that everything he wrote in his dialogues (or letters) or taught in the Academy should express, or at least be consistent with, this systematic thought, though admittedly sometimes in a strange, baffling and enigmatic way. Of course the effort to answer these questions about participation and imitation continues, and should continue, among modern scholars and philosophers because it is so philosophically stimulating and involves continual re-reading of texts which are always worth re-reading. But all that we need to note for the purposes of our present exploration is, first, that *methexis*-language does not necessarily, seem to bring in any idea of "image" or "mirroring" at all, but, if it is used with image language, will influence those who use it in the direction of preferring the "natural" to the "artificial" image, of thinking that things here below are better represented as related to their archetypes as reflections or shadows of them rather than as paintings or statues of them: and, second, that, whatever Plato's own views at any time may have been about the relative merits of the two kinds of language, by choosing the image of the craftsman in what turned out to be by far the most influential of his writings about the relationship of the world of sense to the World of Forms, the *Timaeus*, he gave a strong push to later Platonic thought in the direction of preferring *mimēsis*-language to *methexis*-language, the "artificial" to the "natural" image. We shall see the full significance of both these considerations when we come to consider Platonic mirroring in Plotinus.

But before we turn to this it will be desirable to spend a little time in clearing, not only our discursive and defining thought, but our imaginations and feelings, of anachronisms about images. This is often a necessary operation before embarking on discussions of terms, even if they are to be concerned exclusively with our own contemporary milieu, especially if some element of valuation is going to come in. Simple-seeming words like "love," "family," "city," "bread" or "God" may have very different feelings and imaginations connected with them for different people, and not only the definable content but the tone and emphasis of what they say about them may be determined by very different hidden pictures and feelings as well as assumptions. And this is obviously still more likely if the discussion is to be about other times and cultures than our own, and the original terms to be discussed are in other languages. The unspoken differences may be so wide and deep that an agreed verbal definition of the terms to be discussed will not be sufficient to deal with the situation, though this Socratic precaution is always useful. This is all very elementary, but the preliminary business of imaginative and emotional clarification is so often neglected, especially in this case, that it seems worth trying to clarify how ancient Greek associations, feelings, and imaginations about *eikōn*, *eidolon* or *mimēsis* differed from our own about "image" and "imitation" or "representation" – what the ancients' image of an image was. Let us begin the process of clarification with the artificial image. What we need to clear our imaginations of here are any associations of ancient *mimēsis* with photographic images and the sort of ultra-naturalistic imitative art which prepared the way for their present rather terrifying dominance of our imaginations and feelings. (Of course, if one considers the photographic process in itself, one can raise interesting questions about whether the image resulting from it should be considered as "natural" or "artificial:" it is very much on the border-line. But when one encounters a photographer hung round with the formidable and formidably expensive technology of his skill, or considers the images as we are continually subjected to them, especially on the television screen, where they often seem to be well on the way to devouring their originals – do those efficiently imaged public figures Mr. X and Mrs. Y really any longer exist? If one unbuilt the carefully built image, would there be anything there at all? – one's imagination about the photographic image is decisively directed to seeing it as purely artificial.) The images of the ancient Hellenes, which were in their imaginations when they speculated about *mimēsis*, were not at all like photographic images. They themselves can mislead us here, because they tend to talk, especially about painted or sculptured images, in a way which suggests extreme photographic naturalism. But when one turns from what they say about the art to the art itself as far as we know it, one soon realises that this is a testimony to the powerful imaginative cooperation which lookers and listeners in the ancient world were prepared to give to the artist. Classical Hellenic artistic images were mimetically closer to those of the great traditional arts of the East than to those of nineteenth-century Europe. This is most obviously apparent in what for Plato was the most powerful, even dangerously powerful, *mimēsis* of human character and fortunes, the drama with the singing which was an integral part of it. If we could (as we certainly cannot) put on a performance of a fifth-century Greek tragedy which not only corresponded exactly in every detail with the original production but was instinct with the living spirit of the ancient dramatic tradition, we should be well advised, if we wanted any real imaginative and emotional participation by the audience, to fill the theatre with Japanese and Indians who knew and loved their own traditional dramatic presentations of ancient myths and legends. And if we establish in our imaginations the figure of the masked singing actor as our image of *mimēsis* we shall not do too badly.

But to clarify our imaginations still further it will be as well to add a couple more illustrations of the difference between ancient Hellenic and modern naturalistic or photographic images. One is taken from the most "naturalistic" or "representational" (in the modern sense) of all Greek arts, sculpture, the other from the most "realistic" (again in the modern sense) sort of Hellenistic literature. It would be hard to find a more brilliantly, or appallingly, successful example of academic naturalism in painting than Sir Frederic (later Lord) Leighton, President of the Royal Academy from 1878 to 1896. Leighton liked to paint classical subjects, and was particularly renowned in his own time for his classical draperies: even his warmest admirers had to admit that the flesh which those draperies revealed, as far as Victorian propriety allowed, did look a little like wax. Now I have heard (this was art-school gossip of the early 1920s at second-hand, and I cannot document it in a proper scholarly way) that Leighton used to perform extraordinary operations on the draperies in which he encased his models, involving gum arabic and all sorts of stiffening, to get the folds of those draperies to look properly "classical." And if one looks at the Elgin Marbles in the British Museum one can see exactly what he was trying to do, and, given his general artistic depravity, why he was trying to do it. He was trying to depict with photographic naturalism, as folds in real draperies on living bodies, details which belonged to the in fact highly stylized and non-naturalistic conventions of fifth-century sculpture. This seems to bring out rather vividly the difference between even the most naturalistic ancient images and the images of 19th-century photographic realism or photography.

For my literary example I am introducing yet again (they appeared in *Eranos 53-1984*) that loquacious couple Gorgo and Praxinoa from the Fifteenth Idyll of Theocritus, who have occupied an obsessive little corner in my imagination since I first met them. This, of course, means that their portrayal by Theocritus is realistic in the sense that it is all too easy to imagine them as real people. But let us look carefully at one particularly vivid little scene. The pair have just pushed their way successfully into the palace to see the queen's sacred show, and are loudly admiring the Adonis statue. A gentleman in the crowd objects strongly to their chatter, and espe-cially to the horrible cooing noises they are making by speaking broad Syracusan. Praxinoa replies vigorously, asserting in no meas-ured terms the right of Syracusans – as the two claim to be – to speak broad. The interesting thing from our point of view here is that both sides in this interchange are in fact speaking in the rather artificial literary Doric in which the whole poem is written, and are of course conversing in metrically correct hexameters. Theocritus' ideas about realistic representation are clearly rather different from those of a modern novelist or dramatist. For him, as for any Greek poet, the conventions of the *genre* in which he is writing take precedence over other considerations. (If he had been writing Old Comedy in the manner of Aristophanes he might have permitted himself a little bit of realistically imitated or caricatured Syracusan.)

When we turn from the artificial to the natural image, we may think at first that less clarifying adjustment of the imagination is required. Reflections and shadows are, after all, much the same in all cultures. But we may, none the less, do well to haul our imagina-tions away from the nicely illumined mirrors in their bathrooms and set them somewhere like the shores of Cézanne's Lac d'Annecy. Ancient *katoptra* were, after all, very different from modern looking-glasses, and considerably less uninterestingly efficient as reflecting mediums. Those beautiful bronze mirrors which we see in museums cannot always have given a very accurate reflection, especially if the maid had neglected her duty of polishing, and the mirror was in any case somewhat dented from the last occasion when the mistress had used it to beat her over the head for her negligence, or because she was feeling somewhat dissatisfied with her own appearance. In any case, men did not often look in mirrors, unless they were dandies or exquisites, which philosophers were not supposed to be, and Plotinus certainly was not. It is doubtful if he ever looked into the sort of mirror one might find on a dressing-table. The reflections which would be in his imagination would be those in the country girl's mirror, the lake or pool or clear reach of a stream, in a place, perhaps, of broken sunlight where images and shadows neighbour each other and intermingle.

This exercise in the clarification of the imagination was undertaken for the sake of the imagination and its accompanying feelings rather than to produce any results which can be conceptually formulated in general terms: but it may be useful and interesting to see whether anything can be formulated in this way. It does not seem to me to be necessarily true that the comparatively stylized and non-naturalistic character of ancient artistic images led to a greater conscious distancing of image from archetype and artificer, that the ancients felt that their images were further from reality than we feel our photographs to be. And it does seem to be true that the traditional non-naturalistic image can operate much more easily as a sign, a token of the presence and power of the archetype. We shall understand the full importance of this in the thought of Plotinus later.[1] What has been said about natural images, reflections, will become important when we come to consider the somewhat phantasmal and illusory character which the image always has but which is never the whole truth about it and may not always be of the first

1 Cp. Ugo Bonanate, *Orme ed Enigmi nella Filosofia di Plotino*, (Franco Angeli, Milano 1985).

importance. We shall need then to keep in our imaginations the broken sunlight and the interplay of images and shadows.

II

The preference of Plotinus, shown in the passage quoted at the beginning of this paper, for thinking of this world as a shadow or reflection rather than a picture of the divine and eternal, is a good starting-point for understanding the profound transformation of Platonism which he brought about. By speaking of "transformation," I do not mean to suggest that Plotinus took something which could be called "the Platonism of Plato" or "the Platonism of the Old Academy" and turned it into something quite different. I am not at all sure, as I indicated above, that there were any such "somethings." I would say, rather, that Plotinus, by meditating on what attracted him and held his attention in the vast store of rich and informal thinking which is to be found in the *Dialogues,* and thinking critically about the discussions and controversies which had arisen between Plato's time and his own, produced a kind of Platonic philosophy – genuinely Platonic because it represented what Plato genuinely meant to him – which was profoundly original and has been extremely influential. It was to a considerable extent a response to the challenge of Aristotle's denial of transcendent Forms and to perceived inadequacies in the generally rather second-rate Platonism of his immediate predecessors and contemporaries: but also a response to other contemporary challenges, notably that of the Gnostics. Ugo Bonanate (see note 1) has recently published some interesting observations on this. But Plotinus' meditations on Plato carried him to a deeper level than that of polemic: and by putting mirroring and shadowing in the centre of our thought and imagination we shall be better able to understand his interpretation of the central Platonic doctrine of the dependence of the whole world of our inner and outer experience on the eternal, and what changes this interpretation involves in his apprehension of the

VI

eternal. What his preference for the mirror-reflection rather than the picture enables him to bring forward and stress is, first, the intimacy and immediacy of the relationship of all below it to the eternal, and, second, the direct spontaneity of the eternal's creative self-diffusion. The closeness of the two worlds, that of images and that of archetypes, is well brought out at the end of the passage from the Sixth Ennead with which we began: "here the image has its existence in the strict and proper sense from the prior original, and comes to be from it, and it is not possible for what has come to be to exist cut off from it." (13-15). This kind of immediacy is repeatedly stressed in the *Enneads*. Perhaps its strongest expression is in a chapter of the treatise *On the Intelligible Beauty* (V 8 [31] 7) to which we shall need to return in another context: "The only possibility that remains, then, is that all things exist in something else, and, since there is nothing between (*oudenos de metaxu*), because of their closeness to something else in the realm of real being something like an imprint and image of that other suddenly appears, either by its direct action or through the assistance of soul – this makes no difference for the present discussion – or of a particular soul." (12-16) We should note in this passage the appearance of *indalma*, "imprint," which for Plotinus is a synonym for *ichnos*, "track" or "trace," alongside *eikōn*, "image." It is important for our understanding of Plotinus' preference for the reflection or shadow that we should continually remember that the image for him is always also a trace or sign, and that what is essential about a sign is that it indicates a presence. It is like a fresh track or trail which one might see in the woods or on the sea-shore, and would recognize, with delight or alarm, or a mixture of both, as showing that whatever made it was very much about in the neighbourhood. Images for Plotinus are very much signs of that presence of the divine of which he is always so intensely aware. (Of course the artificial image can also operate as a sign if one comes to regard it as what Greek Christians still call an *eikōn*.) The same sense of closeness, of the immediacy of contact and presence, pervades the discussion of the everlasting entry of *psychē*, which we translate inadequately but inevitably as "soul," into body in the first Porphyrian division of the great work *On Difficulties About the Soul* which occupies the major part of the Fourth Ennead. Here the images of fire, light and shadow, and even "illuminated shadow" (IV 3 [27] 10, 7-8) are extensively used. But there is also another great and strange image which is worth considering to add depth to our understanding of the closeness of the two Platonic worlds in Plotinus, and also of the kind of distinction and separation which he still perceives as existing between them. "The universe lies in soul which bears it up, and nothing is without a share of soul. It is as if a net immersed in the waters was alive, but unable to make its own that in which it is. The sea is already spread out and the net spreads with it, as far as it can; for no one of its parts can be anywhere else than where it lies." (9, 36-42) What this image conveys with great force is the vastness and the independence of the living eternity in which our world is immersed as well as being a reflection of it. There is enough sea for all the extent of the net, and more, and the net cannot net the sea. The eternal world contains the temporal, as the One contains the eternal. It seems that we are inside that great animal whose tracks we see everywhere in this world. But of course, as we are *psyché*, we also are that animal, and, if we are considering where to look for it in our present circumstances, we can say that it is inside us.

The direct spontaneity of the production of the reflection- or shadow-image by the archetype is certainly a most important reason why Plotinus prefers it to the picture painted by the artist as a representation of the relationship between the Platonic archetypal and image-worlds. The main argument of the chapter just quoted from the treatise *On the Intelligible Beauty* is that the Divine Intellect, *Nous*, which in post-Aristotelian Platonism is usually held to be the demiurgic principle symbolized by the craftsman of the *Timaeus*, and in Plotinus is identical with the Platonic World of Forms, does not carefully plan its work and then carry it out like a human craftsman. Plotinus is here, and frequently elsewhere in the *Enneads*, deliberately opposing the literal interpretation of the *Timaeus* adopted by some of his Platonist predecessors, notably

Plutarch and Atticus, in which the Demiurge is presented as very like a human demiurge or artist-craftsman, though of course perfectly good and wise and working on a much larger scale: and in opposing this he is opposing the kind of teleological view of the world shared by Platonists and Stoics, and enthusiastically adopted by Christians, which sees it as an artefact made by the Great Divine Artist for a good purpose. We should, however, be careful here not to exaggerate the difference between Plotinus and Plato and those who followed Plato in speaking of the world in teleological terms, including Aristotle. To begin with, we should not misunderstand the older Hellenic teleologists by supposing them to think that the good purpose for which the Divine Artist made his work of art was a purpose external to that work. The *Timaeus* set the tone for the whole later development. "He was good, and none that is good is ever subject to any notion of grudging. Being without grudging, then, he desired all things to become as like as might be to himself . . . God's desire was that all things should be good, nothing, so far as might be, bad." (29E-30A tr. A.E. Taylor) The purpose of the cosmos, realised in its present everlasting or endlessly recurrent existence, is simply to be itself, as good a cosmos as possible: and the purpose of each and every thing in it is to contribute to this universal goodness simply by being itself at its best. Aristotle's biological teleology, which seems to exclude the idea of conscious divine planning, concentrates very much on the immanent self-realisation and self-preservation of each particular species. But none of the Hellenic teleologists who prefer to keep closely to Plato's language of artificer and artefact see the purpose of the artefact as one which can only be realised in another world or another age. The cosmos for Stoics does not point beyond itself at all: and for Platonists it only points beyond itself in the sense of being the best possible image on its own level of the eternal. Plotinus is entirely at one with his predecessors on this. Where he differs from them is in wishing to exclude the sense of sharp difference and distance given by too close a concentration on the artificer-image, as we have seen, and also in rejecting anthropomorphic ideas of divine deliberation and planning which he finds rather silly in themselves (as the Epicureans had vigorously pointed out) and incompatible with his own understanding of divine activity. But here again we should not misunderstand the precise nature of his difference with earlier and later teleologists. Plotinus, when he prefers the "natural" to the "artificial" image, and excludes divine deliberation and planning, and speaks, as he often does, of the creative outgoing of the divine in terms of emanation or radiation, does not at all intend to present the divine activity which creates and directs the cosmos in terms of blind unwilled natural process. He remains as firmly committed as Plato, or as any of his Stoic or Middle Platonist predecessors and contemporaries, to the vision of the beauty and order of our world as the product and expression of divine wisdom and goodness. When someone, perhaps a Christian,[2] attacked his view of the self-diffusion of the Good by saying "since the nature of the Good happens to be as it is, and does not have the mastery of what it is, and is what it is not from itself, it would not have freedom, and its doing or not doing what it is necessitated to do or not to do is not in its power" (VI 8 [39] 7, 11-15 tr. A.H.A.): he replied at length, with some indignation and great force, by presenting, in his treatise *On Free Will and the Will of the One* (VI 8 [39]), one of the most impressive accounts of the freedom of God to be found in Western philosophical and theological literature. And in those very passages in which he argues most powerfully against divine deliberation and planning, chapter 7, already referred to, of the treatise *On the Intelligible Beauty* (V 8 [31]), and the first three chapters of his greatest exposition of the nature of Divine Intellection *How the Multitude of the Forms Came into Being, and on the Good* (VI 7 [38]); he makes it abundantly clear that the wisdom which he sees in the divine is higher and more effective than planning, that there is thought there, not absence of thought, and thought quite unlike but incomparably superior to the anxious discursive deliberation and planning of the artisan. He expresses this very well towards the end of V 8, 7:

2 A. H. Armstrong, "Two Views of Freedom" in *Studia Patristica* XVIII, (Pergamon Press, Oxford 1982) [this volume, study XI].

You can explain the reason why the earth is in the middle, and round, and why the ecliptic slants as it does; but it is not because you can do this that things are so there; they were not planned like this because it was necessary for them to be like this, but because things there are disposed as they are, the things here are beautifully disposed: as if the conclusion was there before the syllogism which showed the cause, and did not follow from the premises; the world-order is not the result of following out a train of logical consequences and purposive thought: it is before consequential and purposive thinking; for all this comes later, reasoning and demonstration and the confidence produced by them. (7, 36-44: tr. A.H.A.)

Plotinus objects to the crude anthropomorphism of the literal interpreters of the *Timaeus* and other contemporary theists, but perhaps we can detect a more subtle anthropomorphism in his own account of divine creativity. We may be able to be aware, when he is speaking of divine wisdom and goodness, of what seems to have been for him and his disciples the highest and best kind of human being, whose virtue is immediate and spontaneous; who does not have to turn from inner contemplation to be fully aware of and attentive to others, and who immediately and spontaneously does what is right in every changing circumstance without having to spend much time deliberating and making choices; and who radiates goodness to all around just because of its powerful presence within.[3]

It will be useful at this point to introduce another great Plotinian theme which I find easy to relate to the theme of mirroring, the theme of Dreaming Nature. It will help us to understand the intimacy and immediacy of Plotinus' awareness of divine presence and action here below, and the unity of his many-levelled world. There is not, perhaps, anything very difficult or undesirably personally eccentric about bringing dreams, reflections and shadows very close together in one's mind and imagination, but I do have a personal reason for doing so. In the 1950's my elder brother, the painter John Armstrong, with whom I had little contact, who had never, as far as I know, read a line of Plotinus, and who had a strong objection to the importation of any sort of religious or philosophical symbolism

3 Cp. I 4 [46] 9-10: III 8 [30] 6, 37-40: Porphyry, *Life of Plotinus* 8-9.

into his paintings, painted a picture which I thought when I first saw it, and have continued to think in the years during which I have possessed it, was the best illustration I have ever seen to any part of the *Enneads*. It represents a lake in which buildings are reflected, and on the bottom of which, among the reflections, reclines a very beautiful dreaming figure. This I recognize, for my own Plotinian purposes, as the dreaming Nature of the treatise *On Nature and Contemplation and the One* (III 8 [30]). This is in fact the first part of the great work, strangely divided in Porphyry's edition, of which the treatise *On the Intelligible Beauty* with which we have already been concerned is the second. Its general theme is given in the first sentences, which are worth quoting not only for their own sake and present relevance but because they tell us so much about the spirit of Plotinian Platonism:

> Suppose we said, playing at first before we set out to be serious, that all things aspire to contemplation, and direct their gaze to this end – not only rational but irrational living things, and the power of growth in plants, and the earth which brings them forth – and that all attain to it as far as possible for them in their natural state, but different things contemplate and attain their end in different ways, some truly, and some having only an imitation and image of this true end – could anyone endure the oddity of this line of thought? Well, as this discussion has arisen among ourselves, there will be no risk in playing with our own ideas. Then are we now contemplating as we play? Yes, we and all who play are doing this, or at any rate this is what they aspire to as they play. (1, 1-12: tr. A.H.A.)

Dreaming Nature appears in chapter 4, after another powerful attack on the artisan model for thinking about divine creative activity. (Plotinus remarks here that levers or crowbars are not used in making the material world,[4] nor is its creation at all like making wax dolls – 2, 3-9.) She introduces herself as follows, when she is asked why she makes:

---

4 This, which appears elsewhere (V 8, 7, 10-11: V 9, 6, 22-3) seems to be an allusion to the sort of Epicurean attack which is to be found in Cicero, *De Natura Deorum* I.8.19: *quae molitio? quae ferramenta? qui vectes? quae machinae?*

You ought not to ask, but to understand in silence, you, too, just as I am silent, and not in the habit of talking. Understand what, then? That what comes into being is what I see in my silence, an object of contemplation which comes to be naturally, and that I, originating from this sort of contemplation, have a contemplative nature. And my act of contemplation makes what it contemplates, as the geometers draw their figures while they contemplate. But I do not draw, but as I contemplate, the lines which bound bodies come to be as if they fell from my contemplation.[5] (4, 3-20)

And Plotinus comments:

If anyone wants to attribute to it understanding or perception, it will not be the understanding or perception we speak of in other beings; it will be like comparing the consciousness of someone fast asleep to the consciousness of someone awake. Nature is at rest in contemplation of the vision of itself, a vision which comes to it from its abiding in and with itself and being itself a vision; and its contemplation is silent, but somewhat blurred. (4, 22-28)

---

5   In my note on this passage in the Loeb edition (*Plotinus* III, Loeb Classical Library 1967, pp. 368-9) I said: "Though this is not a precise allusion to anything in Plato, Plotinus is thinking in terms of something like the construction of the regular solids which are the figures of the primary bodies in *Timaeus* 53C-55C. But the intuitive spontaneity of the process here, as contrasted with the careful and deliberate mathematical planning in Plato's symbolical description, brings out clearly an important difference in the mentality of the two philosophers." But Peter Manchester, when commenting on the use of the same word used here (*ekpiptein*) by Plotinus in his account of the origin of time in the treatise *On Time and Eternity* (III 7 [45]11, 7 *hopōs de prōton exepese chronos*) has rightly drawn attention to the fact that it has an established geometrical meaning which it is extremely likely that Plotinus has in mind in both places. He says "A geometrical use of *ekpipto* is familiar since Archimedes (*Spirals* 14), having the passive sense 'to be produced' (said of an extended ray)." (P. Manchester, "Time and the Soul in Plotinus III 7 [45] 11," in *Dionysius* II [1978] p. 124). This is almost certainly correct, and in one way brings Plotinus closer to Plato in the *Timaeus*. But it does not, and was not intended to, contradict my original observation in so far as this was intended to stress Plotinus' objection to a view of the Demiurge (for which Plato's text provides a good deal of support) which makes him very like the Newtonian Deity as seen by William Blake. Plotinus' own cast of mind does not seem to have been mathematical, but he has a proper Platonic acquaintance with and respect for the discipline. This does not, however, lead him to think of God as a mathematician. His divinity has no resemblance whatever to Urizen.

This being, *Physis*, is that last and lowest outgoing of *Psychē*, whose creative activity springing from a contemplation as if in sleep[6] constitutes the material cosmos and gives it such reality as it has. I do not now think it very profitable to enquire too closely whether or not Plotinus sometimes treats *Physis* as if she was a distinct "hypostasis." What I said even when I was attempting to maintain that he did still seems to be true, and worth taking more seriously than I did then: "Of course in Plotinus' system the distinction of hypostases is thought of as the mental recognition of real distinctions within a unity. The One interpenetrates all below it, and each of the lower hypostases derives its reality from submitting itself by contemplation as *hylē* to the higher from which it proceeds. The higher is the form, the principle of reality, to the lower, and so there is no very sharply defined frontier between the Beings."[7] This interpenetration of the levels is what his talk about mirroring and dreaming is intended to convey. To understand it fully, we need to remember that *Psychē* in the Platonic tradition does not have a special world of her own. There is the intelligible world, which, after the sharp Aristotelian distinction between *Nous* and *Psychē* came to be generally accepted, was thought to be the special realm of Divine Intellect, and there is the world perceived by the senses, and *Psychē* is the link between them. But she does not link them by possessing an intermediate realm of her own but by being an inhabitant of the one and constituting the other. In Plotinus she, so to speak, translates the intelligible world which she always inhabits into the sense-world by casting the reflections and shadows which make it up or, in her last outgoing when she is called *Physis*, by

6 This is well described in the geometrical context by Manchester: "In both places we see *ekpipto* used for a productive, ordering outflow which is an activity (*energeia*) but not an action or a deed (*praxis*)." (i.c. n.5)

7 A. H. Armstrong, *The Architecture of the Intelligible Universe in the Philosophy of Plotinus* (Cambridge 1940: reprinted Amsterdam, Hakkert 1967), p. 86. On the meaning of *hypostasis* in the Neoplatonists see H. Dörrie, "Hypostasis" in *Nachrichten der Akademie der Wissenschaften in Göttingen, Philol.-hist. Klasse 1955,* 35-92: B. Dalsgaard Larsen, "Jamblique dans la Philosophie Antique Tardive" in *De Jamblique à Proclus* (Vandœuvres-Genève 1975) pp. 14-15.

VI

dreaming the dream which it is, of which the content is supplied by her waking consciousness in the eternal glory of the intelligible. And the activity in which she does this is the activity by which that higher world of *Nous* exists, *theōria*, contemplation. This is what he is expounding in the treatise (III 8) with which we are at present concerned, which is the first part of his great anti-Gnostic work.[8] To see clearly the relevance of this in a work directed against the Gnostics we must of course bear in mind the indissoluble union in the Neoplatonism of Plotinus and his successors between contemplation and creativity. Genuine Neoplatonic contemplation is always productive. This is because it is in its highest form on the level of *Nous*, and always aspires to be, the vision which is union with the Good, only possible through assimilation to the Good, and the Platonic Good is intrinsically productive and creative. Proclus' statement when he is speaking of the providence of the gods, "For it is the mark of goodness to bestow on all that can receive, and the highest is not that which has the form of goodness but that which does good" (*Elements of Theology* 122, p. 108, 19-21 Dodds: tr. E. R. Dodds), sums up the whole tradition from Plato onwards. It is creative contemplation which holds all the levels of the Neoplatonic universe together and ensures that the reflections, shadows and dreams which it produces as our cosmos here below are true signs and icons of the intimate and immediate presence of the Good.

Though *Psychē* does not have an intermediate world of her own, human *psychai*, which are parts of the hypostasis *Psychē*, have a distinctive intermediate psychic activity of their own, that of *dianoia*, discursive or defining reason. This activity seems to be peculiar to humans. Gods do not have it or need it: the cosmic gods

8 There seem to be good reasons for regarding the whole of this, which comprises the Porphyrian treatises III 8 [30], V 8 [31], V 5 [32] and II 9 [33], and not only its polemical appendix II 9 which is entitled *Against the Gnostics*, as being an exposition of what Plotinus regarded as authentic Platonism which he intended as an answer to and refutation of the claims of his Gnostic friends and acquaintances. V. Cilento entitled his excellent edition of the great work, with translation and commentary, *Paideia Antignostica* (Le Monnier, Firenze 1971).

no more employ reasoning in their administration of the universe than the Demiurge reasoned and planned its making. Nor of course do animals and plants reason, though they may be said, as Plotinus says at the beginning of this treatise, to contemplate: the earth, from which the plants grow, is a goddess, whose activity is above, not below reason, and all things that appear to us inanimate share in her life;[9] and their forms are the last traces of *Psychē*, the figures which *Physis* makes in her dream. So it would not be true, for Plotinus, or for any Neoplatonist, to say that all things think, or are thoughts, in the ordinary sense in which these terms are used as applying to discursive reasoning: but Plotinus can say that they contemplate or are contemplation, and Theodore of Asinē that "all things pray except the first,"[10] because all things are in the great contemplative return which is the other side of the creative outgoing from the Good. Discursive thinking, then, is a peculiarly human activity, but not of course the only or the most important psychic activity: a great deal goes on below it, and we only become our true selves when we rise above it to share in the eternal contemplation, and ultimately vision-union, of *Psychē* in *Nous*: though it is the indispensable means in our present condition of attaining that higher level. We can only go beyond thought through thinking. But a psychic life and world confined to or totally dominated by discursive reasoning would for Plotinus be as squeezed, cramped and confined as the life and world of Blake's Urizen.

This is probably a fair assessment of the status of the distinctively human activity of reasoning in the thought of Plotinus. But because, not only in the Platonic but in the whole Hellenic philosophical tradition, it is the indispensable way to any higher awareness of the divine and eternal mirrored here below, it is very easy for discursive, defining thinking to take over and expand so as to dominate, well beyond the limits which it should have in Plotinian Platonism, the psychic lives of those influenced by Hellenic philosophy or its later derivatives. This discursive takeover has of course been particularly

9 *Enneads* IV 4 [28] 22.
10 Proclus *In Timaeum* I. 213, 2-3 Diehl.

apparent in Western Christian and post-Christian thought and intellectual and cultural institutions from late antiquity onwards. It is by no means only to be observed in, and should not be exclusively associated with, the later mediaeval scholasticism which developed after the rediscovery of Aristotle, or the predominant tendencies of European thought after the scientific revolution of the 17th century. It is already clearly detectable, in an indubitably Neoplatonic form, in that late antique and early mediaeval Christian platonic human-ism, the intellectual culture based on the Seven Liberal Arts of the *trivium* and the *quadrivium*, the origins and early development of which have recently been so illuminatingly studied by Ilsetraut Hadot.[11] It is important to be aware of this if we are, not only to arrive at a properly informed understanding and appreciation of the Platonic tradition, but to realise how much there is to be said from the point of view of Plotinian Platonism in support of some modern attacks on "Greek" or "Platonic" intellectualism, even when from a historical point of view they seem rather ill-informed and undis-criminating.[12] One of the most powerful and lastingly influential attacks on the domination of the discursive reason has been that made by William Blake. Blake, as Kathleen Raine has shown, was deeply influenced by Neoplatonism.[13] But he often presented his most profoundly Platonic insights, which were extremely heretical from the point of view of correct Christian Biblicist theology, as true Christian religion, in the strongest opposition to Plato and Aristotle and the Greeks.

The perfect, archetypal form of mirroring or imaging contempla-tion is of course in the thought of Plotinus that to be found in the Platonic intelligible world, the World of Forms which is Divine Intellect, *Nous*. *Psychē* in her highest and purest contemplation is

---

11 I. Hadot, *Arts libéraux et philosophie dans la pensée antique* (Études Augusti-niennes, Paris 1984).

12 Werner Beierwaltes is an excellent guide in the study of the sort of problems indicated here, especially where German thought is concerned. See his *Identität und Differenz* and *Denken des Einen* (Klostermann, Frankfurt 1980 and 1985).

13 Kathleen Raine, *Blake and Tradition* (Princeton University Press 1968).

the reflected image of the contemplative life of *Nous*: though in virtue of that contemplation she is also a full member of the world of *Nous* and can live on the level of that world. It is this characteristic Plotinian ambiguity, which, like other Plotinian ambiguities, should not be ignored or artificially reduced to harmony or explained away, which gives *Psychē* in his thought her breadth of range and her power to hold the worlds together: a breadth and power which she to some extent retains in the thought of the later Neoplatonists in spite of their strong disapproval of Plotinus' tendency to vagueness and ambiguity about the distinction between the hypostases and their own insistence, due to the strongly definitory character of their thought, on making this, and many other distinctions in the intelligible, very sharp indeed.[14] *Psychē*, then, both shares in and reflects the archetypal and ultimate contemplation of *Nous*. When her contemplation is thought of as mirroring and imaging that of *Nous* its content is the World of Forms, the intelligible cosmos which *Nous* is and which *Psychē* mirrors in the material cosmos which she in union with *Nous* creates by her contemplation. But *Psychē*, and even human *psychē*, is often seen by Plotinus as not merely contemplating but being that intelligible universe: "For the soul is many things, and all things, both the things above and the things below down to the limits of all life, and we are each one of us an intelligible universe . . ." (III 4 [15] 21-23) A passage in the treatise *On The Knowing Hypostases and That Which is Beyond* makes particularly clear how easily Plotinus can pass from one way of thinking to the other without denying the validity of either:

> Sense-perception is our messenger but Intellect is our king. But we too are kings when we are in accord with it; we can be in accord with it in two ways, either by having something like its writing written in us like laws, or by being as if filled with it and able to see it and aware of it as present. And we know ourselves by learning all other things by such a vision, either learning a vision of this kind according to the knowing power, by that very power itself, or ourselves becoming it; so that the man who knows himself is double, one knowing the nature of the reasoning which

14 On *Psychē* in the later Neoplatonists see J. Trouillard, *L'Un et L'Âme selon Proclos* (Les Belles Lettres, Paris 1972).

belongs to soul, and one up above this man, who knows himself according to Intellect because he has become that Intellect; and by that Intellect he thinks himself again, not any longer as man, but having become altogether other and snatching himself up into that higher world, drawing up only that better part of soul, which alone is able to be winged for intellection, with which someone there keeps by him what he sees. (V 3 [49] 3, 44-4, 15 : tr. A.H.A.)

And when *Psychē* in this way is *Nous*, her contemplation, mirroring and imaging is the same as that of *Nous*, and to this very strange and paradoxical mirroring and imaging we must now turn. There is of course no mirroring or imaging in the self-contemplation of *Nous* as self-contemplation: it is far too intimate for that, "light transparent to light." (V 8 [31] 4, 6) What is mirrored or imaged in this archetypal contemplation which is the intelligible world is the First, the Origin of all reality, the transcendent One or Good: so that *Nous* and *Psychē* are in their contemplation true images of God: and all human souls which take part in that contemplation and the material cosmos and all things in it which spring from it are not only the products of that ultimate self-diffusive goodness but have, in their various ways and degrees, the form of good and so are images and signs of God. But this ultimate and archetypal contemplative image or mirroring is an image in a very strange sense indeed, because it is an image of the unimageable, of that which no image and likeness can be made. In fact at this point the concept and the imagination of image or mirroring break completely, as all our concepts and imaginations break if we follow with understanding any of the paths in Plotinus' thought which lead to the Good, as all paths in his thought do: one has to go out at the end into the unknowable where there is no path any more. This is why the study of it can have a peculiarly liberating effect on our thinking and sensibilities, as I tried to show last year, following in the steps of Jean Trouillard.[15] Of course, if we have been really trying to think in a Plotinian way about the archetypal image which is the real cosmos in *Nous* we shall not have been trying to apply to it the sort of clearly

15 A. H. Armstrong, "The Hidden and the Open in Hellenic Thought" in *Eranos 54-1985* [this volume, study V].

defined concepts which are useful in our distinctively human activity of logical discourse. The great visionary descriptions of the intelligible cosmos in the *Enneads*[16] are simply not tidily reducible to coherent and systematic conceptual patterns. The thinking of *Nous* is not at all like the sort of thinking peculiar to and generally engaged in by human *psychai* when they remain on their own level. He says:

> The wise men of Egypt, I think, also understood this, either by scientific or innate knowledge, and when they wished to signify something wisely, did not use the forms of letters which follow the order of words and propositions and imitate sounds and the enunciations of philosophical statements, but by drawing images and inscribing in their temples one particular image of each particular thing, they manifested the non-discursiveness of the intelligible world, that is, that every image is a kind of knowledge and wisdom and is a subject of statements, all together in one, and not discourse or deliberation. (V 8 [31] 6, 1-9: tr. A.H.A.)

The thinking of *Nous* is perhaps rather more like the dreaming of Nature than Plotinus would be prepared to admit, and the silence which Nature recommends to her questioners in the passage quoted above, and often both recommended and spoken of in connection with divine activity by the Neoplatonists, may be more helpful in arriving at an understanding of it than the chatter of philosophical discourse, though that too has its necessary place.

It is in Plotinus' descriptions of how this ultimate imaging of the unimageable and mirroring of that which casts no reflection occurs that we can observe best how very active mirrors are in Plotinus, at all levels but the lowest. At every stage in this great cosmos of reflections (this word is used here with deliberate ambiguity) down to the dreaming of Nature the mirror does not just passively receive the reflection, but, because it only reflects in this sense because it is reflecting in another, that is, contemplating, it plays its part in creating the mirror-image and gives it the character appropriate to its level: that is, because it is that reflection or image which it creates in contemplation, it can be said to bring itself into that being which

16 Especially V8 [31] 3-4 and VI 7 [38] 12-15.

is none the less given it from above.[17] And it is because the mirror is active in contemplation in this way that the image is true and living. It is only in the last and strangest mirror, the mirror which does not exist, the darkness of matter, that there is no contemplative activity, and so the image is false and dead: to this we shall turn later. But at the highest level, that of the imaging of the unimageable, where the reflection is the world of real being, the intelligible cosmos which is Divine Intellect, creative contemplation is at its most intense and productive. Without it, in fact, there would be no image, that is, no cosmos, at all: and that of course is exactly what happens in that higher vision which is union of *Nous*, drunk and in love and out of its mind, with the One which eternally co-exists with the contemplation in which it creates itself as World of Forms.[18] (If any contemporary philosopher wishes to say that all this is philosophically unintelligible, I shall be delighted to agree with him.) Plotinus describes the reflecting, imaging, contemplation of *Nous* with great power in the treatise *How the Multitude of Forms Came into Being, and on the Good*: and at the end of his account explains, as far as he can, why he cannot put what he has seen up there into images and concepts:

> That, then, is the Good, but Intellect is good by having its life in that contemplation: and it contemplates the objects of its contemplation as having the form of good and as the ones which it came to possess when it contemplated the nature of the Good. But they came to it, not as they were there, but as Intellect itself possessed them. For that Good is the principle, and it is from that that they are in this Intellect, and it is this which has made them from that Good. For it was not lawful in looking to him to think nothing, nor again to think what is in him: for

17 The relationship of this way of thinking in Plotinus to the later Neoplatonists' doctrine of the *Authupostata* is unclear: it may not be as close as one is at first inclined to think. See John Whittaker, "Proclus' Doctrine of the Authupostata" (with discussion) in *De Jamblique à Proclus* (n. 7, pp. 193-237).

18 VI 7 [38] 35, 19-33. In my own reflections on these two eternal states of *Nous* since 1984, I have often found it helpful to bring before my mind's eye the first two of Shizuteru Ueda's three Zen pictures (the third serves me very well as a mind-picture of Plotinus). Shizuteru Ueda, "Die Zen-Buddhistische Erfahrung des Wahr-Schönen" in *Eranos 53-1984*, pp. 197-198.

then Intellect itself would not have generated them. Intellect therefore had the power from him to generate and to be filled full of its own offspring, since the Good gave what he did not himself have. But from the Good himself who is one there were many for this Intellect: for it was unable to hold the power which it received and broke it up and made the one power many, that it might be able so to bear it part by part. Whatever it generated, then, was from the power of the Good and had the form of good, and Intellect itself is good from the many which have the form of good, a good richly varied. And so, if one likens it to a living richly varied sphere, or imagines it as a thing all faces, shining with living faces, or as all the pure souls running together into the same place, with no deficiencies but having all that is their own, and universal Intellect seated on their summits so that the region is illuminated by intellectual light – if one imagined it like this one would be seeing it somehow as one sees another from outside: but one must become that, and make oneself the contemplation. (VI 7 [38] 15, 10-32: tr. A.H.A. cp. V 3 [49] 11)

It should by now have become fairly clear that the Platonism of Plotinus is very different from a number of other Platonisms, including quite probably the Platonism of Plato himself (if Plato was a Platonist). It even shows some striking differences (of which Iamblichus and Proclus were very much aware) from later Neoplatonisms, Hellenic and Christian. But is it possible to sum up, in the speciously precise discursive language which must inevitably be used by a historian of philosophy, in what these differences consist? It is certainly very difficult, and when one starts to try to do it one feels rather like Plotinus' net trying to catch the sea (above p. 156). Even more, perhaps, than with other great philosophers of our tradition, the only way to get inside Plotinus, as he says we must get inside the intelligible world (above), and so to understand the distinctive quality of his transformation of Platonism, is to read continually in the *Enneads*: of course it helps considerably to attempt to translate his writings into one's own language, as many Plotinian scholars from Ficino onwards have found. But here is yet another brief attempt, concentrating on the differences between him and other Platonists as our present direction of attention requires, to explain the distinctive quality of his Platonism. Attempts, of which there are many, which concentrate more on what he has in common with Plato and other Platonists, or with Aristotle, or with patristic and mediaeval Christian thought, are of course also valid and helpful to understanding. One characteristic of his thought, which consideration of it from the point of view of our main theme of mirroring has brought out very well, is the translucency and interpenetration of the levels which any Platonist must recognize in his universe. This is the direct and inevitable consequence of understanding the relationship between these levels in terms of mirroring contemplation and seeing the lower as an image, shadow or trace of the higher which can only exist by the continual presence of the higher in it: and it brings with it a certain imprecision about the boundaries between these levels. Plotinus' thought about reality can properly be described as, in a sense, hierarchical. But it is as remote as possible from the human models most commonly used in hierarchical thinking, those of the imperial court or the ecclesiastical establishment, with their clear-cut separations and rigid distinctions of status, which have greatly influenced some other Platonisms. The most important aspect of this drawing together and interpenetration of the levels is the closeness in Plotinus of the intelligible and sensible worlds and the way in which he apprehends the intelligible in terms of the sensible, which is its natural image or reflection. Bréhier, in a remark quoted with approval by Schwyzer, once said "C'est trop peu de dire que Plotin a le sentiment du monde intelligible: c'est plutôt chez lui sensation."[19] The intelligible cosmos in Plotinus includes everything in the sensible cosmos, above all life and so in a strange way endless novelty and variety, and this is apprehended with sensuous vividness. Plotinus understands the Platonic World of Forms in terms of direct sense-awareness: he does not reduce it to the conceptual skeleton to which even the bodily world of our immediate experience here below has to be reduced to be manageable in scientific discourses, whether "scientific" is understood in the older sense of *epistemē* or *scientia* or in a more modern empiricist way. And the movement of contemplation

19 E. Bréhier, *La Philosophie de Plotin* (Boivin, Paris 1928) pp. xi-xii: quoted and extensively illustrated by H.-R. Schwyzer in his authoritative survey of the language of Plotinus in *Plotinos* (Druckenmüller, München 1978) col. 526-7.

VI

172

through all the mirroring levels of his universe acquires a distinctive freedom because it culminates in and must always at every level be open to the awareness of the presence of that which cannot be mirrored or imaged, which the last Platonic Successor at Athens, Damascius, did not hesitate to speak of, in a most powerful celebration of the inadequacy of all language at this point, as *to ouden*, "the nothing."[20]

Many Platonists of other kinds, in Plotinus' own time, and since, have found the characteristics of his Platonism to which I have been drawing attention disturbing and annoying, and have either dismissed them as far as possible from their minds or tried to reform his thought to a degree of epistemic order and tidiness which is sometimes rather excessive on their own admitted principles: this is of course particularly necessary if one is concerned to bring his Platonism into conformity with the dogmas of a revealed religion. But I have found myself that his kind of Platonism has certain advantages, which make it at least worth commending the study of the *Enneads* to those who are simultaneously attracted to and repelled by Platonism as they at present understand it. It does seem, in my own experience, to make it easier to converse with, and even sometimes partly to understand, the sages and saints of India and the Buddhist traditions of the further East. It makes it easier to perceive at least some of the genuine and powerful reasons which have prompted some modern attacks on "Platonic" or "Greek," "rationalism" or "objectivism" or even "traditional metaphysics:" without necessarily agreeing with all that is said in them or being always attracted by the alternative ways of thinking which are offered. And it really does seem to have something to offer to many profoundly religious people in our world who are disillusioned with and repelled by religion as it is generally presented to them in Western or Westernized societies. The best short summing up of what that something is which I have encountered occurred in a paper which a student at Manhattanville College wrote for me in the 1960's. She

20 Damascius, *Dubitationes et Solutiones* 2.5.2-9 Ruelle.

said "Plotinus really did help me. My favourite thing about him is
that he didn't organise his Good."[21] These are certainly the sort of
grounds on which it has seemed to me so well worth while to bring
Plotinian Platonism into our discussions here at Eranos.

III

We must now return from the heights of the intelligible world,
where *Nous* creates the image of the imageless, to the waters of the
world of sense, and see how for Plotinus the reflections and
shadows which play on those waters are not only true signs and
natural images for those who understand their nature but can bewitch and mislead those who do not, and take them for the ultimate
realities. The images of mirroring in the Enneads with which we
shall be concerned here are those of Dionysus and Narcissus, which
have been so well studied by Jean Pépin and Pierre Hadot.[22] The
mirror of Dionysus is alluded to once in the *Enneads*, in an account
of the descent of human souls, "But the souls of men see their
images as if in the mirror of Dionysus and come to be on that level
with a leap from above: but even these are not cut off from their
own principle and from Intellect" (IV 3 [27] 12, 1-4 tr. A.H.A.). The
story of Narcissus is used as an illustration of human self-delusion
in the famous treatise *On Beauty*: "For if a man runs to the image
and wants to seize it as if it was the reality (like a beautiful reflection
playing on the water, which some story somewhere, I think, said
riddlingly a man wanted to catch and sank down into the stream and
disappeared) then this man who clings to beautiful bodies and will
not let them go, will, like the man in the story, but in soul, not in

21 Quoted in A. H. Armstrong "The Escape of the One" (*Studia Patristica*, Berlin
   1975 = *Plotinian and Christian Studies* XXIII) p. 88.
22 J. Pépin, "Plotin et le Miroir de Dionysos" in: *Revue Internationale de
   Philosophie* XXIV (1970) pp. 304-20; P. Hadot, "Le Mythe de Narcisse et son
   Interprétation par Plotin" in *Narcisses: Nouvelle Revue de Psychanalyse XIII*
   (Printemps 1976) pp. 81-108.

174

body, sink down into the dark depths where intellect has no delight and stay blind in Hades, consorting with shadows there and here." (I 6 [1] 8, 8-16 tr. A.H.A.)[23] This leads immediately to the great exhortation to set out on the journey to our own country and our father which so deeply impressed Augustine and many others, that journey for which Plotinus' directions are "shut your eyes and change to and wake another way of seeing, which everyone has but few use" (the last words of the chapter).

Hadot rightly stresses that in both these images of mirroring it is human *psychai* which see their reflections and are attracted by them.[24] There is no question of any misleading or enchantment of cosmic *Psyché* in Plotinus: her bringing into being of the material world is not the result of any narcissistic passion for her image in matter which entraps her in the lower darkness: it is, as we have seen, a casting of reflections and shadows, a making of natural images, both inevitable and spontaneous, which are entirely good on their own level and the last stage in the great self-diffusion of the transcendent Good, and this casting of images leaves *Psyché* herself unchanged and unaffected: even human *psychai* in Plotinus are not essentially changed or affected by embodiment: "their heads are firmly set above in heaven." (IV 3, 12, 5: tr. A.H.A.) Hadot contrasts this strongly with the narcissistic account of the coming into being of the material world which is to be found in the Hermetic *Poimandres* (14). Here the *Anthropos*, the Gnostic Archetypal Man, displays himself to Nature down below and falls in love with his own reflection in her: he descends and unites with her in a passionate embrace and so produces mortal humanity. We are here in quite a different world of thought and imagination from that of Plotinus.

The allegorical interpretation of the mirror of Dionysus as applying to the experience of human *psychai* in the world here below is

---

23 A second allusion in the *Enneads* (V 8 [31], 2, 34 ". . . looking at *his own* image") makes it clear that the figure here is that of Narcissus, not, as some have thought, of Hylas (Hadot, *loc. cit.* [n.22] p.99 n.1).

24 *loc. cit.* pp. 100-101.

also to be found in the later Neoplatonists Proclus and Damascius,[25] where the exegesis of the particular passage in Plato with which they are at the time concerned seems to them to require it: but they also have a cosmic interpretation of the whole myth of the rending of Dionysus by the Titans to which the mirror belongs (the mirror was one of the toys with which the Titans attracted the child Dionysus away from his nurses and guardians). The application to individual souls and the cosmic application are closely connected in their minds, and are indeed for them the same interpretation applied on different levels: and, as the cosmic application has a strongly non-Gnostic and indeed anti-Gnostic character, it will be worth considering it briefly here to confirm Hadot's judgement of the difference between the uses of the image of mirroring in Plotinus and in the *Poimandres*. It is to be found in a number of places in the 5th and 6th century Neoplatonic commentaries on Plato where the formation and ensoulment of the material cosmos, with its sharp divisions and separations, by the divine powers is in question. It is this which, for the later Neoplatonists, is symbolized by the tearing to pieces of Dionysus by the Titans; it means for them the creative presence of the divine in the world of spatial and temporal separation. And this is of course for them an entirely good divine activity, not a passive suffering inflicted upon the divine by evil enemies. They express this by saying that the Titans who rend Dionysus are also gods:[26] or,

25 Proclus, *Commentary on Alcibiades I* 19, 43-44 Westerink: Damascius *Commentary on the Phaedo* I.129 p. 81 Westerink: 111.14 Norvin (L. G. Westerink, *The Greek Commentaries on Plato's Phaedo II. Damascius*, Amsterdam-Oxford-New York, North Holland Publishing Co. 1977; this commentary was published under the name of Olympiodorus in Norvin's 1913 Leipzig edition, but has been shown by Westerink to be a report of lectures on the *Phaedo* by Damascius).

26 Damascius I 9 p. 33 Westerink. The whole first section (1-13) of this commentary, which reproduces a great deal of a commentary on the *Phaedo* by Proclus with critical observations by Damascius, with Westerink's notes, provides much information on the late Neoplatonic interpretation of this myth, as does also the commentary by Olympiodorus on the *Phaedo* edited by Westerink in his first volume (see previous note).

176

more remarkably, by saying that the divine demiurgic activity which forms this world of separation and division is "Dionysiac," as if Dionysus in the material creation was rending himself.[27] And their understanding of the mirroring is correspondingly positive: the casting and following of his reflection by Dionysus is divine and beneficial activity. The god Hephaestus makes the mirror, or the reflection of Dionysus in it.[28] And Proclus has a remarkable passage on the smoothness of the outer surface of the universe (*Timaeus* 33 B8-C1), in which he says "The Theologians also have for long made the mirror a symbol of the aptitude of the All [the material cosmos] to be filled by Intellect. This is why they say that Hephaestus made a mirror for Dionysus, and when the god had looked into this and seen his image he proceeded to the whole divided creation."[29] Of course for the Neoplatonists the self-rending, Dionysiac, aspect of divine activity in the material cosmos is only one side of it: it is eternally correlated with the harmonizing, integrating activity of Apollo (who collected and put together the pieces of the body in the original story): so that the activity of the Demiurge, Proclus says in the passage just quoted, is not only "Dionysiac" but "Apolline." And human *psychai* aspiring to return to unity through *Nous* with the One, while accepting their disintegration here below as a good and divine dispensation, will need and receive not only the reintegration by Apollo but that maintaining in some way of the original unity effected by Athena (who in the original story preserved the heart of Dionysus), as Proclus and Damascius teach in their commentaries on the *Alcibiades* and *Phaedo* referred to above (n. 25). It is worth while observing, before we leave this positive cosmic interpretation of the myth, that the understanding of the rending of Dionysus as self-rending, not only

27 Proclus *In Timaeum* II 197, 14-21 D.
28 Proclus *In Tim.* I 142, 20-28 D: 336, 29-337, 1 D. It should be noted that the commentators attribute this positive interpretation of the myth to "the theologians" or "Orpheus," and the late Orphic poems which were part of their canon of Scripture may well have contained it (see below on its appearance in the Stoics).
29 Proclus *In Tim.* II 80, 19-24 D.

by the Neoplatonists but perhaps by the "theologians" whose authority they invoke, may well have been facilitated by the Stoic interpretation known to Plutarch, in which the myth symbolizes the cyclic self-transformation of the Stoic God from pure divine fire into all the changing diversity of the world: as divine fire he is Apollo, as the multiplicity of material things he is Dionysus – always in Hellenic thought the two have to be kept together and both adverted to if one is to have any adequate idea of the divine.[30] It is really remarkable that Hellenic thinkers, confronted with a story whose original Orphic tellers intended it to explain and express their profound sense of alienation as divine beings trapped and imprisoned in human bodies in this dark lower world, seized it so promptly and twisted it so firmly to express a very different evaluation of our experience. It illustrates very well how difficult it was for most Hellenes to sympathize with, or even fully to understand, the deep alienation from this world of Orphics or Gnostics and why, even in the most Orphically influenced Pythagoreans or Platonists, cheerfulness has a strong tendency to break in.

Plotinus would have found all this rather fanciful: he did not share the enthusiasm of his successors for myths and theologians, though he will refer to them when it suits his purpose: but he would not have disagreed with the doctrine.[31] As we have seen, the casting of reflections and shadows is for him a good and natural proceeding in itself. And the following of their reflections in the mirror by human *psychai* is by no means simply a fall, a going astray and a disaster, as he makes quite clear in the long account of their descent which the allusion to the mirror of Dionysus introduces in IV 3, and

---

30 Plutarch *De E Delph.*, 9.388 F-389 A-B.

31 It may be guessed that the tone of the allusion to the mirror of Dionysius quoted above (p. 173) implies a knowledge of a positive allegorical interpretation of the Orphic myth: this is perfectly possible, but it would be going well beyond the evidence of this one casual remark to say that it is certain. It is, however, interesting to reflect at this point that, as we have seen (above pp. 169-70), a breaking up and multiplying, not mythologically symbolized, occurs in the *Enneads* at the formation of the archetypal image, the world of real being which the world of space and time mirrors.

178

in his earlier reconciliation of the apparent contradictions in Plato in IV 8 [6]. What is wrong according to Plotinus in our commerce with images, what leads to a fall too deep, a culpable straying, a self-imposed exile, is to take the images too seriously, to become obsessed with them, to try to grab at and cling to them, and so to become isolated and imprisoned in a petty world of bodily needs and desires. But the images themselves are good and beautiful on their own level and in their limited way, and, because they are natural images, reflections and shadows, the eternal beauty is immediately present and accessible in them if we make the effort required to apprehend it. We are close here to the theme of the non-attached enjoyment of the beauties of earth of which I spoke at Eranos in 1984.[32] Even when Plotinus is using images of mirroring to emphasize the potentially delusive and distracting character of the reflections and shadows which are the material cosmos and the way they can bewitch us into illusion, there remains enough which is positive in his account of them to make his kind of Platonism attractive to those of us who are uneasy with, and perhaps at times repelled by, other forms of Platonism which (as Plato himself often seems to do) increase the distance between image and archetype and sharpen the contrast between the ways of apprehending them. Our consciousnesses are nowadays pretty firmly settled on the bottom of the lake, down among the broken lights and shadows and reflections. We cannot be as sure as the ancients of our ability to raise our heads above water into the light of the eternal: though this does not mean that we should disbelieve or ignore those in past or present, in West or East, who appear to have some claim to have done so. One reason for this lack of confidence is that the brilliant and technically admirable developments of philosophical discourse in modern times have made it very much less likely than even Plotinus thought that the path of discursive reason will lead us to awareness of rather than disbelief in an objective eternal reality quite outside and independent of the dreams and images of the lake, or the *psyché*. There is

32 A. H. Armstrong, "The Divine Enhancement of Earthly Beauties" in *Eranos* 53-1984 [this volume, study IV].

a good deal to be said in our present circumstances for a form of Platonism which will lead us into, at times rather puzzled and hesitant, conversation with William Blake and other poetic and imaginative persons, as against one which will conduct us in a stately logical progress into the lecture-room of the late Dr. Thomas Aquinas or the late Professor Hegel: and of course out again on the other side to take part perforce, if we are wholly or principally committed to the way of epistemic discourse, in the demolition of "scientific" theology or metaphysics. Philosophical discourse remains necessary to a modern Neoplatonist. But its function will seem more and more to him not that of building a sure way to God, but of clearing from the way the obstacles its own older forms have created.

We encountered at the top of Plotinus' cosmos of mirrors a mirror which reflects that which casts no reflection and images that which cannot be imaged. And at the bottom, where we now are, we become aware in some odd way of a mirror which is even more strangely unlike other mirrors in that it reflects without in any understandable way being there at all. We encounter this strangest of all Plotinus' images of mirroring in one of his most difficult treatises, that *On the Impassibility of Things Without Body* (III 6 [26]). In the second part of this he is concerned, as he often is, with the exegesis of Plato's *Timaeus*, and in particular with the account of the recipient of forms in the material cosmos in Timaeus 49-51. This he identifies as his *hylē*, the "matter" of the material cosmos. And in chapter 13 and 14 he compares *hylē* to a mirror whose presence we are not aware of because it is invisible; and it is invisible because it is absolute non-existence. It is this non-existence which seems to give the images of this lower world the dead, ghostly, inauthentic character which they always have for Plotinus in comparison with the real beings of the intelligible cosmos, the manifold image of the Good. It is because of this that they can be for us dangerous and misleading illusions and lead us down like Narcissus into the darkness. But Plotinus, even in the context of his discussions of *hylē* as the principle of evil, does not allow us to forget that they remain images of the eternal beauty and, if we understand them rightly, can help and encourage us in our ascent in contemplative recollection through the images to the imageless. At the end of the last and strongest of his identifications of *hylē* as principle of evil, in the treatise *On What Are and Whence Come Evils*, he says "But because of the power and nature of good, evil is not only evil: since it must necessarily appear, it is bound in a sort of beautiful fetters, as some prisoners are in chains of gold, and hidden by them, so that though it exists it may not be seen by the gods, and men may be able not always to look at evil, but even when they do look at it, may be in company with images of beauty to remind them." (I 8 [51] 15, 23-28: tr. A.H.A.)

To pursue this subject further would take us too far from our mirrors into the much-discussed problems arising from Plotinus' accounts of matter and evil. I have written something on this recently elsewhere.[33] But it may help our understanding of Platonic mirrors and images to return briefly in conclusion to the Athenian Neoplatonist doctrine of *hylē* of which I spoke at *Eranos* in 1984.[34] In the Athenian Neoplatonists Syrianus and Proclus this ultimate invisible and formless mirror is no longer only a dark negativity which has to be there if the self-diffusion of the Good which is its diffraction in images is to reach its furthest possible limit, and is that ultimate limit. In being this, for the Athenians it is the ultimate manifestation of the Dyad or *Apeiron*, the Infinite, one of the two first principles of all reality proceeding directly from the One or Good, and by all Pythagorean and Platonic tradition the feminine one, coupled with the masculine *Peras*, the principle of limit and form. And Proclus says that from this mother of all reality come into being "all division and generative making and procession to multiplicity."[35] So it would appear that the demiurgic power which

33 A. H. Armstrong, "Dualism" in *Plotinus amid Gnostics and Christians* ed. David T. Runia, Free University Press, Amsterdam 1984,[this volume,studyXII].
34 A. H. Armstrong, "The Divine Enhancement of Earthly Beauties" (see n. 32) pp. 78-80.
35 Proclus, *Platonic Theology* III 8, 21-22, p. 32 Saffrey-Westerink.

makes the material cosmos as a divided multiplicity of images is only Dionysiac in this way as well as Apolline, as we have seen that it is (above pp. 175-77), because it derives not only from the masculine but from the feminine principle of all reality who is herself in her last theophany the mirror in which that multiplicity of images is reflected. But this Infinite is also the theophany of that in the ineffable First which makes it impossible to think or image it. She presents through all the levels of mirroring the symbol of the escape of God, of that which makes it ultimately impossible to organize the Good. So at the bottom of the cosmos of mirrors as well as at the top the image of mirroring breaks, as all concepts and images break. At the top there is nothing that can be reflected, at the bottom the reflections are in nothing. The ultimate dark is the same as the glory which is beyond and in and contains the images, the liberating glory of the Nothing.[36]

---

36 Those who have heard or read Professor Ueda's paper on the Zen experience of beauty given at Eranos in 1984 (see n. 18) will realise that I am here using the Zen doctrine which he so well expounded to help my understanding of the Neoplatonists. That I find it quite natural to do so indicates that there is an important point of contact here between our two traditions. But I was of course quite familiar with the Neoplatonic awareness of the Nothing before I knew anything of Buddhism (of which my knowledge remains minimal). And it will help our drawing together if we remember that the resemblances to his own tradition which Professor Ueda rightly detects in Eckhart and Angelus Silesius derive in them from a Neoplatonism transmitted to the Christian world principally (though not exclusively) through the Dionysian writings. If this is studied in its original Hellenic form it will be found to be freer from the anthropocentrism which Ueda rightly observes in Eckhart. Important differences between the two traditions will certainly remain, but they may turn out not to be much greater than those between Indian and Far Eastern Buddhism so illuminatingly displayed by Professor Klimkeit at the same Eranos meeting. ("Die Welt als Wirklichkeit und Gleichnis im Buddhismus Zentralasiens" in *Eranos 53-1984* pp. 83-126)

VII

NEGATIVE THEOLOGY
MYTH AND INCARNATION

There are few, if any people who have done more than Jean Trouillard to
open our eyes to the depth and richness of the thought of the last Hellenic
Platonists, above all of Plotinus and Proclus. My own debt to him is immense,
and I know others, of very different ways of thinking, who would say the
same. But he has not been content simply to expound these venerable thinkers
as period pieces, belonging to a past time and irrelevant to the concerns of
our age. He has tried to show that they can speak to our condition, and do
something to illuminate the religious and philosophical perplexities of our
own time (though not, as we shall see, by providing dogmatic solutions). This
has sometimes brought upon him the charge of inventing a «Neo-Neoplatonism»
of his own (a very Platonic thing to do). But his concern for the contemporary
may be a very important reason for the depth of his insight into the ancient.
And it is because of this that I dedicate in his honour this odd attempt to
show the relevance of some of the late Platonic ways of thinking which he has
so well explained to us to the crisis of religious thought in our own time.

It will be as well to begin by explaining what this large vague phrase
«the crisis of religious thought» means to me. What seems to me to have been
happening for a very long time, but to have become particularly apparent
recently, is the progressive breakdown of any and every sort of «absolutism».
By «absolutism» I mean the making of absolute claims for forms of words
and ways of thinking about God as timelessly and universally true (including
of course the absolute claim that all God-talk is meaningless and hopelessly
incoherent). These claims can be made in various ways. They can be made by
prelates, preachers and theologians asserting the absolute, unique and universal

claims of one special revelation : or by philosophers of the older style (including of course systematic Platonists) who claim that their metaphysical system is the one absolutely and universally true philosophy - and, of course, those of their newer-style opponents who claim equally dogmatically that *their* philosophy provides the one infallible method of disposing of all this metaphysical and religious nonsense : or by the believers in a *philosophia perennis* in the Huxleyan sense, a single tradition which underlies all the great religious traditions and is uniformly confirmed by all religious experience. There are, of course, plenty of absolutists of all these varieties still with us. But their influence is generally confined to restricted circles : and outside these circles, and I think increasingly within them, absolute claims and assertions are now subjected to immediate critical questioning, and generally found wanting or dubious : historical claims are questioned historically, and dogmatic non-historical statements (e.g. about the personality of God or the Trinity) are questioned philosophically.

Two points must be made here, which will probably indicate to many what a conservative and old fashioned paper this is. The first is that questioning does not mean outright rejection : that would be just another, and unpleasant, form of dogmatism. In the field of Christian theology the rejection of «absolutism» does not mean that «radical» positions are always to be preferred to «conservative» ones. Many «radical» positions are very silly : many «conservative» ones deserve serious consideration and are supported by excellent scholarship. Nor does critical questioning mean wholesale rejection of the great systematic philosophies. This paper is permeated by the deepest qualified affection and critical respect for the great late Platonists, Hellenic and Christian, who were in some ways very systematic thinkers. And even if one finds the idea of a *philosophia perennis*, in any sense, implausible, one can still agree with its exponents who insist that living tradition is necessary for any art, including the art of living. What the rejection of «absolutism» means is that all dogmas become hypotheses : and one does not arrive at an unhypothetical principle of demonstration or guarantee of certainty. (God is not such a principle or guarantee). One therefore simply continues the discussion, probably for ever. One must stand away from the tradition one respects, as Aristotle stood away from Plato and Aristotle's personal pupils from Aristotle : and stand away not to propound an improved dogmatism of one's own, but to go on asking more and more questions. This paper is conceived in this spirit, as a contribution to a completely openended discussion, not as a final solution to anything. The second point is that when claims to possess an exclusive revelation of God or to speak his word are made by human beings (and it is always human beings who make them) they must be examined particularly fiercely and hypercritically for the honour of God, to avoid the blasphemy and sacrilege of deifying a human opinion. Or, to put it less ferociously : the Hellenic (and, as it seems to me, still proper) answer to «Thus saith the Lord» is «*Does* he?» - in a distinctly sceptical tone, followed by a courteous but drastic «testing to destruction» of the claims and credentials of the person or persons making this enormous statement.

What are the reasons for this breakdown of «absolutism»? The first, and oldest, is, probably, steadily growing intellectual dissatisfaction with the arguments produced for the various and incompatible absolute positions. This springs from a very venerable element in our tradition, the sceptical in its Academic form (1), which has revived particularly strongly in Western Europe since the Renaissance, and been powerfully reinforced in the last two centuries by the development of critical philosophy and critical history (modern critical historians and scholars are perhaps the truest spiritual descendants of the Academics in our world). The second, which is also ancient (it can be traced back to Herodotus), but which has developed very powerfully in my own lifetime, is an intense and vivid sense of our own historical limitations. We are aware, both by experience and our study of history, of the immense and irreducible diversity of human beliefs and ways of thinking. We know sufficiently well that not only our own thought but that of the founder and teachers of any religious group or philosophical tradition to which we may adhere is limited and determined by historical circumstance, by time, place, heredity, environment, culture and education : even quite small differences in the circumstances of our education (e.g. going to a different university, or even a different college in the same university) might have made our religious and philosophical beliefs quite different, by causing us to be influenced by different people, to read different books etc. And we think this matters, and is not to be casually dismissed with a few rude remarks about «relativism», as is still sometimes done. We should think it crudely and antiquatedly arrogant to be certain of our certitudes, especially in religious questions, without unattainable confirmation by the agreement of all those, of all beliefs and ways of thinking, saints, sages and scholars, who are or have been competent to consider the belief for which certainty is claimed. This lends straight to the third reason for the breakdown of «absolutism». This is comparatively modern (though it is anticipated to some extent in pre-Christian antiquity) and its strong and full development and increasingly wide dissemination are becoming more and more notable in our own time. It is the vast and unprecedented increase in our knowledge of other ways of faith, piety and thought about God than our own, which has more and more both led to and been helped by a growth of understanding, respect, and sympathy for them and willingness to learn from them. Especially if this is not merely gained by reading, but also by direct acquaintance with other ways and personal friendship with those who follow them, this produces an irrevocable change of mind and heart, which both strengthens and is strengthened by our sense of historical limitations. Our new awareness includes, of course, an awareness of the divergences, tensions and contradictions within our own tradition and the value of many ways in it which diverge from those authoritatively accepted. We have become conscious of the folly and arrogance of «not counting» people ; of simply dismissing from consideration (as some philosophers and theologians still do) those who do not conform to the official orthodoxy of the group to which we belong. We have learned at last, I think once and for all, to believe that there is no one universally true or universally saving way : that many different paths lead to the great mystery.

At this point some religious persons will no doubt want to say «But what about *real* faith? What about the Leap, the Wager, the Great Option? Throw away these rationalistic hesitations and commit yourself, if you want to know what true faith is». I am unable genuinely to accept this peremptory and dramatic invitation (I have tried hard enough), because, if one really looks around one and stops «not counting» people, one finds that one is being invited to leap in altogether too many directions at once : and one can only discriminate between them by returning to the, probably endless and inconclusive, critical discussion of claims, credentials and arguments. And even if there was only one direction to leap in (and some Christians still talk as if this is so) it would be impossible without returning to the critical examination of the claims and credentials of the clergyman summoning me to faith, and other related matters, to distinguish faith from gross credulity, which is not religiously or morally virtuous, especially in an academic. I cannot, with regret, accept the view that our experience or awareness of God can in itself justify or guarantee one particular dogmatic and exclusive faith. This is because I hold the view that this experience (even at its lower levels) is strictly ineffable ; we naturally try to interpret it, always inadequately, in the language of the religious tradition to which we belong, but the experience does not justify or guarantee the interpretations (not that we can think or say what it is «in itself» or compare it with the interpretations). Yet this whole paper is based on faith in and dim awareness of the Unknowable Good, which I cannot and do not want to get rid of, but which remains tentative, personal, not absolute or exclusive, and making no demands on others.

What, then, has the old Neoplatonic «negative theology», and other related aspects of the later Platonic tradition, Hellenic and Christian, to give to those who have experienced the breakdown of «absolutism» but still want to believe in and worship God? I can only offer what I myself have found helpful. Trouillard has written most illuminatingly on this subject, and I have stumblingly tried to follow in his footsteps (2) (and have also learned very much from the Greek Orthodox Abbess Maria, who really lived the «negative theology», to its ultimate point). I shall not here repeat much of what can be found better elsewhere. But it must be stressed that what seems likely to be helpful is the fully developed negative theology, in which we negate our negations (which does not mean that we simply restore the original positive statement with a «super» attached, though this language is often used by the ancients because they cannot find anything better : perhaps the «pre» language often used by post-Plotinian Neoplatonists, «pre-being», «pre-intellect» etc. is somewhat less misleading nowadays than «super-being» or «super-intellect»). This leads us to the state of mind in which we are not content simply to say that God is not anything, but must say and be aware that he is not not anything either : and, in the end, not even to know that we do not know. It is a strange kind of liberation from thinkings and languages which enables us to use them freely and critically, always with a certain distance and detachment. (There are of course a number of kinds of human language, poetic, musical, those used in the visual arts, and mathematical, as well as the rather clumsy and limited prosaic-discursive kind normally used in philosophy and dogmatic theology - which by no means escapes metaphor (3) : of course, if we use this last we must use it precisely, and according to the rules of the game as played in our particular environment, as the great Neoplatonists did excellently). Having got this far, we can of course use positive terms about God as freely as negative, provided that we prefix something like the favourite *Hoion* of Plotinus («as if», or «in a manner of speaking») to indicate their inadequacy. I can agree with a great deal which Christopher Stead says about the desirability of using «being» or «substance» terms about God, on the appropriate occasions, and could supply him with some excellent Neoplatonic texts in which they are freely and quite consistently used in a context of radical negative theology (4). It seems that the traditional terms «beyond being» or «non-being», or «nothing» applied to God are most significant when used in their proper Hellenic context in which being is closely correlated with intelligibility : real being is intelligible being. They mean, then, that God is not a somebody or something who can be discursively defined or discerned with intuitive precision. It is not that his intelligibility transcends our limited and fallen human intelligences, but that he has no intelligible content : Trouillard has explained this very well (5). It is this ability to use positive terms in a peculiar way which may make the negative theologian sympathetic to «myths», as we shall see. I prefer, myself, to call what I am talking about «icons» (6), partly for reasons of my own not unconnected with Eastern Orthodox theology and piety, and partly because «myth», since about the 5th century B.C. has had, probably for most people in the Western tradition, the rather narrow and derogatory meaning of «more or less poetic fiction». I shall, however, use «myth» (in an extended and complimentary sense) in this paper in order to relate it to contemporary theological discussions.

Before proceeding to discuss myth it should be made clear that what has been said about «negative theology» so far is perfectly compatible with conservative Christian orthodoxy. The Eastern Christian tradition as a whole and many perfectly orthodox and traditional Western theologians insist that all our language about God is inadequate, that our statements about him are only «pointers» to, or «icons» of his unknowable reality. But they hold that certain statements only are divinely revealed or authoritative, and so are privileged pointers or uniquely authorised icons, and that the Incarnate Christ is the one and only perfect icon (to use patristic language) of the supreme divinity. Reasons for disagreeing with this have nothing to do with the «negative theology» as such. They spring from the attitudes of mind discussed earlier which have led to the general breakdown of «absolutism». For those in whom this breakdown has taken place, however, the «negative theology» can, I think, do something useful. It can, sometimes, prevent them from giving up the whole business of religion in disgust - the usual reaction - and help them to remain at least dimly aware that there is really somebody or something there «behind» or «beyond» (to use the inadequate spatial metaphors which we must all use in this context) the dubious stories and inadequate concepts and definitions. It may help to give some expression to a deep, obscure anonymous faith which remains untouched by the breakdown of «absolutism», though as the result of this breakdown it insists on remaining anonymous. And those who arrive (not necessarily by a Neoplatonic route) at understanding that a radically apophatic faith permits the use of very positive language in a peculiar way may come to understand the expressions of their traditional religion «mythically» or «iconically» : and not just as «myths» or «icons» made up by men but as a multiple and varied revelation of images through which the Good communicates «iconically» with all of us, of all religious traditions, according to our several needs, that we may all have something through which to sense his presence and worship him.

If we understand «myth» in this way, as part of the expression of what happens when the Unknowable, so to speak, seems not content to remain aloof in his ineffable obscurity but «turns» and comes back to us as the painter of many icons not made with hands in that «outgoing» which «Dionysius» calls his «ecstatic *eros*» (7), we may see better how we should use the term and how widely it can be extended. The sense to be given to «myth» in the context of this way of thinking will obviously be strongly positive. It will often be practically equivalent to something like «general» or natural, revelation (this involves, of course, human participation, and human error and inadequacies, in expressing what God suggests). In this way it will come close to the significance of myth (and ritual) as understood by Proclus, whose accounts of the function of mythical and mathematical imagination are most illuminatingly correlated and discussed by Trouillard (8). Myths and the rites and arts which express them can provide true ways to God, though of course they can also mislead. (The superbly and fruitfully ambiguous valuation of art in relation to philosophy and religion by Iris Murdoch in her very Platonic - though not Neoplatonic - book on Plato and the artists (9) should be carefully studied by anyone who wishes to understand its dangers, uses, and, in the end, inescapable indispensability). But myth for Proclus is exclusively poetic or imaginative myth : and he would not have been at all pleased if we extended the term to cover his own (or, as he thought, Plato's) systematic philosophical theology. But the breakdown of «absolutism» seems to have made it necessary to see systematic theology «mythically», as well as the alleged historical facts contained in some particular revelations. The most abstract and logically constructed treatments of the Henads or the Trinity can only function for us «mythically», if they function at all. (One can, and should, of course criticize the logic, as one can criticize the historical evidence or the expressive quality of the images in other kinds of «myth» : but these separate and distinct kinds of criticism will not necessarily deprive the «myths» to which they are applied of all power and value).

It may help to clarify the way in which I regard the Christian story and Christian doctrine as «mythical» if I compare my position briefly with those of a small selection of others. I am not conscious of any strong differences with Maurice Wiles, though our different environments and preoccupations may lead to rather different theological conclusions. I admire the scholarly caution and religious discretion with which he pursues the argument, and find his comparison between the way in which Christian thought about the Creation and the Fall has developed and the way in which Christian thought about the Incarnation might reasonably develop fruitful ; and his statement (derived, like so much else in contemporary discussions, from Strauss) that a myth may have a historical element may be a very useful corrective to extremist positions (10). With Don Cupitt, and others who think like him, my difference is rather sharp, and may be of some general significance (11). It is not that I object to his history. His treatment of the evidence seems to me at any rate plausible. But (to say something which, from inherited reverence, I have refrained for some time from saying) I do not find the Jesus of good critical Biblical scholars very impressive or interesting. I am not even sure that the only people in the first century A.D. with whom I can conceive myself having much in common would have done so, that is to say, Greek-speaking people with some degree of Hellenic philosophical culture, for instance in the neighbouring Decapolis. This reconstructed Galilean rabbi, this Jesus (or these Jesuses) of scholarship, seems very restricted, not only in period but in place and culture (12). It seems unlikely that the «Jesus of scholarship» can ever attain even the limited universality, even in our transitory Western culture, of the «Christ of history». (I am using here the excellent terminology of Wilfred Cantwell Smith. The «Jesus of scholarship» in the Jesus reconstructed by scholars. The «Christ of history» in the «mythical» or «iconic» Christ, the Christ who has mattered in Christian history). I owe a personal debt of gratitude to the Biblical scholars and theologians, conservative and radical, to the de-mythologizers and de-Hellenizers from Bultmann onwards, and to those who, with excellent pastoral intentions, have forced the Bible so much on our attention in the non-Reformed churches in recent years. They have shown me something that I was too obtuse and traditionalist to notice before, but is of

VII

the greatest historical significance. Our Inherited Conglomerate (as Gilbert Murray and E. R. Dodds would call it) (13) is breaking up. The Biblical and the Hellenic elements are, apparently now finally and irrevocably, coming apart. And, if they come apart, it is not as certain as Christian theologians and preachers seem to suppose that most of those who remain at all interested in the matter will choose the Biblical and reject the Hellenic. In my own case my remote forefathers (if they were ever genuinely converted to anything) were pretty certainly converted to a strongly «mythical», Hellenized form of Christianity, and the succeeding generations, Roman Catholic or Anglican, retained this form, on the whole, and interpreted the Bible in its light. The faith of my fathers centred on the «Christ of history». The tradition handed down to me was the «myth», and in my own religious wrigglings of earlier years I think I was, at first unconsciously, trying to get further from the Bible and nearer to the «myth», in a strongly Hellenic, Mediterranean form for which I still have much affection. (Of course my Christian parents and teachers in the earlier 20th century took very good care to see that I should be well educated in Greek poetry and philosophy, which carry Hellenic religion). I really do not think that I have much reason for allegiance to «authentic», «truly Biblical» Christianity, whether radical or conservative. And, now that because of the breakup of the Conglomerate, I have to choose between the Biblical and the Hellenic, I shall choose the Hellenic, though I can only choose it as «myth». And it may be that a good many other people, less well informed than I am about our own older tradition, will make the same choice: either because it has really been the strongly Hellenic elements in the theology and piety of the Conglomerate which will be discussed later which have attracted them, or because it is the «myth» which has inspired the great Christian visual art and music which may be doing more than anything else to keep something of Christianity alive in our own day, or because they are drawn to Indian or esoteric Islamic ways which are often (for whatever reason) very much closer to Neoplatonism than they are to Jewish-Biblical ways of faith, thought and piety (14).

To conclude this essay, let us attempt to see what a «mythical» treatment of the central Christian doctrine of Incarnation might look like. It must be stressed here again that there is no question of dogmatic rejection of traditional doctrines, but of well-grounded doubt, suspense of judgement, the reduction of the doctrines to endlessly discussible hypotheses. In this position one is perfectly entitled to consider as acceptable more conservative and traditional hypotheses than those just discussed, when they are well based on excellent scholarship, like those of C. F. D. Moule (15), provided that they are still considered as hypotheses, and not used apologetically to justify a return to «absolutism». And this means that, within the limits imposed by free and sound scholarship and history, a closer hypothetical linking of the «Jesus of scholarship» and the «Christ of history» might be attempted than has been

54

suggested above. We are not bound to believe that the «myth» has no historical foundation or core, even if the extent of the historical element in it must probably remain for ever undefinable. But it should also be made clear again that the rejection of «absolutism» and questioning of claims and demands extends beyond the claim that Jesus was God Incarnate in an unique sense. It extends to all claims made that any revelation of God has unique and universal authority or that any people or community has been brought into an unique and special relationship with him. If anyone demands faith, submission or territory as a representative of the unique People of God, he should be taken all the way back to the covenant with Abraham and his claims tested every step of the way by the intensest criticism that can be brought to bear, for the honour of God. Criticism can be inspired by religious fervour as well as dogmatic faith.

Even if one is prepared to consider, tentatively, as tenable the hypotheses of the more conservative New Testament scholars who really are scholars and not apologists (some of course, rather bewilderingly to the layman, speak now in one capacity and now in the other) one will probably have to go fairly far in separating the fully Hellenized «Christ of history» from the «Jesus of scholarship». (It is, at least, reasonably certain that Jesus was a Jew, and this makes a difference). I have already shown my preferences if this has to be done (16). What then, can an irremediable gentile like myself make of the centre of the Christian «myth», the doctrine of Incarnation? A good deal, in fact, and some of it surprisingly traditional ; and I should describe my «mythical» interpretation as «expansionist» rather than «reductionist». The method I apply here to the thought of the Greek Fathers is of course heretical in the strict sense, a process of *hairesis* or selection. (There is a good deal of *hairesis* in orthodox theology, especially nowadays). For this reason I bring them in, not to claim their authority, but to acknowledge my debt to them. The characteristic which I have discovered in their thought struck me most forcibly when reading «Dionysius», and particularly the *Divine Names* (17). Though it can certainly be observed over a much wider area (18) and I do not regard it in «Dionysius» as an Athenian Neoplatonist deformation of Christianity, it will make for brevity and clarity, and be appropriate in a paper in honour of Trouillard, if I discuss it in a «Dionysian» context. The first point which impressed me was that, though the language, and I am sure the belief, of the author of the Dionysian writings about the Trinity is perfectly orthodox, *Trias* is only one of the (all inadequate) names for the unknowable God, the Thearchy, interchangeable with others : and his Trinitarian theology is rather in the background and only comes into use when required for the purposes of his simplified, and in a sense Christianized, Neoplatonism. It is not grounded in, and has not much connection with, the historic Incarnation (19). About this, again, the author's language and faith is quite orthodox. But, as with *Trias*, «Jesus» is, in the Christological passages of the *Divine Names*, just another name for the ineffable Thearchy, whose whole function in these

VII

passages he takes over, and the details of his earthly life are interpreted entirely symbolically (20). What this seems to mean is that what really matters to «Dionysius» (and perhaps to many others, in the Greek-Christian tradition especially, though individual cases need particular and careful examination) (21) is the outgoing of the unknowable Godhead in his theophanies and ecstatic *eros*, which is creation, and his leading all things back to himself by that same *eros*, in its return, which is redemption. And both of these are cosmic and universal, not strictly tied to a particular human person or historic event, though the historic Incarnation is of course seen as the exemplar, guarantee and centre of the whole creative-redemptive process and the principal means of redemption.

When one has realized that this sort of distinction between an universal and a particularist understanding of Christian doctrine related to the Incarnation can be discovered in our Christian tradition, and that the emphasis (especially perhaps in the «Dionysian» tradition) lies sometimes more on the universal than the particular, some consequences may begin to appear to one who is conscious of the «breakdown of absolutism» and the grave doubts that must now exist about the Incarnation in its historical particularity. If one retains some sort of faith in the Unknowable Good, one may still want to be able to see not only God's creative, but his saving work as extending from everlasting to everlasting, not only to every human being, but to every being in his universe (anthropocentrism is one of the disadvantages of conservative Christianity) (22) : and to hold that God so works because the cosmos is in him and he is united with it (though «inexpressibly», as the Fathers say about the Incarnation) from the beginning with an intimacy which the hypostatic union of developed Christology cannot surpass. This is part of any Platonic faith, because the Platonic Good is self-diffusive, and being good means doing good (23). And I (because of my Christian background) can think of no better way of speaking of this ineffable outgoing of the Good in his *eros* than in terms of the everlasting and universal mission of Logos and Holy Spirit. Others will legitimately prefer other ways of speaking. I know that I only use these words because my parents and teachers, the books I have read, and perhaps most effectively of all, the great liturgies and arts of Christendom have taught me to. If I had been brought up in India, or a Buddhist or Islamic country, I should have used different «myths» or «icons». And even within our own tradition many of anonymous faith but (often with good reasons) deeply anti-Christian, will prefer other ways of speaking. But, if the negative theology carried through the double negation, leads, as it often does, to this sort of belief in cosmic incarnation, then the Christian «myth» can come to have a very powerful and positive effect as a «myth». It will not give us the kind of assurance possessed by all the Fathers and traditional theologians who believe (as they do) in the unique Incarnation fully and completely as historical fact and the dogmas in which its meaning was explained as divinely guaranteed : but we must be content with a more tentative and uncertain faith nowadays. And accepting a myth is not like accepting a creed. It leaves room for free reinterpretation, imaginative and intellectual development, and plenty of criticism of details and variation of emphasis (even the most orthodox and conformist Christianity allows, and has always allowed, for plenty of all these, though theologians have sometimes pretended otherwise). But, in the end, I can think of no better representations of the faith I hold, if they are interpreted in the free and universal way I have suggested, than the great theological and artistic «icons» of traditional Christianity.

NOTES

1   The Academic rather than the Pyrrhonian is, I think, the strongest scep-
    tical element in our tradition. It differs from the Pyrrhonian in admitting
    degrees of probability, and so leaving room for enthusiasm, and even a
    degree of commitment (though not absolute commitment). See the gene-
    rally excellent statement of the difference between the two traditions by
    the Pyrrhonian Sextus Empiricus (*Outlines of Pyrrhonism* I, 226-231) :
    though it does not seem to be true that, as Sextus asserts, the Academics
    fell into the elementary mistake of stating dogmatically that they knew
    that they did not know, or that Carneades in any way illegitimately
    smuggled certainty as an ultimate norm into his theory of probability :
    see A. A. Long, *Hellenistic Philosophy* (London 1974) pp.94-99.

2   J. Trouillard «Valeur critique de la mystique Plotinienne» in *Revue
    Philosophique de Louvain* 59 (August 1961) pp.431-4 : «Raison et Mys-
    tique chez Plotin» in *Revue des Etudes Augustiniennes* 20 (1974)
    pp.3-14 : «Théologie négative et autoconstitution psychique chez les
    néoplatoniciens» in *Savoir, faire, espérer : les limites de la raison* (Publi-
    cations des Facultés Universitaires Saint-Louis, Brussels 1976) pp.307-
 * 321 : A. H. Armstrong «The Escape of the One» in *Studia Patristica*
 * *XIII* (Berlin 1975) pp.77-89 : «Negative Theology» in *Downside Review*
    Vol 95, No. 320 (July 1977) pp.176-189.

3   «Of course he [Plato] used metaphor, and metaphor is basic ; how basic
    is the most basic philosophical question». Iris Murdoch, *The Fire and
    the Sun* (Oxford 1977) p.88.

4   See Christopher Stead, *Divine Substance* (Oxford 1977) Ch.X, *Conclu-
    sion*. Plotinus uses a great deal of positive «substance» language about
    God, in the way described, in VI 8 [39] where in my view,
    (see tnis volume, study XI)   he is arguing, patiently though not
    without irritation, with a Christian theist much concerned about the free
    will of God. But the Neoplatonic work which uses substance and know-
    lege-language most strikingly (and quite coherently) of God in a context
    of extremely radical negative theology is the Anonymous Commentary
    on the *Parmenides* so admirably studied and edited by P. Hadot in his
    Porphyre et Victorinus (Paris 1968 : text of the Commentary in Vol.II),
    especially IV and V (pp.74-83 Hadot : Fol. 94^V and Fol. 64^V). It is not
    quite as certain as Hadot supposes that the commentary is by Porphyry.
    **But it is a most original Neoplatonic work, of great importance for the
    development of negative theology.**

5   In «Théologie négative et autoconstitution psychique....» (see note 2)
    pp.312-313 : «Dès lors, la notion de «Dieu caché» change de sens. Le
    Dieu de saint Augustin et de saint Thomas est caché parce que, étant la

plénitude infinie de l'intelligibilité, sa trop grande clarté nous éblouit, comme le soleil regardé en face offusque nos yeux. L'Un néoplatonicien est nocturne parce qu'il refuse tout contenu intelligible et toute pensée. Il est au-delà l'ordre de connaissance. Il n'a donc pas de secret, c'est-à-dire d'essence qui se déroberait au regard.

Cela ne veut pas dire qu'il ne peut se communiquer et qu'il reste muré dans une transcendance inaccessible». What follows, on the immanent interior transcendence of the One as an «inexhaustible starting-point», always before, never attained by, thought is very relevant to a proper understanding of what I mean by «myth» in its extended and positive sense.

6 For my curious use of «icon» cp. «Negative Theology» (see note 2) pp.188-189.

7 *Divine Names* 4. 13 (712 A-B).

8 In «Le Merveilleux dans la vie et la pensée de Proclos», in *Revue Philosophique de la France et de l'Etranger*, 1971, pp.439-452 ; section 3 «La fonction de l'imagination» pp.447-452. The principal source for the views of Proclus on poetic myth is *In Rempublicam* I 368-407, 69-205 Kroll, especially 368-378, 71-86 Kroll.

9 *The Fire and the Sun* (see note 3), especially pp.69-89.

10 I refer particularly to his «Does Christology Rest on a Mistake» in *Religious Studies* 6. 1. (March 1970) pp.69-76 and his second essay in *The Myth of God Incarnate* (London 1977) «Myth in Theology», pp.148-166. I also find very satisfying his treatment, both historical and theological, of a most important and difficult theme in the «myth», that of Resurrection, in the *Appendix* to his *Remaking of Christian Doctrine* (London 1974), pp.125-146. I find this much more satisfying than the summary dismissal of the Resurrection by both sides in the older controversy between Jaspers and Bultmann (originally published in book form as *Die Frage der Entmythologisierung* : English translation (*Myth and Christianity*) first printed in paperback New York 1958 and frequently reprinted since). In many ways, however, my position is fairly close to that of Jaspers, and I agree with much in his defence of liberalism and his appreciation of the religious value of myth.

11 I have in mind particularly his essay in *The Myth of God Incarnate* (see previous note) «The Christ of Christendom», pp.133-147, and his numerous and vigorous defences of his position since, generally on radio or television.

12 On the historical Jesus I am at present in general agreement with the position of Dennis Nineham in his somewhat devastating *Epilogue* (pp.186-204) to *The Myth of God Incarnate* (see note 10), which shows clearly what very awkward questions a serious critical study of the evidence can raise.

13 Cp. Gilbert Murray *Greek Studies* pp.66f : E. R. Dodds *The Greeks and the Irrational* (University of California Press 1951) pp.179-180.

14 I have discovered this by experience in dialogue with an Indian and an Isma'ili friend. If they spoke the language of their own traditions and I spoke the language of Neoplatonism, we understood each other without much need of interpretation. P. Hadot, in his profound interpretation of Hellenic philosophy as a whole, *Exercices Spirituels* (*Annuaire de l'Ecole Pratique des Hautes Etudes*, 5e Section, T.*LXXXIV* pp.25-70) has demonstrated that we have in our own Western tradition a rich and varied store of the sort of wisdom for which many people now look to the East.

15 In *The Origins of Christology* (Cambridge 1977). The excellent hypotheses - clearly presented as such - of the chapters devoted to a scholarly consideration of the New Testament evidence do not, unfortunately, seem to me, even if they are taken as certain conclusions from that evidence, to support sufficiently the apologetic conclusion.

16 Those of others will, of course, be different. It is perfectly possible to make a «Jesus of scholarship», even before he goes out of fashion, the historical foundation of a «myth» : and for very many people a Semitic rather than a Hellenic form of «myth», incarnational or non-incarnational, Jewish, Christian or Muslim, will be the right and necessary one. My own reasons for especially disliking un-Hellenic or de-Hellenized Western Christian or post-Christian Biblical «myths» would take too long to explain adequately : it would be necessary to deal with such subjects as the disjunctiveness of Biblical monotheism, the «meaning of history», and the harm done in real history by the idea of an Elect or Chosen People in its various forms. (Or course in many of them the Gentiles of the «myth» will include or be Jews).

17 My belief that what I had noticed in «Dionysius» was really there was strengthened by discovering that Dr. Bernhard Brons had noticed the same phenomena and forcibly described them in his scholarly studies of the Dionysian writings *Gott und die Seienden* (Gottingen 1976) and «Pronoia und das Verhaltnis von Metaphysik und Geschichte bei Dionysius Areopagita» in *Freiburger Zeitschrift fur Philosophie und Theologie* 24 (1977) 1-2 pp.165-186. Of course, as the theological position of Dr. Brons seems to be almost the exact opposite of my own, he notes these characteristics of Dionysian thought with disapproval.

18 It has often been observed that the Fathers of the Alexandrian tradition, in particular, seem more interested in the «incarnability» of the Logos and the universal theandric union of God with humanity as a whole than in the particular historic Incarnation, and something of this persists in Greek-Christian theology and theology influenced by it in the West. E. P. Meijerings «Cyril of Alexandria on the Platonists and the Trinity» in *God Being History* (Amsterdam-Oxford-New York 1975) pp.114-127

is of much interest in this connection.

19 For the way in which «Dionysius» speaks of the Trinity see, e.g. *Celestial Hierarchy* VII 4 (212C) : *Ecclesiastical Hierarchy* I 3 (373C-D) : *Divine Names* I 4 (592A) 5 (593B) : II 7 (645B-C) : III 1 (680B):XIII 3 (980D-981A) ; *Mystical Theology* III (1038A) and V (1048A ; cp. Letter II). On the way in which «Dionysius», as is generally supposed, adapts Athenian Neoplatonism to Christian purposes by a certain conflation of the Neoplatonic One and the Neoplatonic Nous, see the most recent discussion by S. Gersh *From Iamblichus to Eriugena* (Leiden 1978). It is agreed that «Dionysius» is not a «hierarchical» thinker in the sense of Proclus (cp. my «Negative Theology» (see note 2) pp.181-184) and that he uses very positive language about God's being , knowledge and action while strongly maintaining an extreme apophatic theology. But there are unsolved, and possibly insoluble, questions as to the precise relative importance of the contributions made to this Dionysian Christian Platonism by the distinctively Christian side of the theology which he inherited (especially from the Cappadocians), by the predominantly pre-Plotinian Platonism which was the philosophy most used by fourth-century theologians, and, possibly, by a return, which might have been deliberate, to a more Plotinian-Porphyryian kind of Neoplatonism (see *supra* note 4).

20 The principal Christological passage is *Divine Names* II 9-10 (648A-649A) : cp. XI 1-2, 948D-953B where *Eïrene* and «Jesus» or «Christ» seem to be interchangeable divine names.

21 In view of his great influence, the universal sweep of his vision of creation and salvation, and his intense devotion to the Incarnate Lord (who is much more than a symbol to him, however allegorically he interprets the details of his earthly life), Origen deserves particularly careful investigation on this point. And I do not wish to lump together the great thinkers, from Maximos onwards, who have more or less followed the Dionysian tradition under any superficial generalization.

22 See my «Man in the Cosmos» in *Romanitas et Christianitas* (Amsterdam-
*   London 1973) pp.5-14.

23 The main Platonic authority for this conviction for later Platonists has of course been *Timaeus* 29D-30B : though it pervades the theology of the Dialogues. My way of putting it is a summary paraphrase of Proclus, *Elements of Theology*, Proposition 122 (especially p.128, lines 19-21 Dodds).

ADDITIONAL NOTE.

I had written this paper before the publication of Dr. E. P. Meijering's excellent book, *Theologische Urteile uber die Dogmengeschichte : Ritschl's Einfluss auf von Harnack* (Leiden 1978). This does a very great deal to clarify the nature, origin, and much of the development of what I have described as «Biblical» theology, and in the author's final critique of Harnack suggests approaches to the Bible, Greek philosophy, and the theology of the Christian Fathers which, if they were widely followed, might lead to the transformation rather than the desintegration of our Inherited Conglomerate.

Additions to note 2

* Berlin 1975 = Plotinian and Christian Studies XXIII
* July 1977 = Plotinian and Christian Studies XXIV

Addition to note 22

* Amsterdam-London 1973 = Plotinian and Christian Studies XXII

VIII

The Self-Definition of
Christianity in Relation
to Later Platonism

The subject of this paper is what was probably the most important part of the effort made by the Christian community, after it
became a predominantly non-Jewish community, to define itself
in the world of late Hellenic culture within the frontiers of the
Roman Empire. It seems, however, desirable to preface this particular study with a more general personal view of the complexity
and urgency of the early Christian community's enterprise of
defining itself as a distinct entity, neither Jewish nor Hellenic but
with links of varying degrees of closeness to both sides. The first
part of this enterprise, the self-definition of Christianity in relation to Judaism, falls outside the scope of this paper. But it should
be mentioned here, as the decisions taken at this stage, theoretical and practical, had important effects when the community
came to work out its attitude to the Hellenism, both popular and
philosophical, of the *oecumene*, the Roman Empire. Two parts of
this enterprise of self-definition over against Judaism are particularly interesting in this connection. One is the rejection (perhaps
more gradually and after harder struggles than we are generally
inclined to suppose), by the majority of Christians, of the way of
early Jewish Christianity; the refusal, that is, to continue as a
distinctive group within Judaism, heretical and unpopular no
doubt, but still unmistakably Jewish, even if with many Gentile
convert members. It was this which made possible the development of a great church of the Gentiles which had to come to some
sort of terms with the world of Hellenic thought and culture
simply because that was the world to which its members, includ-

Christianity in Relation to Later Platonism

ing the leading thinkers and teachers of the church, fully belonged.

The other is the rejection by the majority Christian community of one of the most radical efforts at self-definition which has ever been made. This was the attempt by the Christian Gnostics and Marcion to separate Christianity finally and utterly from Judaism by ensuring that Christians and Jews did not worship the same God. The essential affirmation of the pessimistic Gnostic way of thinking, springing from a very deep sense of alienation from the world, seems to be that the true believer and his true God are in fact in the fullest sense alien from this world, which is an evil place, a prison and a trap, created by an inferior, ignorant and limited or downright evil being, who is of course identified with the God of the Jews, the creator and giver of the Law. This is important for our purposes, as, though the Gnostic faith was probably in its original intention anti-Semitic, it was also deeply anti-Hellenic, and its adoption by the general Christian body would have made any real coming to terms with genuine Platonism (or Stoicism) impossible. This seems to me to be true in spite of the fact that it was easier for some Gnostics than for orthodox Christians to make use for their own purposes of allegorical interpretations of Near Eastern and Hellenic mythology and, at least in the case of the Valentinians, of themes drawn from popular Platonic philosophy, and that the Carpocratians even went so far as to include representations of Hellenic philosophers among the sacred images which they anticipated the orthodox by some centuries in venerating. [1] Notwithstanding these superficial uses and influences, Gnostic feelings and beliefs about the world are in fundamental conflict with that conviction of the essential goodness of the cosmos and the rational necessity for its existence which was basic in most Hellenic philosophy, especially in the two most influential schools of the early centuries of the Christian era, the Stoic and the Platonist. Even the most pessimistic and dualistic Platonists and Pythagoreans of the second century CE could not rid themselves of the conviction that the cosmos was essentially good: they could not repudiate the Timaeus. And, from Plotinus in the third century onwards, the spirit and doctrine of later non-Christian Platonism became in general (Porphyry is perhaps to some extent an exception) more and more strongly world-affirming. Not only the great and passionate attack on the Gnostics which concludes one of the finest works of Plotinus, but much else in the Enneads, sets the tone for this move away from pessimism about the world. Epicureans, of course, did not think that the cosmos was at all good, and Sceptics suspended judgment on this, as on all other matters; but neither school was widely influential at the relevant time.[2]

The rejection of the radical solution of the Gnostics was therefore an important moment in the self-definition of the majority Christian community, the great church of the Gentiles. It both held it closer to Judaism and made it possible for it to receive a good deal from the Hellenic philosophy of the world in which it was developing. It is of course hard to deny that considerable Gnostic elements have survived unconsciously in traditional Christian literature, teaching and practice. But, in that ever more complex inherited conglomerate which is historic Christianity, they have been in continual tension and conflict with the authentically Jewish and Hellenic elements, as these have often been with each other. It will be well at this point, for the sake of clarity in any subsequent discussion, to state clearly that alienation from this world, dualism, and Gnosticism do not all mean the same thing. One can feel profoundly alienated from the cosmos, as the Epicureans did, without being either a dualist or a Gnostic. The classical example of conflict-dualism, the Zoroastrian orthodoxy of Sassanian Persia, is the most strongly world-affirming of religions, both in theory and practice. And the sense of world-alienation and the very peculiar sort of dualism which persist as one element in the Pythagorean-Platonic tradition are very different indeed from the Gnostic faith and temper.[3] It may also be as well, as it is relevant to our main theme, to note that, contrary to the opinion of a number of ancient and modern writers, the Gnostics were 'theologians', not 'philosophers', to use a much later distinction rather anachronistically. That is, they were primarily engaged in expounding special revelations given to privileged groups of people (in their case, of course, very special and esoteric revelations which were the private property of small privileged groups) rather than in setting forth with the maximum rational coherence the insight into divine things which, in principle, the god-given power of thought of virtuous and intelligent men has always been able to attain everywhere in the cosmos (my description of 'philosophy' is of course designed to be appropriate to the period we are considering). As far as a difference of attitude to special revelations played a part, as it did, in the process of self-definition, the acceptance of any form of Gnosis by the great church would not have made it easier for it to come to

Christianity in Relation to Later Platonism

any sort of terms with authentic Hellenic philosophy. In saying this, I have not forgotten the veneration of the latest Neoplatonists for the Chaldaean Oracles and the Orphic poems, nor the more generally relevant fact that late antique philosophers as well as expounders of special revelations were intensely traditionalist. But very complex questions arise here,[4] and the evidence seems to me strongly against any attempt to bring Gnostics and even post-Iamblichean Neoplatonists together under any sort of comprehensive generalization. Anyhow, they all had different revelations, and, as is usual in such cases, would have fought like cats about their respective merits.

From about the middle of the second century CE, the attempts of the majority Christian community to define its position in relation to Hellenic philosophy became clearly visible. We should not of course neglect the influence and use of ideas derived consciously or unconsciously from Greek thought, perhaps generally through Hellenized Judaism, in the New Testament writings. The fact that they were there, and the way in which they were used, made a difference to the range of possibilities open to Christians in dealing with Hellenic philosophy. But to discuss them would fall outside the limits of this paper and my own competence. To make our terms of reference as precise as possible, we shall be concerned in the rest of this paper with the thought of the probably small educated minority of Greek and Latin-speaking Christians to whom Hellenic philosophy was of serious concern and whose reactions to it played an important part in the formation of traditional Christian doctrine. I shall not venture into the important field of non-Greek-speaking Christianity in the East, of which I know next to nothing, and I shall not speculate very much on what the ordinary uneducated churchmen thought about what the intellectuals were doing. I think, however, that we should beware of the tendency to think of the opposition between philosophically inclined and antiphilosophical Christians as one between intellectuals and 'simple faithful': just as we should beware of the tendency to think that in the great theological controversies in and through which Christian doctrine developed one side was necessarily more Hellenized than the other (of course, to accuse the other side of being Hellenes was a powerful polemical weapon). Both tendencies seem to me to lead to over-sweeping and often ill-founded generalizations.

The educated Greek- and Latin-speaking Christians within the

Roman Empire from the second century of our era onwards, with whom we shall henceforth be concerned, were people who had a strong conviction that their Christian faith and way of life was independent of, superior to, and in many ways opposed to Hellenic religious and philosophical culture. They were conscious of close links with the Jews, though they also believed that their faith and way of life were superior to and had superseded the faith of Israel (and traces of Christian anti-Semitism can be perceived very early). But at the same time, they were, as has already been said, fully part of the world of late Hellenic culture. Their minds had been formed, consciously and, still more importantly, unconsciously, within it. And they had a very strong sense of a universal missionary vocation. They were to bring the whole world to Christ and preach the gospel to all creation. This, of course, meant for them that they had to preach it in terms which their educated contemporaries could understand. If they had seen the full complexity and difficulty of their universal task as we can now see it with our broader and deeper understanding, even only taking into account the whole known Eurasian civilized world of their time, their confidence might perhaps have faltered and they would certainly have been very much less successful in their task. But, like most educated men of their time and for many centuries later they had no idea of the real range and depth of the diversity of religious thought and culture. The men of the Hellenic world had indeed an interest and respect for ancient Oriental wisdom which was particularly strong in the period with which we are concerned. But they had little idea of how great and fundamental the differences might be between their philosophies and genuine Oriental traditions of thought. If the philosophers looked to Persia or India they saw their own versions of Platonism or Pythagoreanism there. If they looked (occasionally) at Moses, they saw in him a good Stoic or a philosophical forerunner of Pythagoras and Plato. The Christians, having established to their own satisfaction that they were the true heirs of ancient Israel, could of course make a powerful apologetic appeal to this veneration for ancient Oriental wisdom. But they had no idea of what it would really have been like to proclaim the gospel simultaneously, in the appropriate languages, to Greek philosophers, Zoroastrian divines, sages versed in the Veda, the Upaniṣads and the Gītā, Buddhist monks and learned Confucians, in terms more or less acceptable and comprehensible to each and every one of them. What they were in fact seeking to formulate was an ecumenical (in the ancient, not the modern sense), not a universal doctrine, one comprehensible and acceptable to the Graeco-Roman world: and in this more modest and limited task they succeeded in the end moderately well.

Christianity and the platonic tradition

The most important part of the task of intellectual self-definition in relation to Hellenic culture undertaken by educated Christians from the second century onwards was the determination of what they could accept and what they must reject in contemporary Platonic-Pythagorean tradition. Stoicism was, certainly, still widely influential in the second century, and Aristotelianism, Scepticism and Epicureanism very much alive, and all of them probably persisted well into the third, or even later, as distinct schools of thought. But it seems that, for the most part, Stoic and, to a lesser extent, Peripatetic ideas were taken seriously by the Christians only in so far as they formed part of a sort of philosophical *koinē* which was used in the interpretation of Plato by Platonists in various ways according to their philosophical purposes and temperaments. The encounter with Stoic ethics was certainly important for Christians and left a deep mark on Christianity. But much Platonic moral teaching was influenced by Stoicism (though other Platonists preferred a more Peripatetic attitude), and much of the Stoic element in developed traditional Christian moral theology probably got into it as much from Platonists influenced by Stoicism as directly from Stoics. Stoic physical theology, which most Platonists rejected, was not generally attractive or interesting to Christians, with a few exceptions, the most notable being the very anti-philosophical Tertullian. It seems quite probable that a main reason for the rejection of Stoic physical theology by most Christians was their sense that it left no room for any transcendence of God and for that discontinuity between Creator and creation discussed below (pp. 89–91). This was of course true as far as the letter of orthodox Stoic doctrine was concerned. God and the cosmos were, ultimately, identical: though Stoic practical piety sometimes had a strong sense of transcendence (cf. e.g. the *Hymn of Cleanthes*).[5]

Peripatetic influence during the period of the formation of Christian doctrine was modest and secondary, and wholly exercised as part of the philosophical common inheritance used by

Platonists. Aristotle for Christians of this time was a rather particularly suspect philosopher, generally regarded much as anti-Aristotelian Platonists regarded him: and in so far as Aristotelian (or Stoic) logic was used or taken account of, it was as part of the common inheritance, which Platonists often used without hesitation, though not always uncritically. I shall consider uses and influences of Scepticism briefly at the end of this paper. Epicureans were, of course, outside the pale for everybody, and Christians (though sometimes coupled with them as *atheoi*) were not constructively interested in them,[6] except for the intellectually insignificant and uninfluential Arnobius. I think, therefore, that I am justified in following the usual practice in concentrating attention on the encounter of Christians and Platonists.

In doing so I propose to treat the Platonism of the first centuries of our era as a continuous whole, and not to make the sharp distinction usually made by modern historians of philosophy between 'Middle' and 'Neo' Platonists. I have three reasons for this. The first is that, though the distinction is useful for some purposes and will no doubt continue to be used, modern scholars are coming more and more to agree with the ancients that there is no real break in the continuity of the later Platonic and Pythagorean tradition after the revival of dogmatic Platonism and the obscure beginnings of what is generally known as Neopythagoreanism early in the first century BC (though Neopythagoreanism seems likely to go back at least into the second). The ancient philosophers with whom we are concerned, of course, not only saw their tradition as continuous from the end of the Sceptical Academy, but traced it back to Plato himself and his colleagues and immediate successors in the Old Academy, and sometimes still further back to Pythagoras: and modern scholars are becoming more and more inclined to agree with them, at least as far as the Old Academy is concerned. It would be widely agreed in modern times that attempts to read later Platonism back into the written or unwritten teachings of Plato himself are, at best, highly speculative and uncertain: though they may stimulate the development of very attractive and interesting modern versions of Platonic philosophy, like that of J. N. Findlay. An original philosopher should not be expected to read the ancients in the same way as a historian of philosophy. As far as Pythagoreanism is concerned, the agreement between ancients and moderns would be less. Neopythagoreanism seems to most modern scholars to be decidedly 'Neo', and to depend more on

Christianity in Relation to Later Platonism

'Pythagoreanizing' ways of thinking in the Old Academy than on genuine early Pythagoreanism. When it comes to the relations between Middle and Neoplatonism, the ancients regarded Plotinus as a great philosopher in an existing Platonic tradition rather than the originator of a new philosophy which made a break with previous tradition: and again modern scholars are coming to think that this is the right way to look at him. Many of the ideas characteristic of his philosophy are to be found in his predecessors, though generally in an inchoate and often rather incoherent form. His greatness lies not in making a clean break and a new start with an entirely new kind of Platonism but in thinking through again, in the light of his own living experience, the confused inheritance bequeathed to him by his rather second-rate predecessors, and shaping it into a religious philosophy of extraordinary power and influence, strongly developed (often in disagreement with Plotinus on important points) by his pagan successors.[7]

My second reason is the time-lag which occurred before what we call Neoplatonism could have attracted, or did attract, any serious attention from Christians. In his lifetime, even when he was teaching publicly in Rome (from approximately 244 to shortly before his death in 270), Plotinus was probably known of by only a few serious philosophers outside the quite small circle of his hearers at Rome. That he was so known is evidenced by remarks of Longinus (see note 7) but it is not clear, even so, that anyone knew much about him or was much interested in him who had not had some contact with the circle of Ammonius 'Saccas' in Alexandria, which was probably very small and obscure indeed, in spite of the later eminence of some of its members (of whom Longinus was one). His writings, in Porphyry's edition, the *Enneads*, were not put into general circulation till the first decade of the fourth century.[8] How widely the earlier edition of Eustochius was known to Christians or anybody else is not certain, though it may be the source of the extracts from Plotinus in the *Praeparatio Evangelica* of Eusebius of Caesarea. There seems to be no clear evidence that Christians read Plotinus and Porphyry before about the middle of the fourth century. And if we turn from the reading of Christians seriously interested in philosophy to the sort of philosophical instruction that those of them who received a traditional Hellenic higher education may have encountered in their younger days, it becomes even clearer that the influence of Plotinian and post-Plotinian Platonism and the need of taking up a position in relation to it cannot have been felt till a late period in the process of Christian self-definition in relation to Platonism, when the main lines of agreement and difference had been firmly established.

In the second and third centuries any philosophical instruction that an educated Christian received would have been in pre-Plotinian Platonism and other still living forms of Hellenic philosophy. It should not be assumed from the fact that Origen the Christian probably studied with the teacher of Plotinus, Ammonius, that he learned 'Neoplatonism' from him. The probabilities point the other way, though the question can never be finally settled, as we know practically nothing about the teaching of Ammonius, since we have no reliable evidence for its content: this has not, of course, deterred some modern scholars from writing a great deal about it. But we should also be perfectly clear that any formal Platonic instruction which Christians received in the great Hellenic philosophical schools of the fourth century is likely to have been pre-Plotinian in type. We know comparatively little about fourth-century Platonism, but it seems clear that the official Platonic teaching at Athens was not what modern scholars would call 'Neoplatonist' till about the end of the fourth century (though there may have been Neoplatonic philosophers resident at Athens throughout the last quarter of the century) and that at Alexandria the transition to full Neoplatonism came later, about the middle of the fifth century.[9] The Neoplatonism in both cases was the Neoplatonism of Iamblichus and his successors, an often sharply critical rethinking and development of the thought of Plotinus with some reference back to pre-Plotinian Platonism and Pythagoreanism. It seems in accordance with the evidence to say that the Platonism of Plotinus and Porphyry was not taken into serious account by Christians before the Cappadocians (especially Gregory of Nyssa) in the East in the middle of the fourth century, and by Marius Victorinus at about the same time and the circle of Ambrose and, above all, Augustine somewhat later in the West: and that the later Neoplatonism of the tradition of Iamblichus and the fifth-century Athenian philosophers Syrianus and Proclus did not make any serious impact on Christian thought before the author of the Dionysian writings, who may be dated, according to one's assessment of the somewhat nebulous internal evidence, more or less where one pleases in the fifth century, but not before.

My third reason for treating later Platonism as a continuous

Christianity in Relation to Later Platonism

whole is perhaps rather less of a commonplace. It is that, on the whole, the Christian understanding of this philosophy, at least in the centuries which mainly concern us, was, with few exceptions, relatively superficial. This has been noted before,[10] but its full significance is not always understood. It means that the more profound, subtle, difficult and original the ideas of a Platonic philosopher were, the less the Christians were likely to understand them in their full depth, range and power, especially when they were fundamentally at odds with some of their own Judaeo-Christian presuppositions at a level deeper than that of the surface hostilities of ancient polemic. Therefore, when Christians, even of the spiritual and intellectual stature of Augustine, read a Hellenic philosopher of the stature of Plotinus,[11] they were likely to grasp less of the content of his thought than they would have done if they had been reading Plutarch or Atticus. And what they did comprehend, whether with approval or disapproval, was more likely to be common Platonic school tradition (of which there is a great deal in Plotinus and his successors) than the great original Neoplatonic developments of that tradition. Since this is so, it seems to me to be likely to lead to a juster assessment of the whole intellectual situation of the age of the Fathers if one speaks only of Neoplatonism or anti-Neoplatonism when any of these great original developments are in question, and otherwise speaks and thinks in more general terms of the interaction of Christianity and later Platonism. One needs to be careful here in several areas, some of which we shall be exploring a little later. A notable one is that of the fully developed Plotinian and post-Plotinian apophatic theology, some of the rather startling implications of which for the Christian theologian are perhaps only beginning to be seen in our own time. In saying that the early Christian thinkers' understanding of Platonism, and especially that of Plotinus and his successors, was superficial I do not wish to imply that their own thought was necessarily superficial – it would be absurd to say this of Origen or Augustine – or that anything better could be expected of them. Most of the great Christians, like most educated men of late antiquity, had had a more thorough rhetorical than philosophical training, and a rhetorician is the last person to understand any different or difficult thought. Too much understanding would damage his rhetorical effectiveness. And their philosophical as well as their rhetorical learning and accomplishment was mostly employed in apologetic, protreptic or polemic (anti-pagan or anti-heretical), and this again was not helpful to deep understanding. Ancient controversy was generally carried on, by Hellenic philosophers as well as Christian theologians, at a deplorably low intellectual and ethical level. In any case, is not a real desire for thorough and sympathetic understanding of other people's philosophical and religious positions a comparatively modern and still by no means universal phenomenon?

During the symposium, some exception was taken to the suggestion that the Christian understanding of Neoplatonism was generally somewhat superficial. A good deal depends here on how one understands 'understanding'. If one thinks that one can 'understand' all sorts of religions and philosophies, at least well enough to dismiss them with well-founded intellectual confidence or to award them grades, like a university examiner, with reference to one's own preferred norm, one will find it easy to suppose that the Fathers 'understood' the Neoplatonists. But if (as has been my own experience) one finds that it takes a lifetime to arrive at a partial and imperfect understanding of any really great philosopher, and is very conscious of the limitations and imperfections of even serious modern scholarship and interpretation, one may be less confident, and may find one's lack of confidence confirmed by reading both Fathers and Neoplatonists.[12]

In considering the specific points where educated Greek and Latin-speaking Christians of the Roman Empire in their encounter with Platonism were influenced by or found it necessary to disagree with the Hellenic philosophers, we shall have to take into account not only conscious but unconscious agreement or divergence. This is because we are dealing with people, as has already been said, who belonged fully to their own period and culture and whose minds had been formed by a normal Hellenic education. Dr E. P. Meijering has recently rendered a useful service to patristic scholarship by reminding us of this: one of the most effective ways in which he has done so is by directing a good deal of his attention to Christian thinkers who are generally, and rightly, supposed not to have been very philosophically minded or deeply interested in Hellenic philosophy, such as Irenaeus, Athanasius, or Cyril of Alexandria, and showing how much ordinary late Platonism is to be found in their thought.

The first point of difference between Christians and Hellenic philosophers which we shall have to consider is the primacy of a special revelation as the essential source of divine truth insisted on by the Christians. This is indeed important, but the conflict here should not be over-simplified, as it often has been, into a straight-forward opposition between an appeal to faith and an appeal to reason, or between revealed religion and philosophic rationalism. On the side of the Hellenic philosophers, the kind of insight, possible only to men who were truly good and wise, to attain which was the goal of a philosopher, went far beyond rationality as we usually conceive it and was experienced as a participation in or illumination by the divine *Logos* or *Nous*, available from the beginning and (it was generally thought) most clearly and strongly in ancient times, to the few who were able to attain it, the blessed philosophers of antiquity, above all the great founders Pythagoras and Plato; though in every generation the philosopher had to reconquer for himself, by most demanding moral and intellectual effort, the true ancient philosophic wisdom, starting this effort under the guidance of his often deeply venerated personal teacher. Beyond the great founding philosophers there were other sources of divine wisdom, non-philosophic in form though needing true philosophy to interpret them rightly – inspired poets, alleged teachings of ancient oriental sages, and oracles of the gods – and some at least of these were thought of as revelations. (The degree to which such venerable, non-philosophic and even non-Hellenic sources of wisdom were in practice taken seriously probably varied a good deal according to the temperament and training of different philosophers. It may be that Plotinus is exceptional in the lack of serious interest he shows in anything outside the Platonic philosophical tradition; and that sturdy individualistic rationalist Galen, who refused to have his intellect fettered by even the tradition of a particular Hellenic philosophy, was certainly quite exceptional in the late second century, and knew it.)[14]

On the Christian side there is a long tradition, extending from Justin and Clement of Alexandria in the second century on through the early centuries of the Christian era, the Middle Ages, the Renaissance, and beyond, which finds in the special divine revelation which it accepts the best and truest philosophy in its most perfect form. Revelation contains, and can be shown by the right sort of exegesis to contain, the fullness of philosophic wisdom. Philo of Alexandria was the forefather of this tradition, and to a great extent he determined both the kind of studies of Hellenic philosophy and the exegetical methods which were necessary to justify this claim. For those who thought like this, of whom the greatest, perhaps, was Origen, though particular philosophers might be wrong on particular points because they presented the ancient wisdom in a garbled and perverted form, there could be no ultimate clash between the truth of revelation accepted not only with faith but with understanding and the highest intellectual enlightenment which could be attained by a philosopher. They were the same thing, and this could be shown by someone sufficiently equipped, illuminated and able in the interpretation of scripture and the Hellenic, especially the Platonic, philosophical tradition. This (with of course many modifications and variations of method and emphasis) was the faith of a long line of great Christian thinkers in East and West who made the greatest contribution to the formation of traditional Christian doctrine and scriptural interpretation.

There is, however, a greater difference between the Christian and the Hellenic philosophical attitude to divine revelation than might be gathered from what has been said so far. This is shown by the existence on the Christian side of an alternative view of the relationship between revelation and philosophy which was not possible for any Hellenic philosopher, however reverential in his attitude to very dubious revelations. This alternative was fideism. For those who hold to their revelation in this way the opposition of faith and reason is indeed absolute. Human reason is utterly helpless to grasp any divine truth and there can be no philosophical wisdom, enlightenment or liberation. Philosophy is not only helpless to attain divine truth. It can be no help in understanding it either. When one has found faith, to speculate on the doctrines one believes can only lead one into error. It may be that this attitude to their faith was the most widespread among the ordinary uneducated members of the Christian communities. But it was by no means confined to the 'simple faithful' as opposed to the intellectuals. It received, of course, its most brilliant and paradoxical exposition from 'that typical ultra-conservative Christian intellectual Tertullian, an extremely clever and well-read man.[15] Its most sophisticated form (revived at the Renaissance) in which the arguments of the Sceptics are used to support a fideist position will be considered briefly in the last section of this paper. Here we need to note that the existence of fideism as a live option for intelligent Christians points to a real difference between the attitude of Christians to their special revelation and the veneration of the most traditionalist Hellenic philosophers for the teaching of the ancients or for divinely

Christianity in Relation to Later Platonism

inspired poets and divinely revealed oracles. (It should be observed in passing that any belief which philosophers – especially later Neoplatonists – held in a divinely inspired inner meaning in the stories of the ancient poets or the oracles of the gods did not at all commend them to Christians. The more generous-minded among them, following Justin and Clement of Alexandria, might concede that the great philosophers had been enlightened by the universal *Logos* and might sometimes prefer this explanation of their approximation to divine truth to the less creditable one that the philosophers had plundered and garbled the Jewish scriptures. But heathen cult and mythology belonged to the devil, and the only inspiration which could be detected in them was diabolical. For this reason the survival of records of the old sharp hostility to the poets and their tales about the gods in the books of the venerated philosophers of the past, especially Plato, helped considerably to convince the Christians that Hellenic philosophy as such was not inextricably bound up with heathenism and could be used for Christian purposes, in spite of the very different attitude of most contemporary philosophers, who instead of rejecting the ancient myths allegorized them as reverentially as Philo or the Christians allegorized the Old Testament.)

Perhaps the central point of this difference betweeen Christians and Hellenic philosophers is to be found in the adjective 'special' which I have attached to 'revelation'. For a traditionalist Hellenic philosopher the divine wisdom which was expounded with unsurpassable accuracy and completeness by Pythagoras and Plato and hinted at enigmatically in the myths and oracles was there from the beginning, in principle discoverable everywhere in the world and by all men by the divine light of intellect which shone for all who could see it, even if few had the capacity and were prepared to make the tremendous effort to do so. For the Christians the primary revelation in which alone the fullness of divine truth was contained was a special and particular one, given in stages to a particular community of men, of which the central and most important part consisted of a record of facts firmly believed to be historical, the mighty acts of God done in and for that community. A special revelation with a core of sacred history both had in itself and conferred on the community in which it had been given, and which had the duty of preserving and proclaiming it, a different and more precise (though not necessarily more powerful) kind of authority than that of the primal and universally diffused divine illumination which the philosophic intellect could recognize, or the 'voices from on high' to which Plotinus summoned his hearers to listen in their souls (*Enneads* V.1.12.14–20). This was recognized as well by those, like Clement of Alexandria and Origen, who were willing and anxious, like Philo before them, to discover universal philosophic truth in the scriptures as by Irenaeus or the deliberately extremist Tertullian. And it gave the community, the church, and its increasingly authoritarian chief teachers, the bishops, an authority of a density and force which was certainly never possessed by those decidedly nebulous entities, the philosophical 'schools' – in so far as they ever really existed.[16] This authority was generally recognized by those anxious to find the perfect and universally true philosophy in the revelation as well as by others, although Origen, with his perhaps unique sense of the intellectual freedom of the man led and enlightened by the Spirit, seems at times to have had his doubts about it.[17]

The sense of the unique importance and authority of the special revelation which marks off Christians so clearly from Hellenic philosophers was intensified by two other convictions. One was that the effects of the Fall of man had reduced human capacity for the knowledge and understanding of divine truth so far, if they had not destroyed it altogether, that without a special revelation, and special grace and enlightenment by the Spirit only given in the Christian community, no man could attain more than a very imperfect knowledge, if even that, of divine saving truth. This conviction was far sharper and stronger than any views held by the most pessimistic second-century Pythagoreans or Platonists about the effects on man's capacity for knowledge of the divine of the fall (or descent) of his soul into body and the world of the senses. It reached its sharpest and most exaggerated forms in the Latin-speaking West. But, in the softer and vaguer form in which I have stated it, it was general also in the Greek-speaking East. And behind it and reinforcing it there may be a deeper difference between Christianity and the Hellenic Platonism with which it was interacting. This was the Christian sense of a (non-spatial) gap, not simply a distance or a transcendence but a discontinuity, between God and his Creation. It was perhaps this, united with the sharp sense of man's fallen state just referred to, which impelled Christians most strongly to believe in their special revelation and unique incarnation, although it is perhaps possible to state belief in both in a way which does not require this sense of discontinuity. This, however, will be better discussed further in a properly theological context, when we have turned, as we now should, to consider what Christians accepted from the Platonists and what they did not in formulating their doctrine of God.

The doctrine of God

The first, most important and deeply influential way of thinking about God which most serious Christian theologians took, probably as much unconsciously as consciously, from the Platonists was the conviction that he was what the philosophers called a *Nous*, an incorporeal being, eternally changeless and incapable of being affected in any way. This was what Platonically influenced Christians meant when they insistently repeated the scriptural 'God is spirit'.[18] (The Johannine text is a particular favourite of Origen's.) Of course the words used both in Greek and Latin, *pneuma* and *spiritus*, were used in the normal philosophical discourse of the time, by Platonists as well as Stoics, in a Stoic rather than a Platonic sense, as meaning that the entity referred to was precisely not incorporeal, but a very subtle and superior sort of body: and Tertullian understood *spiritus* in this sense of God.[19] But the Platonic sense which the great Alexandrians, Clement and Origen, and others gave to the scriptural word prevailed and has persisted. Of course the doctrine that God is incorporeal, changeless and impassible is very difficult to square with a great deal in scripture. However, the firm exegetical methods inherited from Philo enabled ancient and mediaeval Christian thinkers to deal with this quite easily. Modern theologians have seen deeper difficulties arising about the compatibility of the doctrine with Christian belief in the incarnation and passion of Christ, and it is certainly at variance with much Christian piety. None the less, this Platonic doctrine is very deeply rooted in traditional Christianity and will not (and in my opinion should not) be easily abandoned.

But, however Platonic the Christian interpretation of 'God is spirit' became, there remained certain differences between the theism of the Christians and that of the philosophers. A very important difference, with far-reaching consequences, between Christians and at least one side of the Pythagorean-Platonic tradition concerns the Christian sense of discontinuity between God and his creation. It may need to be stressed that this does not mean any sort of spatial absence of God from his world. Divine omnipresence was generally believed in.[20] It means rather a kind of ontological discontinuity, a belief that the creation, even if it has and requires God's continual presence and creative activity to keep it in being, really is other than God and has a sort of separate substantiality of its own. The Neopythagorean (probably in most cases) and Neoplatonic way of looking at the relationship is rather different. Most philosophically serious Neopythagoreans seem to have thought in terms of a generation of the universe from the primal One by a kind of self-explication through the First Principle's production either of a pair of principles, a second One as principle of limit and a principle of indefinite multiplicity (Eudorus)[21] or of the principle of multiplicity, the Indefinite Dyad, alone, which it forms and limits itself (the Pythagoreans known to Alexander and Moderatus).[22] This kind of view of the world's generation does not seem to have been held by the most influential of those who regarded themselves as Pythagoreans, Numenius, whose system is an unclassifiable amalgam of various strains of Platonic and Pythagorean thinking, with perhaps some Gnostic influence.[23] But it was probably an important source of the great vision of Plotinus and his successors of the divine life and light springing from its transcendent source, the One or Good, and descending in unbroken continuity through levels of self-manifestation of diminishing clarity and excellence to the material world, the lowest, but in its rank and circumstances the best possible, of theophanies. It should be noted that this great outgoing and self-diffusion of the Good leaves the Good himself unchanged and undiminished in his ineffable transcendence, and the same applies to each successive level of divine self-manifestation in its degree.[24]

This Neoplatonic view of creation as theophany did not generally commend itself to Christians before the author of the Dionysian writings, with whom it entered the Christian tradition and eventually received one of its clearest, most powerful and most influential expositions in the *Periphyseon* of Eriugena. The Christian thinkers of the decisive period of self-definition to the late fourth century of our era, because of their sense of discontinuity between Creator and creation, are much closer to other Platonists, of the second century, especially to what may be called the 'fundamentalist' group, best represented for us by Plutarch and Atticus. These interpreted the *Timaeus* perfectly literally, and consequently believed in a God who designed and created a world distinct from himself in or with time. A glance at two points of controversy may make the difference between the two ways of thinking clearer. Plotinus, as is well known, strongly disliked the idea of 'artisan' creation, of God as the Great Architect of the Universe,[25] which satisfied fundamentalist Platonists, Jews and Christians. Behind this difference may possibly lie the distinction between the 'substantial' and the 'insubstantial' image, which Edward N. Lee has shown to be essential for the proper understanding of Plato, and which was known to Plotinus.[26] Fundamentalist Platonists, Jews and Christians, when thinking of creation in terms of archetype and image, thought of God making a sort of statue or portrait of himself. For Plotinus and his successors the cosmos was more like a shadow or reflection of God, cast perhaps on or in a medium which is ultimately his own infinity. The persistent controversy, too, between Christians and most Hellenic philosophers about whether the world was created in or with time and would have an end or was everlasting, may have been carried on so enthusiastically on the Christian side because a world with a temporal beginning and end was obviously easier to think of as discontinuous with its eternal Creator. It is interesting that Origen, at his most boldly speculative, will not positively assert more than the eternal pre-existence of creation in the *Logos*, thereby leaving room both for discontinuity between the Creator and a separate, substantial creation and for a temporal beginning of the world.[27]

But however close the Christians were in their understanding of creation to the 'fundamentalist' Platonists, there was one very important difference between them, of which the Christians were fully conscious. This was that for the Platonists (as probably for Plato himself) the Creator was not omnipotent. He did the best he could in difficult circumstances, confronted everlastingly by an independent principle of irrational disorder, the evil soul which was in, or continually attacking, matter, and was the principle and cause of all moral and physical evil. This conflict-dualism was held not only by Plutarch and Atticus (in somewhat different forms) but, in a very pessimistic form, by Numenius.[28] It can easily be derived from some passages in Plato.[29] But it seems likely that the second-century Platonists were moved to accept it whole-heartedly partly by their knowledge of Zoroastrian conflict-dualism (this is explicit in Plutarch).[30] The Christians rejected passionately this limitation of God's omnipotence by an independent principle of evil. And, as the second-century Platonists were the philosophers whom the Christians knew best, this became for them, along with creation in time (though here they sometimes recognized that there was conflict between the philosophers) a conscious point of sharp difference between philosophy and the Christian faith. However quasi-Zoroastrian or even quasi-Manichaean Christians sometimes were in thought and practice, in their attitude to the devil and all his angels and their power in the world, they insisted that the origin of evils must be looked for in the voluntary fall of created spirits, superhuman and human. The great system of Origen expounded in the *Peri Archōn*, though later condemned as heretical, is no more than a magnificently coherent and, in the end, nobly optimistic working out of this basic principle. And, in their reaction from second-century conflict-dualism, Christian theologians eventually come to adopt the same view of evil as the later Neoplatonists, that it can have no independent or substantial existence but is entirely negative, a privation of good. The influence of the Athenian Neoplatonic school is particularly clearly apparent in the fullest exposition of this doctrine by 'Dionysius'.[31] (Plotinus' doctrine of matter and evil seems to me to mark an interesting and complex transition stage in the movement away from the conflict-dualism of Numenius to the late Neoplatonist position: it was probably not very influential.)

We must now consider the most important point, as it seems to me, where Christian thinkers, with few exceptions, remained in a Middle Platonist position, and failed fully to understand the distinctively Neoplatonic development of that position. This is in their use of negative or apophatic theology. In the revived Platonism and Pythagoreanism of the three centuries before Plotinus (and in contemporary Gnosticism) there quite often appears a tendency to use negatively superlative language to express the extreme transcendence of the First Principle, to which or whom our thought cannot, or can only with great difficulty, attain. Sometimes this use of negative language seems to be hardly more than rhetorical, an attempt to speak of transcendence in more superlative negations than anybody else. Sometimes the negations are combined with a clear affirmation that the First Principle is a *Nous* (notably in the author of the *Didaskalikos*).[32] But sometimes, especially in philosophers of Pythagoreanizing tendencies, there seems to be a serious attempt to say that the originative One must be something higher than *Nous* or being (which for Platonists or Aristotelians means definable and so intelligible being, the correlative of intellect).[33] This seems to go back to

92

Christianity in Relation to Later Platonism

Speusippus, Plato's nephew and successor (whose doctrine Aristotle probably misunderstood),[34] and seems to have become the basis of an exegesis of the second half of Plato's *Parmenides* fairly early in our period.[35] Before Plotinus, however, the position remains rather confused. Apophatic and kataphatic theologies remain in a rather indigestible mixture, and even when a serious negative theology was asserted its implications do not seem, as far as we know, to have been worked out (though Speusippus may have gone further in this direction than our evidence permits us to see clearly). But the thought of Plotinus is dominated by the negative theology of the One or Good beyond the One-Being which is *Nous* and World of Forms, and he at least begins to draw the radical consequences of such a theology, of which perhaps the most radical is that mind-language is quite inapplicable to God, who neither thinks nor is thinkable, a theme which pervades the *Enneads*, especially the fifth and sixth. Perhaps neither he nor any ancient Neoplatonist saw the full consequences which a radically apophatic way of thinking about God might have for any dogmatic theology, philosophical or revelational, although Damascius, the last head of the Athenian Neoplatonic school in the age of Justinian, seems to be coming at least very near to doing so. But radical apophatism seems to be becoming a very lively form of theology again in our own times, and it is possible that the ancient Neoplatonists, if we are prepared to develop and apply their thought boldly, may have something to contribute to contemporary theological debates.[36]

But, however that may be, Christians on the whole, at least before 'Dionysius', and generally after him, remained in a Middle Platonist rather than a Neoplatonist position. (The Christian, 'Dionysian' development of Neoplatonic negative theology raises intricate questions, including that of the sense in which the Neoplatonic *Nous* thinks or is thinkable, which cannot be dealt with here.) Christian thinkers had indeed, in many cases, a strong sense of the ineffable mystery of God (at least in part inherited from Philo, in whom it seems to have Jewish as well as Hellenic antecedents). But they also felt a strong need (this was perhaps an essential part of their pursuit of self-identity and self-definition) to make positive, sharply defined, and increasingly elaborate statements about him which were so certainly true that anyone who disagreed with them was certainly wickedly and perversely wrong. So, from Clement of Alexandria onwards, God seems to appear in their discourse, as in much pre-Plotinian Platonist discourse, as an ineffably transcendent spiritual being about whom it is possible to talk a great deal, and that in very definite terms. Gregory of Nyssa, in the later fourth century, provides a very interesting example of this apophatic-kataphatic mixture. He has a very deep awareness of God's ineffable mystery, and develops an original and impressive negative theology in his mystical works, especially the *Life of Moses*, to which Plotinian Neoplatonist apophatism seems to have made some contribution. He also uses negative theology very powerfully for polemical purposes against Eunomius the Anomoean Arian, who in his opinion 'knew' altogether too much about God. But when it comes to his own dogmatic Trinitarian theology, like the other Cappadocian Fathers he seems after all to know, and to be able to say, a good many very definite things about God.[37]

The decisive doctrinal change or development in the fourth century from what is generally called 'subordinationist' theology to the post-Nicene doctrine of the co-equal Trinity and the unity of operation of the Divine Persons in creation and redemption has generally been taken as a moment of the utmost importance in the self-definition of Christianity over against Hellenic philosophy. It is held that pre-Nicene Trinitarian theology, especially that of Origen, shows the influence of the Platonic descending hierarchy of three gods, the First Principle, the Second *Nous* or *Logos*, and the World-Soul. The Trinitarian theology of the Council of Nicaea, as developed and clarified in the subsequent controversies, on the other hand, is supposed to show a clean break with the Hellenic belief that there can be degrees of divinity, that it is possible to be more or less God, and a move to a more intransigently monotheist Trinitarianism. Of course there is much truth in this. The descending hierarchy of two or three principles is not uncommon in Middle Platonism and becomes the basic structure of Platonic philosophical theology from Plotinus onwards, considerably elaborated by Iamblichus and his successors, but still clearly discernible. And pre-Nicene theology is generally one of God's (that is to say, the Father's) work in the world, creating, revealing, redeeming and sanctifying through the *Logos*-Son and the Spirit, whose intermediary and instrumental activities are separately perceptible. This is particularly evident in the theology of Origen, which does look in this way very Middle Platonist. But I do not propose to make so much of it as is usually done in this context, both because it has been so much discussed and for two other reasons. The first and most important is that even if 'subordinationist' theology has a somewhat Middle Platonic appearance, it looks even more like such inchoate Trinitarian theology as may be found in the New Testament, especially the Johannine and Pauline writings (which Origen, after all, knew rather well). This means that we cannot evaluate the degree of Hellenic philosophical influence here without determining how much of it there is in the thought of the New Testament writers and their Hellenistic Jewish background. This is a difficult enterprise, and one which I have already admitted my incompetence to undertake. And it raises the rather awkward question: in what sense is a doctrinal development which moves away both from contemporary Hellenic Platonism and from the New Testament a Christian doctrinal development? This question becomes somewhat more pressing if my second point is considered. In the late third century there was a development within Neoplatonism itself which strikingly resembles the move from 'subordinationist' to Nicene Trinitarian theology in the Christian church. This was Porphyry's development of the thought of Plotinus, recently brought into clear view by P. Hadot.[38] Porphyry, it appears, not only clearly articulated the 'horizontal' triad of Being-Life-Intelligence which is latent in Plotinus' accounts of the eternal generation of *Nous* and is of great importance in the elaborate theological structures of Neoplatonism from Iamblichus onwards, he also identified the first member of the triad with the unknowable First Principle. This was a transient development, as Iamblichus and his successors vigorously rejected it, in their desire to preserve hierarchical subordinationism and accentuate the ineffable transcendence of the One (which Porphyry himself seems to have stressed extremely strongly). And there is no clear evidence that it had any major influence on the development or formulation of Nicene or post-Nicene Trinitarian theology. But it was influential enough, at least in the West, in the fourth century, and sufficiently close to the Nicene position, for the great philosophical theologian Marius Victorinus, who is impeccably orthodox from a post-Nicene point of view, to use it very effectively in the exposition and defence of the Catholic theology of his time against the Arians.[39] Now if we are to say that a doctrinal development which not only moves somewhat further away from the New Testament than earlier Christian theology, but also moves somewhat closer to the thought of the most anti-Christian of Platonic philosophers, is an important moment in Christian self-

VIII

definition, it does raise a rather large question about what exactly 'Christian self-definition' means.

There is however an important difference between all forms of Christian *Logos*-theology and Platonic *Nous*-theology which merits more attention than it has received. In Platonic theology *Nous* is the one god who is all the gods. He has therefore always been immediately present and accessible everywhere in that cosmos which is his material self-manifestation and reflection to those good and wise men who can understand the true inner meaning of their traditional myths and cults. Plotinus expressed this best of all Platonic philosophers. He says of *Nous*, 'For he encompasses in himself all things immortal, every intellect, every god, every soul . . . '; and he prays, 'May he come, bringing his own universe with him, with all the gods within him, he who is one and all, and each god is all the gods coming together into one: they are different in their powers, but by that one manifold power they are all one: or rather the one god is all: for he does not fail if all become what he is . . . '. And in his great challenge to the intransigent Judaeo-Christian monotheism which he encountered in his Gnostic friends he says:

It is not contracting the divine into one but showing it in that multiplicity in which God himself has shown it which is proper to those who know the power of God, inasmuch as, abiding who he is, he makes many gods, all depending upon himself and existing through him and from him. And this universe exists through him and looks to him, the whole of it and each and every one of the gods in it, and it reveals what is his to men, and it and the gods in it declare in their oracles what is pleasing to the intelligible gods.

(*Theos*, which I think I have here rightly translated 'God', seems to refer in this passage, as it does sometimes elsewhere, to the One or Good.)[40]

On the Christian side, through all variations and developments of Christian doctrine from the New Testament onwards, the emphasis is very different. Even when the Divine Ideas which are the archetypes of all creation were thought to be contained in the *Logos*, and he was conceived as working in the world and illuminating the minds of wise and good men from the beginning of time, as he was by Justin and Clement of Alexandria, this universal content and operation of the *Logos*, though insisted on and important for theology as well as apologetic, was not central to Christian faith and piety. For Christians the *Logos* was only adequately and effectively accessible in his unique incarnation in

96

Christianity in Relation to Later Platonism

Jesus Christ, revealed in the scriptures and the teaching of the church. That there is one and one only mediator, Christ, is central to all traditional Christian doctrine, of whatever form. And the incarnate *Logos* is most emphatically *not* 'all the gods'. Even in later centuries when Christian thought and piety became more deeply Hellenized, and Christ was apprehended more and more in the multiplicity of his saints, this glorified mystical body of his, which in so many ways replaced that ancient company of gods and spirits of which Plotinus spoke, was always ecclesiastically limited. There was no room in it for the gods, spirits, saints and sages of mankind outside the church of Christ. Worshippers of saints and their images have talked quite as ignorantly and fanatically about 'heathens' and 'idolators' and behaved quite as intolerantly towards them as those Christians who held to or revived the stricter Jewish view of the implications of monotheism. We are back here with the themes, touched on earlier, of particularity with universal claims and sense of discontinuity. And the great division between Hellenic and Semitic monotheism, whose nature we can perhaps now see more clearly, is by no means of merely historical interest. It is reappearing, because of and in a form appropriate to the religious circumstances of our own time, in the Christian body itself.[41]

Conclusion

It might be expected that, before ending this paper, I should say something about more practical matters, about the ways in which Christians differentiated themselves from Hellenic philosophers in their attitudes to the body, sex, the material world and social and political institutions. But I do not propose to do so. This is partly because I do not find it useful to consider ethical, political and social theory without also considering practice. I think one must look at what people do as well as what they say. And to appreciate the ways and the extent to which there was any distinctive self-definition of Christianity over against Hellenic philosophy in the field of private and public behaviour one needs to look very closely at how Christians thought and acted when they came to power in the ancient world. One can only consider such questions as the effect on Christian attitudes to body, sex and the material world of the acceptance of the philosophical doctrine of the incorporeality and immortality of the soul along with the maintenance of the doctrine of the resurrection of the body, or of the ways in which Christian attitudes to the state and the cosmos may have been determined or influenced by the churchiness which is, in various forms, a distinctive characteristic of Christian societies, in the context of a full discussion of the thought, life and institutions of the Christian Empire, with perhaps some glances onwards to Byzantium and the medieval West; and this would take us far beyond the limits of this symposium and my own competence. Further, I am inclined to think that such a discussion would show a stronger reason for not saying much about these matters of practical philosophy in a paper on Christian self-definition, and that is that there is really very little to say. Even the sincerest conversion to Christianity made little difference here, if our standard of comparison is the life and thought of late Platonic philosophers. And such differences as may be detected in a Christian saint's way of living and thinking as compared with that of a good and intelligent Hellene of the same period are not always improvements from any but an extremely ecclesiastical point of view.[42]

To conclude I shall make a few remarks on the influence on the thought of both Platonists and Christians in the early centuries of our era of Scepticism in its two forms, Academic and Pyrrhonian. This is worth noting, not perhaps because it was very important at the time, but because the presence of elements of Scepticism, sometimes latent or unconscious, in the thought of this formative period, may have had a good deal of influence on later developments. From the Christian point of view, Scepticism is only of value as a polemical weapon. A genuinely Sceptical attitude of mind is the enemy of faith, and part of the intellectual preparation for the acceptance of the faith may have to be a thorough refutation of Scepticism. Augustine's *Contra Academicos* is the classical example. But none the less, the formidable battery of arguments assembled by the Pyrrhonian Sceptics to refute the dogmatic philosophers, which we know best from the work of Sextus Empiricus,[43] could be employed by Christian controversialists to support a fideistic position, or at any rate to demonstrate the inadequacy of philosophy and the urgent need of divine revelation. The use of Pyrrhonian Scepticism to support fideism is excellently illustrated by Book III of the *Divinae Institutiones* of Lactantius. It was of course vigorously revived in the Renaissance, the great example being Montaigne's *Apologie de Raimond Sebond*.[44]

On the non-Christian Platonist side the position is a little more

Christianity in Relation to Later Platonism

complex. The general attitude to Scepticism, both Pyrrhonian and that of the Sceptical Academy, was perhaps one of disapproval. This is certainly true of the philosopher whose views on the subject we know best, Numenius, as we can see from the long fragments of his work *On The Divergence of the Academics from Plato* preserved by Eusebius in his *Praeparatio Evangelica* (the fact that Eusebius thought them worth quoting at such length in his context tells us something about the Christian attitude to Academic Scepticism).[45] But Dillon has discovered some (admittedly rather scanty) evidence of a more sympathetic attitude to Scepticism in Philo (this, however, may be independent of any Middle Platonic influence) and Plutarch (in the titles of some lost works).[46] More important is the possibility that Scepticism may have had an influence of some kind on the development of Neoplatonic apophatic theology and the rejection of the 'artisan' idea of creation, two points at which we have noticed considerable divergences between the Hellenic Neoplatonists and the Christians: there is, however, never likely to be sufficient reason to regard this as more than a possibility, though work on the subject is proceeding. But it does seem very likely that in the tolerant religious pluralism of some of the last defenders of the old religion in the West we can discern a coming together of the urbane Academicism of Cicero with a Porphyrian type of Neoplatonism.[47] Cicero, of course, was extensively read, then and later, by Christians, and has carried his Academicism down the centuries with him. So the mention of his name may serve to introduce what is perhaps the most important thing to say about the relationship between Christian thought and Hellenic philosophy. This is, quite simply, that, not only in the first centuries of the Christian era, but ever since, the Hellenic philosophers have always been there, as independent witnesses to a variety of other possible ways of thinking about God, man and the world, which are always available to Christians who wish to question the prevailing orthodoxy or re-define their faith, and available to them within their own tradition, and indeed until quite recently as a normal part of the content of their formally Christian education.

Notes

1. For the Carpocratians see Irenaeus, *AH* I.25.6. For Naasene exegesis of mythology see Hippolytus, *Ref.* V.7–9, and for that of Justin the Gnostic Hippolytus, *Ref.* V.26–27. Though there does seem to be some knowledge and use of Platonic themes by the Valentinians (and perhaps other Gnostics) it is advisable in the present state of our knowledge not to try to be very precise about specific influences of particular Neopythagorean or Middle Platonist philosophers or groups on Gnosticism, or of Gnostics on the philosophers.

2. For a fuller discussion of this whole subject see my 'Gnosis and Greek Philosophy' in *Gnosis* I.* The Plotinus treatise *Against the Gnostics* (II.9 [33]) is the concluding part of a work editorially dismembered by Porphyry: the three earlier parts, in their correct order, are (II.8 [30], V.8 [31] and V.5 [32].

3. On these points see my chapter referred to in n. 2.

4. I have attempted to discuss some of them in my paper 'Pagan and Christian Traditionalism in the First Three Centuries A.D.', to be published in *Studia Patristica*. That the post-Iamblichean Neoplatonists were genuine Hellenic philosophers is becoming more and more generally recognized by competent scholars. Note the accounts of them by A. C. Lloyd in the *Cambridge History of Later Greek and Early Mediaeval Philosophy*, Cambridge 1972, Part IV; and by R. T. Wallis, *Neoplatonism*, London 1972, chapters 4 and 5. There is a full and very judicious discussion of their theurgy in A. Smith, *Porphyry's Place in the Neoplatonic Tradition*, The Hague 1975. This does not of course exclude their being 'theologians' in the philosophical manner of the best traditional Christian thinkers.

5. During the course of the symposium Professor Rist suggested that

the influence of Stoicism was waning in the second century, especially in the East of the Empire, and that this was why Eastern Christians, especially, adopted a Platonic kind of philosophy quite naturally. The proposal deserves more serious consideration than can be given to it here.

6. Though A. Long in his *Hellenistic Philosophy*, London 1974, notes that Lactantius and Augustine sometimes refer to Epicurus with 'qualified approval' (very qualified, and entirely for anti-pagan apologetic purposes, e.g. in Lactantius, *Divinae Institutiones* III.17, though Lactantius certainly knows Lucretius well, and frequently quotes him to support a point).

7. For the way in which the eminence of Plotinus, precisely as a philosopher in a continuing Platonic tradition, was recognized by a learned and critical contemporary Platonist who did not agree with him philosophically, see the remarks of Longinus in Porphyry, *Life of Plotinus*, chapters 19 and 20. Our evidence for the thought of the Middle Platonists is patchy and of very varying quality and value: and most modern work on them, till fairly recently, has been in the form of articles, many rather inaccessible. Two good surveys of the history of Platonism before Plotinus, with ample references to sources and selective bibliographies of modern literature written from rather different points of view, are P. Merlan in the *Cambridge History of Later Greek and Early Mediaeval Philosophy*, Cambridge 1967, reprinted with small corrections and additions 1972, Part I, pp. 14–132, and John Dillon, *The Middle Platonists*, London 1977. On the Neopythagorean side, the important recent work of John Whittaker should be mentioned, as it confirms and strengthens the case for Neopythagorean influence on important aspects of the thought of Plotinus made long ago by E. R. Dodds in 'The Parmenides of Plato and the Origin of the Neoplatonic One', *Classical Quarterly* 22, 1928, pp. 129–42: see J. Whittaker, 'Epekeina Nou Kai Ousias', *VC* 23, 1969, pp. 91–104; 'Neopythagoreanism and Negative Theology', *Symbolae Osloenses* 44, 1969, pp. 109–25, 'Neopythagoreanism and the Transcendent Absolute', ibid. 48, 1973, pp. 77–86.

8. This is the date generally accepted by Neoplatonic scholars: the publication was after 301 and probably before 305. See H.-R. Schwyzer in Plotinos (Alfred Druckemuller Verlag, Munchen 1978) col. 487 ff.

9. On fourth-century Neoplatonism and the School of Athens see the Introduction to *Proclus: Théologie Platonicienne* I, (ed. H. D. Saffrey and L. G. Westerink), Paris 1968, pp. xxxv–xlvii; R. T. Wallis, *Neoplatonism*, chapters 4 and 5. On the Platonism of Alexandria see

A. C. Lloyd in the *Cambridge History* (see n. 4), pp. 314–19; R. T. Wallis, *Neoplatonism*, pp. 139–42; I. Hadot, *Le problème du néoplatonisme alexandrin: Hierocles et Simplicius* (Etudes Augustiniennes, Paris 1978).

10. See E. Gilson, 'Le Christianisme et la tradition philosophique', *RSPT* 2, 1941–42, p. 242, quoted and developed by J. Trouillard in *La Purification Plotinienne*, Paris 1955 in the remarkable section 4 of chapter VII, 'Liberté plotinienne et surnaturel chrétien', pp. 122–32. Trouillard has developed his thought considerably since, but this section is still well worth reading.

11. On Augustine's degree of understanding of Plotinus I am in agreement to some extent with Robert J. O'Connell. See his *Augustine's Early Theory of Man*, Cambridge, Mass. 1968, 'Epilogue', pp. 283–89. But I am inclined to think that there is more, rather than less, that Augustine did not understand in Plotinus than O'Connell sees. The possibility should not be neglected that Porphyry may have had something to do with the hardening, narrowing and shallowing of Plotinian Platonism which can be detected in Augustine, who certainly read a good deal of Porphyry as well as Plotinus. Porphyry's influence on people's understanding of Plotinus down the centuries has been considerable and often, I think, unfortunate.

12. Reference here may be made to Professor G. C. Stead's 'Ontologie und Terminologie bei Gregor von Nyssa' (in English) in *Gregor von Nyssa und die Philosophie* (eds. H. Dörrie *et al.*), Leiden 1976. Stead's judgment of Gregory of Nyssa's philosophical understanding is rather harsher than mine would be.

13. See E. P. Meijering, *Orthodoxy and Platonism in Athanasius*, Leiden 1968, and the articles collected as *God Being History*, Amsterdam/Oxford/New York 1975.

14. For further discussion of the sort of traditionalism and veneration for ancient wisdom mentioned here see my 'Pagan and Christian Traditionalism in the First Three Centuries A.D.' [= this volume, study IX]. On Galen see R. Walzer, *Galen on Jews and Christians*, Oxford 1949, with my comment in the paper just mentioned, p.431, n.48.

15. The contrast of attitudes described in this and the preceding paragraph has been very often discussed. An excellent and judicious summary account is to be found in R. A. Markus, *Christianity and the Roman World*, chapter three, 'The Crisis of Identity'.

16. Many discussions in Dillon's *Middle Platonists* will give some idea of the most recent views on the philosophical 'schools' of the Roman Imperial period. When a modern critical scholar directs his close attention to a philosophical 'school' it has a distinct tendency to disappear: see John Lynch, *Aristotle's School* (Berkeley & Los Angeles 1972); John Glucker, *Antiochus and the Late Academy* (Gottingen 1978). One of the very few pieces of reliable evidence (perhaps the only one) which we have about how the headship of one of the great schools at Athens and the school property was transmitted (by the individual testamentary disposition of the scholarch) is the correspondence between the Empress Plotina and the head of the Epicurean school in 121CE. See A. Wilhelm, *Jahresheft des oesterr. arch. Inst.* 2, 1899, p. 270; H. Dessau, *Inscriptiones Latinae* II.1,

Berlin 1906, No. 7784, p. 827; cf. H. Diels, *Archiv für Geschichte d. Philosophie* 4, 1891, pp. 486ff. I owe this reference to Dr Peter Kussmaul.

17. Cf. *Commentary on John* I.25.160–66; XIII.13.83–85. For Origen's opinion of important and self-important bishops see *Greek Commentary on Matthew* (ed. Klostermann) XVI.8. For further discussions of Origen's attitude to the earthly church and its bishops see F. H. Kettler, *Der ursprüngliche Sinn der Dogmatik des Origenes*, Berlin 1966, where the evidence is very fully collected, and some speculations of my own in 'Pagan and Christian Traditionalism in the First Three Centuries A.D'. The resemblances and differences between Origen's beliefs about the true, spiritual church and those of Tertullian in his Montanist period (cf. *De Pudicitia* 21) are rather startling.

18. John 4.24. See Origen's great refutation of corporealist interpretations in his *Comm. John* XIII.21.123–24.145.

19. *Adversus Praxean*. 7.

20. There is an excellent statement of the common Hellenic-Christian doctrine of universal divine presence, in the context of a discussion of the 'sending' of the Son, of which Plotinus would have approved (though he might have felt it made belief in the incarnation rather unnecessary) in Augustine, *De Trinitate* II.4.6–5.7.

21. Simplicius, *In Phys.* 181.10ff. (ed. Diels).

22. Diogenes Laertius VIII.25; Simplicius, *In Phys.* 230.41–231.25 (ed. Diels). This passage on the doctrine of Moderatus is quoted by Simplicius from Porphyry, and it cannot be certain that Porphyry did not reword and explain the teaching of Moderatus to bring it closer to that of Plotinus: we cannot therefore be quite sure that Moderatus anticipated the teaching of Plotinus about the three hypostases as completely as is now generally held.

23. It is now easy to study the evidence for the thought of Numenius in the excellent Budé edition of the fragments by É. des Places, Paris 1973.

24. For a succinct statement of this by Plotinus see *Enn.* V.2 [11]; 1.1–3; 2.24–29. The rather elementary confusions which tend to arise when people argue about whether this Neoplatonic doctrine is 'monist' or 'pantheist' or not are usefully cleared up by Plato Mamo in his 'Is Plotinian Mysticism Monistic?', *The Significance of Neoplatonism*, Old Dominion University, Norfolk, Virginia 1976, pp. 199–215.

25. The clearest and fullest expression of this rejection of 'artisan' creation is V.8 [31].7.

26. Edward N. Lee, 'On the Metaphysics of the Image in Plato's Timaeus', *The Monist* 50, 1966, pp. 342–67. For the distinction in Plotinus see VI.4 [22].9–10. [this volume, study VI].

27. Origen, *Peri Archōn* 1.4.

28. For conflict-dualism in Plutarch see *De Animae Procreatione in Timaeo* 6, 1014D–1015C; *De Iside et Osiride*, chapters 45–50, 369A–371E. In Atticus cf. Proclus, *In Tim.* I.381.26–382.12 (ed. Diels). In Numenius, see fr. 52 (ed. des Places) (Test. 30 Leemans).

29. *Laws* X, 896E–897D, combined with *Timaeus* 52–53.

30. *De Iside et Osiride*, chapters 46–47, 369D–370C.

31. *Divine Names* IV.18–35.

32. On the authorship of this scholastic survey of Platonic doctrine see now J. Whittaker's articles 'Parisinus Graecus 1962 and the Writings of Albinus', Parts 1 and 2, *Phoenix* 28, 1974, which give good reasons for restoring it to the obscure Alcinous to whom it is attributed in the manuscripts and no longer, with all modern scholars, regarding it as a work of Albinus.

33. The best account of pre-Plotinian negative theology is to be found in the articles by J. Whittaker referred to in n. 7.

34. The most important passages for understanding what the authentic doctrine of Speusippus might have been are those to which P. Merlan drew attention in his *From Platonism to Neoplatonism*, 2nd ed., The Hague 1960, chapter V: Iamblichus, *De Communi Mathematica Scientia* 4, pp. 15.5–18.12 (ed. Festa); Proclus, *In Parmenidem* (from the part of the commentary which only survives in Latin translation) (ed. and tr. R. Klibansky, C. Labowsky and E. Anscombe, Plato Latinus III), London 1953, pp. 38.32–40.5. There is a good discussion of all the evidence, including Aristotle's, in J. Dillon, *The Middle Platonists*, pp. 12–18.

35. See the article by E. R. Dodds referred to in n. 7.

36. Negative theology in various forms is of course widely fashionable at present. But the pioneer in developing and applying it in its distinctively Neoplatonic form is J. Trouillard. See his 'Valeur Critique de la Mystique Plotinienne', *Revue Philosophique de Louvain* 59, August 1961, pp. 431–44; 'Raison et Mystique chez Plotin', *Revue des Etudes Augustiniennes* 20, 1974, pp. 3–14; 'Théologie négative et autoconstitution psychique chez les Néoplatoniciens', *Savoir, faire, espérer: les limites de la raison*, Brussels 1976, pp. 307–21. I have tried to follow in his footsteps in my 'Escape of the One', *Studia Patristica* 13, Berlin 1975, pp. 77–89 and "Negative Theology", *Downside Review* 319, July 1977, pp. 176–89 [= Plotinian and Christian Studies XXIII and XXIV].

37. The literature on Gregory of Nyssa is enormous. A good brief survey of the most important works (in chapter 1, first part) and up-to-date bibliography are to be found in Kerstin Bjerre-Aspegren, *Braütigam, Sonne und Mutter*, Lund 1977.

38. P. Hadot, *Porphyre et Victorinus*, 2 vols., Paris 1968.

39. See the great SC edition of the theological works of Marius Victorinus by P. Henry and P. Hadot (2 vols., Paris 1960) and the work of Hadot cited in the last note. What is being said here is not, of course, that developed post-Nicene Trinitarian doctrine, even in the form which it takes in Marius Victorinus, is simply a form of the 'Porphyrian' doctrine of the Being-Life-Intelligence triad. All that is suggested is that it belongs much more to the world of thought of late third-to fourth-century Neoplatonism than to that of the New Testament and the Christian

thought of the first and second centuries of our era.

40. The passages quoted, in my own translation, are V.1 [10].4.10–11; V.8 [31].9.14–19 (the remarkable spiritual-intellectual exercise which precedes this prayer should be read to see that the idea of 'coming' here implies no distance or discontinuity): II.9 [33].9.35–42.

41. See especially the work of my friend and colleague at Dalhousie University, Wilfred Cantwell Smith, who has perhaps done more than any other Christian writer of our time to make clear what is in question here and to commend a religious pluralism which is totally removed from indifferentism and lack of faith. One of the best of his many statements on this is a simple-seeming one, his little book *The Faith of Other Men* (paperback ed.), New York 1965. There is much of interest also in the volume *Truth and Dialogue* (ed. John Hick), London 1974, including a remarkable dialogue between W. C. Smith and the editor. But the literature on this subject is now becoming very extensive indeed. An important recent volume is *The Myth of Christian Uniqueness* ed. John Hick and Paul F. Knitter (S.C.M. Press, London 1987). It should be noted that the Platonic position illustrated by my quotations is not 'syncretistic'. All the gods are really different, though difference does not mean separation or division, and all are contained in a greater unity and derive from the transcendent One. No thinkers have ever been more conscious of the immense diversity of heaven than Plotinus and the later Neoplatonists. This non-syncretistic character persists in the last statements of opposition to intransigent Christian monotheism by defenders of Graeco-Roman tradition in the West. See Symmachus, *Relatio* III.10 (= *Ep.* 61) (PL 18.391C), *Uno itinere non potest perveniri ad tam grande secretum*, which, especially in its context, makes clear that the paths are different; and Maximus the Grammarian (Augustine, *Ep.* XVI.4) *Dii te servent, per quos et earum atque cunctorum mortalium communem patrem universi mortales, quos terra sustinet, mille modis concordi discordia veneramur et colimus.*

42. Two extremely enlightening discussions, which on the whole confirm what I have said here, are, on attitudes to body and the material world, Chapter I of E. R. Dodds, *Pagan and Christian in an Age of Anxiety* and, on the practical consequences of the conversion of the Empire to Christianity, A. H. M. Jones, *The Later Roman Empire*, Oxford 1964, and *The Decline of the Ancient World*, London 1966. The latter is an abbreviated version of the former, without its overwhelmingly massive documentation and detailed discussions of evidence; see especially chapter XXIV.

43. Probably second or early third century. But the (unfortunately unpublished) work of Dennis House of Dalhousie University shows quite conclusively that the date of Sextus (and everything else about him) is much more uncertain than many modern scholars suppose. A thoroughly Pyrrhonian attitude should be adopted to statements about Sextus Empiricus, and the 'Sceptical School' in general, in modern scholarly literature.

44. On the influence of Scepticism on Christian writers see A. A. Long, *Hellenistic Philosophy*, pp. 237 and 244–46 and the further references there

233

given.

45. Numenius, *Fragments* 24–8 (ed. des Places) (1–8 Leemans).

46. J. Dillon, *The Middle Platonists*, p. 144 (citing Philo's *De Ebrietate* 162–205 and *De Josepho* 140–2. The first seems to be taken straight from Aenesidemus, the second is clearly based on Plato, *Timaeus* 43Aff.); and p. 188 (Plutarch, titles of lost works from the Catalogue of Lamprias).

47. See the passages cited in note 41 and P. Hadot, *Marius Victorinus*, Paris 1971, chapter III, pp. 6–9.

Addition to note 2

* (ed. Barbara Aland et al., Vanderhoeck & Ruprecht, Gottingen 1978 = Plotinian and Christian Studies XXI).

Pagan and Christian Traditionalism
in the First Three Centuries A.D.

Let us be clear to begin with, about what is meant by "traditionalism" in this context. It is something which goes far beyond the unconscious influence or the free use of traditional material. And it does not mean an attitude to the authorities of the tradition to which one regards oneself as belonging which is respectful but at the same time genuinely critical. This latter attitude is excellently summed up in a few sentences from a sermon of a Christian Platonist of a later century, the Cambridge divine John Smith. "Whilst we plead so much our right to the patrimony of our fathers, we may take too fast a possession of their errors, as well as of their sober opinions. There are *idola specus* – innate prejudices and deceitful hypotheses that many times wander up and down in the minds of good men, that may fly out from them with their graver determinations. We can never be well assured what our traditional divinity is: nor can we securely enough addict ourselves to any sect of men. That which was the philosophers' motto ἐλεύθερον εἶναι δεῖ τῇ γνώμῃ τὸν μέλλοντα φιλοσοφεῖν we may a little enlarge and so fit it for an ingenuous pursuer of divine truth: 'He that will find truth, must seek it with a free judgement and a sanctified mind'."[1] We may find as we study the ancients something in the freedom of spirit with which Origen the Christitian or Plotinus handled the traditions which they regarded as sacred which reminds us of this admirable statement. But they like other thinkers, Christian and pagan, of their time (and John Smith himself and other Christian thinkers of the 17th century and the whole period between it and the age of the early Fathers), would have accepted a restriction on that freedom which many, even among the small minority who have any respect whatever for ancient tradition, would no longer be prepared to accept. They would hold, that is, that there was one traditional authority which was an authority in the full sense, a body of teaching in which the fulness of universal truth was contained and with which it was not permissible to disagree, though of course it had to be interpreted rightly and intelligently. For many, perhaps most, of those few of us now-a-days who still try to believe in some way in a traditional religion and have some veneration for the past, this kind of restriction can no longer hold. For a number of converging reasons, one or

---

[1] John Smith Discourses I, most conveniently accessible in Gerald R. Cragg The Cambridge Platonists (New York 1968): the sentences quoted are on p. 84.

two of which may emerge from this paper, it has become a matter of obligation for us to approach even the most sacred authority and the most venerable tradition in the free critical spirit so admirably expressed by John Smith and to make no exception for Scripture or the most authoritative Church pronouncements.[2] This makes it all the more necessary to study the ancient form of traditionalism as seriously and sympathetically as possible, and to show clearly the degree of genuine freedom and rationality which was possible within its limitations.

We should note at this point that in most cases in the first Christian centuries, among both Christians and pagan philosophers, what we are dealing with is the acceptance of *one* traditional authority, not an undiscriminating blanket acceptance of everything handed down from antiquity. For practically all Christians the Bible stood alone and unchallenged as the one traditional authority in the full sense: though some gnostic sects, the Carpocratians and Naassenes, may have attempted to bring pagan philosophies or mystery-religions into their authoritative tradition.[3] Among the pagan philosophers there were certainly those, like Antiochus of Ascalon in the 1st century B.C. who held that all the great ancient philosophers had taught essentially the same doctrines: the same over-ecumenical attitude is to be found in Hierocles in the 5th century A.D. and was probably not uncommon among the less thoughtful enthusiasts for the ancient philosophical tradition in the intervening period. But the more serious philosophers generally recognised one and only one traditional authority in the full sense. This is obviously true for Epicureans. Stoics are rather more eclectic, but on the whole the conservative Stoics of the Empire seem to have held firmly and exclusively to the main lines of Old Stoic dogma. Genuine Aristotelians are rather difficult to find in our period, but there is no doubt that for the great Alexander of Aphrodisias Aristotle was the one sufficient authority. And for the Platonists, with whom we shall be mainly concerned in this paper, Plato (often coupled with Pythagoras) is the only full traditional authority. Of course the traditional authority might be thought of as presenting in its perfected form a much more ancient wisdom going back to time immemorial. This will be discussed later in the paper, as will also the degree of authority attached to Christian Church and pagan school tradition.

But before we begin to discuss ancient traditionalism in its full and proper sense, the acceptance of an absolute traditional authority, it will be as well to glance at the very large areas in which the kind of free critical examination of earlier thought recommended in my quotation from John Smith could proceed completely freely and without inhibition. Because the thinkers of the

---

[2] Maurice Wiles's books The Making of Christian Doctrine (Cambridge 1967) and The Remaking of Christian Doctrine (London 1974) are excellent examples of this sort of total critical rethinking of the tradition.

[3] For Carpocratian reverence for ancient philosophers see Irenaeus Adv. Haer. I, 25, 6. For Naassene exegesis of mystery-cults and pagan mythology see Hippolytus Ref. V 7–9.

first three centuries A.D. recognised, for the most part, one and only one specific tradition which was for them fully authoritative, there was a great deal of older thought which they could consider freely and criticise uninhibitedly, rejecting what they found unreasonable and unacceptable from the point of view of their own tradition and accepting whatever they found useful for the elucidation and development of that tradition. The so-called "eclecticism" of the philosophers of our period is in most cases, where the more serious thinkers are concerned, a matter of this sort of critical selection and adaptation of useful material from other traditions. The way the Platonists made use of Aristotle and their attitude towards him are particularly interesting in this connection. Aristotle, in spite of his unsparing criticism of Plato, stood in some ways very close to Platonism, and, as is generally recognised, considerable Aristotelian elements are to be found in some forms of Middle Platonism and in Neoplatonism. But Aristotle was never quite accepted into the Platonist canon, so to speak, of Scripture: he never became in the full sense a traditional authority for Platonists. Their attitude towards him varied considerably. Alcinous[4] quietly and without acknowledgement incorporates a great deal of Aristotelian thought into his introductory account of Platonism. Atticus[5] attacks Aristotle in the most passionate tones. Numenius proposed to "separate Plato from Aristotle, Zeno and the Academy".[6] But we have most material for judging the attitude of Plotinus and later Neoplatonists. Plotinus, who had read Aristotle and his commentators extensively and uses a great many Aristotelian ideas, approaches Peripatetic thought with a critical respect very satisfactory to a modern scholar or scholarly philosopher. He thinks that Aristotle does disagree with Plato, and is wrong when he does so, but he takes his ideas seriously, discusses them thoroughly and intelligently, and often finds them worth adopting and adapting. Porphyry and the later Neoplatonists treat Aristotle more respectfully, study and comment on him more closely and thoroughly, and are inclined to minimise the degree of his differences with Plato. But his works are never part of Scripture for them. He is not a traditional authority in the full sense. Most of them (Hierocles the partisan of universal agreement is an exception)[7] think like Plotinus that he disagrees with Plato on important points, and do not hesitate to criticise him when he does.[8] The interac-

---

[4] Professor J. Whittaker's articles ("Parisinus Graecus 1962 and the Writings of Albinus 1 and 2, Phoenix 28 (1974) 3 and 4) give ample reasons for restoring the Didaskalikos to the obscure author to whom it is attributed in the MSS and no longer attributing it to the eminent Albinus.

[5] Ap. Eusebius Praep. Ev. XV 3–9.

[6] Fr. 24 des Places (1 Leemans) 1. 68–69 = Eusebius Praep. Ev. XIV 4. 728 D.

[7] Ap. Photius Bibliotheca III 214 p. 129 Henry (173 A).

[8] The carefully qualified attribution of a limited authority to Aristotle in the lower parts of philosophy by Syrianus in his introduction to his commentary to Books M and N of the Metaphysics should be compared with such criticisms as those of Proclus In Tim I. 252. 11-254. 18: 262. 5–29: 266. 19-268. 23 Diehl which though respectful, are sufficiently deci-

IX

tion of Platonism and Aristotelianism in late antiquity was continuous and fruitful: but the two never fused into a single tradition, then or later.

For the Christians, as has been said, the Bible (as read in the Churches and interpreted by the holy Fathers as soon as there were any) was the sole absolute traditional authority with which it was not permissible to disagree. This meant that the whole of Greek philosophy was free to them for critical reading, selective acceptance or rejection, and adaptation according to the requirements of their own sacred and authoritative tradition. This must be taken into account in assessing the relative degrees of freedom of thought and originality of Christians and pagan philosophers respectively. Here I must reluctantly disagree with a remark made by Dr. H. Chadwick in his admirable chapter on Origen in the Cambridge History of Later Greek and Early Mediaeval Philosophy[9], which represents a point of view fairly widely held among Christian scholars. He says "The Platonism of Celsus, Porphyry, and, for that matter, Plotinus is in its feeling and temper a scholasticism bound by authority and regarding innovation and originality as synonymous with error. They would not have understood an attitude such as that expressed by Origen when he writes that 'philosophy and the Word of God are not always at loggerheads, neither are they always in harmony. For philosophy is neither in all things contrary to God's law nor is it in all respects consonant'." Surely Plotinus, and other Platonists too, could have understood Origen's attitude here perfectly well if they could have overcome the distaste induced by his selection of a barbarian traditional authority. It does not differ greatly from the attitude of Plotinus to Aristotle. Philosophy for Origen was not a traditional authority, but was something to be taken seriously, examined critically, and its conclusions favourably received when they agreed with the traditional authority which he did accept, rationally interpreted. And this is just how Plotinus, as we have seen, regards Peripatetic philosophy. And the later Neoplatonists were perfectly capable of examining earlier philosophers whom they did not regard as authoritative in the full sense, notably Plotinus and Porphyry, accepting their conclusions when they agreed with what they regarded as the reasonable interpretations of Plato and other great traditional divinely inspired authorities, and rejecting them when they did not. Both pagans and Christians of this period were capable of independent and critical thinking in much the same cojndi tions and within much the same limitations. It has been maintained that the much sharper contrasts and conflicts between the Judaeo-Christian and the Hellenic traditions produced more striking and important originalities than the debates between pagan Hellenic philosophers – that they led to the discovery of the concept of personality, the philosophy of Being, and other interesting things. But these large claims do not seem to stand up very well

sive in tone and free of that awestruck reverence for sacred authority of which Proclus is eminently capable.

[9] Part II ch. 11. p. 186.

to close critical examination. It does however remain true that an exceptional degree of freedom and independence can be discerned in the thought of Origen the Christian, as in the thought of Plotinus. Both were later regarded, by their Christian and pagan successors respectively, as deplorably original. An attempt will be made later in the paper to suggest very tentatively a possible reason for this exceptional freedom.

We now need to consider the reasons for the prevalence of this sort of traditionalism in our period and later. It will make for greater clarity if at this point we consider pagan and Christian traditionalists separately, though without losing sight of the very great deal which they had in common. Among the pagans, one important reason for the general swing back to tradition was fear, the sense that inherited ways of life and thinking were disintegrating from within, or, later, under attack from without by those unpleasant and aggressive barbarizers and deserters to an alien way of life and thinking, the Christians. Another particularly strong reason for the traditionalism of later antiquity, which has been given particular prominence by Heinrich Dörrie and others[10], was the general conviction of the age that the oldest is always best, that we live in an age of decadence, at a low point on the universal cycle: that the ancients were nearer to the gods and the beginning of things and therefore knew much more about them than we can: the true, unalterable and unimprovable Logos was revealed in the beginning. It is certainly important to remember this if we are to understand the thought of late antiquity rightly. It was a conviction shared by both pagans and Christians, and the argument from superior antiquity which is based on it played a particularly important part in Jewish and Christian apologetic[11]: though the Christians' conviction of the antiquity of their revelation has theological implications which go deeper than mere polemic, and will be discussed later. This is why Plotinus had to set Amelius and Porphyry to demonstrate elaborately and at great length that the books of the gnostics were recent forgeries, not documents of ancient Oriental wisdom.[12] If the Gnostics had been able to make people believe that their "book of Zoroaster" was really by that ancient sage it would have become immediately highly authoritative.

But I am not entirely satisfied that this explanation of the traditionalism of late antiquity, if it is presented without qualification or reference to the earlier history of Greek thought, accounts completely and satisfactorily for the phenomenon. We need to remember that there was a very strong tendency

---

[10] cp. J. H. Waszink "Bemerkungen zum Einfluss des Platonismus im Frühen Christentum" Vig. Christ. 19. 1965. 129–162: H. Dörrie "Die platonische Theologie des Kelsos in ihrer Auseinandersetzung mit der christlichen Theologie" N. A. G. phil.-hist. 1967, 23–55.

[11] For a fine, vigorous, exaggerated example see Tertullian Apologeticum 19: but the argument is very common, and can be found in much more reasonable people than Tertullian.

[12] Porphyry, Life of Plotinus 16.

to traditionalism, to following ancestral custom in art, literature and social behaviour, even in classical Greece, which would easily extend to philosophy when it had developed to a certain point, when the philosophers had produced intellectual structures which looked to some at least of their contemporaries as complete, final and satisfying as a Doric temple. The fascination of classical Greek literature and thought for us is at least partly due to the fact that they were the products of a society which was both a primitive agricultural, and therfore intensely traditionalist, community and an intensely sophisticated one, with a more than normal proportion of intellectually mature, independent-minded, critical and questioning people. We should have a more vivid idea of the particular flavour of the mental life of a Greek intellectual if we remembered more often and more vividly the sort of things Socrates and Plato (and the women of their families) did when they fulfilled their religious obligations as Athenian citizens. Perhaps, at least when we imagine the great writers and thinkers, we are still too much under the spell of the old classicist picture of gentlemen in white robes singing beautiful hymns before dignified marble statues. We tend to forget the blood and the phallic symbols and images, the lively piglets and lumps of very dead pork with which the most highminded and critical intellectual would inevitably find himself involved when he carried out the normal public and private rituals many of which went back to the Stone Age. Anything which at any period had been brought to what seemed an ultimately satisfactory form by the ancients was repeated with very little change to the end of antiquity by their descendants. And a great deal of this instinctive social and religious traditionalism persisted into late antiquity alongside the self-conscious revivalism and archaism and respect for the ancients based on a theory of primeval revelation and universal decadence prevalent among the tiny educated class.[13]

Further, it seems to me that late Greek traditionalism is perfectly compatible with the belief found among so many Greek intellectuals in the 5th and 4th centuries B.C. in progress up to a point.[14] Man, these intellectuals thought, had indeed progressed from a brutish state. His political institutions, his practical skills, and, eventually, his philosophy, had developed from primitive beginnings to their present much improved condition. But in the phrase "Man *had* progressed", the accent must be on had: progress, it was generally thought, was now finished. A Greek, long before the Roman Imperial period with its general conviction of the decadence of the present

---

[13] A particularly important type of social and cultural traditionalism, which came to have increasing religious significance, was the veneration of the educated classes for the literary classics of Greek and Roman antiquity, which has been so extensively studied by Marrou and others, and was maintained, as they have shown, by the unchanging forms of ancient literary education from early Hellenistic times onwards. This of course was an important reason for the conviction of philosophers that philosophic wisdom was to be found in the ancient poets, mentioned in the next paragraph.

[14] See W. K. C. Guthrie in The Beginning (London 1957) and E. R. Dodds The Ancient Concept of Progress (Oxford 1973).

420

and the superiority of antiquity, might well hold that philosophy had progressed up to a point, but that point was the high point, and all change
thereafter must be decadence, or, at best, clarification of the essential
doctrines and modification of detail. Aristotle, like many great philosophers
since, seems to have thought in this way about his own philosophy. It is
of course true that the thinkers of late antiquity generally believed and were
sometimes seriously concerned to show that the teaching of the great philosophers whom they regarded as supreme traditional authorities presented
in perfected and fully developed form an immemorial wisdom which was
expressed symbolically in the myths told by the ancient inspired poets and
could be found in the teachings of still more ancient Oriental sages: true
philosophy for them had in some way to go back to the beginning of things.
But the degree to which this belief in the immemorial antiquity of the doctrines discovered in the traditional authority was important seems to have
varied a good deal according to the temperament and outlook of individual
thinkers. Plutarch thought it worth while to show at length in his Isis and
Osiris that all the Oriental wisdom known to him agreed with the teaching
of Plato as he understood it. Numenius also clearly considered it important
to show that the teachings of Brahmins and Jews and Magi and Egyptians
agreed with those of Plato and Pythagoras.[15] And to judge from a story told
by Proclus on the authority of Porphyry[16], it seems that the inspired authority of Homer was of quite desperate importance to that rather commonplace
person the pagan Platonist Origen (I hope it is not any longer necessary to
demonstrate that he was a different person from Origen the Christian). This
Origen is reported to have continued bellowing for three days, purple in the
face and streaming with sweat, in furious protest against the idea that Plato
could possibly have meant to suggest that Homer and other ancient inspired
poets were unfit to describe the achievements of the philosophic warriors of
antediluvian Athens in their war with Atlantis.

But when we turn to Origen's greater fellow-student of Ammonius,
Plotinus, the picture is rather different. There is a good deal of evidence in
the Enneads that he shared the general conviction that philosophic wisdom
was to be found allegorically expressed in ancient poetry and mythology.
But, as Cilento has shown[17], this was not a matter of much importance to

---

[15] Fr. 1 a and b des Places (9 a and b Leemans): 8 des Places (17 Leemans).

[16] Proclus In Tim 19 D-E. I 63, 24 ff. Diehl (=fr. 10 Weber). Origen's views (though not
necessarily his emotionalism about them) were shared by the conservative Platonist Longinus (l.c.) The following comments by Porphyry and Proclus are interesting. Porphyry
clearly did not in this context regard Homer as a philosophical authority (though he takes
him considerably more seriously in the De Antro Nympharum). Proclus's concluding settlement of the question is an excellent example of the calm ingenuity with which the later
Neoplatonists reconciled sacred texts and showed to their own satisfaction that there was
really no quarrel between poetry and philosophy, Homer and Plato.

[17] "Mito e Poesia nelle Enneadi di Plotino" Entretiens Hardt V (Les Sources de Plotin)
(Vandoeuvres-Genève 1960) pp. 245–310.

him. And the story of how he tried to go East to study Persian and Indian philosophy suggests that he also shared the general belief in ancient Oriental wisdom[18], though there is very little trace of this in the Enneads[19], and again it does not seem to have been very important to him. As regards philosophy earlier than Plato, his casual references to the Pre-Socratics suggest that he thought that Plato had improved on them very considerably. His attitude to Pythagoras is particularly interesting. For Numenius before him, and for Porphyry and still more Iamblichus after him, that comparatively ancient sage was a traditional authority if anything more venerable, though less universal, than Plato. Pythagoreanism and Platonism formed a single tradition of which the true founder was Pythagoras. But Plotinus twice attacks views which he knows to be attributed to the Pythagoreans – their identification of time with the whole heaven and the famous soul-harmony doctrine.[20] In neither case does he commit himself to saying that the Pythagoreans actually held the views attributed to them by others, and in the second he says clearly that he thinks they have been misunderstood. But he makes no attempt to expound or defend what he considers to be the true Pythagorean doctrines, and is clearly not very much interested in them. And in another passage, from the treatise On the Descent of the Soul[21], in the course of a very rapid survey of Pre-Socratic views on the fall of the soul, he remarks that the "the riddling statements of Pythagoras and his followers on this and many other matters" are no clearer than those of Empedocles (though of course Empedocles makes himself still more obscure by writing poetry). This is hardly even polite to Pythagoras, and suggests an attitude to Pythagoreanism rather more like that of Aristotle than that of Iamblichus. Plotinus was a firm traditionalist in the ancient manner, but it does not seem that he thought that the oldest philosophy was always the best. His one traditional authority in the full sense, the one ancient sage with whom he does not consider it permissible to disagree, is Plato.[22] And it is important to notice that even the more extreme admirers of remote antiquity refer to the most ancient wisdom to confirm, not to criticise, their much more recent supreme traditional authority, who always remains central and uniquely important, and is never thought of as declining from or distorting the primeval Logos.

---

[18] Porphyry Life ch. 3, 15–17.

[19] In the most important passage, the observation on hieroglyphics in V 8 (31) 6 he is careful to leave the question open whether the sages of ancient Egypt arrived at their admirable representation of the non-discursiveness of the intelligible world ἀκριβεῖ ἐπιστήμῃ . . . εἴτε καὶ συμφύτῳ (1–2).

[20] III 7 (45) 2 and 8: IV 7 (1) 84.

[21] IV 8 (6) 1, 17–22.

[22] I have discussed the attitude of Plotinus to Plato at some length in my "Tradition, Reason and Experience in the Thought of Plotinus" Plotino e il Neoplatonismo in Oriente e in Occidente (Rome 1974) pp. 171-194 [= Plotinian and Christian Studies XVII] and given some reasons for doubting Professor Rist's view that Plotinus did occasionally think it permissible to disagree with Plato (pp. 178-180).

Christian attemps to appeal back to the primeval revelation in its pure form in the Jewish Scriptures from the garbled versions given by the Greek philosophers were very ill received by their pagan contemporaries, just as Christians were not best pleased when Jews or pagans suggested that their religion was a recent perversion of the ancient Jewish tradition.

The traditionalism of the Christians of our period and later centuries is first of all to be attributed to the fact that they were men of their age and shared its spirit and outlook. What Dr. Meijering has so well demonstrated about the Father's adaption of certain contemporary ideas [23] applies with even more force to their traditionalist outlook. As he says "One does not choose a 'Zeitgeist', but the 'Zeitgeist' has us in its grip whether we like it or not." [24] As a result of their necessarily independent and hostile attitude to Hellenic pagan rites and the Jewish ceremonial law they were not bound in the same way as their pagan contemporaries by the instinctive traditionalism of Mediterranean societies in matters of religious practice which I mentioned earlier. [25] This contrast became more marked, as far as the philosophers were concerned, in the fourth and succeeding centuries when the last pagan Platonists committed themselves to the defence of all the antique cults and observances of Mediterrranean paganism. But as far as thought was concerned the Christians were as traditionalist as any of their contemporaries. They looked back to a supreme traditional authority with which they held that it was not permissible to disagree even more clearly and firmly than the pagans. And they were convinced, and demonstrated at great length, that the teachings of this supreme authority, the teachings of Christ and his Apostles recorded in the New Testament, were in all essentials the same as those of the Old Testament, the most ancient of Oriental traditions going back to a time long before the earliest of the poets whom the pagans regarded as inspired, and making by comparison Greek philosophy seem, when this was required for apologetic purposes, a very modern and dubious affair. The Christians, as is well known, were very conscious of the apologetic advantage which their claim to possess an immemorial Oriental wisdom gave in their world, and asserted and exploited it to the full. But it would be a grave misjudgement to dismiss the Christian conviction of the unity of the Testaments as nothing more than the result of the spirit of the age or as a successful apologetic device. There were deep religious reasons for it, of which controversy with Gnostics and Marcionites made Christians of the Great Church fully conscious. To maintain the unity of the revealed tradition from the beginning was for them to maintain the unity of God's action in the world. It meant that the Redeemer was also the Creator: that the same God, the same Logos and

---

[23] In the papers collected in his God Being History (Amsterdam-Oxford-New York 1975): cp. also his earlier book Orthodoxy and Platonism in Athanasius (Leiden 1968).

[24] op cit. "What could be the Relevance" p. 150.

[25] p. 419. This sort of instinctive traditionalism, of course, asserted itself with great force in the Church of later centuries.

the same Spirit had acted, spoken, given life and inspired in the beginning and throughout all the ages who continued to do so with even greater fulness and clarity in the new dispensation. This was the orthodox Christians' essential defence in principle against the absolute supernaturalism of the Gnostics, the complete dichotomy between the life of the elect and the irrelevant, futile or evil world in which they found themselves: and it could be the foundation of a very positive attitude to God's good creation and magnificent hope of its total redemption: though it must be admitted that very orthodox Christians who were horrified by Gnostic or Marcionite theology have not infrequently adopted an attitude of practical Gnosticism towards God's creation, or considerable parts of it. Irenaeus' superb exposition of this great theme is well known: and it has recently been very precisely discussed and compared with relevant aspects of the thought of Plotinus in one of the best of Meijering's excellent articles on Irenaeus.[26] It will therefore be unnecessary to discuss it further here, except perhaps to comment briefly on Meijering's mild criticism of some remarks of my own, in a comparison of pagan Neoplatonist and Christian attitudes to the cosmos which I offered in honour of Professor J. H. Waszink.[27] I had detected in general in the Christian thought of the first three centuries and later, as compared with the Platonism of Plotinus, a certain shift of religious emphasis from the natural to the ecclesiastical cosmos resulting in a new and radical sort of religious anthropocentrism, which I suspect may have had far-reaching and rather undesirable consequences. Meijering is undoubtedly right in implying that I should have paid more explicit attention to the doctrine of the unity of Creation and Redemption which he and Irenaeus expound so well: and he is also right in drawing attention to the obvious fact, which I omitted to mention, that the Christians, though they disagree with the Platonists, agree with the Stoics in their anthropocentric view of Divine Providence[28] (this may possibly have had some influence on the monstrous development of theoretical and practical anthropocentrism in post-Renaissance European thought, in the teeth of the discoveries of modern science about the universe and man's place in it). But it still seems to me to be possible that I might have been right as well: that even given the noble doctrine of Irenaeus, and given that it was shared by many other Christian teachers and preached to the faithful of many Christian congregations, the material cosmos as a whole might still have had less religious relevance for Christians than for pagan Platonists, and that there may have been, even in these first centuries, a perhaps at first small but decisive shift towards a "churchy" view of the sacred.

---

[26] "God Cosmos History" Vigiliae Christianae 28. 4. December 1974 pp. 248–276, reprinted in God Being History pp. 52–80.

[27] "Man in the Cosmos" Romanitas et Christianitas ed. W. den Boer et al. (Amsterdam-London 1973) [= Plotinian and Christian Studies XXII].

[28] H. Chadwick, Origen Contra Celsum (Cambridge[2] 1965) X f.

Though the Christians had such deep and good reasons for maintaining the unity of their tradition back to the primal revelation, and found such apologetic advantage in the maintenance of its antiquity, they were of course even more effectively safeguarded than the pagan philosophers from any unthinking assumption that the oldest was always the best. They were as unshakably convinced of the immeasurably superior fulness and power of the revelation given in Christ Incarnate and recorded in the New Testament to that given in the Old as they were of the essential unity and continuity of the two. Their supreme traditional authority was both noticeably more recent and far more authoritative in comparison with earlier utterances of the universal Logos than any great classical Greek philosopher, even Pythagoras or Plato, could seem to the most devoutly traditionalist pagan contemporary. I do not propose at this point, or any other, to make much of the sharp distinction which some might wish to introduce between the authority of "revelation" for the Christians and "reason", even of the most venerable traditionally guaranteed sort, for the philosophers. To do so would, I think, misrepresent the position of the ancient philosophers, who, in our period certainly, and quite often before, were not "rationalists" in any sense in which the word would naturally be used nowadays. The kind of spiritual or intellectual insight, possible only to those who were good as well as wise, which was alone the mark of real philosophical attainment among the ancients, went far beyond rationality as we usually conceive it, and was felt as a participation in and an illumination by the one divine Logos, however precisely it was conceived. Plotinus is the least "supernaturalist" of the Neoplatonists. But he was continually aware of the lifting love and enlightening radiance which came to him from the transcendent Good through the noetic world in which he felt himself rightfully at home. (The difficulties which a modern translator encounters in rendering the Greek word *Nous* perhaps indicate something of what is in question here.) [29] And Porphyry unhesitatingly attributes his master's philosophic attainment to divine guidance.[30] The later Neoplatonists after Iamblichus had a still more explicit sense of the need for divine help and guidance in philosophy, but to discuss their position and its implications would take us too far outside our limits. But for the pagan philosophers the action of God on the human mind is universal and continual; the divine light is always available to all men according to their capacity to attain it. Till we come to the later Neoplatonists, they do not think much in terms of particular revelations. And the Christians *were* thinking in terms of a particular revelation given to special groups of men, the old and the new Israel: groups, moreover, which were thought of in some way as representing the whole human race. We encounter here the paradox which has been a great source of strength to the Church in ancient times, as of increasing weakness in more modern ones: the universal claims of a so-

---

[29] cp. the interesting remarks of Cilento and others in Entretiens Hardt V pp. 421–425.
[30] Life ch. 23.

ciety which in fact is, and always has been, obviously particular and peculiar. It was this vivid awareness of a recent particular revelation with universal claims which transcended and at the same time fulfilled and was con-
tinous with the earlier revelation which led to the development of the form
which some early Christian thinkers gave to the general Judaeo-Christian
conviction that God works out his purposes in human history. This was the
great doctrine of God's gradual education of the human race through his
progressive self-revelation, again best expounded by Irenaeus[31], and explicitly extended by Clement of Alexandria[32] to the divine education of the
Greeks through philosophy, a doctrine which goes well beyond the classical
Greek ideas of intellectual progress referred to earlier.

A distinction which is not always sufficiently clearly made in considering
ancient traditionalism is that between the authority of the original teaching
of the Founder of Church or School and the authority of the continuing
tradition, the interpretation of that teaching in the church or school itself.
It would be simple, but rather over-simplified, to dismiss the question of the
differences here apparent between pagan philosophers and Christians by
saying that the Church and a philosophical school are very different sorts
of entities. This is true, but the differences between them are interesting
and deserve a little closer examination in this context. In studying any
philosophical school of our period, especially the Platonist, which was most
important and about which we know most, we discover that though the
authority of the Founder was absolute, the authority of school tradition was
very slight indeed. Ancient philosophical traditionalism was not "scholastic"
in any very meaningful sense of the word. The authority of the School
was no sort of court of appeal. There was plenty of the "I read it in a book
therefore it is true" sort of mentality about, and unintelligent and unoriginal
people, then as now, simply reproduced what they had been taught or read.
But the attitude of serious philosophers to their predecessors as well as their
contemporaries in the School was highly independent and critical. It is now
well established that this was the attitude of Plotinus to the commentators
who were read at his lectures and the school traditon in general.[33] But the
most interesting evidence here comes from Numenius, now so much more
accessible to us thanks to the admirable new edition of the fragments by
Professor des Places.[34] In the fragments which Eusebius has preserved of his
acidulous and unfair, but penetrating and often entertaining book On the
Disagreement of the Academics with Plato he shows himself an extreme

[31] Adv. Haer. IV 9, 11, 14, 20, 28. cp. Meijering art. cit. pp. 259–260 (pp. 63–64 of God
Being History).
[32] e.g.: Strom. 1. 5, 28, 1 with its precise parallelism of the educative functions of Greek
philosophy and the Jewish Law. cp. Salvatore Lilla Clement of Alexandria (Oxford 1971)
ch. 1 where many further references are given.
[33] H. Dörrie "Plotino-Tradizionalista o Innovatore" Plotino e il Neoplatonismo (Rome
1974) 195–201 is one of the latest and best treatments of the subject.
[34] Paris 1973.

IX

426

traditionalist in the sense in which the word has been used in this paper. He says of Plato's immediate successors καὶ γὰρ με δάκνει ὅτι μὴ πᾶν ἔπαθόν τε καὶ ἔδρων σώζοντες τῷ Πλάτωνι κατὰ πάντα πάντῃ πάσην ὁμοδοξίαν.[35] And he goes on, very strikingly for a Platónist, to praise Epicureans for their devout and absolute fidelity to the teachings of their master and their condemnation of innovation as impiety.[36] It is clear that ὁμοδοξία with Pythagoras and Plato is as important to Numenius as ὀρθοδοξία to the most traditionalist Christian. But his attitude to the School is in the highest degree disrespectful. Any dogmatic and traditionalist Platonist would of course have had to repudiate the rather long sceptical period in the history of the Academy, and the fact that there had been this period may have affected the Platonic attitude to school tradition in general, though there is no evidence that it differed greatly from that of the other dogmatic schools. (The Epicureans, as Numenius remarks, claimed to have no distinct school tradition at all, but simply to preach from generation to generation nothing more or less than the pure gospel of the Founder). Numenius, however, extends his disapproval well beyond the Sceptical Academy. Antiochus, the restorer of dogmatic teaching in the school, is dismissed as an innovator.[37] And, more remarkably still, Plato's immediate successors, including his immediate disciples and close associates Speusippus and Xenocrates and Polemo, Xenocrates' convert, are accused of giving up a great many of Plato's ideas and distorting (στρεβλοῦντες) others[38] − though Numenius might have been expected to be sympathetic to them because of their Pythagoreanizing tendencies as well as their closeness to Plato. The traditionalism of Numenius, though rigid and absolute, is a traditionalism of return to the sources rather than of maintenance of a continuing tradition − one might almost speak of it anachronistically as a Liberal Protestant traditionalism.

It is fairly easy to see some reasons for the lack of authority of the continuing traditions of the philosophical schools in this very traditionalist age. The pursuit of philosophical wisdom was always an individual matter, the struggle to follow a personal vocation, though it was generally begun under the guidance of an often deeply revered master and carried on in a group of like-minded friends. The philosophical schools were never institutionalized even to the extent of the Churches of the first three centuries. There was nothing in late antiquity resembling a mediaval or modern university. And it is important to realise that the headship of such rudimentary institutions as there were (such as the Platonic Academy at Athens) or the holding of an official chair conferred no authority whatever on a philosopher. The Platonic Diadochi in the lifetime of Longinus and Plotinus were clearly quite insignificant persons who enjoyed no prestige of office among Platonists.[39]

[35] Fr. 24 (1 Leemans) p. 63, 16–18 des Places.
[36] l. c. lines 23–31.
[37] Fr. 28 (8 Leemans).
[38] Fr. 24 (1 L.) ad init. p. 62 des Places. [39] Porphyry, Life chs. 15 and 20.

There were no philosophical bishops, no persons in the philosophical world who were recognised as having authority to teach, and special divine assistance to enable them to do so rightly, in virtue of their office. It is possible that European attitudes to official Christianity may have been considerably influenced by the existence at the beginning of this alternative, unofficial, individual way of thinking about and teaching religious truth and the remembrance and persistent revival of it in later centuries. The bishops have never had it quite their own way because there has always been at least the danger of an outbreak of philosophy in the ancient manner and attempts at inoculation with an episcopally approved philosophy have never been very successful.

We all know that on the Christian side things were very different, at least in the Great Church. The rather Epicurean view of tradition so well expounded by Irenaeus was generally accepted. Sects and heresies there had indeed been, perhaps from the beginning, but the main tradition had always been and remained one, uniform and unchanging. To discover what Christ and his Apostles (between whom difference was inconceivable) had truly meant to teach, one only needed to consult the contemporary teaching of the Churches; and this meant more and more clearly from the second century onwards the teaching of the bishops. There are many ways of looking at and accounting for this much greater emphasis on the community and its continuing tradition in the Christian Church than in the philosophical schools. One reason for it which seems to me important is that for the pagans God's self-revelation was natural and universal and needed no special body to carry it other than that of the cosmos and the whole community of its intelligent inhabitants, especially of course those of Hellenic culture. The great philosopher who was accepted as the authority in a particular school had seen with incomparable clarity what God had to say to men in the universe, but he had seen what in principle was available to all. But the Christians, as has been said before[40], were thinking in terms of a special revelation given at one particular time, and such a special revelation requires a particular body to carry it, and special divine assistance and safeguarding to ensure that it continues to be reproduced authentically in each succeeding generation: this is particularly important if the core of the revelation consists in a number of what are asserted to be historical facts, which must not be allegorized away or deprived of their true significance by a too free interpretation.

But, though great emphasis on the continuing tradition of the Church is indeed characteristic of the Christian thought of our period, ecclesiastical traditionalism was not yet as rigid as it became increasingly from the fourth century onwards. (To discuss the various reasons for this increasing rigidity and elaboration, and the rather similar rigidity and elaboration which developed in the pagan Platonic school of the fifth and sixth centuries would

[40] p. 424.

require another paper.) But the Church in our period had not so much to say authoritatively as it had later, and here and there, especially at Alexandria, a good deal of freedom is apparent in the attitude to what it did say. Clement of Alexandria and Origen the Christian are thoroughly traditionalist in the sense that they hold that all truth is contained in the doctrine of Christ preached by the Apostles and contained in the Scriptures and that no genuine seeker after truth can go outside or disagree with this inexhaustibly vast body of authoritative teaching, the letter of which, at least, is transmitted in the Church of which they are loyal members. But Origen, to a considerably greater extent than Clement, feels himself free to go very far beyond the ordinary elementary teaching of the Churches here below and their bishops, and does not take a very high view of these or regard their authority with profound respect.[41] He moves in the great world of the Scriptures with extraordinary freedom and confidence in his spiritual insight, and propounds original doctrines highly disconcerting to the ordinary Churchman with great assurance and absolute conviction that they represent the real meaning of Scripture. There is a certain likeness here to the freedom with which Plotinus handles Plato and the confidence which he has that his spiritual insight will enable him to attain the deepest truths of Platonic doctrine; though there are also important differences. Origen is much more concerned with detailed exegesis than Plotinus (he resembles Porphyry more closely here), though his methods are such that this does not inhibit his original insight. And there is another way in which a peculiar spirit of freedom seems to manifest itself in the teachings of the great pagan and the great Christian. In both the spirit of man can range freely through the spiritual universe from the summit to the lowest depths. There are of course most important differences between Origen's vision of the cyclic history of the community of free spirits and Plotinus' more static conviction that the self has no bounds or limits which it cannot transcend. But in both of them the spirit is free, able to transcend all limits till it reaches union with God[42], not fixed in its appropriate place in a rigid hierarchy. And I think that it is possible that this conviction of unlimited spiritual freedom may have something to do with the ease and freedom of their exegesis of traditionally authoritative texts.

---

[41] I find F. H. Kettler's view of Origen on the whole convincing. See his "Der ursprüngliche Sinn der Dogmatik des Origenes" (Berlin 1966). On Origen's attitude to the earthly Church ἡ νομιζομένη (or ὀνομαζομένη ἐκκλησία) cp. the mass of passages collected by Kettler from the works which survive in Greek in his enormous note 190 (pp. 48–51), and especially the passage from the Commentary on John on 4. 21 (worship in spirit and in truth, XIII 16. 240, 11 ff).

[42] W. Theiler has noted this characteristic of the thought of Origen, but makes no comparison with Plotinus, and because of his mistaken reliance on the Hierocles text in Photius as a source of information about Ammonius, makes it a point of separation between Ammonius and Origen: "Ammonios der Lehrer des Origenes" Forschungen zum Neuplatonismus, Berlin 1966) pp. 30 ff.

If it is really possible to detect an unusual spirit of freedom and originality which set Origen the Christian and Plotinus somewhat apart from their contemporaries, and made them both seem deplorable innovators and heretics to their more conservative traditionalist successors, it is tempting, though hazardous, to speculate that the man who taught them both, Ammonius, might have had something to do with it. During this last year a seminar at Dalhousie University, under my direction, set itself to examine the scanty evidence yet again in the faint hope that we might find some light on this mysterious figure. As was to be expected, we emerged from our studies knowing no more about any doctrines which Ammonius may have taught than Professor E.R. Dodds[43], that is to say next to nothing. But, considerably to our surprise, we found ourselves with a very vivid impression of the sort of man he might have been. We came to see him as a man of the highest spiritual attainment, what my Oriental friends, on whose help in understanding the thinkers of late antiquity I increasingly rely, call a "Mahatma" or a "Hakim": a man who, by example perhaps more than precept, inspired confidence in his pupils that it was possible to ascend to the summit of the spiritual world (however the nature of that summit and the reasons for that possibility were conceived, and these may have been matters which were discussed endlessly and inconclusively in his circle). With this may perhaps have gone a freedom in handling traditional texts which would be a natural consequence of his consciousness of spiritual achievement. This at least would have been the sort of man of whom Plotinus could have said τοῦτον ἐζήτουν, and with whom he could have stayed happily for eleven years[44]: and the sort of man who could have done something to bring out the spiritual confidence and powerful originality of Origen the Christian. (Origen the pagan, from what little we know about him, does not seem to have taken light from his master in the same way: but the closest associates of great philosophers do not always seem to appreciate their masters fully or share their deepest insights. Numenius was, after all, probably not so far wrong about Speusippus and Xenocrates.[45] Theophrastus was never very comfortable with Aristotle's metaphysics. And if we see Ammonius as a sort of late antique Socrates, we might see Origen the pagan as his Xenophon.)

I have given some reasons for not taking very much account of the distinction between "revelation" and "reason", except in the form of a distinction between a universal and continuous and a particular, once-for-all divine self-communication or self-manifestation. But it is important that we should take account of the distinction between "authority" and "reason", and I shall conclude this paper by discussing briefly how the traditionalist pagans and Christians of the first three centuries, and later, saw the relationship between the two. In this context I would define a reasonable man, one who

---

[43] "Numenius and Ammonius", Entretiens Hardt V, pp. 24—61 (with full discussion).
[44] Porphyry, Life ch. 3.
[45] above p. 426.

genuinely and seriously recognises the necessity of reason, as one who feels obliged to try to give an account of what he believes which is coherent and internally consistent and also in accord with all human experience which is available to him. In this sense I believe that the best and greatest thinkers, pagan and Christian, of our period and the succeeding traditionalist centuries, were eminently reasonable men. There were of course plenty of Christians in our period, of whom the best known example is Tertullian[46], who insisted very strongly on the weakness and corruption of human reason due to original sin and saw their traditional authority as opposed to, authoritative against, and overriding human reason. This is a position which it has always been tempting for Christians to adopt, and many less anti-rational Christians than Tertullian, men like the Cappadocian Fathers and Augustine, who did try very hard to make reasonable sense of the authoritative tradition, sometimes use this sort of language (it would be unkind, but not altogether untrue, to suggest that it is particularly attractive to controversialists when they get into intellectual difficulties and find themselves faced with rational arguments to which they cannot think of an answer). It is a position which can be (and frequently was) powerfully supported by the arguments from the disagreements of the philosophers so ingeniously used by the ancient Sceptics, which were particularly well set out in our period by Sextus Empiricus. But it is quite alien to the minds of any of the philosophers of late antiquity who made positive contributions to religious thought. It is not to be found in the later Neoplatonists, Iamblichus and his successors, who are so often unfairly accused of gross superstition and irrationalism. If we are to make a fair comparison between Christians and pagans and appreciate the real rational strength of ancient traditionalism we need to pay more attention to a very different view of the relation between authority and reason which is generally current in our period.

According to this, tradition is accepted as authoritative because in it is found the perfection of wisdom. It is assumed with complete confidence that whatever is found in the documents of traditional authority will, if properly investigated, turn out to be perfectly reasonable and, in all essentials, consistent. There can therefore be no question of a clash between reason and traditional authority: the two cannot be opposed. All important truths are to be found in the Scriptures or in Plato: and right interpretation of them will show that their teaching is both perfectly coherent in itself and alone adequate to give a reasonable account of all human experience. This seems to me to be the position of Plotinus and other pagan Neoplatonists, and Justin, Clement and Origen and, on the whole, of most of the most intelligent traditional Christians in succeeding centuries. It is important, if justice is to be done to them that this should be fully understood.[47] They are not traditiona-

---

[46] See e.g. De Praescriptione Haereticorum 6–12.

[47] This and the four sentences immediately following are taken from my Rome paper, Tradition, Reason and Experience in the Thought of Plotinus, p. 173.

lists or authoritarians in a way which requires the conscious perversion of reason to comply with the demands of traditional authority. When confronted with a piece of apparent nonsense in the tradition, they do not accept it as higher sense, or ineffably superior to sense. They, so to speak, take hold of it by the scruff of the neck and shake it till it makes sense. They apply whatever exegetical violence is necessary to produce an interpretation in accordance with reason. Their confidence in the total reasonableness of the traditional authority is absolute and unbounded, and their confidence in their own ability to interpret its teachings in the only rational, and therefore the only right, way, is hardly less so. This absolute confidence at once in authority and reason is the source of the intellectual strength and creativity of the Fathers and the great philosophers of their age.[48] But it is a confidence which most of us cannot share. We are too deeply affected by a sense of historical relativity to accept the teaching of any traditional authority as absolutely definitive and all-sufficient and we are too vividly conscious of our own relativity and limitations to believe that our methods will bring us to final and universal truth. Whatever we learn from the ancients, and I believe that we can learn very much, will have to be received in a spirit of honest tentativeness and perennially questioning uncertainty which would have horrified our teachers.

---

[48] Something should be said here about the very different attitude of the great Galen, esteemed by his contemporaries as a philosopher as well as a physician, at the end of the 2nd century A.D. This has been admirably discussed and documented by R. Walzer in his well known and often quoted Galen on Jews and Christians (Oxford 1949). Galen was certainly not a traditionalist in the sense in which the word has been used in this paper and could, as Walzer abundantly shows, be called a "Hellenic rationalist" without further explanation or qualification. But Walzer was rather inclined to see Galen as more typical of the pagan Hellenic thought of his own period and the preceding century than I think that he actually was. Galen himself was fully conscious that his independent-mindedness, his explicit refusal to give unqualified allegiance to any tradition, philosophical or medical, was most uncommon in his own time. This is particularly clear in the passage De pulsuum differentiis iii 3: VIII 656. 8 Kuehn so well discussed by Walzer (pp. 37ff.). And I think that anything like it had been uncommon and untypical for some considerable time before him: it did not represent the attitude of most professed philosophers. As for Walzer's very interesting discussion of possible Galenic influence on Theodotus and his group of Monarchians at Rome (ch. III, p. 75ff), it does not seem to show that they were not traditionalists in the sense in which the word has been used here. Even if we accept as exact everything said by the heresiologists about their Hellenizing rationalism, it only shows them as engaging in just the sort of exegesis which has just been described, with all the help which Hellenic logic could give them. And their alleged passion for emending the text of the Scriptures is in its way a sign of extreme traditionalism. If the sacred and authoritative text cannot be made by the most vigorous exegesis to give a thoroughly reasonable sense, then the text as it stands in the available MSS cannot be correct. It must therefore be emended till it does give a reasonable sense.

X

Philosophy theology and interpretation
the interpretation of interpreters

This is an attempt to understand the traditionalist religious thinkers of the Mediterranean and European worlds in the period before the rise of the universities and the official separation of theology from philosophy. To come to some comprehension of the unity of their thought, and of the manner in which they interpreted ancient wisdom and how it differed from our own interpretative activities, is likely to be helpful, and may even be essential, for those who wish to maintain some living contact with the wisdom of the past in our own very different world of thought.

To begin with, let us enquire what sort of an activity philosophy was in the Mediterranean world in the first centuries of the Christian era. What did philosophers think their business was, and how did they proceed? It is a commonplace that philosophy was, for the serious philosophers of this period, an all-embracing activity requiring total engagement. The philosophic wisdom which was sought, though it might be the attainment of *theoria*, was not a matter of "theory" having little, if any, relation to life and conduct. Progress towards it required reformation of life, and attainment of it would mean complete transformation of life. This must never be forgotten. But what we need to enquire for our present purposes is how the philosophers went about their business on what we, with our more compartmentalised way of thinking, would call the "theoretical" or "intellectual" side. Plotinus, the one great philosopher of the period, whom we can see closely and clearly at work if we illustrate what we are told in Porphyry's *Life* by a close study of his own writings, provides an excellent example of the assumptions and methods of a late Hellenic philosopher, though perhaps an exceptionally favourable and impressive one. This is later Greek philosophy at its best: but what we are told by Porphyry and can gather for ourselves from the Enneads does not seem incongruous with our evidence about his Platonist predecessors and successors[1]. The impression we gain from Porphyry's *Life* (especially chapters 8 and 13) and from reading the Enneads is of a philosopher who is determined not to depart consciously from the traditional teaching which he regards as authoritative, that of Plato: who is equally determined to satisfy the most rigorous demands of rational discussion and discourse, to answer all questions which can be asked on the level of discursive reason, in spite of his considerable doubts about its status and capacity: and whose thought is guided by his constant, illuminating,

---

[1] I have tried to discuss this more fully in my "Pagan and Christian traditionalism in the First Three Centuries A. D." [= Plotinian and Christian Studies IX].

direct experience or awareness of the spiritual realities which he tries, with conscious inadequacy, to discuss and describe². The particular blend of tradition, reason and experience which we find in Plotinus is of course unusual in the relative (by no means absolute) freedom with which he moves within the tradition, in the power of his reasoning, and the transforming and contagious intensity of his experience. But surely some blending of these three elements, varying both in the quality of the elements and the proportion of the mixture according to the periods, environments and persons concerned, is generally characteristic of late antique and early mediaeval thought. And it seems to leave no room for a separate intellectual discipline which can be called "theology" as distinct from that highest philosophy which interprets sacred tradition rationally in the light of the philosophers' experience of God. Christians in the first centuries found it quite natural to present their doctrine to the educated world as the one true philosophy. (It would be interesting, but irrelevant here, to consider the grounds of tradition, reason and experience on which the Hellenes rejected this claim). And they did not for many centuries feel the need to distinguish and define a theology distinct from philosophy³.

Even, however, if they did not do so, we may at least be able to detect some characteristics of Christian thought, even in the first centuries, which prepared the way for the later separation. The weight of their primal authority, Scripture as read in the community, was greater (though the degree of difference should not be exaggerated) than the weight of their primal authorities was for Hellenes before Iamblichus. (The use of the word "read" in the last sentence should be noted. It seems useful in the course of the present investigation to use it in the large sense which it and its equivalents in other European languages can have, when one speaks of "reading" a text with one's students. This includes exposition and, where it is appropriate and relevant, application to our own circumstances). And it was not only that saving and transforming wisdom could be found there by the spiritual and intellectual search of illuminated men-even Origen clearly admitted that simple faith saved the simple. There was always for Christians the possibility of an kind of fideism, the defiant assertion of an irrational faith to which God had given the victory over reason⁴. The authority and institutional weight of the community itself was also much greater for Christians. For a Hellenic philosopher the only decisive authority was that of the founder of the school to which he adhered and, sometimes, of a loved and revered personal master. The authority of the school counted for very little⁵, largely because the philosophical "schools" of late antiquity seem to have

---

² For a more detailed and documented account see my "Tradition, Reason and Experience in the Thought of Plotinus" in Plotino e il Neoplatonismo in Oriente e in Occidente (Roma 1974) pp. 171-194, [= Plotinian and Christian Studies XVII].

³ Albertus Magnus still does not make exactly this distinction: see R. D. Crouse "Philosophia Ancilla Theologiae" in the proceedings of the Fifth International Congress of Mediaeval Philosophy held in Madrid in 1972; the conclusions of this are summarized in "St. Thomas, St. Albert, Aristotle: philosophia ancilla theologiae" in: Tommaso d'Aquino nella storia del pensiero I (Naples 1975) pp. 181-185.

⁴ I have discussed this further in "The Self-Definition of Christianity in relation to Later Platonism" in: Jewish and Christian Self-Definition I: The Shaping of Christianity in the Second and Third Centuries ed. E. P. Sanders (London 1980) pp. 74-99. [this volume, study VIII].

⁵ Further discussion in "Pagan and Christian Traditionalism" (see n 1).

had far less corporate substantiality and institutional continuity than we are sometimes inclined to suppose. We may give ourselves very false impressions if we talk carelessly about the "Sceptical School", or describe the informal circles of Ammonius at Alexandria or Plotinus at Rome as "schools". But for Christians, even in very early times, it was extremely important to belong to the holy community, the people of God, and to choose rightly, when occasion arose, among the various communities which claimed that title. This meant remaining within the limits (admittedly very much more liberal at first than they afterwards became) of what the community considered tolerable belief and tolerable interpretation of apostolic teaching. It is important also that the Christian communities from the second century had teachers who claimed an *ex-officio* charisma. One of the reasons for the eventual separation of philosophy from theology may well be that there have never been bishops among philosophers. This weight of the community and of the traditions, decisions and doctors it accepted, of course grew enormously from the end of the third century onwards[6]. All this meant that, though the kind of intellectual activity pursued by Christians and pagans in the centuries we are considering remained a single kind of activity, it became among the Christians more and more what we should call "theological" and less and less what we should call "philosophical". And this, combined with the fact that a more "philosophical" kind of philosophy, recognized as pre-existing, outside, and not dominated by Christian tradition, continued to be studied as a preparation and to provide tools for the great work of interpreting sacred tradition, pointed the way forward to the eventual separation of theology and philosophy into distinct disciplines, with all its consequences.

We can, perhaps, best sum up what the thinkers of the period with which we are concerned had in common in a way which does not obscure the differences between them by saying that what they are all engaged in is *interpretation*[7]. Does this set them apart sufficiently from thinkers of other periods? Theology, in the normal Christian sense, must always be predominantly interpretation, and it plays a much larger part in even the most antitraditionalist and anti-authoritarian philosophy than is generally admitted. But the Hellenic philosophers of the earlier part of our period are unusually close to "theologians", as we should call them, in the degree to whilch they consciously regard their task as an interpretation of a tradition which is sacred and authoritative for them, and it is partly this which makes them so difficult to distinguish from the "theologians": though only partly, because one must also take into account their preferred subject-matter, which is God, and the large ancient conception of "reason". It seems, then enlightening to think of all our thinkers, both Hellenes and Christians, as interpreters of a special sort, which may be qualified as "traditionalist." They are engaged in the reading of sacred documents (in the large sense of "reading" already explained): and they are reading them with special sorts of diffidence and confidence about their task, diffe-

---

[6] Cp. R. A. Markus "The Problem of Self-Definition: From Sect to Church" in: The Shaping of Christianity in the Second and Third Centuries A. D. (see n. 4) pp. 1-15.

[7] And of course increasingly as we pass from late antiquity to Byzantium and the mediaeval West, interpretation of interpretation: for this in Eriugena cp. Dominic O'Meara. "L'Investigation et les Investigateurs dans le De Divisione Naturae" in: Jean Scot Eriugena, et l'Histoire de la Philosophie (Paris 1977) pp. 225-233.

rent from our own. If we investigate these it may prove to be helpful in enabling us to understand better both their originality and their dependence on their sources.

The greatest of their diffidences is one which we can to some extent share with them. This springs from the strong awareness that our great subject of study, God, always escapes us: our nets of thought and speech cannot catch him in the reticulate articulations which are necessary for all intelligible discourse. This awareness is strongest, most fully developed and most powerfully expressed and transmitted in the central Neoplatonic tradition of "negative theology" but is not necessarily confined to Neoplatonists either in ancient or in modern times. There is a real continuity here between our different worlds. But the difference between them is apparent in the way this liberating negative assurance is related to our several ways of faith and belief. The traditionalist interpreters generally do not doubt the powers of their thought and speech to apprehend and express, truly even if inadequately, everything in the spiritual or intelligible world below the highest. Nor, however deeply and thoroughly they accept Neoplatonist "negative theology," do they doubt that certain authoritatively guaranteed ways of thinking and speaking about God are privileged ways with an unique, divinely given power to help us towards him. They can therefore still believe that there is one true philosophy or one and one only divine revelation. Many of our contemporaries, including some whom we must respect, remain of course in this position. But those of us from whose point of view this paper is written have been driven out of the sanctuaries of archaic certitude by the pressures of contemporary experience and above all by the demands of the discipline of critical history soon to be discussed. And in these circumstances the awareness conveyed by the "negative theology" provides a ground of faith in the unknown and unknowable God which remains unshaken in the dissolution or relativizing of our beliefs and an endless stimulus to further criticism of all "God-talk," whether archaizing or self-consciously modern.

Another great diffidence of the traditionalist interpreters is that which springs form their conviction of the immeasurable superiority of the ancient sources of their tradition. This is something we can never quite share, though we may have reacted much too far in the opposite direction. For them the Scriptures or the Dialogues of Plato represented a wisdom far greater than any they or their generation could originate. They could add nothing to it except clearer explication. Their task was to interpret, not to innovate, because anything new must be inferior, if not positively false and evil. We, on the other hand, are too easily inclined to think that we and our contemporaries have more of the fullness of wisdom than is to be found in ancient writings, and to regard the blessed ancients as superannuated figures mainly of historical interest (in the derogatory sense of that phrase). We may be able to some extent to correct this conceit by study, but we can never quite return to the innocent immediacy of the reverence for the ancient wisdom of the traditionalist interpreters. However deeply we may come to revere the past, we are conscious of difference and distance in a way they were not: and this leads us from considering their diffidence to considering their confidence.

There are two sides to this confidence. One is an absolute confidence in their great authorities which does not only inspire the diffidence just mentioned, the sense of inferiority and inadequacy, the fear of introducing new thoughts because anything new must certainly be worse. It involves some very positive convictions. There is the conviction that the whole of wisdom is contained in the traditional authority. There is no question which the ancients cannot answer. Interpreters may have to dig deep, far below the surface of the sacred texts: they may have to build great edifices of interpretation on a few words, to make much of hints and copiously fill out elliptical statements. But in principle it is all there: there is at least nothing of serious importance which we need to know for enlightenment or salvation about God, man or the world which is not contained in whatever is Scripture for the tradition if it is read in the proper way[8]. And necessarily bound up with this is the conviction that this whole is consistent and coherent. The divine and ancient Logos cannot contradict itself. This is a double confidence which it is hard for many of us to share now-adays. We are conscious of the difference, distance and multiplicity of wisdoms and worlds of thought in an way in which the older traditionalists were not, and we are sadly aware that none of the ancient wisdoms, nor all of them put together, if to put them together were possible, can answer all the questions which we must ask. We see that, even if we can learn very much from an ancient world of thought, it is always a different world of thought and not our world. Its frontiers are remote, and its limitations other. And we are forced by the pressure of our historical – critical studies of the revered ancient documents to admit that they are not only inadequate and in some ways unsatisfying but inconsistent and incoherent: and we do this (or at least we should do it) not in a spirit of arrogant and destructive cocksureness, a conviction that the ancients are antiquated muddlers and that we alone can think coherently and have all the answers, but in a sober conviction of our responsibilities as historians to our own consciences and our own time. When we speak of ourselves as historians, we mean something which the great traditionalist interpreters of the past would not have quite understood. And this brings us to consider the other side of their confidence.

This is a confidence in their methods of interpretation which, in spite of the diffidence already mentioned about their merits as independent thinkers, was in principle absolute. Origen interpreting Scripture, or Plotinus interpreting Plato, or Eriugena interpreting Scripture and Holy Fathers, was sure that what he discovered would not only be perfectly conformable with reason, but with his reason, and that his reason, guided by the continual inner illumination of *Nous* or *Logos*[9] would be adequate to discover the anciently expressed but timeless truth contained in his sacred documents: and would be able to do so without abandoning or changing the contemporary and customary procedures of discourse and search, which were not for him contemporary but equally timeless. An ancient traditionalist had little sense of the barriers of time or the strangeness of the past. Plotinus, who seems to have had less reverence for antiquity as such than most other thinkers of late antiquity, does complain, in a quite Aristotelian manner, of the obscurity and inadequacy of some Pre-Socratic statements[10]. But he does not regard

---

[8] The attitude of the Gnostics here was rather different. See Elaine Pagels "Visions, Appearances and Apostolic Authority" in: Gnosis FS f. H. Jonas (Göttingen 1978) pp. 415-430. But the Gnostic reliance on continuing revelation through visions did not commend itself to the church or the Platonic School and is not likely to be very acceptable to modern scholarly interpreters.

[9] On the Hellenic philosophers' sense of inner illumination from above see my "Pagan and Christian Traditionalism in the first three centuries A. D." in: Studia Patristica (see n. 1).

[10] IV 8 (6) 1: V 1 (10) 8.

them as stating another kind of philosophy, but as stating the one true philosophy rather badly. Parmenides and Plato's Parmenides are expounding essentially the same doctrine, the true Platonic doctrine as Plotinus understood it (he of course would have omitted that last qualification). But Plato's Parmenides expounds it better.

This kind of confidence is one which those of us, at least, who have been sufficiently trained in the exacting and at times devastating disciplines of critical history can no longer share. Those who have been trained in other kinds of discipline, or who have successfully subordinated their scholarship to the requirements of some dogmatic system wrongly supposed to be timeless and universal, or at least treated as if it were, still quite often seem to display it. But this does not commend their conclusions to us. We are conscious that there are many houses of language and countries of the mind, none of them timeless or universal, all marked off more or less strongly from each other by differences in space and time and all the manifold particularities of history, and that our own thought-worlds and language-houses (in any representative gathering of historians there will be several) are as limited as any. We can never completely unify the frontiers of our own thought with those of the thought-worlds of the ancients whom we try to interpret, and if we could succeed perfectly in this we should no longer be able to interpret them to our contemporaries. Even where our evidence is perfectly complete and adequate for interpretation and we are equally well informed about and well fitted to understand all of it, which is almost never the case, the very scholarly disciplines to which we have to submit ourselves in the pursuit of understanding and the self-conscions attitude which we have to assume towards their thought-worlds and our own and those of our contemporaries (to say nothing of many intermediate thought-worlds) prevent perfect assimilation: for all our strivings to understand and interpret are given their particular character by our own limited historicity, and we know it. We are finding more and more that histories of interpretations are an indispensable part of our scholarly equipment. But anyone who writes a history of interpretations is inevitably interpreting those interpretations in his own particular way. We cannot by this method, any more than by any other, free ourselves into timeless universality. We may become free of Harnack, but only in the ways in which an Englishman or a Dutchman of the late twentieth century can become free of Harnack; and that means that in other ways we are bound[11].

And if we turn, as we often should, from interpreting without much personal commitment to trying to learn from the great ancient interpreters, again we must be aware of difference, distance and limitations. All great teachers have known and desired that those who learnt from them would make what they learnt their own, but the ancient traditionalists did not realise what a change this might involve, how much otherness might come between master and disciple, especially if the disciple is a reader of a much later generation. Plotinus and Eriugena were not entirely conscious of how much they transformed the spiritual food they received from the Blessed Ancients or the Holy Fathers in digesting it. We must be much more vividly aware than they were that

---

[11] The reference is, of course to E. P. Meijering's Theologische Urteile über die Dogmengeschichte: Ritschl's Einfluss auf von Harnack (Leiden 1978), which I have found a most enlightening and liberating book.

Whatever Miss T. eats
Turns into Miss T.

We have lost irrecoverably the noble innocence of our fathers, that assurance of belonging together with our ancient masters in a timeless and all-encompassing thought-
world which is perhaps essential to any living traditionalism. But perhaps this very loss
of innocence, this sense of difference which has been so laboured in the last paragraphs,
may enable us both still to learn from the great traditionalists in the only way we can
and to understand them, and particularly to understand both their great originality and
their dependence on their sources (not, of course, only their explicitly recognised authorities). That is, it may do so if we fully recognise and accept it. If we do not, we shall
do no more than lament the past and strike archaic attitudes. We can learn from them,
and in learning understand something about them, if we do consciously what they did
unconsciously. In learning from them we have to digest and transform, to make what
they give us our own in a way which changes it, and we have to know clearly and say
honestly that we are doing so. And in the process of getting to know what we are doing
we can see that they were doing the same thing, creative learning by an assimilation
which changes both the assimilator and what is assimilated, but doing it, as was justified
in their place and time, without our nagging historical consciousness and conscience.
And to see this will give us a genuine, though never perfect, understanding both of their
great originality and of their dependence on their sources, including not only those documents which they are explicitly "reading" to us but other sources which they have assimilated so thoroughly that they do not advert to them. In determining (in so far as this
is possible) what these are and in situating our great traditionalists as precisely as we can
in their several countries of the mind we shall turn to the other side of our historical-in-
terpretative activity.

This is the attempt (never of course completely successful) to keep ourselves out of
the picture and present the ancients "as they really were" – a phrase which, if we are to
remain honest, we must always put in inverted commas. The two sides of our activity or
enterprise, the personal-hermeneutic and the "objective" historical, cannot and should
not be completely separated, especially if we have that strong and particular attraction
to the persons we are trying to interpret which alone makes worth-while interpretations
possible. (Historians need to remember that not everybody can interpret everybody.
This is one reason why large-scale interpretative histories of thought, religion and culture are generally so unsatisfactory). Perhaps the best way of distinguishing the two is to
say that in both there is a dialogue between interpreter and interpreted, and this dialogue is written by the interpreter: this is why the line of demarcation between historical
novels and history can never be as precise as historians would like. But in the personal-
hermeneutic dialogue the interpreter will have no inhibitions about talking himself very
freely, and quite often saying, explicitly or equivalently, things like "It seems to me,
Blessed Ancient, that what you *really mean* must be this." In the more severely historical kind of dialogue the interpreter will try to say as little as possible, and will not, if he
is properly conscious of his own limitations, speak about "the real meaning". He will try
to let the interpreted do nearly all the talking and as far as possible speak for himself.
(Of course the "interpreted person speaking for himself" will inevitably be a character

X

14

in the interpreter's history). He will try to let him display his thought in its own setting, with all in that thought and its setting which must seem to us strange, remote, inconsistent, incomprehensible, and so unassimilable and unusable. If we bring what we can learn from this kind of dialogue together with what we can learn from the kind where we learn personally by interpretation, we may come nearer to seeing the great ancient traditionalists, and others we may study, a little more clearly: not, of course, "as they really are." We could never do this even if the evidence was complete, reliable and completely comprehensible. But when we come to see them, not as moments in the progression of a procession of general ideas but as people living and learning somewhat (not altogether) like ourselves, by reading and interpreting with the resources available to them what books they could get hold of and discussing, acrimoniously or otherwise, with those they happened to encounter, we may come to know them a great deal better. We shall see better their real originality in one view with their deep indebtedness to others in their past and present, understand better what they have given to their future and our past, and perhaps be able to speculate a little more intelligently about what they may give to our future as we experience the liberation from our thin slice of time which they can give us in our present.

XI

Two Views of Freedom
A Christian Objection in Plotinus
Enneads VI 8. [39]7, 11-15?

T HE treatise *On the Voluntary and the Will of the One* (*Enneads* VI 8 [39]) is the profoundest discussion of the metaphysic of will and freedom in ancient Western philosophical literature. A careful study of it, especially of the τολμηρὸς λόγος ἑτέρωθεν σταλείς (ch. 7, 11-12) and Plotinus' exasperated but thorough and serious reply to it, seems to me to bring out an important difference in ways of looking at freedom, human and divine, which (though not always consciously perceived) is apparent in Greek philosophical discussions from Aristotle onwards, and has had a considerable influence on, and at times produced considerable tensions in, Christian thought about the freedom of God.

The tension or difference of emphasis which I detect here may be expressed as follows. On one side the essence of freedom is perceived as being free to *be oneself*, which means, in the strongly teleological forms of thought which predominate in Greek thought from Plato onwards, to be oneself at one's best, to energize according to one's full and complete *energeia*, to realise which is one's good and goal; and to be so without external limitation, constraint or impediment — external, that is, to one's true nature or selfhood. On the other, the essence of freedom is seen as consisting in an absolutely undetermined power of choice between alternatives, a liberty of opinion not restricted or determined even by one's own nature. The two are not as a rule stated in Hellenic or in patristic or in mediaeval Christian thought as absolutely mutually exclusive. Those who prefer the first will generally admit that, at a certain level, freedom must express itself in choice between opposites: those who prefer the second will often admit that when one reaches the highest and most perfect possible self-realization one has passed beyond choice — the blessed in heaven, for most Christian theologians, cannot choose to be other than they are or do other than they do, and are no less free for that.

Plotinus begins VI 8 with an analysis of our concept of human freedom and ascends

XI

from there, with considerable trepidation but admitting that he has no better starting point, to consider the freedom of the Good or One. It will therefore be necessary, if we are to understand his thought in its proper context, to glance briefly
at earlier Greek thought about the freedom of man. His starting-point in the first
chapters of VI 8 seems to be Aristotle's most influential discussion of the subject
in the third book of the *Nicomachean Ethics*.[1] Aristotle is of course treating the
subject from the point of view of moral responsibility and in the down-to-earth,
practical, approximate way appropriate to moral philosophy as he understands it. In
spite of his careful and useful distinctions he leaves a good deal unclear, and can
be quoted on both sides in the difference about the nature of freedom with which we
are dealing. Joachim explains and illustrates this lack of clarity excellently in
his *Commentary*.[2] The problem is to see exactly what Aristotle thought about προαίρεσις ('purpose'). Joachim sums up the two possible interpretations, between which
the evidence from Aristotle's writings does not permit us to decide, as follows:
'according to the first interpretation, the προαίρεσις is the all-important factor
in determining the issue, but the προαίρεσις itself is nothing mysterious or miracul-
ous. On the contrary, it is the expression of man's nature — the nature, that is, of
a reasoning and deliberating, as well as a desiring, being. According to the second,
our good and bad actions express a 'deliberate decision' which appears to emerge
without intelligible development, and without intelligible connexion with the rest
of man's nature and the environment in which he lives. Aristotle himself, as far as
I can judge, wavers in such a way that passages can be quoted in support of both of
the above lines of interpretation'.[3]

The Epicureans are not relevant to this discussion as part of the background of
the thought of Plotinus or most Christian thinkers. But they are worth mentioning
here as the Hellenic philosophers who passionately championed the view that the
power of absolutely undetermined choice is the essence of human freedom. For them
indeterminacy is built into our nature by the famous (though not too clearly attest-
ed) doctrine of the atomic 'swerve'.[4] The Stoics are very relevant indeed, and much
in VI 8 derives from Stoic thought. Here the problem of human freedom and responsibility appears in its most acute form because it is considered in a setting of
determinism and cosmic optimism. Stoic determinism is theoretically absolute[5]: and
this applies in the sphere of human will and freedom. Freedom for Chrysippus means
acting from our own inner resources, our own nature moving itself by its own forces
in response to external circumstances. But our nature, and so our response, seem to
be determined.[6] Yet the Stoics, as austere moralists, need to assert, and do assert
continually, that at least 'assent' is properly attributable to us, that we can
genuinely accept our destiny as our destination and be blamed if we do not. There
are immense problems here for the Stoics, which they never really solved. But perhaps
no one else did either. The Middle Platonists certainly failed to deal with the

question satisfactorily. Their distinction between lower 'fate' (εἱμαρμένη) and higher 'providence' (πρόνοια) is not helpful here.[7] But it does carry with it the Platonic belief that our selves transcend this world at their highest and have their true
home in the intelligible, and therefore, in their true nature, are free from the
causal nexus, the fate or necessity of the physical world. This is an important part
of the thought of Plotinus. But neither the Middle Platonists nor, I think, anyone
else in antiquity refuted the 'soft' determinism of Chrysippus, according to which
our experience of freedom is our experience of the spontaneity, the genuine self-
expression, of our determinate natures. As Dillon says[8], 'This [countering with dogmatic assertions] I fear, we will find to be the case generally with Middle Platonic
efforts to deal with Fate and Free Will. Only Plotinus in *Enneads* III 2-3 comes
seriously to grips with the problem, and he only succeeds ultimately in demonstrating its insolubility'.

One can see from this summary and unoriginal account why a Greek philosopher of
the time of Plotinus would be inclined to think of freedom as freedom to be one's
true self rather than freedom of undetermined choice, though the latter concept was
by no means unfamiliar to Hellenic philosophers. But before we examine how Plotinus
deals with his Platonic-Aristotelian-Stoic inheritance, since the main discussion in
VI 8 is about the freedom of God, we should glance at the Greek philosophical background of this side of the discussion. There is not very much of it. It was not,
perhaps, till the time of Plotinus, or shortly before, that, probably due to Jewish
and Christian contacts, questions about God's freedom became serious and important.
Plato uses will-language of God or the gods, especially in the deliberately mythical
and anthropomorphic story of the Craftsman in the *Timaeus*, notably the speech to the
created gods (41 A-D), which had great later influence, and in the somewhat 'popular'
theodicy of *Laws* X (903-7). But he does not discuss the question of God's freedom:
and Aristotle and the Stoics are even less interested in it. This does not of course
mean that they deny it. Perhaps it would be fair to say that for both it is inconceivable that the divine should be other than it is or do other than it does, but this
does not mean that it is bound or compelled by any sort of necessity. The Stoic God,
so far from being compelled by necessity, is the very substance of necessity or fate.
He is anything but a blind compelled compulsion. Marcus Aurelius says, quoting
Euripides: 'The earth is in love with the rain and the majestic sky is in love. The
universe also is in love with making what is to be. So I say to the universe "I am
in love along with you"'.[9] Σοὶ συνερῶ: that is not the language of a man who feels
himself the puppet of a force of nature. The Middle Platonists do not have much to
add on God's freedom. Atticus, in the second century A.D. stresses Plato's teaching
on divine will in his 'fundamentalist' interpretation of the *Timaeus*[10]: and this may
have influenced some third-century Platonists. But he does not really develop Plato
or discuss any problems about God's βούλησις. The emphasis is a natural one in a

400

polemic against Aristotle's denial of Providence: and, as Dillon has pointed out[11], we cannot be sure how far the teaching of Atticus is adequately or accurately represented by this contribution to inter-school squabbling which attracted Eusebius for his own apologetic purposes.

Let us now turn to Plotinus. Before considering the free will of the One in VI 8 we should look closely at the model of human freedom with which he is working. As Dillon in the quotation above remarks, his fullest and most serious treatment of the question is in the great work *On Providence* (III 2-3 [47-48]). And, as Dillon also observes, this, by the very seriousness and clarity with which it presents the problems, demonstrates their untimate insolubility. No solution which Plotinus suggests seems to him perfectly satisfactory. In the end the problems of why there is wickedness in a divinely ordered world, and how the moral responsibility on which he insists can be reconciled with universal providence, remain unsolved. But one thing which is important for our purposes does seem clear. Plotinus does not appear to feel any need to assert a principle of free action in man which is totally undetermined. Our free actions, for which we are held responsible and must take the consequences, are indeed our own, but they are according to our natures, higher and lower, which are part of the organic structured unity of the intelligible or the disjunct harmony-in-conflict of the sense-world.[12] Man for Plotinus is a very complex being and can act according to various parts of his nature, and be himself on a number of different levels, with varying consequences. In his arguments against Stoic or Stoicizing Platonist and astrological determinism[13], which are based on the Middle Platonist distinction of πρόνοια and εἱμαρμένη mentioned above (p. 399), what Plotinus is really concerned to maintain is that soul at its best transcends the realm of physical necessity and is a real cause of action higher than the εἱμαρμένη of the sense-world, to which we are subject at our lower levels. Our thoughts and actions are not determined by the World-Soul or the stars. We are in that sense absolutely free, if we rise to the level at which freedom is possible. Plotinus is not interested in asserting a pure and absolute contingency of will, a total freedom of man to determine once and for all his own nature and destiny. His model of freedom is that of freedom to be oneself.

In the first chapters of VI 8 which are concerned with human freedom the position is even clearer, because the question is not as in *On Providence* 'Who is to be blamed for wickedness here below? Is it just to hold God or man responsible?' but 'Where and when are we truly free? At what level and in what activity of our selves do we attain true freedom?' In VI 8, where we are not looking for someone to blame, the wicked who act by lower passions and impulses have not even will (τὸ ἑκούσιον), let alone the power of self-disposal and self-command (τὸ αὐτεξούσιον).[14] True freedom, true autonomy and independence, τὸ ἐφ'ἡμῖν, is only attained when we are on the νοῦς level (as higher ψυχή, our higher self, always is even if we do not consciously choose to live on that level), when nature and activity and thought and will are one, when we are not enslaved to or struggling with passions or dependent on external circumstances to attain our purposes: when we are in, and all our activity is directed towards, the Good. This is true freedom, the unhindered activity of our true self at its best.

In chapter 7 of VI 8 Plotinus begins by wondering whether it is right to carry his discussion of freedom beyond Noῦς up to the Good. 'How can one bring the very lord and master of all things of value after it which sits in the first seat, to which all things else want to ascend and depend on it and have their powers from it, so as to be able to have something attributable to themselves — how can one bring it [down] to what is attributable to you and me? To a point where Noῦς also was only dragged with difficulty, though it was violently dragged'.[15] Then he introduces the τολμηρὸς λόγος ἑτέρωθεν σταλείς, the 'rash statement sent in from elsewhere' (line 11), which says 'Since [the nature of the Good] happens to be as it is, and has not the mastery of what it is, and is what it is not from itself, it would not have freedom, and its doing or not doing what it is necessitated to do or not to do is not attributable to itself'.[16]

This has been interpreted in various ways. Bréhier[17] and Cilento[18] wanted to take it as a statement of Gnostic doctrine. Their parallels are not very convincing, though with our present vastly increased knowledge of Gnostic literature it might be possible to find better ones. But both the wording and the place of the λόγος in the treatise suggest an objection rather than a positive counter-statement of a doctrine different from that of Plotinus. Harder and Theiler[19] take it as an objection introduced by Plotinus himself, translating ἑτέρωθεν in its commonest meaning, 'on or from the other side'. This has a good deal to be said for it. Plotinus often argues with himself in this way. He obviously takes this objection seriously, reiterates it in various forms, and is not at all easily satisfied that it has been answered.[20] But the indignation which it clearly arouses in him and his feeling which pervades the rest of the treatise that it utterly misrepresents what he thinks about the Good would be easier to understand if it was the objection of a real opponent. And, though the meaning of ἑτέρωθεν adopted by Harder and Theiler is the commonest, it means 'from elsewhere', not 'from or on the other side' in two passages which Plotinus might have had at the back of his mind, Plato *Laws* 707c7 and Aristotle *Eth. Nic.* 1121a34. It seems likely, though not certain, that we are dealing with an objection which Plotinus had actually heard, perhaps from a visitor[21] to his circle at Rome. On this assumption I would paraphrase it and supply the positive counter-statement somewhat as follows: 'Your Good just happens to be good and has to be good: it is like that by nature and can't help it: so it is not free but compelled to diffuse its goodness eternally by the necessity of its nature. But the God in whom we believe does just what he likes. He creates as and when he chooses by the act of his free and sovereign will'. Now someone who talked like that in the third century would most probably be a Christian, and very likely a Christian who was passionately opposed to Gnostic emanationism and inclined to confuse the teaching of Plotinus with it, as others have done since. This assumption makes it possible to suppose on my hypothesis that the indignant anxiety of Plotinus to refute the objection is inspired, as Bréhier and Cilento thought, at least partly by his desire to distinguish his position from that of the Gnostics.

There are two directions in which we can look to find a kind of Christian teaching which could have inspired such a criticism. One is to the kind of Christian Platonism, represented in the third century by Methodius of Olympus, which G.C. Stead detected in the background of the Arian controversy[22], which laid much emphasis on creation by an act of divine will. (While perfectly prepared to believe that people of this way of thinking existed, I would not myself wish to think of them as forming any sort of 'school', or to locate then too precisely at Alexandria or elsewhere, or, for reasons already given, to attach too much importance to the influence of Atticus on their thought.) Methodius is certainly an extreme advocate of the indeterminacy view of human freedom.[23] On divine freedom, however, his position is rather less extreme, and he has, perhaps, more than he would have liked to think in common with Origen, who has a good deal in common with Plotinus. Origen in the *Contra Celsum*[24] is very indignant with Celsus for alleging that Christians get out of difficulties by saying 'anything is possible to God'. He has already stated clearly and emphatically that God's omnipotence is limited by his divinity, goodness and wisdom[25], and he replies to the allegation of Celsus by saying that Christians believe as firmly as philosophers that God cannot do anything ugly (αἰσχρόν) or contrary to nature in the sense of either sinful or irreconcilable with reason. And in the *De Principiis* in the great chapter of the first book on the Son[26], he shows all things eternally created in the Son whom it is inconceivable and impious to suppose that the Father would not eternally beget, create or radiate (good New Testament terms which Origen regards as all meaning the same thing). Origen seems completely uninterested in asserting any sovereign indeterminateness of God's will. This contrasts strongly with his account of the wills of created beings. It is of course central to his whole theodicy and account of divine creation and education that these are and remain absolutely and permanently indeterminate.[27] Methodius certainly criticizes Origen's doctrine of eternal creation.[28] But he does so, not on the ground that it limits or inhibits the freedom of God's will but that it makes God dependent on creation, makes him *need* creation in order to be God. Plotinus would have agreed with him that this cannot be so: he insists continually that the One does not need what springs from him. And in the *De Autexousio*[29], after a pious remark on the inscrutability of God's will, Methodius thinks it necessary to show that there are excellent reasons why God should create, namely *i)* that he did not think it right that his skil

(τέχνη) should remain unexercised and undisplayed and *ii.)* that he could not really
be good without anyone to benefit by his goodness. Plotinus would have found the
first reason ridiculous[30], but might not have objected too much to the second. Perhaps we might say that Plotinus, Origen and Methodius all start from a simple Platonist, thoroughly Greek, conception of God's omnipotence, in which the primary truth
about God is that he is good and wise, and it is impious and insane even to frame
the hypothesis that he could be other than he is or do other than he does. But nevertheless Methodius does say in the *De Creatis*[31] that the Father made all things instant-
aneously from non-existents by a *bare* act of will (γυμνῷ τῷ βουλήματι), and he shows
himself as passionately opposed to the eternity of the world in *De Creatis* II-VII as
he is to pre-existing matter in the *De Autexousio*. It is therefore perfectly possible
that a Christian influenced by Methodius or some closely related theologian, who was
looking for a stigma to beat a pagan dogma, should have produced the objection in
Chapter 7.

There is, however, another possible Christian source of influence which is nearer
to the circle of Plotinus at Rome. This is the teaching of Hippolytus. Hippolytus is
inclined to use extreme indeterminacy-voluntarist language about God's freedom, insisting that God does just what he likes in creating.[32] In one passage[33] he carries
this so far as to say, addressing mankind in general, that (I paraphrase) 'God knew
perfectly well what he was doing when he made you a man: if he had wanted to he
could have made you a God, as he did the Logos'. Surely no Christian theologian has
ever carried this kind of voluntarism further. And a Christian influenced by Hippolytus (who died about 236) might quite probably have been a casual auditor of the
lectures of Plotinus in the middle 260's — we know from the case of Thaumasius[34]
that such people sometimes made remarks.

The reply of Plotinus to the objection occupies the rest of the treatise (chapters
7-21). It is impossible to paraphrase this close-packed argument which, as always,
is both based on and an exhortation to seek an awareness of that transcendent Good
in union with whom we are 'more than free and more than independent'.[35] What is important for our purposes is to note the way in which the language of will and freedom
is used throughout, and especially clearly and forcibly in the last chapter (21).
Plotinus, in order to combat the objection, is prepared to use this language, as he
uses other positive ways of speaking of the One in this treatise, with continual
warnings of their utter inadequacy. Substance, Act (ἐνεργεία), Love, Wakefulness or
Super-Knowledge are all used as 'divine names', and the Good is spoken of as creating himself. And though every term is negated, its use implies also the negation of
its contrary. This is always true in Plotinus, but is more explicit in this treatise
than elsewhere.

As with the other terms, he warns continually against using 'will' in any way
which would imply duality. The 'will' of the Good is not to be thought of for a

moment as other than his 'self' or 'substance'. 'He is all will,' Plotinus says, 'and there is nothing in him which does not will, therefore not that which is before the will. He is, then first himself his will'.[36] And he remains true to the concept of freedom with which he began the treatise by absolutely excluding any possibility of choice between alternatives from the freedom of the Good in willing both himself and his products (it seems self-evident to Plotinus that the Good in 'willing' himself 'wills' his self-diffusion). He remarks 'to be capable of the opposites belongs to incapacity to remain with the best'.[37] All other beings are freest when they are so perfectly conformed to the Good they seek as to be incapable of choosing the bad. And it would seem to Plotinus a blasphemous absurdity even to imagine for a moment the Good 'willing' anything other than himself. This implies no constraint on his freedom: his freedom *is* just being himself: πρώτως αὐτός καὶ ὑπερόντως αὐτός.[38] And in so far as we are united to him his selfhood is perfect freedom, for us as for him. In so far as we live on any lower level he is also our 'necessity and law'[39] in that he produces the law in producing that level and gives us our destiny to return to him. But at the highest he is our freedom as he is his own. He is free to be the Good, and we are free to be good.

One would have thought that later Christians might have welcomed this great portrayal of a God who, in our inadequate human way of speaking, is himself the self-diffusive Good which he freely wills and the free will with which he wills it, without even the possibility of distinguishing God, good, and will which this language inevitably suggests. But of course they did not, at any rate in the context of creation. The hold of the view of freedom as essentially undetermined choice on Christian minds, especially in the West, has been so strong that room has had to be made for it at the top. There has also been a technical theological reason for rejecting the doctrine of Plotinus, the need to make a very sharp distinction between eternal generation and creation, which was strongly felt after Nicaea and the Arian controversy, though by no means always before, as the passages which I have referred to from Origen and Hippolytus show. So to this day a commonplace Christian objection to Neoplatonism is very much on the lines of the τολμηρὸς λόγος: and about 400 A.D. the author of Pseudo-Justin *Quaestiones Christianorum ad Gentiles* vigorously attacks in the third question[40] a well stated Hellenic position which is substantially that of Plotinus. But to establish fully the grounds for the Christian rejection of the Plotinian position, and still more to trace all the clashes and tensions between the two ways of looking at freedom with which we have been concerned even in the thought of the Fathers, would be a very large undertaking. It will, however, I think, help to clarify many discussions if we realise fully that this duality exists and is deeply rooted in Hellenic philosophy.

REFERENCES

1. III 1109b30-1114b25: cp. *Eudemian Ethics* 1225a9ff.
2. *Aristotle: The Nicomachean Ethics*. A Commentary by the late H.H. Joachim edited by D.A. Rees (Oxford 1951) pp. 107-111.
3. *op. cit.*, p. 110.
4. Lucretius II 251-293: Cicero *Nat. D.* I 69.
5. See for example: *S.V.F.* II 944, 945, 959, 967.
6. *S.V.F.* 974 (=Cicero *De Fato* 39-44), 979, 1000.
7. Very useful and well-documented discussions of the thought of various Middle Platonists about fate, providence and free will can be found in J. Dillon *The Middle Platonists* (London 1977) by reference to the Table of Contents.
8. *The Middle Platonists*, p. 211.
9. ' ἐρᾷ μὲν ὄμβρου γαῖα, ἐρᾷ δὲ ὁ σέμνος αἰθήρ.' ἐρᾷ δὲ ὁ κόσμος ποιῆσαι ὃ ἂν μέλλῃ γίνεσθαι. λέγω οὖν τῷ κόσμῳ ὅτι σοὶ συνερῶ (X 21).
10. Eusebius *P.E.* XV 801bff.
11. *The Middle Platonists*, pp. 248-251.
12. III 2, 10, 11-79: III 3, 2-5.
13. III 1 [3] and II 3 [52].
14. ch. 3, 17-26.
15. πῶς δὴ αὐτὸ τὸ κύριον ἁπάντων τῶν μετ'αὐτὸ τιμίων καὶ ἐν πρώτῃ ἕδρᾳ ὄν, πρὸς ὃ τὰ ἄλλα ἀναβαίνειν θέλει καὶ ἐξήρτηται αὐτοῦ καὶ τὰς δυνάμεις ἔχει παρ'αὐτοῦ, ὥστε δύνασθαι τὸ ἐπ'αὐτοῖς ἔχειν, πῶς ἂν τις εἰς τὸ ἐπ'ἐμοὶ ἢ ἐπὶ σοὶ ἄγοι; ὅπου καὶ νοῦς μόλις, ὅμως δὲ βίᾳ εἵλκετο; (lines 6-11)
16 ...ὡς τυχοῦσα οὕτως ἔχειν, ὡς ἔχει, καὶ οὐκ οὖσα κυρία τοῦ ὅ ἐστιν, οὖσα τοῦτο ὅ ἐστιν οὐ παρ'αὐτῆς, οὔτε τὸ ἐλεύθερον ἂν ἔχοι οὔτε τὸ ἐπ'αὐτῇ ποιοῦσα ἢ μὴ ποιοῦσα ὃ ἠνάγκασται ποιεῖν ἢ μὴ ποιεῖν. (lines 12-15).
17. In his *Notice* to VI 8 in vol. VI 2 of the Budé edition (Paris 1938).
18. *Paideia Antignostica* (Florence 1971) pp. 25-26 cp. p. 225.
19. *Band* IV b of the Harder-Beutler-Theiler edition (Hamburg 1967) p. 372 ad loc. cp. the translation in B. IV a, p. 19.
20. cp. especially chp. 12, 2-3 : πάλιν γὰρ ἡ ψυχὴ οὐδέν τι πεισθεῖσα τοῖς εἰρημένοις ἄπορός ἐστι.
21. A visitor like Thaumasius (*Life* 13,12) rather than a regular attendant. There is no reason to suppose that any non-Gnostic Christians were members of the group of Plotinus' friends and disciples.
22. G.C. Stead 'The Platonism of Arius' in *J.T.S.* N.S. XVI 1 (April 1964) pp. 16-31.
23. *De Autexousio* and *Symposium Logos* 8 and the final dialogue 292-302.
24. IV 14.
25. III 70.
26. I 2, especially 2, 29-30 and 10.
27. *De Principiis* I 5.3, 7.2, 8.3: II 1-3, 9.1.
28. *De Creatis* II-VII pp. 494-498 Bonwetsch.
29. XXII 2-11, pp. 202-6 Bonwetsch.
30. cp. II 9 [33] 4, 13-15. But IV 8 [6] 5, 29-32 should be taken into account in assessing the distance between Plotinus and Methodius here. What Plotinus would have objected to in this passage might perhaps have been not so much the reasons given for creation as the idea that God has to advert to them and decide to create at a particular time.
31. IX p. 498 Bonwetsch.
32. *Contra Noetum* (Hippolyte *Contre les Hérésies: Fragment* ed. P. Nautin, Paris 1949) 8 (p. 249,25 Nautin), 10 (251, 11-253, 8. N).
33. *Philosophoumena* ('Ελέγχος) 10. 32-33. (*P.G.* 16.3.3450A).
34. *Life* 13.12.
35. ch. 15,21.
36. πᾶν ἄρα βούλησις ἦν καὶ οὐκ ἔνι τὸ μὴ βουλόμενον· οὐδὲ τὸ προ βουλήσεως ἄρα. πρῶτον ἄρα ἡ βούλησις αὐτός (21, 14-16).
37. Καὶ γὰρ τὸ τὰ ἀντικείμενα δύνασθαι ἀδυναμίας ἐστι τοῦ ἐπὶ τοῦ ἀρίστου μένειν (21,5-7).

406

38. ch. 14,42.

39. ch. 10,44. As has already been remarked (p. 398) in considering the Stoic God, to *be* necessity is something very different from being *bound* by necessity.

40. *Corpus Apologetorum Christianorum Saeculi Secundi* ed. J.C.Th. von Otto (Jena 1848) Vol. III 2 *Quaestiones Christianorum ad Gentiles* III pp. 282-305 (*P.G.* 6.1427C-1444B). The Christian question alleges that the pagan God creates τῷ εἶναι καὶ οὐ τῷ βουλέσθαι οἷον θερμαίνει τὸ πῦρ τῷ εἶναι. The Hellenic reply seems to be based on VI 8. The Christian refutation insists that God's βούλησις must be separated from his οὐσία (οὐσία being πρὸς ὕπαρξιν and βούλησις, πρὸς ποιήσιν) if God is not to be said to create by necessity of nature.

XII

2. Dualism Platonic, Gnostic, and Christian

There are a number of terms whose use or abuse in a large, vague, fluctuating way can confuse our understanding of the history of thought and sometimes our own theological and philosophical thinking: this has often been true of 'dualism', as also of 'pantheism', 'Platonism', 'Gnosticism' and 'Christianity'. It seems to me an important part of the task of historians of thought to give such terms the precise and varied contents which they should have in varied contexts and environments. I see our work rather as Cézanne saw his painting when he said that he wanted to 'do Poussin over again from nature'. In this paper I shall try to give precision and variety to some senses in which 'dualism' can legitimately be used when we are discussing the thought of the early centuries of our era, with particular reference to the Pythagorean-Platonic tradition, Gnosticism, and Christianity. I shall consider mainly one of the ways of thinking which can properly be described as dualist: cosmic dualism, which sees the whole nature of things as constituted by the meeting and interaction of two opposite principles: though I shall also briefly discuss two-world dualism, in which there are two kosmoi or levels of reality, that of our normal experience and a higher one (which may itself be conceived as complex and many-levelled).

Cosmic dualism, the dualism of two opposite principles, can take, and in the period which we are considering did take, a number of different forms. We may begin with a suspiciously tidy-looking scheme, which, as we shall see, will require some qualification and modification.

1. The two principles may be thought of as both unoriginated,

independent and everlastingly operative in the nature of things.
They may be perceived as (a) intrinsically opposed and in perpetual conflict (or conflict as long as this world lasts). This
gives a conflict-dualism of what may be called the Iranian pattern. In this case one principle must be qualified as 'good'
and the other as 'evil', and one is expected to take the good's
side. Or (b) they may be conceived as equally independent, but
working together in harmony. This seems to be prevalent in Chinese thought, and is certainly very well expressed by the Yang-
Yin symbol. Its most radical and fiercely original expression
in the Greek world is in the thought of Heraclitus: here it
takes a very dynamic form, and the conflict and tension, which
any doctrine of cosmic harmony which is sufficiently attentive
to experience must recognize, is powerfully emphasized.
2. Or the second principle may be thought of as derived from
and dependent on the first. (I shall refer to this second principle as the 'dark other', to avoid prejudging various questions
about it which will arise.) This derived and dependent 'dark
other' may be thought of as either (a) in revolt against, or at
least opposed to, the first principle or (b) working in accord
and co-operation, at least passive, with it.

This very neat generalized classification of four possible
forms of cosmic dualism is a useful starting-point for thinking
about the subject. But when we begin to apply it to the dualisms with which we are here concerned, we shall find that it has
to be used with a good deal of caution and qualification. This
is particularly true when we are considering the various forms
which cosmic dualism takes in the Pythagorean-Platonic tradition.
The thinkers of this tradition range over all the four varieties
of cosmic dualism listed above, but profess them, for the most
part, in distinctive ways and with important modifications. When
they think of the two principles as independent they do not maintain an absolute and unqualified conflict-dualism: and even when
the 'dark other' is thought of as dependent for its existence on
its opposite it is not, through most of the history of Platonism,
accepted and qualified as 'good': though at the very end, in the
final and most fully and carefully thought out form of Platonic
dualism which we find in Syrianus and Proclus, we do arrive at a
dualism of cosmic harmony which can be very well symbolized by

the Chinese Yang-Yin circle. As we shall see, a great deal depends on what one means in various contexts of thought by clas-
sifying the 'dark other' as 'evil'.

In the earliest form (or forms) of Pythagorean dualism
known to us the two principles (or groups of principles) seem to
be independent and everlastingly coexistent. This is clearly
brought out in the Pythagorean Table of Opposites.[1] And we learn
from this that the light, male, limiting, ordering principle is
qualified as 'good' and the dark, female, indefinite principle
as 'evil'. But we need to consider carefully the sense in which
the 'dark other' seems to be thought of as principle of evil in
early Pythagoreanism. As the principle of indefinite multiplicity it is (or can be) the principle of formlessness, disorder
and irrationality, and so opposed to the good principle of light
and musical order. But both principles are absolutely necessary
if there is to be a cosmos at all. They are the parents of the
numbers which are the very stuff of reality; without both, number and the great musical order of the whole cannot exist. And
the necessity and goodness of the cosmos is something which early
Pythagoreanism may be held to affirm with less qualification than
later Platonism and Pythagoreanism, in that for pre-Platonic
Pythagoreans there was only one cosmos, not two, a higher and a
lower. This very qualified and, from the viewpoint of darker and
more passionate dualisms, attenuated understanding of the sense
in which the 'dark other' is evil persists, with varying feeling-
tones and shades of emphasis, throughout the later Platonic-Pytha
gorean tradition.
In Plato we find two forms of cosmic or two-opposite-princi-
ples dualism which were influential later. (I do not believe
that in Laws X 896e-897d Plato is talking about a cosmic evil
soul, though later Platonists interpreted the passage in this
way.) These two forms are, first, that contained in our reports
of his discussions in the Academy about the generation of the
Ideal Numbers from the One and the Indefinite Dyad. I do not

---

1. Aristotle Metaphysics A 5 986a22-26. I accept the view that Aristotle is
much our best and most reliable source of evidence for pre-Platonic Pythagoreanism.

propose to say much about this because I do not think we know
very much.[2] But I do not think that there is any sufficient evidence to suggest that the Dyad is derived from the One; the two
principles seem to be independent. And it seems clear that, if
the Dyad is one of the principles from which the Ideas or Forms
are generated, Plato can only have thought of it as a principle
of evil in some very peculiar sense, even more attenuated than
the Pythagorean. Aristotle does say that the principles are respectively τὴν τοῦ εὖ καὶ τοῦ κάκως αἰτίαν,[3] of things being in
a good state or going well or of being in a bad state or going
badly, but this should not be pressed too far.

The dualism of the One and the Dyad influenced later Pythagorean thought and is very important for the Neoplatonists, as we
shall see. But much the most influential form of Platonic dualism is that symbolically presented in the great myth of the Timaeus. Here the material universe (there is nothing in the Timaeus
about the genesis of the eternal world of Forms which is its paradigm) comes to be through the encounter of two independent principles or powers: that of the Craftsman looking to his Paradigm,
Divine Reason active in the formation of the visible cosmos, and
that strange, not properly knowable, turbulence of place, which
is the receptacle, mother and nurse of becoming and accounts for
the element of irrational necessity or brute fact which we find
in the world. Of the innumerable questions which have arisen
through the centuries about this powerful symbolic presentation
of the world-forming activity of the divine, two concern us here.
One is, what exactly is there about the other principle which is
really 'dark', which we (or later Platonists) might want to call
'evil' even if Plato does not do so? It is certainly responsible
for the fact that, though this is the best of all possible material worlds, everything is not absolutely for the best in it, but
only as good as possible: it is responsible for all those faults
and failings which make it lower and worse than its paradigm, the
World of Forms, and which it would be blasphemous to attribute to

---

2. I agree on the whole with the sceptical assessment of the evidence for
Plato's oral teachings given by Gregory Vlastos in his review of H.J.Krämer
Arete bei Platon und Aristoteles, Gnomon 41(1963)641-655, reprinted in Platonic
Studies (Princeton 1973) 379-403.

3. Aristotle Metaphysics A 6 988a14.

the Divine Craftsman; in this sense we can, if we like, call it,
in a rather abstract and uninformative sense, a 'principle of
evil'. But of course the Timaeus insists most strongly both that
there ought to be a material universe, that its existence is an
inevitable consequence of the generous goodness of the divine
(29e-30a): and that it is itself as divinely good as it is possible to be on its own level, a 'visible god' (92b7). The element
of turbulent, disorderly irrationality in our world, the fact
that it is not perfect and absolute cosmos, seems to be a necessary condition for the existence of any material cosmos at all.
And it is surely rather inadequate, and may be misleading, to describe this as a 'principle of evil'.

The other question which we need to ask for our purposes is,
how does the good divine power deal with this element the opposition of which it has to overcome? Plato's answer is famous, and
deserves continual meditation. Divine intelligence works in the
world by persuasion: it persuades necessity to co-operate with it
(48a). To bring out the full force of this and show how central
it is to Plato's thought I should like to quote the conclusion of
Cornford's Epilogue to his running commentary on the Timaeus,
Plato's Cosmology. Cornford is here comparing the trilogy of dialogues which he supposes Plato intended to write, Timaeus, Criti-
as and Hermocrates with the Oresteia of Aeschylus. His supposi-
tions about how Plato planned his trilogy are speculative and may
be wrong, but this does not affect the force and rightness of the
understanding of Plato which he derives from the comparison.[4]

> The philosophic poet and the poet philosopher are both consciously con-
> cerned with the enthronement of wisdom and justice in human society. For
> each there lies, beyond and beneath this problem, the antithesis of cos-
> mos and chaos, alike in the constitution of the world and within the con-
> fines of the individual soul. On all these planes they see a conflict of
> powers, whose unreconciled opposition entails disaster. Apollo and the
> Furies between them can only tear the soul of Orestes in pieces. The
> city of uncompromised ideals, the prehistoric Athens of Critias' legend,
> in the death-grapple with the lawless violence of Atlantis, goes down in
> a general destruction of mankind. The unwritten Hermocrates, we conjec-
> tured, would have described the rebirth of civilized society and the in-
> stitution of a State in which the ideal would condescend to compromise
> with the given facts of man's nature. So humanity might find peace at
> the last. And the way to peace, for Plato as for Aeschylus, lies through
> reconcilement of the rational and the irrational, of Zeus and Fate, of
> Reason and Necessity, not by force but by persuasion.

---

4. F.M.Cornford, Plato's Cosmology (London 1937) 363-364.

XII

It makes a great difference, both in theory and practice,
which of the privileged images of divine action in the world
available to them cosmic dualists adopt. They may, as we shall
see, image the divine as a redeemer liberating the children of
light from this dark world, or as a general leading the armies of
light against the forces of darkness.[5] But Plato in his great
cosmic story chose, and by choosing bequeathed to later generations, the image of the craftsman working on his rather awkward
and recalcitrant material, humouring it and persuading it to take
as well as it can the form of the unchanging goodness and beauty
which is his model. It is an image the contemplation of which
produces a very different attitude to the world from a passionate
longing to escape from its miseries or the partisan pugnacity of
the conflict-dualist.

In post-Platonic Pythagoreanism we find that, probably for
the first time in the history of the tradition, the 'dark other'
is generally held to be derived from the One. The most interesting form of the doctrine for our purposes is to be found in a
well-known account of the teaching of Moderatus of Gades given by
Simplicius on the authority of Porphyry.[6] In spite of recurring
doubts as to whether Moderatus has not been somewhat Neoplaton-
ized in transmission, I think his account of the generation and
nature of the other principle must be accepted as genuine pre-
Neoplatonic Pythagoreanism. It is criticized by Numenius,[7] and
there is nothing quite like it in the Neoplatonists. Moderatus
says that the Unitary Logos, intending to produce from himself
the genesis of beings, by self-privation made room for quantity.
This quantity is identified with the disorderly, irrational,
formless principle of the Timaeus, and probably with the Dyad.
It is the principle of evil in the material world in so far as it

5. In the third part of the great theodicy of Laws X, in 906, the gods are
compared to generals, as they are to skippers, charioteers, doctors, farmers
– and sheepdogs, and the everlasting war against evil in which gods and spirits
are our allies is mentioned (906a5-7); but this is very incidental, and the
main point of the comparisons is to show how unlikely it is that the gods are
corruptible.

6. Simplicius In Phys.230.34-231.27 Diels. See P.Merlan in A.H.Armstrong
(ed.), The Cambridge History of Later Greek and Early Mediaeval Philosophy
(Cambridge 1967) 90-94.

7. Numenius fr.52 Des Places (test.30 Leemans) 15-24.

is the principle of avoidance of and deviation from form. But
it is produced by the Unitary Logos as the first stage in its
creative activity and it is clear that without it there can be no
ordered multiplicity, at least of material beings, no cosmos at
all. And at the end of the passage it seems that the 'dark other',
in spite of its persistent tendency away from form and towards
non-being, is pretty thoroughly overcome by the formative power
of the divine numbers (231.20-27). Moderatus remains in this way
in the tradition of early Pythagoreanism and the Timaeus. His
dualism is a qualified and mitigated dualism, compatible with a
good deal of cosmic optimism.

The Platonists of the first two centuries A.D. whom we need
to consider carefully in the present context are those represented for us by Plutarch and Atticus, who are grouped together by
later commentators because of their very emphatic dualism as well
as on account of their insistence on taking the Timaeus literally
as an account of creation in time. Both belong to my first group
of dualists, those who hold that the two cosmic principles are
both unoriginated, independent, and everlastingly opposed. At
first sight they may appear as rather uncompromising conflict-
dualists of Iranian type. Plutarch in his treatise On Isis and
Osiris does speak with approval of Iranian dualism;[8] and is led
to use a good deal of conflict-dualist language elsewhere in the
treatise by his identification of the evil soul which he finds in
Plato with the enemy of Osiris, Typhon or Set. But when we come
to look at him and Atticus more closely we shall find that their
positions are rather interestingly different from straightforward
conflict-dualism. Like some Gnostics, they think in terms of
three principles, not two. There is the principle of light, form
and order, the dark, disorderly evil soul, and between them matter, which is sharply distinguished from the evil soul. In Isis
and Osiris Plutarch makes clear that matter, which is identified
with the goddess Isis, is not just neutral but divinely good,
with an innate passionate love for the Good himself, who is Osiris. This is very finely stated in chapter 53. And the evil soul
which is Typhon can disturb and damage, but cannot intrinsically
effect, the beauty and goodness of the cosmos which results from

---

8. Chapters 46 and 47, 369D-370C.

XII

the union of these great divine male and female principles. And
when we turn to the very interesting accounts of the doctrine of
Atticus about the disorderly motion and time which existed before
the making of the world which are given by Proclus,[9] we find that
Proclus does not distinguish his doctrine on the point which concerns us from that of Plutarch. The evil soul for Atticus is, as
throughout the tradition, evil as principle of irrational disorder. But it is clearly distinguished from matter and seems in
the process of world-making to be as totally dominated and transformed by the power of the good, intelligent formative principle
as matter itself[10] (this seems likely to come from Atticus rather
than Plutarch). As Dillon remarks, 'This [the Maleficent Soul],
in terms of Plutarch's Isis and Osiris is an Isis-figure rather
than a Typhon-figure'.[11]

Though the dualism of Numenius sometimes seems to have a
darker and more pessimistic colour, especially when he is thinking about the nature and embodiment of man, his way of thinking
is really not so far removed from that of Plutarch and Atticus.
As already mentioned (p.34), he rejects the Pythagorean view represented by Moderatus of the derivation of the second principle
from the One and returns to the two independent and opposed principles which he finds in the earlier Pythagoreans and Plato. He
seems to associate the evil soul more closely with matter than
Plutarch, and regards its malign influence as extending even to
the heavens.[12] But by the end of the passage on Pythagorean
teaching which derives from him in Calcidius, the victory of the
good principle over the evil of animate matter is strikingly complete: it is not so complete that the evils of this our world are
done away with (no Platonist could ever accept this), but it is
complete enough for matter reformed by divine providential activity to be spoken of not as the adversary but as the consort of
god, the mother of the universe and even mother of 'the corporeal
and generated gods'.[13] And the universe of which matter with its

9. In Tim.1.276–277 and 381–382 Diehl.
10. 382.7–12 Diehl.
11. J.Dillon, The Middle Platonists (London 1977) 254.
12. Calcidius In Timaeum 296–297; fr.52.65–70,82–87 Des Places).
13. Ibid.298 (fr.52.101–102 Des Places).

bad soul is the disorderly and irresponsible mother is, as Numenius says elsewhere,[14] 'this beautiful cosmos, beautified by participation in the beautiful'. For all these philosophers of the
Platonic-Pythagorean tradition who were so troubled by the problem of evil and anxious to find a solution to it, the Timaeus was
naturally of central importance. And in the end it was the spirit of the Timaeus which triumphed in them over whatever tendencies they may have had to darker and more passionate forms of
cosmic dualism.

In the great final rethinking and development of Hellenic
Platonism which begins with Plotinus, which we call Neoplatonism
the view that the 'dark other' derives from the Good itself is
finally accepted as against the dualism of two independent principles. But this leaves room for some variation, within the Platonic limits which should by now have become clear, in the way in
which the second principle is thought of and valued. For Plotinus the matter of this lower world derives from the higher principles, and so ultimately from the Good, and there is a 'dyadic'
or 'hylic' element in the intelligible realm. But in his treatise On the Two Kinds of Matter (II 4 (12)) he attempts to separate the two matters more sharply than is done anywhere else in
the tradition where there is any question of matter at the higher
level; and the relationship of the two matters never seems to be
made perfectly clear. In II 4 and I 8 (51), and incidentally
elsewhere, he speaks of the matter of this world as principle of
evil in very strong terms, while in III 6 (26) he gives a most
remarkable account of its phantasmal and sterile quality, which
makes this our world a kind of ghost-world, incapable of further
productivity. Yet there is no Platonist who more passionately
insists on and defends the divine goodness and holiness of the
material cosmos. And it is intrinsic to his whole way of thinking about the Good that its creative self-diffusion will go on
till the ultimate limit is reached and everything that can have
any, even the smallest, measure of being and goodness has been
called into existence. And this means going on down to the material cosmos, where its matter operates, in a very strange way, as
the principle of evil. The creative process, in proceeding to

---

14. Fr.16 Des Places (25 Leemans) 16-17.

38

the ultimate limit in the generation of positive goodness, evokes the utter negativity which is that limit. For it is as total negativity that matter in Plotinus' universe is the principle of evil. It is perfectly true, in a sense, to say that for Plotinus the dark ὕλη which is absolute and principial evil does not exist. But it is the inevitable cosmogonic approach, which is necessarily a movement away from being and form, to its absolute non-existence which makes ὕλη the principle of cosmic evil, and the approach, closer than is needed, by weaker individual lower souls not perfectly under the command of their higher souls, which enables it to become the principle of moral evil. Its effects in the universe of Plotinus are very limited. They do not extend to the Upper Cosmos, the region of the heavenly bodies, where matter is perfectly obedient and subdued to form.[15] The great embodied gods, including the earth-goddess,[16] are in no way affected for the worse by the 'dark other'. Even in individuals their higher souls are in no way affected by evil and even their lower souls are not intrinsically affected; there can be no substantial change for the worse in them, only a change of direction due to a failure to attend to the higher. In Plotinus' great theodicy, the work On Providence, matter is certainly included as a cause of the evils in this world of ours.[17] But the part which it plays in the justification of divine providence is modest, and a great deal of the work gives an account of cosmic harmony in conflict and tension which is not only in the spirit of Plato but not far removed from the cosmic optimism of the Stoics.

Plotinus has clearly moved a considerable distance from that much more substantial and lively evil principle, the evil soul of the Middle Platonists: and he is moving in a direction which leads towards the final rehabilitation of the 'dark other' by the Athenian Neoplatonists. But I now think that it may be a mistake to dismiss his account of matter as principle of evil by its very negativity as a rather unsatisfactory transition stage in the evolution of Platonic dualism. Plotinus, like the Middle Platon-

---

15. II 1 (40) 4.12-13; II 9 (33) 8.35-36; IV 4 (28) 42.25-26.
16. For the Earth as a goddess see IV 4 (28) 22.26-27.
17. III 2 (47) 2.

ists we considered earlier, does take the evils we experience
here below very seriously, and this may be to his credit. The
'classical' solution worked out by his successors is most coherent and impressive and has much to recommend it. But can it not
sometimes become a little too smoothly complacent in its cosmic
optimism? There is perhaps a way of looking at the doctrine of
Plotinus which is not in the end incompatible with the later Neoplatonist position but which gives a more vivid sense of the reality and seriousness of evil, though I do not wish to suggest
that Plotinus himself always understood it in this way. We are
often inclined, I think, to solidify and reify rather too much
what the ancients are talking about: the language which they use,
of course, encourages this distortion: in the present case the
words ὕλη, silva or materia do rather strongly suggest lumps of
stuff, and as long as there is even the faintest trace of unconscious tendency to look at ὕλη in this way it is very difficult
to understand how what is being talked about can be a principle
of evil precisely as absolute non-existence. But if we suppose
that Plotinus is trying to speak of a kind of necessary condition
if what must be there if the Good is to diffuse itself freely, a
world of bodies in space and time, is to exist at all, it may become easier to make sense of his position. We can see that if
the productivity, the generative power, of divine goodness, is to
go on to its furthest limit, as, since it is absolute goodness,
it is inevitable that it should; if it is to produce not only the
complete and self-contained beauty of the archetype but the imperfect but real beauty of the image which is all that is left to
produce, since the archetypal world contains all that can exist
on its level of real being and perfect beauty and goodness; then
a world must come into being which has a built-in element of negativity, sterility and unreality simply by not being the World of
Forms, just as its harmony must be a harmony of separate beings
in clash and conflict because it is a world of space and time
(this last characteristic is not for Plotinus, any more than for
Heraclitus and the Stoics, necessarily evil).[18] In the end

18. Pierre Hadot's exposition of Plotinus' allegorical interpretation of the
myth of Ouranos, Kronos and Zeus in his great anti-Gnostic work brings out
very well how and why Plotinus thinks it necessary that the diffusion of the
Good should go on beyond the self-contained, inward-looking perfection of the
world of Nous; see P.Hadot,'Ouranos, Kronos and Zeus in Plotinus' treatise

Plotinus remains close to the spirit of the Timaeus, on which he meditated so continually.

In the Athenian Neoplatonists the 'dark other' at last attains full equality of esteem with its opposite principle of light, form and order. The mother of all reality is honoured equally with the father. This first becomes clear in Syrianus, for whom the primal Monad and Dyad which proceed immediately from the One are prior even to the world of real being. They are the co-equal and equally necessary principles of all multiple, that is to say of all derived, reality, of all that comes from and diffuses the Good from the highest gods to the lowest bodies.[19] And they are not only equally necessary but equally valued. Syrianus strongly denies that the Dyad is the principle of evil.[20] He seems to be the originator of the 'classical' account of evil in which it is a παρυπόστασις a by-product, with no existence or principle of its own. As Anne Sheppard puts it:[21]

> The dyad is only indirectly responsible for evil in so far as it is responsible for otherness and plurality, and it is because of these that evil παρυφίσταται in the world. Another way of putting this would be to say that evil is unavoidable because the world is as it is, that it is inevitably involved in the partial and divided condition of the lower realms of the universe.

When the Athenian doctrine is stated like this, it is easy to see that it is not too far removed from that of Plotinus, or, for that matter, of the Pythagoreans and Plato whose teachings Syrianus thought he was expounding. Proclus develops the teaching of his master very powerfully. He shows[22] how the two principles operate at every level of his vast and complex universe, and both in a positive way, and how the 'dark other', the Infinite, is the principle of life, fecundity and creative expansion without which the great diffusion of the Good through all the levels of multi-

---

against the Gnostics' in Neoplatonism and Early Christian Thought (London 1981) 124-137.

19. The doctrine of Syrianus is very well expounded by Anne Sheppard in her contribution 'Monad and Dyad as Cosmic Principles in Syrianus' to Soul and the Structure of Being in Late Neoplatonism (Liverpool 1982) 1-17. Very difficult problems arise, in Syrianus and still more in Proclus, about the place of the primal pair (Monad and Dyad in Syrianus, Limit and Infinity in Proclus) in relation to the Divine Henads, as Sheppard indicates (p.11-12).

20. In Metaph.184.1ff.; 185.15ff. Kroll.

21. Art.cit.10.

22. In Tim.1.54, 176 Diehl; In Parm. VI 1119.4-1123.21; El.Theol. prop.89-92; Plat.Theol. III 7-9.

plicity cannot occur. Jean Trouillard sums up this final development of Platonic dualism very well when he says:[23]

> Chaque être est fait de mesure et d'infinité, d'un et de multiple, de
> clarté et de ténèbres. L'ordre a toujours besoin de s'opposer le dés-
> ordre et de le maîtriser, parce qu'il est une mise en ordre active et
> parce qu'il est soutenu par une puissance de dépassement. Et du moment
> que l'origine est ineffable, elle s'exprime aussi bien par la dyade mul-
> tiplicatrice que par la monade unifiante... Puisque il [le dualisme]
> traverse tous les niveaux et exprime une origine unique, il est pour
> ainsi dire exorcisé. L'abîme symbolise le sanctuaire. Ni le Chaos ni
> la Nuit ne sont le mal. Ils figurent l'Ineffable au même titre que
> l'ordre et la clarté.

One can see very well, if one reads the passages in Proclus on
which Trouillard's account is so solidly based, how this doctrine,
though it corrects and clarifies earlier language and thought,
remains faithful to the essentials of that thought, and even perhaps leaves room for understanding how the 'dark other', though
of the very highest status in the universe after the Good, and
herself wholly good, can be the necessary condition for the existence of evils here below and in this way a 'principle of evil'
in the restricted and peculiar Platonic sense; so that this intense cosmic optimism need not be too fancifully and inhumanely
roseate.

We must now turn to the Gnostics more or less contemporary
with the later Platonists whom we have been discussing. I shall
confine myself here to those represented in the Nag Hammadi Library, and I must apologize for the superficiality of my treatment.
I do not know this literature really well; I must read it in
translation because of my ignorance of Coptic, and I am not at
all sure whether my mental limitations as a Hellenist do not pre-
clude me from any deep understanding of it. However, I will
offer such tentative observations as I can. The first, and the
most important from my point of view, is that it seems to me a
mistake to read the Gnostics as if they were bad philosophers.
Whatever elements in their stories may seem to derive in some way
from their acquaintance with Greek philosophy, they are not doing
the same thing as philosophers. They are not giving explanations
of why things are as they are and accounts of the nature of the
divine powers in terms of concept and system. They are telling

---

23. Jean Trouillard, La Mystagogie de Proclos (Paris 1982) 247.

exciting stories about the often vividly imagined doings and
sufferings of spiritual beings, and it is the stories as told
which give their explanation of the universe. To reduce them to
abstract terms of principles and concepts will do them a greater
injustice than will be done if we do the same thing to those
greatest of Greek philosophers, Plato and Plotinus, who frequently use the language of poetry and religion. To try to turn their
stories into abstract schemes, as it is so convenient for the
comparative historian to do, is likely to be as unsatisfactory as
the attempts which have been made to give an account of Beethoven's
symphonies, especially the Fifth, in similar terms. I shall not
therefore make any systematic effort to place the Gnostic stories
precisely in my original scheme of cosmic dualisms.

Another reason for not attempting to do this is that I find
it difficult to discover in the Nag Hammadi literature anyone or
anything which corresponds closely to the 'dark other' as a major
force in the development of things to their present state. In
other forms of Gnosticism, of course, we do meet with a darkness
and powers of darkness which seem to be in ultimate opposition to
the powers of light in the Iranian manner, though they are generally rather inert and passive by Iranian standards. But in the
Nag Hammadi treatises which I have read the part played by any
ultimate darkness seems decidedly modest. We meet with the important Gnostic idea of darkness as a mirror, the reflection in
which of a higher power is a stage in the genesis of the lower
world.[24] In Zostrianos the darkness is considerably more important, but it seems to denote not a cosmic principle but the whole
lower cosmos from which the Gnostic is being shown the way and
passionately exhorted to escape.[25] It is notable in our present
context that the darkness here is feminine: the message of the
whole treatise is summed up in the exhortation 'Flee from the
madness and the bondage of femininity and choose for yourself the
salvation of masculinity'.[26] (In other treatises, of course, the
feminine is viewed with a good deal more favour: a great deal
seems to depend on how the Genesis story of the fall of man is

24. Hypostasis of the Archons (II 4) 11-14; cf. Poimandres (Corp.Herm.I) 14
Nock-Festugière.

25. Zostrianos (VIII 1) 1.

26. Ibid.131.

interpreted and on how the ambiguous and androgynous figure of
Barbelo is understood.) In the Tripartite Tractate the 'Outer
Darkness', 'Chaos', 'Hades' or the 'Abyss' seems to be just the
place which rightly belongs to the turbulent 'beings of the likeness', and to which they fall down.[27] In the Apocryphon of John
the basic darkness which causes all other evil and darkness seems
to be identified with the ignorant archon and Demiurge Yaltabaoth,
who of course like all Gnostic Demiurges appears late in the
story: he *is* 'ignorant darkness'.[28] The position seems to be much
the same in the Trimorphic Protennoia, but here the demonic,
aggressive evil of Yaltabaoth is more strongly stressed.

My next observation is, I hope, fairly uncontroversial, but
important in our present context. It is that the form in which
the Gnostics apprehend the action of the divine power of good and
light in this world is predominantly that of a Redeemer, Enlight-
ener and Liberator. The down-grading of the favoured image of
the Platonists, the Demiurge, by the Gnostics is of course well-
known. (I shall say something soon about how it continues to
operate even in Gnostics who insist that the creation of the
lower world is part of a great divine salvific plan.) But it is
worth remarking that even though in the end this bad and unhappy
world will be done away and the power of light will then finally
defeat and triumph over the forces of darkness, the image of cham-
pion and war-leader for the great divine power who will bring
this about is not generally favoured. It is the liberation of
the Gnostic children of light from the darkness through the saving enlightenment brought by the Redeemer which is in the centre
of the picture, not the cosmic defeat of the armies of the darkness. This marks a difference, as we shall see, between Gnostics
and non-Gnostic Christians, which is important in practice as
well as in thought. During the centuries of the Christian domination of Europe those who can in some extended sense be called
Gnostics have been decidedly more crusaded against than crusading.

The stories told by Gnostics of this kind have a common feature which seems to me useful in determining their position in
relation both to the Platonist tradition and to non-Gnostic

---

27. Tripartite Tractate (I 5) 78.
28. Apocryphon of John 11.

XII

Christianity. This is the importance given to a fall or failure
in the spiritual world, a break in the middle of the great process of outgoing which determines the character of the subsequent
process and leads in the end to the creation of this lower world.
It is of course a very good kind of plot for a story which sets
out to explain why things are so unsatisfactory here below in
terms of the adventures of higher beings. This picture of some
kind of fall or failure occurs even in stories which stress that
the whole outgoing, including the creation of the lower world, is
part of the great divine plan and which give a comparatively
favourable account of the creator. This is particularly noticeable in the Tripartite Tractate. Here the Logos, the creative
power, acts throughout in accordance with the will of the Father.
It is stressed that his aspiration to ascend to the Father and
desire to create on his own is intended by the Father. 'Therefore it is not right to criticize the movement which is the Logos,
but it is fitting that we should say about the movement of the
Logos that it is cause of a system which has been destined to
come about.'[29] There is certainly something here which is compar-
able (with due caution) with Plotinus' idea of tolma.[30] But as we
read on we find that the Logos 'was not able to bear the sight of
the light, but he looked into the depth and he doubted. Therefore it was an extremely painful division, a turning away because
of his self-doubt and division, forgetfulness and ignorance of
himself and of that which is'.[31] This goes beyond the most Gnos-
tic-like idea in any Platonist, Numenius' concept of the 'split-
ting' of the Demiurge.[32] And in what follows in the Tripartite
Tractate we discover that all the unreality, disturbance, and
trouble of this lower world, the defects and dissensions of the
cosmic powers, the Archons, and the conflict between the powers

---

29. Tripartite Tractate 77 (translation by Harold Attridge and Dieter Mueller
in The Nag Hammadi Library in English (Leiden 1977).

30. On this see Naguib Baladi, La Pensée de Plotin (Paris 1970) and my own
treatment in 'Gnosis and Greek Philosophy' 116ff. (in Gnosis: Festschrift für
H.Jonas (Göttingen 1978) 87-124, reprinted as no.XXI in A.H.Armstrong, Plotinian and Christian Studies (London 1979).

31. Tripartite Tractate (I 5) 77.

32. Numenius fr.11 Des Places (20 Leemans).

of light and darkness which dominates the present state of things,
are due to the weakness and sickness of the Logos which comes
from his attempt to attain to the Father. Here we have a real
'break in the middle', a real fault and failing in the spiritual
world accounting for the origin of an on the whole bad, and transitory material cosmos, which is not compatible with the thought
of Plotinus or with any kind of genuine Platonism.

It is not easy to fit the Gnostic stories which we have just
been considering into any tidy scheme of cosmic or two-principle
dualism. But of course the Gnostics, like the Platonists and the
non-Gnostic Christians, are dualists in another perfectly legitimate sense of 'dualism', that of belief in a duality of worlds, a
higher and a lower cosmos. Something must be said here about
some possible variations of this. We need to look rather carefully at the variants of two-world dualism which we encounter in
the first centuries of our era in order to determine the degree
of 'otherworldliness', that is of hostility to, alienation from,
and desire to escape from this lower cosmos which appears in them.
This seems to depend to a great extent on the way in which the
relationship between the two worlds is conceived or imagined. It
is perfectly correct to say that the Nag Hammadi literature has
shown that not all Gnostics were totally alienated from this world
and committed to a darkly pessimistic view of the cosmos and its
maker. But it must be admitted that a rather dark pessimism does
predominate; and even in those treatises where a comparatively
favourable view is taken of the creator and his creation, the
estimate of the material cosmos does not seem to be high. There
is not very much to be said for it as it appears in the latter
part of the Tripartite Tractate. The sentence in Marsanes '<I
have come to know> when <I> was deliberating that in every respect the sense-perceptible world is [worthy] of being saved entirely' certainly deserves to be quoted to show that not all
Gnostics were utterly alienated and anti-cosmic. But if we also
quote what remains of what comes immediately before, 'Finally the
entire defilement was saved, together with the immortality of
that one [feminine] ...', it does not look as if the material
world, presumably identical with or part of the 'entire defilement', is very much esteemed after all.[33] The most deeply and

---

33. Marsanes (X 1) 5.

strongly world-affirming of the treatises which I have read is
the Writing Without Title,[34] with its loving descriptions of the
paradises of the cosmic Erōs and the symbolic animals of the land
of Egypt.[35] Tardieu describes the spirit and mood of the treatise
(and of the closely related Hypostasis of the Archons) beautifully and accurately:[36]

> Tous les trois [the myths of Adam and Eve, Erōs, and the animals of
> Egypt] expriment la même nostalgie d'une intimité chaleureuse, d'une
> fusion originaire et vital entre l'homme et la femme (cycle d'Adam),
> l'homme et les plantes (jardins d'Erōs), entre l'homme et l'animal
> (cycle des animaux d'Egypte), nostalgie analogue à celle qui préside à
> la genèse des mythes de la bisexualité, de l'age d'or et de la régenera-
> tion.

It is important to remark that here the female and the androgynous (Erōs is androgynous) are very highly regarded: in the telling of the story of Genesis the values are reversed and Eve and
the serpent are good saving powers. This is certainly not a
spirit of mere cosmic pessimism and alienation from this world.
But it is a spirit of nostalgia, and nostalgia is generally understood as a passionate longing for something far away and long ago,
and generally implies that one is fairly miserable about the state
in which one finds oneself. Here we can see an important reason
why it is very easy for Gnostics to be very hostile to and alienated from this present world. In the Gnostic stories the higher
cosmos is remote and we cannot return to it, except in vision and
revelation, till after bodily death. The material cosmos is not
only remote from the world of light but itself a transitory phenomenon; there is no reason to care about it very much.

For Platonists the relationship of the two worlds is very
different. From the Timaeus onwards the essential truth about
the material cosmos is that it is an image, divinely made, of the
eternal world of Forms. (The idea that things in this world are
in some sense images of things in a higher world does of course
occur in some Gnostic writings,[37] as Plotinus notes with hostil-

---

34. II 5.

35. As M.Tardieu observes, this praise of Egypt brings the treatise close to
the Hermetic Asclepius (see Trois Mythes Gnostiques (Paris 1974) 269-272).

36. Ibid.269.

37. E.g. Zostrianus 48,55,113 (a treatise which Plotinus may have known).

ity.[38]   But the archetypes of the images do not usually seem to
be on a very high level or to come into existence very early in
the story and the stress seems to be very much, as a rule, on the
shadowy, phantasmal, and generally unsatisfactory character of
the material image.   In some Gnostics the valuation of body and
the material world may not be very far from the _Phaedo_ or from
the nostalgia for the higher world of _Phaedrus_ 250C, but it never
seems to come very near to the _Timaeus_.   The idea of the world as
image does not seem to be really central for the Gnostics and, at
their most cosmically optimistic, they are very far from regarding it as the everlasting icon of the eternal glory.)   I have for
some time found it useful, in considering the attitudes of Platonists to body and the material universe, to observe that the concept of 'image' allows, and indeed demands, a sliding scale of
valuation.   At the lower end of the scale one says, 'How poor,
trivial and inadequate a thing the image is compared with the
original'; at the higher end 'How beautiful and venerable is this
icon of the eternal glory not made by human hands'.   And many intermediate stages are possible, according to mood, temperament
and context.   We have seen how even in the more dualistic and
pessimistically inclined Middle Platonists, the influence of the
Timaeus prevented the higher valuation of the cosmos as image
from ever being forgotten.   And it is particularly clearly and
strongly evident in Plotinus, in spite of a considerable number
of pessimistically other-worldly utterances.   We can see very
well in him how the beauty of the everlasting image depends on
the continual presence in it of the invisible and eternal archetype; indeed, not only its beauty but its very existence, for it
is a 'natural' image, like a shadow or reflection, which cannot
exist without the archetype's presence.[39]   The two worlds are very
close to each other in Plotinus; so close that many good modern
interpreters of the _Enneads_ find it better and less misleading to
understand his thought in terms of one world, one set of entities,

---

38.   II 9 (33) 26-27.   'Why do they feel the need to be there in the archetype
of the universe which they hate?'   A great deal of II 9 is devoted to severe
criticism of the Gnostics' perverse use of the concept of image and the false
other-worldliness which springs from it.

39.   On the distinction between 'natural' and 'artificial' images see VI 4 (22)
9-10.   A text which well brings out the closeness of the two worlds is V 8 (31)
7.

apprehended in different ways at different levels, rather than two.[40] In terms of comparison with Gnostics, and non-Gnostic Christians, this means that for Plotinus heaven, or the Pleroma, or the World of Light, is not remote and our sojourn there is not something which belongs to the past or the future. The eternal is here and now present in its everlasting image. The only Parousia there will ever be is here and now. And those who are capable and prepared to make the great moral and intellectual efforts to do so can live in heaven and rise beyond it to God here and now. Porphyry was, it seems, more inclined than his master to follow Numenius in regarding this world as a place to escape from. But the Athenian Neoplatonists incline even more strongly than Plotinus to the highest valuation of the image; for them too the One and the Henads and the Forms are intimately and immediately present at every level of their vast hierarchy of being, the highest more intimately and immediately present in this lower cosmos of ours than those of lower rank. And through the sacred rites their presence may be experienced by at least some of those who cannot rise to the austere contemplation of the sage.

I have left myself little room to discuss the formidably complex subject of the forms of cosmic dualism which are to be found in the thought of non-Gnostic Christians. But it will already be apparent that a good deal which has been said in the earlier parts of this paper about both Platonists and Gnostics can be applied to mainstream Christians. The best thing I can do here is to suggest at least a partial explanation for the remarkable variations in Christian theory and practice in terms of the different solutions adopted by Christians to the problems of the evils and imperfections apparent in the world and human beings. Non-Gnostic Christians have generally rejected with great passion and emphasis interpretations of the Jewish and Christian stories which made the creator of the world other than and inferior to the one God and Father of Jesus Christ. They have rejected the kind of 'break in the middle' which figures so prominently in the Gnostic stories. As a result they affirm very strongly the good-

---

40. Cf. two recent articles in Dionysius: K.Corrigan, 'The Internal Dimensions of the Sensible Object in the Thought of Plotinus and Aristotle' 5(1981) 98-126; M.F.Wagner, 'Plotinus' World' 6(1982)13-42.

ness of the creation as well as of the creator, and eventually
classical Christian theology came to accept the later Neoplatonist view of evil as having no real existence, as a parhypostasis.
On this side of Christian thinking Platonic influence has been
strong and deep. In the West as well as in the East Christians
have often arrived at a theophanic view of the material creation
in which it appears as the God-made icon of the eternal glory. I
was myself brought up in an English Christian tradition which saw
no fundamental difference between Platonism and Christianity, and
instinctively and unselfconsciously accepted God's self-revelation in nature as equal in honour to his self-revelation in scripture and church, a way of faith admirably summed up in St.Maximus
Confessor's discussion of the proper interpretation of the white
garments of the Transfiguration in which he concludes, '... the
two laws, of nature and of scripture, are equal in honour and
teach the same as each other, and neither is greater or less than
the other...'[41] But there are of course important differences between the normal Christian creationist position and that of the
later Platonists. The Christians lay much greater stress on God's
will and have a more unbridled and absolute conception of divine
creative power than Plato and his followers; as a result they not
only reject the independent principle of evil of the Middle Platonists but have little room in their thought for the 'dark other',
still so important in the last Neoplatonists, and in general, at
least till quite recently, reject any limitation on God's omnipotence which would mean that he works by persuasion rather than
force. This can result in leading those Christians, like Augustine in his later years, who incline to a gloomy view of the present state of affairs, not only to a pessimism about the world as
great as that of the Manichees but to a way of thinking about God
darker and more terrifying than that of any thorough-going cosmic
dualists.[42]
      The darker view of this world is strongly assisted by the
older and more popular Christian way of explaining its evils.
This is a story-explanation, in terms of persons rather than
principles, about the fall of angels and men, and in this way

---

41. Maximus Ambigua VI, PG 91 1128C-D.
42. Peter Brown brings this out very well in his Augustine of Hippo (London
1967) in ch.32 on the controversy with Julian of Eclanum.

resembles the Gnostic stories. In Patristic thought, and sometimes in later Christian thought, the fall of the angels plays an
important part in the explanation of cosmic or physical evil;
though no other Christian thinker goes as far as Origen in making
the whole creation depend on the fall of the spirits who, according to the depth of their fall, became angels, men or devils; a
doctrine which he is enabled to reconcile with his firm anti-
Gnostic faith that the creation is essentially good (because it
is the work of the perfectly good and wise Father working through
the Logos in whom there is no fault or failing) by his vision of
the whole creative process as one of redemption, education and
purification which will bring all the spirits back to that original state from which they, freely and of their own motion, in no
way impelled by God chose to fall. The vital difference between
the way of thinking of the Peri Archōn and the at first sight not
entirely dissimilar one of the Tripartite Tractate is that for
Origen there is no element of fault and failing, no falling below
the best, in the divine creative act itself. Origen's view was
of course generally rejected by non-Gnostic Christians; but in
less wholesale forms the explanation of cosmic evils by the fall
of the angels has not, perhaps, been uncommon. My father, who
was an Anglican clergyman, reconciled his passionate belief in
the goodness of the creation with the undoubted existence of
evils in it by an interesting Christian adaptation of what is
said in the Timaeus about the part taken by the 'younger gods' in
the formation of the world, which he regarded as perfectly orthodox and traditional. He held that the angels had had bestowed on
them by God limited powers of creation which the devils were not
deprived of, and continued to exercise after their fall by creat-
ingall the things in the world of which my father disapproved,
notably slugs and snails, to which, being an enthusiastic garden-
er, he had the strongest objection.[42a]

But it is when the doctrine of the fall of the angels is
combined with that of the fall of mankind to provide an explanation of the evils which beset humanity here below that we may
find the foundations in Christian thought for a world-view as
dark as that of the Manichaeans or a conflict-dualism fiercer
than that of the Mazdaeans. J.H.W.G.Liebeschütz, in his excellent book on Roman religion, has shown very well how the passion-

42a My father said that he found this doctrine in William Law, I believe correctly. Law took it, as he took so
much, from Boehme.

ate early Christian belief in devils and the identification of
the pagan gods with devils darkened the late antique world-view,
by strengthening the tendency which had already appeared in it to
believe in supernatural personifications of evil:[43]

> The transformation of the gods into demons had a significant psychologi-
> cal consequence. The gods had sometimes been cruel or arbitrary, but
> they could be placated by offerings in quite the same way as arbitrary
> or tyrannous humans. They were not essentially hostile or spiteful.
> Christianity offered man enormously powerful assistance, but it also
> proclaimed the existence of powerful and totally evil adversaries. Life
> became a battle in which men must fight for God against 'the enemy'.

In a footnote he adds:

> There had been a tendency to believe in supernatural personifications of
> absolute evil, especially in connection with magic, in later Greek or
> Roman paganism... But it was left to Christianity to fill the world
> with evil spirits.

Peter Brown has unforgettably described the consequences in Augustine's latest thought of combining this devil-dualism with the
anti-dualist insistence on the omnipotence and sovereign will of
God:[44]

> God had plainly allowed the human race to be swept by his wrath: and this
> human race, as Augustine presents it in his works against Julian, is
> very like the invaded universe of Mani. Augustine had always believed
> in the vast power of the Devil... Now this Devil will cast his shadow
> over mankind: the human race is 'the Devil's fruit-tree, his own proper-
> ty, from which he may pick his fruit', it is 'the plaything of demons'.
> This is evil, thought of much as the Manichees had done, as a persecut-
> ory force. The demons may now have been enrolled as the unwitting agents
> of a superior justice: but it is they who are seen as active and man as
> merely passive.

Here, as Brown shows, we are very close to the Gnostic view of
the world at its darkest, and, though the figure of God is inves-
ted with a transcendent and absolute horror exceeding that of any
Gnostic demiurge or even the Manichaean evil principle, his most
eminent activity in the world in its present state is seen as the
redemption and deliverance of the small number of the elect from
its darkness. For the rest of humanity, of course, there is no
hope at all, as God simultaneously with his work of redemption
pursues his 'awesome blood-feud against the family of Adam'.[45]

---

43. J.H.W.G.Liebeschütz, Continuity and Change in Roman Religion (Oxford
1979) 269 and n.2.

44. Peter Brown, loc.cit. (n.42) 395. The quotations are from Augustine De
Nuptiis et Concupiscentia I xxiii,26 and Contra Julianum VI xxi,67.

45. Brown loc.cit.393; I have referred to this chapter because in it Brown
has said, with great precision and sympathy for Augustine, whatever can decent-
ly be said in defence of his later doctrine. For Manichaean influence on Augustine's doctrine of the massa
damnata see Th. G. Sinnige, "Gnostic Influences in the Early Works of Plotinus and in Augustine", in
Plotinus amid Gnostics and Christians (the volume in which this paper was originally published), ed. D.T.
Runia (Free University Press, Amsterdam 1984) pp. 93–97.

But those Christians who have not the tormented genius of
Augustine for drawing out the full horror of the consequences implicit in some traditional Christian doctrines, and who do not
see the world as so totally devil-ridden as Augustine did in his
later years (and many of his Christian contemporaries did not)
have often come to attach much importance to the third image which
I mentioned (p.34) as available to cosmic dualists, that of the
war-leader, commanding the armies of light against the forces of
darkness. They have found that the qualified conflict-dualism of
the belief that all the evils of this world are due to the sins
of the fallen angels and the men and women whom they have seduced
into following them provides admirable support for the ferocious,
though sometimes quite cheerful, pugnacity, exceeding that of
mainstream Iranian conflict-dualists, which has been a distinguishing characteristic of historic Christianity. The belief
that those whom one regards, at any place or time, as enemies of
authentic Christian faith, civilization, or interests are of the
Devil's party is a powerful stimulus to crusading: that is, of
course, if one does not pay too much attention, as Christians in
this sort of context have generally quite successfully avoided
doing, to where and how Christ chose to overcome evil, and so is
not inhibited by the reflection that the Cross is a singularly
inappropriate symbol for a Crusader.

Those of course who do attend to the meaning of the Cross,
as the best of those who have used the language of 'spiritual
combat' have done, will come to use that language in a very different way and understand the overcoming of evil in very different terms to the polemists and crusaders. In their thought and
practice this strange triumph will be achieved by accepting and
carrying evil and requiting it with good and with love. Most of
us have not got nearly as far as this. But, as we contemplate
the overcoming of evil by the way of the Cross, we may be permitted to observe that the language of conflict-dualism is not really appropriate to it, except in a most violently paradoxical
sense; so that we may come to prefer other images, including the
great Platonic image of the Craftsman, for our struggle in this
imperfect, but good and lovable world.

XIII

THE WAY AND THE WAYS:
RELIGIOUS TOLERANCE AND INTOLERANCE
IN THE FOURTH CENTURY A.D.

The subject I propose may seem to my present audience excessively well-worn. None the less it seems to me of such historical interest and contemporary importance that it is still worth looking carefully again at least at selected themes and moments in the controversies and policies of the period between the recognition of Christianity by Constantine and the final establishment of Christian intolerance under Theodosius. The choice of the way of intolerance by the authorities of Church and Empire in the late fourth century has had some very serious and lasting consequences. The last vestiges of its practical effects, in the form of the imposition of at least petty and vexatious disabilities on forms of religion not approved by the local ecclesiastical establishment, lasted in some European countries well into my lifetime. And theoretical approval of this sort of intolerance has often long outlasted the power to apply it in practice. After all, as late as 1945 many approved Roman Catholic theologians in England, and the Roman authorities, objected to a statement on religious freedom very close to Vatican II's declaration on that subject.[1] In general, I do not think that any Christian body has ever abandoned the power to persecute and repress while it actually had it. The acceptance of religious tolerance and freedom as good in themselves has normally been the belated, though sometimes sincere and whole-hearted, recognition and acceptance of a *fait accompli*. This long persistence of Theodosian intolerance in practice and its still longer persistence in theory has certainly been a cause, though not the only cause, of that unique phenomenon of our time, the decline not only of Christianity but of all forms of religious belief and the growth of a totally irreligious and unspiritual materialism. This is something which many people, by no means only committed Christians, continually and rightly lament. But I am more and more convinced that a principal cause of it has been the general experience of Church teaching and practice and of the behaviour of Christians during the centuries from the imperial establishment of Christianity to our own times. The triumph of Christianity carried in it, as perhaps all such triumphs do, the seeds of future defeat. The Church in the fourth century took what it wanted and has been paying for it, in one way or another, ever since.

It seems also important to examine what happened in the fourth century rather carefully because such an examination may do a good deal to dispel the idea that the triumph of Christian intolerance was the inevitable result of some great spiritual movement sweeping on irresistibly to its goal: or even that it was inevitable given the ancient, and particularly the Roman view of the rights and responsibilities of rulers in matters of religion. I would not deny that what actually occurred was inevitable given the actual balance of forces at the time and the course of preceding events, including the long and, on the whole, successful reign of Constantine and the premature death of Julian: though even so, if Gratian and Theodosius had chosen to continue the religious policy of Jovian and Valentinian I rather than to develop further the intolerance of the sons of Constantine, the triumph of Christianity would have been considerably qualified in ways which might have meant that its consequences for the future would have been less deleterious. But I cannot see any deeper necessity here than that of circumstance and actual balance of forces.

In view of what has just been said, we should clearly start our consideration of tolerance and intolerance in the fourth century by a rather careful general consideration of the ancient world's view of the place of religion in society and of the duties of rulers in matters of religion. The place of religion in society in the later Roman Empire was what it had always been in the Greek and Roman world, as in other traditional societies. Religious cults were all-pervasive and central to the life of society and it was therefore generally agreed, as it had always been, that the maintenance and proper regulation of religious practice was the proper concern of the authorities of the state. Religious concern and anxiety had been deepening and itensifying since the late second century, and this of course made the concern of the authorities, in some cases at least, a good deal more intense. But the line between this late antique period and the centuries immediately preceding it, the age of the Hellenistic kingdoms and the early Roman Empire, should not be drawn too sharply. We may, if we like, speak of the Hellenistic Age as "irreligious" in comparison with archaic Greece or the period with which we are now dealing. But this does not mean that it was irreligious in any modern sense. Old cults, and, for the mass of the population, old beliefs continued: splendid new temples like Didyma were built: new cults, including the very successful one of Serapis, were introduced: and one of the most deeply and passionately religious of philosophies, the Stoic, developed. The massive continuity of the old religion is more impressive that the variations of intensity of religious concern at different periods and in different places and groups. The rise in late antiquity of a new form of sacred absolute monarchy of course intensified the sense of religious consecration and religious responsibility of the ruler, and concentrated it on his single sacred person as representative of the divine on earth, and this is important. In considering the effects on Christianity of what happened in the fourth century we need always to remember that the Church of the Fathers was the Church of the Empire and that its thought and institutions developed in a world in which absolute sacred monarchy claiming universal jurisdiction was the only conceivable form of government. But the Sacred Emperors were exercising essentially the same sort of religious authority, for essentially the same reasons, that the magistrates and assemblies of the city-states, and the archaic kings before them, had exercised from the beginning.

The reasons for this religious concern of ancient authorities should not be misunderstood. There was nothing particularly spiritual or otherworldly about it. The concern of the rulers to keep on the right side of God or the gods, to ensure that the divine-human relationship was as it should be in the societies of which they had charge, was part, and a most important part, of their care for the temporal, this-worldly, well being of their subjects. Divine displeasure might bring pestilence and famine, barbarian invasion, defeat in war, or, perhaps most serious of all from a late antique emperor's point of view, the rise and eventual triumph of a rival claimant to the throne. These temporal consequences were believed to be due to divine displeasure by pagans and Christians alike, and sanctions of this kind could be understood even by the stupidest and most unspiritual of emperors, the sort who, Plotinus ironically suggested, turned into eagles after their death.[2] And even those who did not believe in this sort of divine visitation (and in late antiquity they were probably very few) would inherit from the more sceptical side of the early thought of Greece and Rome a conviction that proper religious observance, whatever that was thought to be, was central and essential to the maintenance of the whole fabric of culture and society.

4

All ancient rulers, then, considered it part, and a most important part, of their duties, to maintain in their dominions a proper relationship with the divine. This was particularly true of Roman authorities, with their passion for order and precise regulation and their vivid sense of the social and political importance of religion. And, as has already been remarked, the way in which the sacred authority of the emperors of the fourth century was conceived made their sense of obligation in religious matters particularly intense. A secular society was inconceivable and impossible in the ancient world, and never more inconceivable and impossible than in the fourth century. But having made these generalizations, we need to consider rather carefully the very various ways in which the general principles were understood and practical conclusions were drawn from them.

The starting-point here must be the obvious and well studied contrast between Hellenic and Roman paganism and Christianity. The old religion was a religion of cult, not of dogmatic belief. This meant that what was thought of as seriously and dangerously displeasing to the divine was anything which endangered the performance of the sacred rites or might bring them into disrespect or neglect. But there was no doctrinal orthodoxy deviation from which might bring down the divine displeasure. People could, and did, think in a great variety of incompatible ways about the gods, and could express their opinions, within rather unpredictable limits set by the prevailing degree of religious concern and anxiety among the general public or the ruling classes. I do not propose to go into any disputed questions concerning the persecution of the Christians. But I may perhaps be permitted the generalization, that the widespread dislike of the Christians, which from time to time intensified into a feeling that something drastic must be done about them, sprang from the awareness of an alien barbarian attack on the sacred rites and the ways of thinking and feeling bound up with them and so on the whole social fabric which they permeated and the whole peace and harmony of human society with the divine. And I can certainly be permitted the obvious observation that the persecutions were decidedly spasmodic. From the edict of toleration of Gallienus in 261 to the great persecution which began in 303 the Church had enjoyed peace and a kind of quasi-recognition sufficient to allow it to acquire and hold property, always a most important aspect of toleration or recognition from the point of view of the imperial administration. And even during the Great Persecution itself there is a good deal of evidence for a

XIII

marked lack of enthusiasm among a good many local authorities, who were very lax in enforcing the imperial edicts, as A. H. M. Jones has noted.[3] It seems that, though when Christians were persecuted the motive was the fear of divine displeasure and social disruption noted in my earlier generalization, this fear was not always very strong and compelling. At the time when the dominance of the old religious ways was complete, there seem always to have been plenty of pagans who were willing in practice to grant Christians at least the same sort of hostile and contemptuous tolerance which was always given to Jews. And this suggests that the apophatic or agnostic pluralism put forward as a ground for tolerance by pagans of the late fourth century was not simply an accomodation to circumstances. I believe myself that it has very deep roots in authentically Hellenic intellectual and spiritual tradition. But before discussing this further it will be as well to consider some aspects of the thought and practice of the greatest of fourth-century Hellenes, the Emperor Julian.

To a great extent I share the now widespread admiration for Julian. I find him the only genuinely likeable human being in his very unpleasant family, and one whom his promise and early performance show to have been likely to have been a great and good emperor. And I am inclined to think that, if he had reigned as long as Constantine and trained a reasonably competent successor (or successors) to carry on his religious policy, that policy might have had a considerable measure of success. Historians, of course, should not speculate too much on what might have been. But it is surely not too fanciful to suggest that, if the Empire had been officially pagan in the time of St. Augustine's episcopate, and its Christian period had been a remote and for many people unpleasant memory, subsequent religious history would have been rather different. But, in spite of my admiration, I cannot regard Julian as a typical or normal Hellene or Neoplatonist. There is no need to say much about the un-Hellenic character of Julian's religious policy. Dr. Athanassiadi-Fowden's excellent book[4] has shown clearly how thoroughly Byzantine it was. Nothing could be more un-Hellenic than his conception of a great Hellenic religious institution coterminous with the Empire, with a dogmatic Iamblichean orthodoxy and a teaching hierarchy, under the control and direction of the sacred Emperor. In this he stands firmly in the line of development from Constantine to Justinian and beyond. Even if his reign had been longer and his re-Hellenization of the Empire reasonably successful, his Hellenic church could hardly have survived as

6

more than a formal institutional framework. The essential variety of paganism could not have been constricted into an orthodoxy.

Julian's position as a Neoplatonist needs rather more careful examination than it has always received. The account by Eunapius of his reception by Aedesius and his pupils at Pergamum and his choice of Maximus as spiritual director is well enough known.⁵ But its implications deserve consideration. It is true that Julian adopted Neoplatonism in its most theurgic and ritualistic form and that he did so in the school of Aedesius at Pergamum. But it is clear from Eunapius that the attitude of Aedesius to theurgy was decidedly reserved.⁶ And the account of Julian's choice of Maximus shows that one of the leading members of the Pergamene group, Eusebius of Myndus, was definitely hostile. It is a mistake, and may lead to considerable distortion of the history of Hellenic Neoplatonism, to speak of an older type of "Plotinian" and "Porphyrian" Neoplatonism and a later "Iamblichean", "theurgic" Neoplatonism as if they were two distinct schools or sects. They were, rather, different tendencies or inclinations (sometimes very definite and passionate) in individuals who continued to feel themselves united in all essentials, which are apparent throughout the history of Neoplatonism from the time of Plotinus to the time of Damascius.⁷ The extreme and exaggerated "Iamblichean" concern with sacred rites is likely to be a reason for the un-Hellenically ecclesiastical character of Julian's attempted Hellenic restoration and also for his extreme dogmatic intolerance. Religious hatreds always seem to be deepest and bitterest when forms, ceremonies and institutions come into the dispute. And there is another, less noticed, feature of Julian's Neoplatonism which would have tended the same way. It is quite remarkable in a Neoplatonist that little, if anything, is said in his theological writings about the unknowable God and our passionate aspiration to him. Apophatic theology was certainly important to Iamblichus, and remained centrally and at times painfully important to the great theurgic Neoplatonists of Athens, Proclus and Damascius. But Julian is decidedly a kataphatic theologian. He concentrates his theological attention and personal devotion on the gods of the Iamblichean noeric order, mediators between the transcendent spiritual world and ours; and above all on his personal patron, Helios-Mithras, that great god of whom the visible sun is sacrament, icon or theophany and Julian himself, the Emperor, the appointed representative on earth. And this again would have influenced him in the direction of dogmatic intolerance. The less

XIII

one thinks one knows about the God of one's faith and aspiration, the easier it will be to see other people's faiths as true ways towards him. Passionate devotion to a highly personalized deity of well-defined character is more likely both to inspire in oneself and to provoke in others of different devotion a passionate and bitter hostility.

I have spoken of Julian's dogmatic intolerance, which indeed is sufficiently apparent. His language about Christianity is as violent as that of any Father of the Church about paganism and heresy. But in fairness to him one must remark briefly on the very moderate degree in which he translated his theoretical ferocity into practical intolerance: and I do not myself believe that if he had returned victorious from Persia he would have moved further in the direction of persecution, though no doubt his practical tolerance of Christians would have remained thoroughly hostile and discriminatory. He shared to the full the conviction of his Christian contemporaries that forced conversion was not permissible. Insult and invective, adverse discrimination, confiscation of the property of dissident groups and prohibition of their worship were permissible. But, in this century, the line was drawn at forced conversion. This is no sound basis for any degree of practical tolerance which we should regard as tolerable nowadays: and the line between prohibiting all expression of religious dissidence and forcing dissidents into at least outward conformity with the prevailing orthodoxy is very difficult to draw in practice and was sometimes overstepped in the fourth century. But Julian drew the line rather further back on the side of tolerance. He never showed any sign of prohibiting Christian worship and teaching in the churches, and I do not believe that if his reign had continued he would have done so. He seems to have had an authentically Hellenic and philosophical conviction that the way to win a battle of ideas was by example and argument, not coercion.

The most extreme example, in the view of Ammianus, of his practical intolerance was of course the decree prohibiting Christians from teaching the pagan classics, which upset the Christians so remarkably. This has been very extensively discussed, and it is clear that Julian's insistence on excluding Christian teachers, the Christians' indignation, and the more easy-going attitude of most contemporary pagans, derive from different ideas about the religious content of the classics which were the basis of the unquestioned and unchallenged common culture of the *oecumene*. Julian, who saw that religious content in the light of his own Byzantine Hellenic orthodoxy, and was perhaps thinking in terms of training a devout pagan ruling elite, naturally wished all classical education to be conducted by teachers of the true faith. Those Christians who thought at all seriously about the matter, like St. Basil, believed that by judicious selection and Christian teaching the classics could be, so to speak, "decaffeinated", their pernicious pagan content neutralized, and what was useful in them turned to wholly Christian purposes.[8] The more easy-going pagans, and probably a good many Christians, most likely thought simply that teaching and learning the classics could not possibly do anyone anything but good, and that the only way to a genuine culture was to get as much of them as one could. It was of course the last point of view which prevailed, with some varying admixture of the second, and it was the, on the whole unselfconscious and easy, acceptance of the ancient classics by Christians from the fifth century A.D. onwards which ensured their survival through the Christian centuries and made them the centre of upper-class Christian education down to my own younger days. But Julian was right in a way. The Hellenic classics could not be purged of their Hellenism and domesticated to the service of the Church. They did not transmit through Christendom a Julianist Hellenic orthodoxy which they did not contain. But they have transmitted a whole complex of ways of thinking, feeling and imagining which are not compatible with Biblicist and ecclesiastical Christianity. The Muses and the Lady Philosophy are not to be recommended as priests' housekeepers.

One must begin any discussion of the tolerant, pluralist paganism of the fourth century with the great statement of Symmachus *Non uno itinere perveniri potest ad tam grande secretum.*[9] But of course the place of this in his appeal for tolerance is very modest and incidental. He bases his main case on good Roman grounds of ancient tradition and more recent precedent, including the precedents of Christian emperors. A better representative of this way of thinking is, as Henry Chadwick has seen,[10] Themistius. The great philosopher-orator to whom even intolerant Christian emperors listened with respect was, unusually for his time, an Aristotelian rather than a Platonist. But he is not unaffected by contemporary Platonism, and the simple theology which is the basis of his appeals for tolerance would have been acceptable, as far as it went, to many Neoplatonists. His surviving oration before Jovian,[11] and the summaries of his even more powerful plea for tolerance to Valens in the church historians,[12] give a good idea of his position. I quote (in my own re-translation from the German) Henry Chadwick's excellent conflation of Socrates and Sozomen[13] (whose summaries differ slightly) as a good statement of the common position of these tolerant pluralist pagans. "The differences of opinion between the Christians are unimportant compared with the three hundred different opinions among the pagans. God's glory is increased by the knowledge that religious differences are only a consequence of his unattainable majesty and of human limitations."

We are considering here a temper of mind rather than a formal, systematic doctrine, and one which can express itself, according to the dispositions and circumstances of different individuals and groups, in a variety of ways from formal scepticism and agnosticism to a passionately apophatic theology. This temper of mind is something which can be clearly detected a very long way back in the history of Hellenic thought. One of the most powerful expressions of diffidence about human knowledge of the divine is also one of the earliest, the lines of that formidable philosophical theologian Xenophanes "No man knows, nor will there be anyone who knows, the truth about the gods and about everything I say: for even if one happened to say the complete truth, yet one does not know it oneself: but seeming is wrought over all things".[14] And anyone who reads Herodotus will be able to see how firmly rooted the *non uno itinere* is in ordinary classical Greek thinking about other people's religions. With more direct relevance to the thought of the fourth century A.D., I would maintain that a great deal can be found in the dialogues of Plato (whether Plato himself intended it to be found there or not) which can lead either towards scepticism or towards apophatic theology. It is easy enough, of course, to find scepticism of different degrees and varieties in the Hellenistic and early Imperial periods: and from the first century B.C., at latest, there begins to develop the apophatic theology to which sceptical criticism of earlier dogmatisms about the divine made an important contribution. This is all much too summary to be convincing, and needs far more elaboration and discussion than is possible here. A very good concise account has been published by the late R. T. Wallis.[15]   But unless we are aware that we are considering here something very widespread and deeply rooted in the whole Hellenic tradition, and not simply the attitude of a group in the fourth century, we shall find it hard to understand the persistent recurrence of this temper of mind throughout the history of later European thought about the divine, not least evident in our own times.

10

In considering the tolerant pagan pluralism of the fourth century we need to observe the coming together in it of a number of different forms in which this temper of mind expressed itself. There is the old simple awareness, clearly discernible in Herodotus, that people are different and understand the divine in different ways, and that there is no good reason to suppose that any one tradition or nation has a monopoly of truth about the divine: this is not in itself very sceptical, agnostic or apophatic. It was well expressed in the late second century, in an entirely pagan context and without reference to Christianity, by Maximus of Tyre: "If the art of Pheidias awakes the Greeks to the memory of God, the cult of animals the Egyptians, and a river others, and fire others, I do not resent their disagreement: let them only know him, let them only love him, let them only remember him":[16] a peroration of which one can hear an echo in the late fourth century in the celebrated conclusion of the letter of another Maximus, St. Augustine's elderly pagan correspondent, "May the gods preserve you, through whom all we mortals whom the earth supports venerate and worship in a thousand ways with concordant discord the common father of the gods and of all mortals".[17] Then there is the urbane and moderate Academic scepticism of which in the Latin West Cicero was the principal transmitter, a scepticism always accompanied by a strong traditionalism in practical religious matters which certainly weighed heavily against the Christians but may also have told against the exaggerated ritualism of Julian. Finally there is the faith, based on deep religious experience, of the Neoplatonists in a God who is simply beyond us, too great for speech or thought, formulated, as has already been suggested, partly though by no means wholly under the influence of sceptical attacks on dogmatism about the divine. This is indeed important, but should not be regarded, in and by itself and out of the wider context just sketched, as the principal or sole cause of tolerant pluralism.

When we think about the mentality of these fourth-century pagan pluralists we should also take into account another aspect of the Neoplatonism of Plotinus and Porphyry, in which it differs most sharply from that of Iamblichus and his successors. This is the conviction that the only true religion is philosophical religion, and that the stories and practices of non-philosophical religion are, at the best, no more than helpful popular expressions of philosophic truth for non-philosophers. This sort of Neoplatonism is of course compatible with the hostility shown by Porphyry himself to the alien barbarian Christian attack on

XIII

the whole of Hellenic thought and culture: but it can also issue in a tolerant pluralism or in considerably more positive attitudes towards Christianity. The kind of probably more or less Porphyrian Neoplatonism which he learnt from Hypatia at Alexandria certainly helped Synesius in his decision to accept episcopal office when that seemed to him the best way of serving the community.[18] And Marius Victorinus moved on from tolerant pluralism to see the post-Nicene theology of the Trinity as the perfect expression of Porphyrian metaphysical religion and so was able to accept Christianity whole-heartedly as the perfection of the ancient philosophy and culture which he loved, in which it could be preserved for the future.[19]

We now pass on to Christian intolerance and tolerance in the fourth century. Here we must return to the difference noted earlier (p. 4) between Hellenic paganism and Christianity. The old religion was one of cult, not of belief. There was no doctrinal orthodoxy deviation from which might bring down the divine displeasure. For Christians dogmatic orthodoxy mattered very much, especially for the bishops who felt themselves responsible for the transmission of the true faith and the preservation in unity of faith of their flocks: and the conclusion was generally drawn that it was an important part of the religious responsibilities of the rulers of the Empire to enforce whatever the bishops of any place or time considered orthodoxy to be, if they wished to avoid the serious temporal and spiritual consequences for Emperor and Empire of the displeasure of an offended God. The general fourth-century Christian episcopal attitude was well summed-up early in the next century by Nestorius in his address to Theodosius II: Δός μοι, ὦ βασιλεῦ, καθαρὰν τὴν γῆν τῶν αἱρετικῶν, κἀγώ σοι τὸν οὐρανὸν ἀντιδώσω· συγκάθελέ μοι τοὺς αἱρετικούς, κἀγὼ συγκαθελῶ σοι τοὺς Πέρσας[20] promises which must have a double tragic irony for later readers when we remember not only Ephesus but that the great future of the Church of the East which heresiologists call Nestorian lay not in the Roman Empire but in and beyond the eastern boundaries of the Persian.

When we turn from Christian bishops to Christian emperors the picture is rather more interesting and varied. I accept as probable H. A. Drake's view of the religious policy of Constantine, very fully expounded and well supported by evidence in his study of *De Laudibus Constantini*:[21] his case does not by any means wholly depend on the division of Eusebius' panegyric into two separate orations delivered to different audiences on different occasions, though this seems a reasonable enough hypothesis. If he is right in seeing Constantine as a sincere Christian who as emperor was always more concerned with the religious peace and unity of the empire than with the triumph of right belief at any cost (and there is a great deal of evidence which points that way) and one who was prepared to the end of his life to extend a large tolerance to paganism: then we can see him as providing a weighty precedent for the policy of the Christian emperors between Julian and Gratian. This deserves a good deal of attention. All three of these sincerely Christian emperors, Jovian, Valentinian I, and Valens, were fully tolerant of paganism. Valens, unlike his brother, considered it his duty to persecute those Christians whom he considered as heretics on what he reasonably thought was the best episcopal advice available to him. This illustrates a point which is always worth bearing in mind when considering Christian intolerance. Christians have in general, till very recently, spoken of and behaved to their brethren with whom they disagreed in matters of faith much worse than they have treated adherents of other religions. Ammianus justly remarks that Christians are worse than wild beasts to each other.[22] He does not say, and would not, at least at the time of writing, have been correct in saying that they are worse than wild beasts to non-Christians.

Valens seems to have agreed fully with his brother, and with Jovian before them, in his tolerance of paganism, and it is in the policy of Valentinian I that we can see fully developed what seems to me a perfectly viable alternative to the Theodosian policy of intolerance, adapted to the conditions of the time and congruous with ancient thought about the religious responsibilities of the ruler. It was, of course, a policy of scrupulous tolerance of paganism, inspired, it seems by a genuine belief that all his subjects ought to enjoy complete freedom of worship,[23] combined with a resolute refusal to intervene in any ecclesiastical disputes or to lend the crushing weight of his authority to any party in the deeply divided Church of his time. Valentinian was a firm believer in Nicene Christianity and a military man of little education, unlikely to be deeply influenced by the ideas of pagan intellectuals (though his brother does seem to have listened with respect to Themistius[24]). And he was certainly not of an easy-going disposition, and showed few signs of benevolence, except to bears.[25] His policy seems very likely to have been prompted, not only by a reasonable belief that it was in the best interests of the peace and unity of the empire but by a confidence that it was according to the will of God, which would have been possible within the limits of the general ancient view of the religious responsibilities of the ruler. And if it had persisted and become the imperial norm followed by rulers of the successor states in the West, its consequences might have been far-reaching. Our religious history would surely have been rather different if in many towns, instead of one great bishop and one great cathedral, there had been in the next few centuries two or three vigorously dissentient bishops and two or three rival cathedrals, together with a pagan temple or two.

The bishops were too strong in the end for a tolerant policy to establish itself. But before concluding I would like to take a look at a very insignificant and, as far as we know, untypical bishop in whom a gleam of tolerance may be discerned. This is Pegasius, Bishop of Ilion in 354, who in 362 applied for and obtained a position in Julian's pagan hierarchy. All we know about his beliefs and practices is contained in a letter of Julian to an unknown correspondent defending his appointment of Pegasius in 362, in which he describes how the bishop had shown him round the holy places of Troy when he visited it in the course of his journey to the court of Constantius in 354.[26] A careful examination of this letter has suggested to me that Pegasius may have been something a good deal more interesting than a cynical opportunist or Vicar of Bray. He said himself in 362 that he had always been a faithful crypto-Hellene, and Julian believed him. But at this point it does seem likely that the opportunity of a dignified and lucrative career under the new régime had considerably coloured Pegasius' presentation, and perhaps his actual recollection, of his earlier position. The letter itself makes clear that there were plenty of people who said that Pegasius had always been a rather bigoted Christian, and threw doubt on the sincerity of his conversion to Hellenism: this in fact seems to be why Julian felt he had to write in defence of his appointment. And it is surely rather unlikely that a Hellenic "mole" should have managed to get himself elected and consecrated bishop even in a small Christian community remote from the centres of Christian life and thought and the attention of the bishops of the great sees. We should also remember that the position of Julian in 354 was very different from his position in 362. On that journey to the court at Milan, soon after the execution of his brother Gallus, he can hardly have seemed a promising patron to anyone. It would have been imprudent to make a large bet on his long survival, and very imprudent to wager anything at all on his changes of succeeding to the throne. It seems, therefore, that we are likely to get as near as we can to the real Pegasius if we do not pay much attention to the way in which he and Julian interpreted his beliefs and behaviour in 362, and attend closely to Julian's very precise account of what he did and said in 354.

When he met Julian at Troy and offered his services as guide he first conducted him to the shrine of the great local hero, Hector. Here Julian was surprised to find fires alight on the altars and the bronze statue of Hector beautifully anointed with oil. He asked Pegasius "Do the Ilians sacrifice?" to which the bishop replied "καὶ τὶ τοῦτο ἄτοπον, ἄνδρα ἀγαθὸν ἑαυτῶν πολίτην, ὥσπερ ἡμεῖς" ἔφη, "τοὺς μάρτυρας εἰ θεραπεύουσιν;" on which Julian comments ἡ μὲν οὖν εἰκὼν οὐκ ὑγιής· ἡ δὲ προαίρεσις ἐν ἐκείνοις ἐξεταζομένη τοῖς καιροῖς ἀστεία. I am inclined to think that Pegasius meant exactly what he said and that he made the comparison which offended Julian because he was a Christian and it came naturally to him as a Christian. They continued their tour to the temple of Athena and the shrine of Achilles (which Pegasius was later falsely accused of having destroyed). Here everything was in good order and the images well preserved, but there is no further mention of signs of cult. Julian did however particularly notice in the temple of Athena that the bishop did not hiss and make the sign of the cross against the demons, as the impious (i.e. Christians) were accustomed to do. Another piece of information in the letter, not connected with the meeting in 354, is that Julian says he has heard "from those who are now his enemies" that Pegasius used in secret to pray to and venerate the Sun. This hearsay evidence seems, because of its source (presumably those pagans who were now objecting to Pegasius' appointment) to be as worthy of belief as Julian's eyewitness account.

How then, in the light of this reliable evidence, are we to understand the position of Pegasius in 354? The most reasonable interpretation seems to me that he was a sincere Christian, though perhaps not one of very deep and passionate faith. I do not find any reason to suppose that his Christian fellow-townsmen were grossly mistaken in thinking him suitable to be elected bishop (or neighbouring bishops in consecrating him) or that he did not perform his episcopal functions of celebrating the Eucharist and preaching with sufficient devotion. But he was a Christian who saw no harm in permitting, and perhaps performing, traditional rites in honour of a great, good and famous pagan hero of his community as they had always been performed in that community: and a Christian who did not find it necessary to regard the Hellenic gods as devils or to do anything but preserve and honour the holy places of the old religion. As for his praying to the Sun, we should remember the importance of the Sun as a religious symbol for Christians as well as pagans, and that a century later St. Leo the Great in a Christmas sermon found it necessary to condemn the behaviour of some members of his congregation who before entering St. Peter's turned at the top of the steps to bow to the rising sun.[27] Pegasius' regard for the Hellenic past went beyond a qualified acceptance of Hellenic philosophy and an uneasy acquiescence in the necessity of a classical education to a real love of Hellenic myth and legend and even to some extent ritual observance. What parts were played in this by love of the ancient poetry, especially Homer, by the spirit of place of Ilion, and, perhaps, by the importance of the tourist trade to the economy of his diocese, we shall never know. It makes Pegasius a most untypical and unconventional Christian bishop, as far as we know. But we should remember that we only know anything at all about him by the chance of Julian's visit, and we cannot be sure that there were not a good many Christians of similar outlook existing unobtrusively in various parts of the empire.

We have discovered enough good sense and good feeling, even among Christians, in the fourth century, to have made a solution to its religious dissensions more tolerant and tolerable than the Theodosian both possible in the circumstances of the time and in accordance with ancient views of the place of religion in society and the religious responsibilities of rulers. I have said enough at the beginning of this paper about what I believe to be the negative consequences of the solution adopted. But I would like to conclude by drawing attention to some inevitable consequences for the Church which I do not myself regard as entirely undesirable. The Church was left as, for a time, the sole custodian of the ancient culture, and has therefore since attracted, and even now may continue to attract, some whose real love is for that culture rather than for Christianity. And by successfully suppressing all other living and traditional forms of worship the Church has become the sole institution for public worship within the bounds of European civilisation. All those who desire to worship God publicly and communally, however variously they may conceive him, must in practice worship him according to Christian rites. These they will naturally and properly interpret in their own various ways, and have their own requirements of the Church which provides them. This is part of the payment for the Theodosian settlement.

NOTES

¹ See Michael J. Walsh "Ecumenism in Wartime Britain (2)" in *Heythrop Journal* XX-III No. 4 (October 1982) 377-394.

² Plotinus *Ennead* III 4 [15] 2, 25-6.

³ See A. H. M. Jones, *The Later Roman Empire* (Oxford 1964) Ch. II.

⁴ *Julian and Hellenism* (Oxford 1981).

⁵ Eunapius, *Lives of the Philosophers* VII 1.

⁶ Eunapius V 1.

⁷ Porphyry calls Amelius, the closest friend and collaborator of Plotinus φιλοθύτης, an epithet which would apply admirably to Julian (*Life of Plotinus* 10): and it is perfectly clear from his biography that though Plotinus refused to join in Amelius' pious practices, he and others always regarded Amelius as the senior member of the group and the one closest to the master. For "Plotinian" attitudes in later Neoplatonism see Damascius *Life of Isidore* fr. 40 pp 35-36 Zintzen and "Ep. Phot." 38 p. 64 Zintzen: cp. my remarks on the difference between the two tendencies in "Tradition, Reason and Experience in the Thought of Plotinus" *Plotino e il Neoplatonismo in Oriente e in Occidente* (Rome 1974) = *Plotinian and Christian Studies* (London 1979) XVII pp. 185-187.

⁸ This approach has recently been attracting some needed critical attention: cp. E. L. Fortin, "Hellenism and Christianity in Basil the Great's Address *Ad Adulescentes*" in *Neoplatonism and Early Christian Thought* (London, Variorum 1981) 189-203: P. Athanassiadi-Fowden, *Julian and Hellenism* (see n. 4) 18-19.

⁹ *Relatio* III 10.

¹⁰ See his article *Gewissen* in *Reallexikon für Antike und Christentum* X (1978) viii d col. 1101-2.

¹¹ *Or.* 5.

¹² Socrates IV 32: Sozomen VI 6-7. The *Oratio de Religionibus* which purports to be a Latin version of this speech is a post-Renaissance forgery.

¹³ H. Chadwick, *art. cit.* col. 1102.

¹⁴ Xenophanes Fragment 34 DK.

¹⁵ "The Spiritual Importance of Not Knowing" in *Classical Mediterranean Spirituality* ed. A.H. Armstrong (vol 15 of *World Spirituality: an Encyclopedic History of the Religious Quest*, Crossroad, New York 1986) pp.460–80.

¹⁶ Maximus of Tyre, *Dissertatio* VIII (*On whether Images should be consecrated to the Gods*), end.

¹⁷ Augustine, *Ep.* XVI.

¹³ I accept the account of Synesius given by Jay Bregman in the latest and best book on him (J. Bregman, *Synesius of Cyrene*, Berkeley-Los Angeles-London 1982).

¹⁹ Here I follow the account of the conversion of Victorinus given by Pierre Hadot in Chapter XV of his *Marius Victorinus* (Paris, Études Augustiniennes, 1971).

²⁰ Socrates VII 29. The association here of temporal and spiritual prosperity with orthodoxy is commonplace. The egocentric use of the first person is less so, but may be due (if Nestorius is accurately and fairly quoted) rather to rhetorical overexcitement than spiritual arrogance. Or it may simply be due to the introduction by Nestorius into his sermon of the figure of Christ addressing the Emperor, so that the "I" is Christ, not Nestorius. Christian preachers have often put their own words into the mouth of their Master.

²¹ *In Praise of Constantine*: A Historical Study and New Translation of Eusebius'

[22] Ammianus XXII 5.4.

[23] Cod. Theod. 9. 16. 9. issued by Valentinian in the names of himself, Valens and Gratian seems to make this clear. Speaking of his consistent policy the emperor says "Testes sunt leges a me in exordio imperii mei datae, quibus unicuique, quod animo inbibisset, colendi libera facultas tributa est. Nec haruspicinam reprehendimus, sed nocenter exerceri vetamus". This, coupled with the exemption, at the instance of Praetextatus, of the Eleusinian and other ancient rites from the prohibition of nocturnal sacrifices (Cod. Theod. 9. 16. 7: for the exemption see Zosimus 4. 3. 2-3), shows a scrupulous tolerance in an area not far removed from the magical practices which the emperors so feared and hated (Ammianus XXVIII 1: XXIX 1-2).

[24] See note 12.

[25] For those charming creatures Mica Aurea and Innocentia, and how good the emperor was to them, see Ammianus XXIX 3. 9.

[26] Julian, *Letter* 79 Bidez-Rochefort-Lacombrade (78 Hertlein, 19 W. C. Wright): 451 D. Spanheim.

[17] St. Leo, *In Nativitate Domini Sermo VII* (PL XXVII) 4. p. 142 Leclercq-Dolle (SC).

XIV

ITINERARIES IN LATE ANTIQUITY

I

Our theme this year is a fascinating one, stimulating both to thought and to imagination, and with rich and various possibilities of development. Let us begin by considering a possible variation in the basic metaphor of a place where ways meet and part and future directions are determined. Our three titles all speak of a *crossing* of ways. In this they follow modern European usage: all our ordinary words for a meeting of ways which are commonly used metaphorically suggest a place where four ways meet or two intersect, more or less at right angles, a *carrefour* or carfax. This has a certain suggestion of clash and conflict about it, a meeting of opposed directions, a place for firm and dramatic decision whether to turn sharp right or left, or push straight on, or turn round and go straight back. In this our languages follow the Latin *quadrivium*. But in ancient Latin usage *trivium*, a place where three ways meet, is commoner than *quadrivium*: and in ancient Greek *tetraodos* with its related forms is very rare indeed, and late. The normal word for a meeting of ways is *triodos*, like *trivium* a place where three ways meet (or one way forks or branches). This suggests an easier and more natural way of going on than the sharp clash and decisive choice of direction at a *cross*roads. At a *triodos* one can take a branch which is not that which one intended to take, almost without noticing. And this way of speaking also brings the road rather closer to a stream (the two were often rather hard to distinguish in ancient Greece, especially in winter): and when we are thinking about spiritual and cultural ways, it is often useful to shift our metaphor from the road to the stream.

But this possible variation does not exhaust the suggestive possibilities of our metaphor. Provided that one is thinking about real ways and not lines marked on a map, there are many things besides direction which may come into one's mind: the landscape through which a way passes, for instance, or the baggage and provisions with which one equips oneself or finds oneself encumbered at the start of the journey. I shall be bearing all these suggestions of the basic metaphor in mind as I try to trace the spiritual itineraries of late antiquity, and shall, as one ought to do, be prepared to abandon the metaphor altogether if it becomes constricting or distorting. And the title of this paper has been designed to introduce some further ambiguity. An itinerary in English usage can mean an actual journey, or the route which one maps out for one's journey, or a route-map or collection of route-maps including ways which it would be possible to take from a given point but which one does not in fact follow.

The "crossroads," or meeting and parting of ways with which I shall be concerned is the spiritual crossroads of late antiquity. It is always undesirable to attempt to limit any historical period too precisely, to give precise dates for its beginning and end. But it seems reasonably accurate, and will be appropriate to our purposes here, to say that the first clear signs of the beginning of a transition from the world of classical Graeco-Roman culture to the rather different world which we have recently come to distinguish from it as the world of late antiquity come in the late second century of our era, and that by the beginning of the seventh century that world of late antiquity had been transformed into the world of the Middle Ages.[1] It is within these limits that what I have called the "spiritual crossroads" is to be found, where the old *oecumenē*, the Mediterranean world with its imperial extensions, passed from the unselfconscious acceptance of an older and more universal kind of religion to the dominance of Christianity. This was the most important meeting and parting of ways in our spiritual history. The way

1 Peter Brown, *The World of Late Antiquity* (London, Thames and Hudson, 1971) still seems to me the best general introduction to this world.

followed from that crossroads determined the direction of the religious and cultural history not only of the Mediterranean world, but of Europe as soon as it emerged, and, during the short and recently ended period of European domination, has deeply and probably irrevocably affected the religions and cultures of the whole world. It is important to notice that it is a *spiritual* crossroads which we are observing, not accompanied by any revolutionary political, social or economic upheaval. The Christian Empire maintained a rather depressing continuity with the pagan Empire. Absolute monarchy with some sacred character continued to be the normal form of political government in Europe till the period of more or less unchallenged Christian dominance was drawing to its end in the 17th and 18th centuries. And the social and economic changes involved in the transition from the late antique to the mediaeval world, both in the Eastern Empire which continued and in the barbarian kingdoms which arose as the Western Empire disappeared, were evolutionary rather than revolutionary and decidedly modest by the standards of recent history: at the end of the process, as at the beginning, society was predominantly agrarian, with an aristocratic ruling class under the monarchs. But the spiritual change of direction at the late antique crossroads was so great and so far-reaching in its consequences that it is necessary to study it carefully if we are to understand ourselves: and all the more necessary now that we have come to the end of the way taken then and are beginning to understand that, if we survive at all as properly human beings, we have to find a new one. In finding a new beginning we need to study the old way and the reasons for its ending which are to be found in its beginning. Eranos has always taken a leading part in this search and study, and I am very glad to have the opportunity of communicating here such conclusions, no doubt insufficiently tentative, complex and ambiguous, as I can draw from a lifetime's study of the the spiritual history of the late antique world, to which I have been drawn by a love of crossroads and frontiers, of mixed cultures and religions and periods of transition.

XIV

108

II

The first itinerary we must trace of those which met at this great crossroads is one which simply passed through them and continued, changing its outward forms to bring them into some conformity with the requirements of newly dominant religions, but with little change in its fundamental character and sense of direction: the way of the ancient and continuing pieties of the countryside, of the peasant religion or folk religion which was that of the vast majority of the peoples of the Mediterranean world and of Europe till recent times, and still survives strongly in many parts of the world. It is very much a religion of this world, venerating the divine powers in nature and the seasonal life of the villages, and moved to its observances by very mundane hopes and fears of gain and loss. But it has spiritual depth and is not simply a sordid affair of giving to the powers in order to get, or of keeping on the right side of them because of fear of what may happen if one does not. It is a piety of harmony and integration with the gods in nature and the dead who have in some way joined them and work with them, which has plenty of room for love and adoration as well as fear and bargaining for advantage. It is an intensely local piety by its very nature, moved by particular sacred places and times, responding to innumerable small precise theophanies: this characteristic is strongly apparent in its surviving forms after the passage through the crossroads. The peasant life which supported it has now disappeared from Western Europe, though only very recently. I have encountered its last vestiges in my own earlier lifetime. I have seen the Hesiodic plough in use, and my older children once rode on the animals treading out the grain on the circular threshingfloor. We do not, I think, yet know how grave the psychological consequences will be if it disappears completely not only from our experience but from our consciousness and imagination, or whether its survival in art and poetry and some aspects and observances of such religion as we still have, will help sufficiently to carry us through till we can find some new way of establishing unity with the divine in nature and a sense of local sancties. At least, since much of this ancient way still survives, sometimes at a very deep level, in our inherited pieties, we should try to keep the instincts and observances which carry it alive. We should sometimes spare the time to make, whether in spirit or by train, the short journey from Zurich to Einsiedeln, and light our candle to the local goddess. We should try to ensure that the customary forms of worship continue in the country churches even though the peasant communities for which they were built and which supported them have disappeared or been changed out of all recognition. And we should strongly develop and cultivate that sense of the presence of God in nature which is to be found in some Christian traditions of piety, which my wife inherited from her Quaker parents and I from my Anglican ones.

We next come to a great spiritual journey which led to the crossroads, but only continued beyond it in a very strange way, perhaps unparalleled in any other religious culture, which we shall consider later. Since Tertullian indulged in a celebrated rhetorical flourish[2] it has been customary to call this and the other great way which it met at that crossroads by the names of cities: and, as I find this convenient for my own purposes, though I do not take it altogether seriously, I shall continue the custom. This, then, is what is usually called the way of Athens, though the name does little justice to its breadth, complexity, antiquity and, in its own sphere, universality. It is the way of reflective Hellenic piety, the spiritual way followed and taught by the great philosophers of the Hellenic and Hellenized worlds. We shall consider it here in the form in which it came to the crossroads and which was of the greatest significance for what happened later. This is Neoplatonism, that great synthesis into which the whole tradition of Hellenic thought and piety gathered itself as it approached the final conflict. But it is important to remember that, precisely because it is a way of philosophers, and of ancient philosophers who were not academically

2 Quid Ergo Athenis et Hierosolymis? Quid Academiae et Ecclesiae? Quid Haereticis et Christianis? Tertullian, *De Praescriptione Haereticorum* VII.

or institutionally organized in a mediaeval or modern manner, it always remains capable of great variation. Hellenic philosophers on their spiritual journey did not march in ranks or keep in step. At most small groups can be discerned, sometimes with the minimal institutional coherence given by the common ownership of a small piece of heritable real estate, more often held together for a time by strong personal loyalty to a revered master and his interpretation of the teaching of the founder of a philosophical tradition.

This final late Platonic synthesis must be described as monotheistic, on any reasonable understanding of the term. In it the whole of reality is derived from and totally dependent on the transcendent first principle, the One or Good, the creative source of all reality and value and the true ultimate goal of all desire. But it is a monotheism which is very different from that developed from Biblical monotheism by centuries of Christian reflection which we usually think of when we are speaking of "monotheism" or simply of "theism". It is now fairly generally recognized that there can be more than one kind of monotheism: the reasons for this recognition have been well and clearly stated in a recent article by Dr John Kenney, who is engaged in a full-scale study of the differences between Hellenic monotheism and what is sometimes called "classical theism". He says:

> There is some tendency in Western thought to assume that monotheism denotes only the very sophisticated concept which emerged as the product of centuries of mediaeval Scholastic refinement. ... We must not think, by force of cultural habit, that this is the only conceptually possible version of monotheism, since doing so forecloses to our understanding other monotheistic options (e.g. deism or process theism) and prejudices anachronistically our recognition of forms of Western monotheism that emerged antecedent to this Scholastic construct. If we realize that monotheism as a core religious intuition can admit of a range of possible interpretations other than the one we naturally assume, then we will be free from a habit of mind that can blinker our assessment of classical religious thought and, indeed, that of other non-Western traditions.[3]

3 John Kenney, "Monotheistic and Polytheistic Elements in Classical Mediterranean Spirituality" in *Classical Mediterranean Spirituality* ed. A. H. Armstrong (Vol. 15 of *World Spirituality*: Crossroads, New York 1986) p. 270.

This Hellenic monotheism grew naturally out of the vast complex of particular and local theophanies or experiences of the divine which were the foundation of the archaic pieties of the peoples of the Mediterranean regions. It was not the result of a break with them prompted by an overwhelming revelatory experience of the One God: and its continuity with archaic peasant religion determines its character. In it the self-revelation of the One is in and through the cosmos and the manifold experiences of humanity, and those who become aware of it, whether by an immediate illuminating experience or rather dimly and indirectly, are not called to deny and reject the multiplicity of gods and sacred wisdoms. Rather, their value at their own level is confirmed by the revelation of their source. This is how its greatest exponent, Plotinus, speaks of the One God and the many gods, in conscious opposition to that intransigent and exclusive monotheism of which the Hellenes were becoming clearly aware as the ways drew near to the centre of the great crossing and the final conflict approached:

> One must rather think that there are other perfectly good men, and good spirits as well, and, still more, the gods who are in this world and look to the other, and, most of all, the ruler of this universe, the most blessed Soul. Then at this point one should go on to praise the intelligible gods, and then, above all, the great king of that other world, most especially by displaying his greatness in the multitude of the gods. It is not contracting the divine into one, but showing it in that multiplicity in which God himself has shown it, which is proper to those who know the power of God, inasmuch as, abiding who he is, he makes many gods, all depending on himself and existing through him and from him.
>
> (Plotinus *Enneads* II 9 (33) 9, 29-39: tr. A.H.A.)

This shows clearly how the developed Hellenic monotheism of the Neoplatonists differs from what has been normally presented as monotheism in the Christian West. It has some characteristics which need to be considered carefully if we are to understand the nature of the final conflict, and a good deal which happened after it. We should notice first that the way in which it grew spontaneously out of the natural archaic religion of the peasants, and grew as, and was always held to be by those who developed it, a piety for the reflective few, means that, however critical some philosophers might be of the old stories attached to the gods, and however contemptuous or indifferent they might be in their attitude to traditional rituals, the continuance of the old cults was generally presupposed, and a complete breakaway, the foundation of a new philosophical religion, was not envisaged.[4] In this way Hellenic monotheism could be described as extremely conservative. But in another way it had extremely radical possibilities. Philosophers, as they drew near to the crossroads, became in one way intensely traditionalist, sure that the wisdom they expounded was ancient wisdom[5] and rallying to the defence of all the ancient myths and cults, and sometimes more recent oracles, and believing that in them and in the teaching of the great ancient philosophers an immemorial divine revelation was contained.

But at the same time, as philosophers, they remained absolutely free in their speculative interpretation of their whole inheritance: and the free criticism and discussion which were part of the very nature of Hellenic philosophy always contain very radical and subversive possibilities indeed. Philosophy in the ancient world, and above all late Platonic philosophy, had a double character which later developments in the West make it rather difficult for us to understand (it is perfectly intelligible in the East). It was a spiritual and contemplative way of life leading to enlightenment and liberation, to a transforming wisdom which enabled those who followed it to the end to live well and happily.[6] But it was a spiritual way which was properly and intrinsically intellectual (it would be practically impossible to say this in Neoplatonic Greek since the

4 See A. H. Armstrong, "The Divine Enhancement of Earthly Beauties" in *Eranos* 53-1984 pp. 64-67; and Introduction to *Classical Mediterranean Spirituality* (see n. 3) pp. xv-xvi.
5 For some necessary qualifications here see A. H. Armstrong, "Pagan and Christian Traditionalism in the First Three Centuries A.D." in *Studia Patristica* xv ed. Elizabeth A. Livingstone (Berlin, Akademie-Verlag, 1984) pp.414-431 [= this volume, study IX].
6 P. Hadot *Exercices Spirituels et Philosophie Antique* (2me Edition revue et augmentée, Paris, Etudes Augustiniennes, 1987); and I. Hadot, "The Spiritual Guide" in *Classical Mediterranean Spirituality* (see n. 3) pp. 444-459.

same word *Nous*, covers all that we mean by both "spirit" and "intellect"): it proceeded by enquiry and dialogue, by asking questions and trying to give answers and criticizing those answers, involving a search for truth which is likely to go on for ever. Even when one philosopher freely following this spiritual way thought he had found a final answer, someone (perhaps one of his own disciples) would immediately challenge and criticize it. Philosophers had plenty of dogmas and could be very dogmatic about them: but they never acquired the overbearing authority of the dogmas of a Church. One very good reason for this was that the symbiosis of traditional cult and philosophic monotheism of which we have been speaking had no place for a separate religious institution, a Church. Public religion was a matter of cult, not of belief and was an affair of the whole community. Its institutions were common community institutions, and the proper people to regulate and direct it were the rulers of the community, whether assemblies or emperors. This of course gave those rulers ample opportunity to manipulate religion for their own political and worldly purposes. The Romans, as Polybius in the 2nd century B.C. already observed,[7] were masters of this skill in religious manipulation, and transmitted it most successfully to the Christian world, where it continued to be used by the authorities of both Church and State.

The last of the great itineraries which led to the crossroads is, of course, that which, in the Tertullianesque manner of naming, is called 'the way of Jerusalem.' But here we encounter a more serious difficulty about the name than the conventional inadequacy of calling the tradition of reflective Hellenic piety and speculation 'the way of Athens.' This is that there was then, and always has been since, another way which, if one tries to take a reasonably detached and non-sectarian view, has a much better claim than the Christian to be called 'the way of Jerusalem.' This is the way of orthodox Rabbinic Judaism: a spiritual way inspired continually by the memory of God's worship in old Jerusalem and based on the loving

---

7 Polybius VI, 56, 6-15.

observance of and exact compliance with the whole Torah, including that great mass of commandments which Christians have,
often with unjustified contempt and derision, discarded as 'ceremonial' or 'ritual.' It is a way which the history of the Jewish people has
shown to be by no means a mere religious legalism. It has been not
just compatible with, but generative of, great love of God and one's
neighbour, holiness of life, a high degree of mystical experience, and
bold and profound religious speculation. My knowledge of it is
superficial, my contacts with it minimal, and I feel little personal
attraction towards it. Such information about it and understanding
of it as I have has come to me, as to so many others, very largely
through the writings of Gershom Scholem, so well known here at
Eranos. But the little that I have acquired has made me think it a
duty of justice to say what I have said. We Christians really should
give up claiming that we have a superior right of ownership or a
monopoly of understanding of the Scriptures which Jesus recognised as the Word of God, or for that matter of Jesus himself, as
Jewish scholars sometimes courteously but firmly remind us.

But this other way of Jerusalem does not play a major part in the
story of the religious crossroads of late antiquity. Jews were certainly present, and vigorously present, in the central conflict at the
crossroads, but not in any decisive force: they had no great share in
determining the outcome. So I shall describe what I am convention-
ally calling the way of Jerusalem in Christian terms, and leave it to
any Jewish hearers or readers to decide how much of the description
applies to them. It is a spiritual way of intransigent and exclusive
monotheism, differing sharply from the inclusive monotheism of
the One God revealed in the many which we found in the Hellenic
thinkers and can equally well find in India. It springs from an
overwhelmingly intense experience of the presence and self-revelation of its God in the particular history of one particular people
whom he has chosen: and finally, in its Christian form, of that
God's decisive entrance into that history in his own person, taking
human nature upon him as the God-man Jesus Christ. This experience was so overwhelming to those who fully underwent it that it

led them to reject and devalue all other ways to God, through the innumerable theophanies and traditional cults, and the reflective piety leading to the One God in the many, of other religious traditions. It was this exclusive intransigence which marked it off most sharply from the way of Athens, and led to the conflict at the crossroads: for this reason it is being strongly stressed here. But there is of course much more to be said about the Christian way of Jerusalem, and very much in its favour as well as against it.

I have spoken of this way as springing from an overwhelmingly intense revelatory experience, and no doubt this is true of its origins, in its Jewish and in its Christian and in its later Islamic form. But it seems likely that the experience in its full intensity has always been comparatively rare among the followers of it in any of its forms. Even a casual reading of the Old Testament prophets will show what a hard struggle exclusive monotheism had to maintain itself among the Hebrews. The Book of Jeremiah shows particularly vividly how little enthusiasm there was for the cult of the One God alone among the rulers and people of Judah on the eve of the Exile. And modern Old Testament scholars and archaeologists have demonstrated clearly how much the early religion of the Hebrews had in common with those of their neighbours, and how much creative censorship and vigorous editing of the traditions of the people of God was necessary to give the Old Testament the strongly monotheistic character which it has in our Bibles. This is not altogether relevant to our main story, and I am quite incompetent to express any opinions worth having on the subject. But there is one thing which has struck me particularly forcibly in my superficial reading: that is, how necessary from the point of view of exclusive monotheism, and how difficult, it was to exclude the feminine from the sphere of divinity. One of the hardest struggles seems to have been that to deprive Yahweh of his Asherah, his feminine consort.[8] The same

8 David Sperling's recent summary account of the evolution of the religion of Israel brings this out very well ("Israel's Religion in the Ancient Near East" in *Jewish*

insistence on at least keeping down the feminine of course has continued and still continues in Christianity. It seems to be generally considered necessary by exclusive monotheists that the One God should be male.

In Christianity, and the Judaism of the New Testament period from which it sprang there was perhaps already at the beginning some tempering of exclusive monotheism: and as the new religion spread to even larger and more heterogeneous groups in the Gentile world, and the effect of the intense original experience diminished (though it has always remained renewable in individual cases) it was inevitably influenced by and in some ways drew closer to the other monotheism of the way of Athens. But it is important, if we are to understand the conflict at the crossroads and the way which was there finally followed, that it retained, and still to a great extent retains, its intransigent exclusiveness. The New Testament writers and the Fathers of the Church held, as those Christians for whom traditional orthodoxy is important still hold, that there is One True God and all other gods are false, and that there is one true faith revealed by him to which all other sacred teachings are at best approximations, to be judged according to their nearness to or distance from that revelation. This was what made conflict inevitable, and it was the, as we shall see, qualified and always somewhat precarious dominance of this exclusive faith which gave its character to the way followed from the crossroads. It should be clearly understood that I have not up to this point been trying to give anything like complete descriptions of the great spiritual ways which led to the crossroads: in particular I have said nothing about what they had in common with each other and with other great religious ways.[9] What I have been attempting to do is to explain

Spirituality from the Bible Through the Middle Ages ed. Arthur Green (Vol. 13 of *World Spirituality*: Crossroads, New York, 1986) pp. 5-31.

9 I have tried to show something of the convergences as well as the differences between the thought of Plotinus and that of Christians of his time and later in an essay "Plotinus and Christianity" which will appear in a volume in honour of Édouard des Places edited by Charles Kannengiesser and Stephen Gersh.

what it was in each that made it inevitable that there should be a crossroads and a conflict, a period of struggle followed by a change of direction.

III

The struggle between the two ways of Athens and Jerusalem began to be intense in the late second and early third century of our era. Exactly when and how it ended, and indeed if it has ended, are questions which, as we shall see, require careful examination. But by the end of the fourth century Christianity was definitively established as the one tolerated religion of the Roman Empire (though local survivals of the old religion continued for long after this date, and Neoplatonic philosophers maintained an open intellectual opposition to the new establishment for more than a century). This way of referring to what is sometimes loosely described as the 'Triumph of Christianity' has considerable implications, which will be examined. The struggle was seen, more and more clearly as it went on, on both sides, as a struggle between the two kinds of monotheism which I have attempted to describe, between God in and with the gods and God without and against the gods. The rather spasmodic and sometimes reluctant persecutions of Christians while the old religion was dominant seem to have been inspired by a deep feeling that the new intolerant because exclusive monotheism threatened man's whole traditional relationship with the divine, the whole complex of inherited pieties which permeated culture and social life. And in the period of Christian domination and increasing intolerance, which began with the conversion of Constantine, the intellectuals who defended the old way appeared more and more as champions of tolerant pluralism, with the exception of Julian and his circle, whose Hellenism was already rather Byzantine. And on their side the Christians after they came into power increased and developed their exclusive intolerance, however much in other ways they were influenced in both theory and practice by the

118

way of Athens: and they maintained it in theory, though their opportunities for practical intolerance had by then become severely restricted, well into my own lifetime, and indeed in some quarters maintain it still.[10]

The form taken by the 'triumph of Christianity,' in which the followers of Jesus of Nazareth grasped eagerly at the wealth and power suddenly offered them, while continuing to maintain, sometimes sincerely, that worldly wealth and power were undesirable and irrelevant, a hindrance to the following of the true way of the Gospels, had important consequences for the Churches. The distinction between the Great Church and the sects, and the conception of orthodoxy as normative and heresies as peripheral, sharpened, hardened and became generally accepted: with the equally accepted corollary that it was the duty of Christian rulers to support the Great Church and suppress all dissident Christian and non-Christian forms of piety. This, in an important way, affected the very nature of Christian institutions. With the closing of the temples and the suppression of religious dissidence the Churches became inevitably, whether they liked it or not, no longer simply assemblies of the faithful united in the Body of Christ, but institutions for public worship, committed to providing sacred rites for all and sundry in the communities they served: and so they remained after the end of the Empire, and to a great extent, even in our present changed circumstances, remain today: and if Christian clergy object, as they often do, to marrying unbelievers and baptizing their children or conducting elaborate services in large ancient buildings expensive to maintain, they should be reminded both that the

10 Cp. A. H. Armstrong, "The Way and the Ways: Religious Tolerance and Intolerance in the 4th Century A.D." in *Vigiliae Christianae* Vol. 38.1 (1984) pp. 1-17: reprinted in *"To See Ourselves as Others See Us,"* ed. J. Neusner and E. S. Frerichs (Chico, Scholars Press 1985) pp. 357-372: this volume is very enlightening on the, now much studied, subject of self-definition against others, which is closely bound up with intolerance, on which see also the volumes of the McMaster project on *Jewish and Christian Self-Definition,* ed. Ben E. Meyer and E. P. Sanders (London, S.C.M. Press, 1980).

maintenance of public worship is an honourable and necessary function, and that the performance of these, as it seems to many of them, incongruous ceremonies is part of the price which still has to be paid for that fourth-century triumph. The bill run up by Ambrose and Theodosius and their likes includes the salary of the Maestro di Cappella and the use of the church by any couples who wish to make their weddings grand social occasions.

Though the leaders of the great churches, with the approval of most of their followers, grabbed the new wealth and power with both hands, there were Christian groups who resisted and tried to maintain the older Christian way, closer to the Gospels, in which the church is the society of saints, separated from and alien to the world and its powers: the best known of these is the Donatist Church of North Africa. They have had their successors throughout Christian history. The monastic movement, too, was in its beginnings a protest within the great Churches against the increasing wordliness resulting from their triumph, and it and related movements have continued to provide and stimulate for many Christians a way of life nearer to the Gospels. But none the less the development took place and the dubious triumph was secured. This should not, I think, be interpreted as the inevitable result of a great spiritual movement marching irresistibly to its goal. I am not a believer in that sort of historical determinism. I think the triumph was due to a great extent to contingent historical circumstances, to the long and comparatively successful reigns of Constantine I and his Christian successors and the early death of Julian in battle, and to the characters and religious dispositions of the great Christian emperors and the bishops who guided them. It was in fact an affair of internal power-politics, as the 'conversion' of whole communities to any religion or ideology tends to be when it is not achieved by conquest from outside. To do something to justify myself for this belief, I shall say something about other ways which were clearly signposted and even followed for short distances at our crossroads, which would have led in rather different directions, before I attempt to describe more closely the way which we actually followed.

XIV

IV

The first of these ways, carefully mapped and clearly signposted, but only followed for a very short distance, was that of Julian's attempted re-Hellenization of the religion of the Empire. Whatever the Emperor himself may have thought, this was not to be a simple return to the old religious ways as they had been before the conversion of Constantine. For all his love of antiquity Julian was very much a man of his time, and the religious reform which he proposed and began to carry out had something distinctly Byzantine about it. There was to be something very like a Great Imperial Church, with a hierarchy under the Emperor whose functions included not only the performance and supervision of cult but doctrinal teaching, moral exhortation and the setting of an example of godly life to their flocks, and the promotion of charitable works. And Julian's personal religion, which he wished his hierarchy to propagate, was not just "Hellenic" or "Neoplatonic" but an extreme form of theurgic Neoplatonism in the manner of Iamblichus.[11] The extraordinary incongruity, from older Hellenic points of view, and unsuitability to the old religion of a Hellenic teaching church with dogmas would no doubt have weakened the reform, but need not have been fatal to it. The distinctive Iamblichean-Julianist colour of the theology might soon have faded, and dogmatic teaching become less important: the hierarchy might have become no more than an administrative framework: Christianity would have survived and flourished and been continuingly influential. But, if Julian had reigned as long and successfully as Constantine and trained a competent successor or successors to carry on his religious policy, the policy might well

11 Julian has recently been extensively studied. The best introduction to his thought and his reforms, solidly based on and documented from his own writings, is the book of Polymnia Athanassiadi-Fowden, *Julian and Hellenism* (Oxford, Clarendon Press, 1981). For an assessment of Iamblichean theurgy and its modern assessors see A. H. Armstrong, "Iamblichus and Egypt" in *Les Etudes Philosophiques* 2-3, 1987, pp. 179-188 (French translation in 4, 1987, pp. 521-532), [= this volume, study II].

have succeeded in essentials. What ensured its failure was Julian's death in Persia in 363, at the age of only thirty-two. If he had returned from his Persian campaign with a moderate degree of success, ruled for many years and been succeeded by another Hellene, Christianity might never have managed to take over the Empire again. It would have survived as a widespread and powerful religion in an essentially non-Christian environment. So the idea of a 'Christian State' or a 'Christian country' might never have emerged, or only sporadically and much later. Though these parallels are dangerous, the outcome for the Empire and perhaps later for Europe might have been rather 'Chinese,' with Christianity occupying something like the position of Buddhism in China, or that which the great Church of the East which heresiologists call Nestorian occupied for centuries in the lands beyond the Eastern frontier of the Roman Empire, and even for a time in China itself: at least the suggestion is worth making to remind us how comparatively recently in our history the vast cultural and religious gap opened between 'East' and 'West' of which we are now so conscious.

The second way which I propose to consider is even more interesting from the point of view of our present discussion, because it was a way of Christian tolerance. If I was to continue to follow the convention of calling the ways by the names of cities, I should have to call it the 'way of Harran (or Carrhae),' after that not very important little town, just within the Eastern frontier of the Roman Empire, which had the unique distinction of maintaining a considerable degree of religious liberty and tolerance to the end of Roman rule in those parts, and after, as Michel Tardieu has shown us in two fascinating recent articles.[12] Though it had a Christian bishop and a number of pilgrimage sites connected with the story of Abraham,[13] most of the population remained pagan, the great pagan temple stayed open, even the Manichees seem to have been allowed

12 M. Tardieu, "Sabiens Coraniques et Sabiens de Harran", *Journal Asiatique* 274 (1986) pp. 1-44; "Symplicius et les calendriers de Harran" in *Simplicius, sa vie, son œuvre, sa sourvie*, ed. I. Hadot, Berlin – New York, De Gruyter, 1987, pp. 40-57.
13 Itinerarium Aetheriae 20.

to worship in public, and most interesting of all, a school of Hellenic Neoplatonists established itself there and maintained itself openly for centuries under Muslim domination. (M. Tardieu thinks that some of the philosophers who left Athens when Justinian closed the Platonic School eventually settled there). But though Harran deserves a mention in any account of the final conflict of Hellenism and Christianity, in spite of the fact that its reasons for maintaining, and being able to maintain, religious tolerance were for the most part entirely mundane and secular, the significance of this way does not depend on its survival on the Roman-Persian frontier till the sixth century and beyond, but on the fact that it was followed by Christian emperors for more than a decade after the death of Julian. Jovian (363-364) and Valentinian I (Emperor of the West 364-375) were scrupulously tolerant in all respects: they seem to have been genuinely anxious that all their subjects, pagan and Christian, should be free to worship according to their various religious beliefs, and they preserved strict neutrality and consistently refused to intervene in the bitter disputes between Christian factions. Valentinian's brother Valens (Emperor of the East 364-378) tolerated pagans, but persecuted with some vigour those Christians whom he regarded as heretics, on the best episcopal advice available to him in his part of the Empire. (They were of course those whom later generations regarded as the Catholic and orthodox party, the upholders of the Nicene creed). This way, in the fully consistent form in which it was followed by Valentinian, the most ferocious of autocrats and of very ordinary intellect and education, had, I believe, solid foundations in contemporary thought and practice: there was nothing anachronistic or eccentric about it, and it seems well adapted to the needs of the time. The followers of the old religious way found it most acceptable, and there seems reason to suspect that there were many more Christians than we know of who would also have found it acceptable, and, if it had continued as Imperial policy, would have settled down to a very comfortable symbiosis with the pagans, and even with those fellow Christians whom the bishops of their particular group urged them to regard as heretics.[14] (We should reflect that, under a policy of strict governmental tolerance and neutrality, there could be, just as in a modern city, two rival cathedrals, with their rival bishops, in the same street, with some pagan temples open for worship a little way up the road in the old quarter of the town. This would have consequences: if one cannot suppress other people, one must learn to live with them). If the way of tolerance had become settled and normal, the accepted religious policy of the Empire, and been transmitted as such to the successor kingdoms of the West, the way we followed from the crossroads could have been very different. We might have found ourselves in a quite modern climate of opinion as regards religious differences, rather like that of England in the late 17th century, before we had reached the Middle Ages: in which case we presumably should not have had the Middle Ages, though what we should have had instead is impossible to conjecture. But for whatever reasons (again I believe they were contingent rather than necessary), the way of tolerance did not continue to be followed, and in the reign of Theodosius we set out irrevocably on the way we were to follow for centuries, the way of Christian domination in which the intransigent and exclusive monotheism of the early preaching embodied itself in Christendom. This is the way which we must now consider.

V

If we need a conventional date for its beginning the best to choose would be that of the prohibition of the ancient cults by Theodosius I in 391: though there were many edicts, both against pagans and dissident Christians, before and after that date.[15] There is some difficulty about giving it a name. There are serious reasons, some of which I have already indicated, against continuing to call it the 'way of Jerusalem': and I do not think that anyone should feel very happy

14 See further A. H. Armstrong, *art. cit.* (n. 10).

15 Cod. Theod. XVI 10.10: issued in the names of Valentianian II, Theodosius I, and Arcadius: but Theodosius was for practical purposes sole emperor.

about calling it the 'way of Christ' if they sometimes read the Gospels and have had the privilege of knowing some of the very few Christians who actually follow that way in its essentials of poverty and non-resistance to evil. The way of intolerant and exclusive Christian orthodoxies supported by the powers of states on which we made the definitive start in the late fourth century may perhaps best be called the 'way of the Romes'. By using the plural I mean of course to indicate Old Rome and New Rome or Constantinople. But if some Russian Orthodox hearer or reader wishes to include Moscow, the Third Rome, I have no objection. It can often be very enlightening when considering this way to bring the Third Rome into the picture, especially in its most recent, post-Christian, phase. It will be difficult to give even the most summary and sketchy description of so complex and strange a phenomenon: though in trying to do so I shall leave out the further complexities and strangenesses which developed later, after it had become the way of Europe and no longer that of the old Mediterranean world, and speak of only those characteristics which were apparent at its beginning. It will be necessary at this point to abandon, or at least to take care not to be confined or inhibited by, our metaphor of the itinerary. But before we do so, let us indulge in a final metaphorical flourish. Let us exploit the metaphor as far as it will go, if not further, and produce a sharply outlined and crudely coloured caricature-frontis-piece to our account which may serve to draw attention to some interesting features.

Let us first consider the most important thing about any itinerary, the direction in which those travelling think they are going. The leaders are, in the characteristic Christian manner, quarrelling continually about almost everything, but they agree in saying that this is a Christian itinerary, a march of the pilgrim Church to the New Jerusalem: though there is never a lack of voices from the ranks saying (and sometimes shouting very loudly) that in fact everyone is going in the wrong direction and this is the broad way leading to destruction, not the narrow way to salvation. Next let us look at the landscape through which the travellers are moving. Not all the mountains which dominate the view look Biblical. Sinai, Moriah and Tabor are by no means always principal features, and Calvary often almost seems to disappear. Other mountains are prominent which the poets in the travelling company, who are always good guides to imaginal landscape, identify as Helicon or Parnassus or Olympus. And in the scenery along the road all those woods and little hills where the travellers frequently pause for rest and refreshment often look very like the sacred groves and high places so abominated by the Old Testament writers. Finally, let us inspect the provisions which are being taken along for the journey. The wines, of which there are a great quantity, do not for the most part appear to have been made from grapes grown on the slopes of Mount Carmel, and many of them look more suitable for Dionysiac than Paschal celebrations: and a great many of those cans of meat, even some of the ones labelled "Lamb of God", seem to contain something very like meat offered to idols.

I will now try to provide a text for this picture, in less picturesque language. If we come to understand the strange complexity of this way, even in its beginnings, we shall, I think, be better able to understand its later course and its end. It was a way in which the ways which led to the crossroads came together, neither fully integrated nor merely juxtaposed, in an uneasy combination peculiarly liable to disintegrate and peculiarly disintegrative in its effects when it does so. The archaic peasant way continued, in changed outward forms, beneath and penetrating the whole, throughout most of its course. Its progressive disappearance during the last two centuries has done much to destabilize that course, and is one important reason for its ending. But, given the close connection of the way of Athens with that primaeval way, it is mainly in the meeting and co-existence in our journeying from the crossroads of the ways of Athens and Jerusalem that the reasons both for the complex richness and spiritual fecundity and the extreme precariousness of our way are to be found. The title which I have given to it, the "way of the Romes" already suggests, as I have indicated, that in and by reason of its very triumph Christianity was deeply affected by the religious way of the ancient cities, above all Rome, the City which became an Empire and reproduced itself imperially at Constantinople. By using the name of Rome in my title I do not at all intend to focus attention here on the Bishop of Old Rome and the church which he rules, or even exclusively on the great churches of Rome and Constantinople. The influence on Christianity of the manner in which it attained domination goes far wider and deeper than that, and is to a great extent independent of the varying institutional relationships between Churches and States: it may be detected even now, after the end of Christian domination, wherever the clergy and faithful of any Christian community think of them- selves as belonging to a "Church", a great public institution, rather than a "sect", and feel, in however vague, easy-going and tolerant a way, that all their fellow-countrymen really ought to be Christians of their particular kind.

But the partial integration of Athens with Jerusalem goes far further than this, and has had far wider and deeper effects. The influence, direct or indirect, of Hellenic philosophy on Christianity is, and must necessarily be, a main subject of study for any body of scholars concerned with Christianity, not only in the patristic and mediaeval periods but in every subsequent period down to and including our own. To try to summarize, or to generalize about, this vast and ongoing body of studies would be useless and misleading. I can best sum up my own sense of the complexity of the state of affairs which they reveal by saying that I can see a great deal of truth in the Catholic humanist view which sees in developed Christian theology, spirituality, and cult much of the best which the older way had to offer integrated under the supreme ruling and correcting authority of the original exclusive monotheism: but also in that of the reformers who hold that authentic original Christianity has been distorted and diluted by these Hellenic importations, and that of anti-Christian humanists who think that what has survived into our way from the way of Athens has been spoilt and weakened by its integration into a Christian-dominated synthesis. The fact that there seems to be some truth in all of these views already shows the strangely mixed and precarious character of our way. It was not only that particular Christian doctrines came to show the influence of Hellenic philosophy through being expounded and argued about in Hellenic terms, which were the only terms available in late antiquity for intelligent exposition and argument. The whole method and practice of Christian theology and personal piety came under Hellenic influence.[16] This was on the whole, in my opinion, beneficial and strengthening to Christianity. But there was one way in which it was not. The Hellenes must take some responsibility for the remarkable and persistent tendency of Christians to quarrel furiously about theology. Any religious way which bases itself in a revelation contained in a scripture is liable to develop an obsessive interest in words which can have undesirable consequences,[17] and Christians disputed from the beginning about the meaning of Scripture and the proper language to use in expressing their faith and formulating their law of life. But Hellenic philosophers had their own interest in language, and were properly concerned with description and definition and the expression of what they believed to be the truth in clear, logically coherent, systematic form. They had within their own tradition means of overcoming too obsessive a concern with verbal definition and system in the Sceptical critiques of dogmatism and, most deeply and powerfully, in the apophatic side of Neoplatonism. But these were not sufficiently generally accepted, or their meaning and powers sufficiently well understood, to prevent ancient, like later, philosophical life being largely concerned with spirited quarrelling over terms and definitions and the maintenance of rival systems by polemical attack and defence. And when this Hellenic disputatiousness combined with the fanaticism about the sacred text, and its divinely guaranteed interpretation, of Biblical monotheism, and the attempt began to be made to express revealed truth with the precision of systematic philosophy, the result was that perennial Christian disposition of mutual hatred

16 P. Hadot, *Exercices Spirituels et Philosophie Antique* (see n. 6).
17 Cp. James Hillman, "On Paranoia" in *Eranos 54-1985*, pp. 308 ff.

grounded in disagreement about the faith which was excellently summed up in the fourth century by a fairly dispassionate Hellenic observer: "No wild beasts are such enemies of humanity as most Christians are deadly dangerous to each other."[18]

But the story of the survival of the old way of Athens in our new way from the crossroads by no means ends with whatever in it could be in some way and to some degree integrated into the thought and piety of the dominant Christian religion. What gives our whole cultural and religious tradition its peculiar and distinctive duality, instability and openness is that we have carried along with us in our spiritual luggage, as part of our intellectual, imaginative and emotional provender for the journey, a vast amount from the old way which could not be assimilated into or dominated by triumphant Christianity. And what we have brought along is not 'doctrine' or 'method' or 'mythology,' something abstract and therefore easily manageable, which can be tidily packed into parcels labelled 'assimilable' or 'unassimilable,' 'wanted on voyage' or 'not wanted on voyage.' What we have brought along is for the most part contained in those formidable, extremely concrete and (with all due respect to Plato) extremely lively entities, the books of antiquity, in a sufficiently diverse, if partial and random, selection. (Of course a few buildings, even fewer paintings, and a larger number of sculptures have also survived, and been helpful to the imagination, but it is on the books that the survival has depended of much from the old way which could not be integrated or controlled). How this came about we may understand better if we look at a particular episode in the fourth century, and try to see its implication.

By general consent on all side, the harshest and most intolerant of Julian's enactments affecting the position of Christians was that which prohibited Christians from teaching the Hellenic classics,

18 Ammianus Marcellinus XXII 5, 4, speaking of Julian's recall of the bishops exiled under Constantius II and his advice to Christians of all parties (which he knew very well would not be taken) to live at peace with each other, each following his own religious way freely.

thereby excluding them from the educational profession.[19] (He by no means wished to exclude Christian children from education: he says this explicitly in his encyclical explaining the rescript. But he wished them to be taught the classics only by good honest believing Hellenes). That Hellenes like Ammianus[20] should find this objectionable is simply an example of that tolerant pluralism of late antiquity of which I spoke earlier. But what the furious Christian reaction to the edict reveals is the original cause of that strange duality and division in our thoughts, imaginations and feelings which has meant that, throughout the time during which we followed the way of the Romes the dominant religion has never been quite able to dominate them. The power of the Graeco-Roman literary culture of late antiquity was so great that nobody in that world could conceive of any other culture, or any other education. The Christians did not eagerly seize the opportunity (explicitly offered them by Julian) to develop a Christian education which would be totally and authentically Christian in the manner in which traditional Jewish and Islamic education are totally and authentically Jewish and Islamic (though a few feeble and futile attempts in that direction were made). They felt themselves unjustly excluded from a common human heritage, and as soon as they were able started to teach the Hellenic and Hellenized Latin classics again – indeed most of them probably never stopped doing so, as it is unlikely that the edict could have been widely enforced in the few remaining months of Julian's life. This episode shows clearly how and why the great writers of the old way were present and working in us from the very beginning of our setting out on the new, operative in our thoughts, feelings and imaginations in varying degrees according to their availability at different places and times, and inspiring other thinkers, poets and artists to give new expression to what they have given us. And this has meant the survival in

19 A Latin text of the rescript is in Cod. Theod. XIII 3.5. Julian's circular letter explaining it is Ep. 42 (Hertlein), 36 (Wright).
20 XXII 10,7: XXV 4, 20.

our consciousness of the old gods and of ways of thinking about the ultimate divinity which belong to the way of Athens rather than to the exclusive Biblical monotheism which was officially dominant. Aphrodite, Venus or Dionē, the goddess with whom Christianity has had the greatest difficulty in coming to terms, was already dancing all over Europe in the Middle Ages. Perhaps one way of expressing the strangeness and instability of our situation during the period of Christian domination would be to say that, though in one sense of the word we have a cultural and religious tradition of exceptional richness and variety, in another sense we have not since the fourth century had a tradition at all. We have not, that is, had a single all-encompassing tradition guiding and inspiring a fully inte-grated religion-culture like that of Islamic or Buddhist countries or the Hindu world. It may be this, and not simply the collapse of what we have been pleased to call traditional Christian culture, which causes so many of those admirable, deeply spiritual and profoundly intelligent and imaginative people in our world who feel so strongly the need of this kind of tradition to look for it outside Europe, to adopt and assimilate themselves to, as far as they can, Islamic or Buddhist or Indian tradition. In Europe it may not even be tradi-tional to be a traditionalist.

But even if we do not have a tradition in the strict sense of the traditionalists we have an ample, if disintegrated and ambiguous, spiritual inheritance, of much of which we can still make use. What has come to the end is the period of attempted Christian domina-tion, not necessarily Christianity itself, still less all the company of pieties and reflections, with their sacred images and signs, whether assimilated or partly assimilated or unassimilated to Christianity, which we have brought along with us from the older world. It was the great passionate will to dominate, which can all too easily develop in exclusive monotheists, the will to destroy or exclude all rival forms of religious thought and piety, to press philosophy and culture into the service of one intolerant creed, which secured the triumph of organized Christianity and in securing it ensured its inevitable defeat. This defeat should not worry Christians too much. They are, after all, reminded every Holy Week that the triumphal entry into the city is the beginning of the march to the gallows, and can find good reason in the Gospels for supposing that they should not wish to dominate anybody or anything. Our belated awareness that the time of dominance and exclusion has ended should make us freer and more friendly. (It is a very belated awareness: in many Christian circles it has only come in my lifetime, and in some it does not seem to have come yet). So we may be better able to learn something from the study of that fatal victory in the fourth century and the ways which led to it: and there is much there which may be of use to us in the future, a future in which all that is reasonably certain seems to be that no religious group will be of much service to the world unless it is prepared to accept equality with others, to practice mutual hospitality, to see theophanies whenever they may appear and hear the Spirit in many winds, and to join with others in a common confession of ignorance before God.

XV

On Not Knowing Too Much About God

The Apophatic Way of the Neoplatonists and other influences from ancient philosophy which have worked against dogmatic assertion in Christian thinking

Christianity stands out among the three great Abrahamic religions in its willingness to make extremely precise dogmatic statements about God. The Christians who make these statements have generally regarded them as universally and absolutely true, since they are divinely revealed, or divinely guaranteed interpretations of revealed texts. Of course from the beginning there has not been universal agreement (to put it mildly) among Christians about what statements should be so regarded and how they should be worded: and the seriousness with which this need for dogmatic precision has been taken is shown by the way in which the inevitable disputes did not only involve theologians but the general body of Christians, and have led to divisions of churches, long continuing and flourishing mutual hatreds, and an overwhelming amount of theoretical and, where opportunity offered (i.e. where a Church party could get a secular power on its side), practical intolerance.[1] Two areas of Church history which seem to me to provide particularly clear evidence of the incompatible verbal precisions demanded in dogmatic statements and the serious consequences of these demands are the Christological controversies of the fifth and sixth centuries and the *Filioque* dispute between East and West (though there is plenty of choice, and others may have other preferences). In both of these, theologians with a real and deep sense of the mystery of God often seem to an outside observer, in spite of their passionate assertions that this is not at all what they are doing and the rhetorical

---

[1] A grim comment on this, which became more and more manifestly true as the Christian centuries went on, was made very early in the period of Christian dominance by a fair-minded non-Christian observer, the historian Ammianus Marcellinus. Speaking of the Emperor Julian's advice to Christians of all parties (which he knew very well would not be taken) to live at peace with each other, observing their own beliefs freely, he says 'Julian knew from experience that no wild beasts are such enemies of humanity as most Christians are deadly dangerous (*ferales*) to each other' (Ammianus XXII, 5.4).

reverence of their language, to be arguing as if the God-Man or the Trinity were small finite objects which they had pinned down firmly in their theological laboratories and were examining under the microscope.

The difference in this way between Christianity on the one hand and Judaism and Islam on the other seems to be largely due to the greater influence of Hellenic philosophy on Christian thinking in the discussions which led to the formulation of authoritative statements of Christian doctrine. It is therefore interesting that this philosophy itself has provided Christians with some powerful means of overcoming their extreme addiction to the imposition of precise dogmatic statements as truths about God in which all must believe.

Hellenic philosophers were from the beginning in the habit of making extremely definite statements about everything, including the divine: and it was of course essential to their particular kind of activity that as soon as a statement, especially about something regarded as interesting and important, was made, someone else (or perhaps the same philosopher later, if he was properly self-critical) would challenge it and argue against it, and probably in the end make a counter-statement, which would then itself in due course be countered in its turn: and so on. Philosophy was for them, as it has generally remained since, intrinsically a conversational activity;[2] and, though vigorous attempts have sometimes been made to close the conversation on particular subjects (notably the subject of the divine) they have never, because of the very nature of philosophy, been successful, and philosophical conversations have continued to be obstinately open-ended. Of course, like all conversations, Hellenic philosophical conversation could take a number of different forms. It could be a discussion between friends, civilized, courteous, and moderately fair-minded, as Plato's earlier dialogues are and as the Seventh Platonic Letter says that any philosophical conversation which is to attain its end must be.[3] Or it could be viciously bad-tempered and unfair, as controversy between the different philosophical schools generally was: a horrid example is the anti-Aristotelian polemic of Atticus preserved by the Christian

---

[2] I prefer to use 'conversation', 'conversational' rather than the more technical and precise-sounding 'dialectic', 'dialectical' because 'dialectic', both in ancient and modern times, has had so many meanings, some of which in the present context would be unduly restrictive or misleading.

[3] Letter VII, 3448, 4–9, 'But by rubbing each of them strenuously against each other, names and definitions and sights and perceptions, testing them out in kindly discussions by the use of questions and answers without jealous ill-will, understanding and intelligence of each reality flashes out, at the highest intensity humanly possible' (trans. A.H.A.).

On Not Knowing Too Much About God

church historian Eusebius.[4] But very much greater philosophers than Atticus, e.g. Aristotle or Plotinus, are not at their best in inter-school controversy. And there is of course plenty of conversation, of a sort, in the ancient as well as in the modern philosophical world, in which the 'dialogue' consists of a series of monologues in which no speaker pays the slightest attention to what the others have said.

At least a smattering of this sort of conversational and controversial philosophy was part of the education of the Christians in the early centuries of our era who thought out and formulated the authoritative Church statements of Christian doctrine, simply because it was part of the higher education of everyone in the very small minority of the population who received any in the Graeco-Roman world. And, since that education was predominantly rhetorical (the old quarrel between philosophers and rhetoricians was long since over), such philosophy as entered and formed the minds of educated Christians generally tended to do so in a somewhat rhetoricized form: that is, with the issues over-simplified and contrasts sharpened, and any tendencies to agnosticism, tentativeness, and serious attempts to understand opposing points of view minimized.[5] It is easy to understand the effect of this sort of philosophico-rhetorical training of the mind on people like the early Christians who already had a deep religious anxiety about words because the divine relevation in which they believed was given in verbal form, as a body of Scriptures claiming divine authority.[6] By noting that this effect was adverse, I do not at all intend to range myself with the de-Hellenizers in the long controversy about the influence of Greek philosophy on Christianity.[7] I believe this to have been on the whole beneficial, and on many points am more inclined to advocate the re-Hellenization rather than the de-Hellenization of Christianity. But for this very reason I think it important to note adverse effects of philosophy, or of particular philosophies, on Christian teaching and practice when I see them. The attempts to express the essential con-

---

[4] Eusebius, *Praeparatio Evangelica* XI, 1–2; XV, 4–9; 12F: Atticus, *Fragments*, ed. E. Des Places (Paris: Les Belles Lettres, 1977).

[5] On philosophy, rhetoric and education in antiquity see I. Hadot, *Arts Liberaux et Philosophie dans la Pensée Antique* (Paris: Etudes Augustiniennes, 1984).

[6] Cf. James Hillman, 'On Paranoia', *Eranos* **54** (1985; Frankfurt: Insel, 1987), 269–324.

[7] The works of E. P. Meijering, notably his books on Von Harnack, *Theologische Urteile uber die Dogmengeschichte* (Leiden: Brill, 1978), and *Die Hellenisierung des Christentums im Urteil Adolf Von Harnacks* (Amsterdam, London and New York: North-Holland Publishing Co., 1985), are to be recommended to those unfamiliar with this predominantly Lutheran-inspired controversy. I agree generally with his conclusions.

tents of the Word of God, which may be better understood as poetry and myth, in terms of systematic philosophical definition do seem to me to have played an important part in developing that distinctive ferality which has marked the attitude of most Christians to others who disagree with them till very recently.

But, of course, to describe Hellenic philosophy in this way is to give a very inadequate idea of it. There was a great deal more to it than the disputes of the schools. We should never forget that aspect of it as 'spiritual exercise', as a quest for enlightenment and liberation, a seeking to attain such likeness to the divine as may be possible for humans, to which Pierre and Ilsetraut Hadot have recently called our attention.[8] And this might often be closely connected with the deep sense of diffidence[9] which is apparent at least in some philosophers from the beginning, which expresses itself in a tendency to self-critical examination in which the principal questions are 'How much, if anything, can we really know, especially about the divine? Isn't wisdom the attribute of the gods? Can we humans ever be more than lovers of and seekers after wisdom (philosophoi)?' This is particularly evident in Plato, and this is important for our purposes, as it was Platonism in the early centuries of our era (as perhaps it has always been since) which exercised the deepest influence on Christian thought of any kind of Hellenic philosophy. The figure of the Platonic Socrates, with his continual profession of ignorance, became for later generations the paradigm of what a philosopher should be. And the Seventh Platonic Letter, in its philosophical digression (342A–344D) expresses with great force the inadequacy of language in dealing with transcendent realities. (The question of the authorship of this is not relevant to our present purposes. In the period with which we are concerned it was accepted as by Plato, and was a text of great authority for Platonists.) And, whatever Plato himself may have intended, there is a great deal in the Dialogues the reading of which can strengthen this tendency to diffidence and encourage the readers to develop it in various ways. It could also, of course, develop independently of any reading or influence of Plato, as a disposition engendered by philosophical reflection on philosophical

---

[8] P. Hadot, *Exercices Spirituels et Philosophie Antique*, 2nd edn, revised and extended (Paris: Etudes Augustiniennes, 1987). I. Hadot, 'The Spiritual Guide', in A. H. Armstrong (ed.), *Classical Mediterranean Spirituality*, Vol. 15 of *World Spirituality* (New York: Crossroad, 1985), 436–459. Cf. A. H. Armstrong, *Expectations of Immortality in Late Antiquity* (Milwaukee: Marquette University, 1987), 22–23.

[9] A. H. Armstrong, 'The Hidden and the Open in Hellenic Thought', *Eranos* **54** (1985), 96–99.

On Not Knowing Too Much About God

encounters, a philosophy, if you like, of philosophical conferences: this was probably the case with Pyrrho.

There are two developments from this original diffidence which, I think, have done something in the past to correct the addiction of Christians to thinking they know and saying much too much about God and may do considerably more in the future, now that the hold of absolute and clear-cut certainties on the minds of religious people is, for a variety of good reasons, steadily weakening and likely to continue to do so in spite of conservative reactions. These are the Apophatic way or Via Negativa of the Neoplatonists and the ancient traditions of Scepticism, the Pyrrhonian and that which developed in Plato's school at Athens, the Academic. The two belong to quite different periods in the history of Hellenic philosophy, the Sceptical to that immediately after Aristotle which it is convenient to call Hellenistic as long as this is not taken to imply too precise a date for its ending, and the Apophatic, which really begins with Plotinus in the third century of our era, to late antiquity. And their main influence on Christian thought has also been exercised at different periods, the Apophatic in patristic and medieval times and the Sceptical from the Renaissance onwards. In view of their common origin in diffidence, their common insistence on the importance of not knowing, and the way in which they can work together harmoniously, in some circumstances, in the minds of religious people, it is tempting to look for some signs of influence of the earlier tendency, the Sceptical, on the later, the Apophatic. But there is little evidence of this, and I do not think that a search for more is likely to get us very far. The dogmatic Platonists of the Roman Empire generally found the sceptical interlude in the history of their school something of an embarrassment, and it seems to me unlikely that Plotinus ever applied his mind seriously to Scepticism in any of its forms, though the possibility cannot be excluded. The following statement by the late Richard Wallis, who before his untimely death had been doing a good deal of research in this area, seems to me to go as far as is reasonably possible in drawing attention to resemblance and suggesting some degree of influence:

How far Pyrrhonism influenced Neoplatonic views on divine unknowability (as later Scepticism certainly influenced Plotinus on other points) remains uncertain. But at least two of its principles are echoed by the Neoplatonists. First, statements about Ultimate Reality are mere expressions of our own attitude thereto; second, negations used of the Supreme must in turn be negated.[10]

[10] A. Wallis, 'The Spiritual Importance of Not Knowing', in *Classical Mediterranean Spirituality* (above n.8) , 465. Wallis's "Scepticism and Neoplatonism", in *Aufstieg und Niedergang der Romischen Welt (ANRW)*, ed.

This certainly indicates that it is worth while taking Scepticism as well as the negative way of the Neoplatonists into account in considering the desirability of not knowing too much about God, and I shall attempt to do so to some extent. But I shall concentrate attention mainly on the Neoplatonic way. This is in accordance with the original intention of this series of lectures and the limitations of my own competence. It is only from the Renaissance onwards that there is any real evidence of serious influence of the ancient Sceptical traditions on Christian thought (as distinct from the polemical trick, very common in early as in later Christian writers, of using Sceptical arguments from the dis-agreements of philosophers as sticks to beat other people's dogmas while maintaining an ultra-dogmatic stance themselves: this I do not find very important, interesting, or attractive). This period lies rather outside our terms of reference, and I know just enough about the Christian thinkers of the sixteenth and seventeenth centuries and later on whom Sceptical influence has been detected to know how little I know.

The Negative Way

That way of thinking towards God which is usually referred to as the 'negative' or 'apophatic' way begins as a serious way of thinking which exercised a strong and deep influence on people who were seriously religious, with Plotinus (205–270CE). There had been anticipations of it in the revived dogmatic Platonism and revived Pythagoreanism of the two centuries before Plotinus, and something like it is to be found in the Gnostics of the same period. There are assertions of the absolute unity and supreme transcendence and unknowability of the first principle of

---

W. Haase and H. Temporini, II 36.2, 912–54, has little to add on Sceptical influence on the negative theology, but does give good reasons for supposing that Plotinus's thought about the divine was influenced at a number of points by Sceptical arguments. David T. Runia, "Naming and Knowing: Themes in Philonic Theology with special reference to the *De mutatione nominum*', in R. van den Broek, T. Baarda and J. Mansfeld (eds), *Knowledge of God in the Graeco-Roman World* (Leiden: Brill, 1988), 69–91, has a very interesting discussion (iv, 82–89) of Philo's theological use of the rhetorical term *katachresis*, the 'abusive' or 'improper' use of language, in which he cites a somewhat analogous use of the word in Sextus Empiricus (*Outlines of Pyrrhonism* I, 207). Though the word *katachresis* is rare in philosophical authors of the first three centuries CE (as Runia notes), and nobody else exploits it theologically as Philo does, the discussion does suggest at least the possibility that there may be some sceptical influence detectable in Plotinus's frequently expressed conviction that all our ways of speaking about the One are improper (particularly evident in VI, 8 (39), 13–18, where he uses the most strongly positive language to be found anywhere in the *Enneads*: cf. also, for the way in which we can use language about the One, VI, 9 (9), 4, 11–14).

On Not Knowing Too Much About God

reality, sometimes placing it above real being (the Platonic Forms) and/or the divine mind which created the universe. Much of the exegesis of the Dialogues of Plato on which Plotinus relies seems to have originated in this period, notably the fantastic explanation of the second part of the *Parmenides*—probably a complete misunderstanding of the intentions of Plato, but one which proved remarkably fruitful. But what made the apophatic way important for later religious thought was the thinking through again, bringing together and developing of these earlier, rather inchoate, ideas by Plotinus, under the pressure of an intense experience of the presence of that which he knew he could not think or speak of, but had to go on trying to do so to keep the awareness awake in himself and wake it in others so that they could share it. In my attempts to speak about this way in its original Hellenic[11] form I shall rely mainly on Plotinus, though without neglecting the developments and clarifications of his thought which are to be found in the later Hellenic Neoplatonists.

The Neoplatonic Negative Way is often described as a way of thinking about God in which it is considered preferable in speaking about him to say what he is not than what he is. Denial gives a better approach to the divine than affirmation. This is true as far as it goes, but rather over-simplified, and can lead to misunderstandings. To understand it better the first thing we need to do is to distinguish between the underlying experience and the intellectual approach to God which it stimulates, and which helps to establish and strengthen it. (It will probably begin to be noticed here that I am rather carefully avoiding the word 'mystic'; and I do not intend to refer to 'ecstasy'. This is in accordance with Plotinus's own usage[12] and will avoid various entirely inappropriate and misleading associations which the words have nowadays.) It is important, however, not to make the distinction too sharp and not to suppose that the experience and the proper following of the intellectual way can be disjoined. This would be anachronistic and misleading. In the Christian tradition, before the disjunctions and

[11] Instead of the rather silly and in intention derogatory word 'pagan', I prefer to use in this context 'Hellene', 'Hellenic' which were used both by the philosophers and their Christian opponents during the period of conflict between Christianity and the old religion when referring to the adherents of the latter and their beliefs and practices.

[12] The adverb *Mustikōs* is used once in the *Enneads* (III, 6 (25), 19, 26), referring not to anything like 'mystical union' but to the secret symbolism of ordinary Greek mystery-rites: the adjective *Mustikos* .and the substantive *Mustēs* do not occur at all. *Ekstasis* may be used once (VI, 9 (9), 11, 23) in the sense of 'being out of oneself' in speaking of union with the One : but here there is a good deal to be said for an emendation of Theiler's which would eliminate the word (see my note ad. loc. in the Loeb Plotinus).

separations of the high Middle Ages, and later, in the West which have led to our being inclined to make very sharp distinctions, first between theology and philosophy, and then between theology and 'spirituality', religious experience and theology went very closely together, as they still do in the Christian East. And for the Hellenes, for whom of course no separation between philosophy and theology was possible, philosophy, and especially that part of it which they called *Theologia*, was always, as has already been said (above p. 132), a 'spiritual exercise', a quest for transforming enlightenment and liberation, a movement towards assimilation to or union with the divine.

The experience which underlies and provides the driving force for the negative way from its beginning and is increasingly realized as it goes on is of course, according to the accounts given of it by those who follow that way in East and West, ineffable, and it is therefore obviously desirable to say as little as possible about it. It would be preferable not to say anything, but it is rather difficult to write a paper about the Negative Way without doing so. Of course it should be made clear at this point that anything I say is second-hand. I do not claim the experience of a true apophatic contemplative like Plotinus, but at most the sort of dim awareness of what he and others are talking about which is necessary for anyone who tries to write or speak about him and which may in fact be quite common: he himself thought that it was universal.[13] What must be said, to avoid a common misunderstanding, is that this growing experience is of something immeasurably positive and that the realization as one follows the negative way to its proper end in the negating of all the negations, that all thought and language is inadequate is immensely liberating and indeed glorifying, because it points on to something that our minds cannot contain. This is why most Neoplatonists[14] retain some positive terms for their goal, above all 'One'

[13] '. . . all men are naturally and spontaneously moved to speak of the god who is in each one of us as one and the same. And if someone did not ask them how this is and want to examine their opinion rationally, this is what they would assume, and with this active and actual in their thinking they would come to rest in this way, somehow supporting themselves on this one and the same, and they would not wish to be cut away from this unity' (VI, 5 (23), 1, 2–8; trans. A. H. Armstrong). It is worth reflecting on the fact that Plotinus regards this as commonplace and generally acceptable. It does something to illustrate the closeness in some ways of Neoplatonic thought to that of India, and the change made by centuries of Christianity in the kind of religious statements we regard as obvious and commonplace, whether we believe them or not.

[14] Iamblichus in the fourth century and Damascius and Simplicius in the sixth separated the absolutely transcendent Ineffable from the One/Good. But Proclus (fifth century), the greatest and most precise systematizer among the

On Not Knowing Too Much About God

and 'Good', though they know very well how inadequate they are. 'One' indicates for them the impossibility of applying to the First the divisions, distinctions and separations which alone make discursive thought and discourse possible, and 'Good' acts as a kind of direction-finder or signpost, indicating that what we are travelling to along the way is more and better, not less and worse, than anything we can conceive. This preserves that consonance between religious and moral convictions which seems necessary to prevent any religious reflection from becoming perniciously insane.

This emphasis on the positive power of the experience which generates and is strengthened by the negative way leads necessarily to a consideration of the attitude of negative theologians to the positive or Kataphatic theology which makes affirmative statements about God. This cannot be one of simple exclusion or rejection, for two reasons. The first is that if one is following a way of negation one has to have something solid to negate: a negative theology needs a positive theology to wrestle with and transcend. And if the negation is to be done properly, one has to understand what one is trying to negate: and 'understand' here must be taken in a serious sense, as involving a great deal of hard study and intellectual effort, and some respect for and good will towards the people who make the positive statement one is trying to negate. This of course applies to negations in general, whether one is following the way of negative theology or not. A really good negation cannot be just polemical or journalistic.[15] The second reason, perhaps, goes rather deeper. The great negative theologians, from Plotinus onwards, are always aware as they follow the negative way that in the end they must negate their negations:[16] if not, they will arrive in the end at an empty space neatly fenced by negative dogmas, which is not at all

[15] Cf. Mary Midgley, 'Sneer Tactics', *Guardian* (Wednesday, 7 October 1977): an excellent comment on negation by flippant dismissal.

[16] There is a good account of the negation of negations at the end of the part of the *Commentary on the Parmenides* of Proclus which survives only in Latin:

Parmenides, then, is imitating this and ends by doing away both with the negations and with the whole argument, because he wants to conclude the discourse about the One with the inexpressible. For the term of the progress towards it has to be a halt; of the upward movement, rest; of the arguments that it is inexpressible and of all knowledge, unification. . . . For by means of a negation Parmenides has removed all negations. With silence he concludes the contemplation of the One (*Plato Latinus* III, trans. Anscombe and Labowsky (London: Warburg Institute, 1953), 76–77).

Hellenic Neoplatonists, does not find this necessary: and Plotinus, I believe, would have thought that it showed an insufficient understanding of the odd, flexible, paradoxical, detached use of language which becomes necessary at this level.

where they want to be. So if the negative theologian finds himself becoming captivated by his negations he will immediately negate them vigorously while continuing to bear them in mind and keep them in balance and tension with the positive statements he is impelled to imply in negating them. (At this point one can see how close negative theology can come to ancient Scepticism, as Wallis noted (above p. 133): though I still think the two should be distinguished.) These reasons account for the vast amount of positive theology which is to be found in the works of the great negative theologians, Hellenic and Christian.

What has just been said leads, I think, naturally to a consideration of a kind of description of the Neoplatonic way often used, especially by Christian theologians, as an 'intellectual' or 'philosophical' way. (This is usually intended to be derogatory: 'merely' is either explicitly said or implied.) This is true in a sense, but requires some explanation and qualification. It is true in the sense that those who follow the negative way of Plotinus know that they can only get beyond thought by thinking with the highest possible degree of intensity and concentration through a long course of critical and self-critical reflection and argument. (In the later Hellenic Neoplatonists the position is complicated by their acceptance of a 'theurgic' way deemed to be in some sense superior to the philosophical. But when they follow the philosophical way this still remains true of them.) But what I said earlier about ancient philosophy as spiritual exercise, and the closeness of the way and the underlying experience, should indicate that one has to broaden the meaning of 'intellectual' considerably and use 'philosophical' in a wide and loose way of which a good many present-day philosophers would not approve. Very hard thinking is certainly going on, but it is by some standards decidedly peculiar thinking. One should never in reading Plotinus forget that the experience is primary and that it is apprehended by him and the other Neoplatonists as something given, light from above, voices from on high, a power given in our nature by the Good as our source which impels or lifts us to the Good as our goal. And we go the way it drives and use what it puts in our way, poetry and myth and symbol and paradox as well as straightforward argument.

There is another limitation on the intellectualism of the Hellenic and traditional Christian, Jewish and Muslim Neoplatonists which must also be taken into account. The positive theologies with which they wrestle and which they seek to transcend are of course the theologies of their own traditions, and they take them as they find them. And the intellectual world in which Neoplatonism developed and passed to Christian thinkers was strongly traditionalist in the sense that the authority of whatever one regarded as the authentic tradition was absolute.[17] This remains true even of a thinker as original and indepen-

[17] Cf. A. H. Armstrong, 'Pagan and Christian Traditionalism in the First

On Not Knowing Too Much About God

dent-minded as Plotinus. He does not think it right to disagree know-ingly with Plato. Of course ancient methods of exegesis, as illustrated by the Fathers of the Church expounding the Scriptures or Proclus expounding Plato's *Timaeus* and *Parmenides*, made it much easier to combine traditionalism with considerable freedom of thought. But the intellectual limitation remained, and did a good deal to hamper some possible developments of the negative way. Its influence was real, powerful, and widespread in the Christian patristic and medieval tradi-tion. It is by no means confined to the Dionysian writings and those influenced by them in East and West. It can be observed in the fourth-century Greek Fathers and in predominantly kataphatic thinkers of the West, most notably Augustine and Aquinas. But it does not affect their theology as pervasively as might be expected. It does not make them more tentative about traditional dogmas, or even their own expositions of them, or more tolerant of dogmatic disagreement. (The same is true of Proclus and other late Hellenic Neoplatonists.) I shall return to this briefly in my conclusion.

The attitude of those who follow the way of negation to the external observances of religion, to sacred rites and sacraments and images, can be a good deal more positive than is sometimes supposed. Plotinus himself had little personal use for or interest in them, and perhaps most apophatic contemplatives become more and more independent of them as they advance on the negative way. But he had no objection to his closest associate Amelius being much concerned with external obser-vances, as long as he himself was not required to take part in them.[18] He recognizes their sacredness and value for the vast majority of human beings who need them, and his occasional references to them in the *Enneads* are always respectful. And at least once he shows himself as ready as his pupil, the great anti-Christian controversialist Porphyry, to defend the whole Hellenic inheritance of cult and myth against the growing assaults of Christianity.[19] He is no more detachable from or

[18] Porphyry, *Life of Plotinus* 10, 33–37. On the significance of this story in the context of what we are told in the *Life* about the position of Amelius in the group see A. H. Armstrong, 'Iamblichus and Egypt', *Les Etudes Philos-ophiques* 2–3 (1987) 182–183 and 188, [this volume, study II].

[19] *Enneads* II, 9 (33), *Against the Gnostics*, 9: the key sentence is 1.35–39. 'It is not contracting the divine into one but showing it in that multiplicity in which God himself has shown it, which is proper to those who know the power of God, inasmuch as, abiding who he is, he makes many gods, all depending upon himself and existing through him and from him' (trans. A.H.A.). I have tried to bring out the full significance of this in 'Plotinus and Christianity', to be published in a volume of essays in honour of Edouard des Places.

Three Centuries A.D.', in *Studia Patristica* **XV**, No. 1, E. A. Livingstone (ed.) (Berlin: Akademie-Verlag, 1984), 414–431, [this volume, study IX].

hostile to his Hellenic religious environment than most great Christian contemplatives who have followed the negative way have been from the rites and sacraments of their churches. And the later Hellenic Neo-platonists, in the period of increasingly intolerant Christian domina-tion, were passionate and committed defenders of their whole religious inheritance against the new religion.

This seems to lead naturally to a consideration of another characteris-tic often attributed to the negative way, to some extent rightly, its interiority, One does indeed advance on the way indicated by Plotinus by an intense introspection. One must seek the principle and goal of one's existence, the Good, within oneself. But Plotinus, who very well knows the inadequacy of all such spatial metaphors, prefers to speak of each lower stage which one passes through on the quest as within the higher, so that Soul and its work, the material cosmos, are in the Divine Intellect and Intellect is in the Good. The Good is immediately present at every level, containing and pervading them all, so that the apprehen-sion of it is always not only of it as discovered in, beyond and containing the self but as in, beyond and containing all things, imparting to them, each in their degree, such reality as they have. The supreme moment of union is indeed one of extreme interiority and complete unawareness of self and all else. But this is rare and attained by few. And because of this intimate and immediate presence of the Good in and containing all things, the heightened awareness of it given by the ultimate experience or such communication of it as is possible makes those who have undergone it, or had it fruitfully communicated to them, more aware of this supreme divine presence not only within themselves but in all external and material things, which makes them each and every one theophanies or icons, and as such holy and lovable. It is a constantly recurring experience of those who study Plotinus that he teaches us to love the world: not in a way which makes us want to possess or exploit the things in it, which would be contrary to the whole spirit of Hellenic philosophy, and also, I believe, of authentic traditional Christianity, but in contemplative enjoyment of the light of the Good shining in and on its beauty. This 'iconic' awareness and understanding of the world is one of the most powerful and pervasive legacies of Neoplatonism to the Christian world, apparent in its art and poetry as much as, or more than, its theology and spiritual teaching.

Ancient Scepticism

I shall now try to say something about the ancient Sceptical traditions and the kind of influence they can exercise on religious thinking. This will be very brief for reasons already indicated, and mainly directed to showing both the differences between Sceptical religious thought and

On Not Knowing Too Much About God

the Negative Way and the possibility, in some circumstances, of their working harmoniously together to mitigate dogmatic fanaticism. I shall concentrate on trying to present Scepticism as an attitude or temper of mind rather than on discussing the details of, and differences between the more highly organized, systematic and coherent forms of Sceptical thinking, the Academic Scepticism of Arcesilaus and Carneades and the Neo-Pyrrhonism inaugurated by Aenesidemus.[20] It would of course be absurd and contrary to the intentions of the ancient Sceptics to present any form of Scepticism as a system, or even a collection, of anti-dogmatic dogmas supported by conclusive arguments: for Sceptics all arguments, including their own, are inconclusive: the investigation must always be pursued further. And there may be a subsidiary reason for presenting Scepticism in the way which I have chosen. In spite of the extent to which the Neo-Pyrrhonian Sextus Empiricus was read and used by Christian thinkers in the Renaissance, I am inclined to think that the most pervasive Sceptical influence in the Christian West has been that of the rather weak and watery Scepticism (as it appeared to his contemporaries and to later connoisseurs of the Scepticality of Scepticisms) of Philo of Larissa, as transmitted by the very widely read and influential Cicero. And this urbane, tentative Philonian or Ciceronian Academic Scepticism certainly transmitted itself as an attitude or temper of mind rather than as the tidy parcel of knock-down arguments so efficiently provided by Sextus Empiricus.

The most important thing to understand about ancient Sceptics and those in later times who have been influenced by them is that they do try to remain genuinely open-minded. Their suspense of judgment is real, and does not conceal a negative certainty. This should be remembered when considering Sceptical views on religion and influence on religious thought. When confronted with a metaphysical or religious dogma (as with any other kind) they do not simply deny or reject it: they enquire into it as long as there are any questions to be asked, but at no stage deny that there is something to enquire into (though they do not, of course, affirm this either). If they are Pyrrhonians they may pursue the enquiry only sufficiently far to rest in inconclusiveness and so ensure their own tranquillity. If they are Academics, who really enjoy arguments and are not particularly interested in tranquillity, they will pursue the enquiry indefinitely. In practical, every-day religious life this Sceptical temper is a strong defence against the fanaticism which is so easily bred by

[20] The precise study of ancient Scepticisms from Pyrrho to Aenesidemus has now been made very much easier by the admirable source-book recently produced by A. A. Long and D. N. Sedley, *The Hellenistic Philosophers*, 2 vols (Cambridge University Press, 1987). Their documentation and discussion of the varieties of Scepticism is particularly full, exact and illuminating.

dogmatic certainty. It will often, especially in its more Pyrrhonian forms, tend to conformism. In Christian terms, the Pyrrhonian will tend to be a conservative churchgoer who does not actually believe anything, or, quite often nowadays, a conservative non-churchgoer who thinks that the services which he does not attend should remain in all respects unchanged. This conformism is what the ancient Pyrrhonians explicitly recommend.[21] But Academics who follow Carneades in regarding probability as an adequate guide in everyday life and are capable of enthusiasm may find it quite compatible with strong support for radical reform and even revolutionary change in religious matters.[22]

The main reason for introducing Scepticism into this paper was that it can provide an alternative means to the Negative Way by which Christians can avoid the temptation to know too much about God. It seems therefore important for clarity to distinguish the ways in which they can affect the religious mind. The Negative Way is a very passionate business. It is the awareness of a supremely powerful and attractive presence which drives one on to go beyond the limited statements of dogmatic theology to that which cannot be thought or spoken. Sceptics have their own passions and their own sense of enlightenment and liberation, but these are different from those of the Negative Way. Pyrrho intensely desired, and probably attained, that liberation and peace of mind which comes from the dismissal from the mind of theoretical conclusions (not of course in favour of practical conclusions but in favour of not arriving at any conclusions at all). The Academics had a passion for argument for its own sake, and delighted in showing their skill, as Carneades did so well, by arguing excellently on both sides of a question, thereby satisfying themselves and demonstrating to others that all the arguments anyone can think of are inconclusive and the matter requires further investigation and discussion, so that they can pursue their favourite occupation indefinitely. All Sceptics operate entirely on the level of discursive reason, which the followers of the Negative Way are trying to get beyond. But these are well aware that they must continually be active on this, as on all, levels. So they may find the Sceptics and their arguments a great help in dealing with those who would set up dogmatic blocks to their further progress. And the

[21] Cf. Sextus Empiricus, *Outlines of Pyrrhonism* II, 2. 'In the way of ordinary life we affirm undogmatically that the gods exist and we give them honour and affirm that they exercise providence but against the headlong rashness of the dogmatists we have this to say': . . . there follows a very full statement of the reasons which make it impossible to be certain that anything is the case about the gods.

[22] There is a good statement of the difference indicated here, of course from the Neo-Pyrrhonian point of view, in Sextus Empiricus, *Outlines of Pyrrhonism* I, 228–231.

On Not Knowing Too Much About God

Sceptics, if they are true Sceptics in the ancient Greek style, though they may not share the faith of the followers of the Negative Way, may be open to it if it comes to them because they have no dogmatic blocks. They may help each other to provide some corrective to Christian dogmatic fanaticism, though how effective this will be will depend very much on the religious circumstances of the place and time and the character of the prevailing kataphatic dogmatism, which the Sceptics need in order to criticize it as much as the followers of the Negative Way need it to wrestle with and transcend.

How far in fact did the two tendencies ever work together after the full development of the Negative Way by Plotinus in the third century? There does seem to be one way of thinking in which it may be possible to detect the influence of both, though I would not be too dogmatic about the Sceptical side. This is the tolerant pluralism of the Hellenic intellectual opposition to the new Christian domination in the fourth century, so well expressed by Symmachus (who certainly read Cicero) and Themistius (an independent-minded philosopher-orator, of pre-dominantly Aristotelian tendency, who might well have known something of the Sceptics).[23] This, however, is hardly relevant to our main subject, as it was furiously rejected by the leaders of Christian thought at the time, and the rejection was maintained throughout the centuries of Christian domination, as it still is by conservative theologians. It is tempting at first sight to see some Sceptical influence in a way of Christian thinking very much more germane to our main concern, the idea of Eriugena, powerfully developed by Cusanus, that our knowledge of God never attains more than the *Verisimile*, is always *Coniectura*.[24] This, however, I think would be a mistake. It is historically most unlikely, and the development can be adequately accounted for by that deep Platonic and pre-Platonic diffidence about the possibility of adequate and expressible knowledge of the divine about which I spoke earlier (p. 132), which is still powerfully apparent in Plotinus. This is of course the starting-point of the Negative Way, of which Eriugena is one of the greatest Western Christian exponents. Its development by Nicholas of Cusa is worth noting, as his influence on the Christian Platonism of the sixteenth and seventeenth centuries was considerable, and it is here that we can see the strong beginnings of an effective

[23] Symmachus, *Relatio* III, 10; Themistius, *Oration 5*, and the summaries of his lost speech on tolerance before the Emperor Valens in the church historians (Socrates IV, 32, and Sozomen VI, 6–7): cf. Henry Chadwick, 'Gewissen', *Reallexikon für Antike und Christentum* **X** (1978), viii d, col. 1101–1102; A. H. Armstrong, 'The Way and the Ways', *Vigiliae Christianae* **33** (1984), 8–11.
[24] W. Beierwaltes, 'Eriugena und Cusanus', in *Eriugena Redivivus* (Heidelberg: O. Winter, 1987), 328–338.

XV

tentativeness about our knowledge of God, effective in the sense that awareness that 'truth is bigger than our minds', that God is beyond our knowledge, is leading, in a way new in the history of dominant Christianity, to the belief that we should be less dogmatic about our own dogmas and more tolerant and kindly to those who disagree with them. We should, however, observe that negative theology is very much in the background in Renaissance Christian Platonism, when it is there at all, especially in England. The Cambridge Platonists are very uneasy with radical negations.[25] Their admirable tolerance was more directly inspired by a moderate, subtle and flexible Scepticism which seems to derive from the Ciceronian–Philonian Scepticism of which I spoke earlier (p. 141).[26]

On the whole it seems that in the earlier period of Christian history, down to and including the Reformation, the Negative Way, though often powerfully present and with a strong influence on the spirituality and thought of individuals, was always kept very much under control and rather in the background. Apophatic theology was very much dominated by Kataphatic, with which, as I have said, its relationship can never be simply hostile or dismissive. The reasons for this are various.[27] But perhaps the most important is that Christian thought throughout this period was traditionalist in the sense which I indicated above (pp. 138–9) and traditionalist in a particularly rigid, exclusive and authoritarian way. It was only when it began to be considered permissible to disagree with the sacred authorities, the Church and the Bible, that the full possibilities of the Negative Way could develop, and in particular that what Jean Trouillard[28] called the 'critical value of

[25] R. Cudworth, *True Intellectual System of the Universe*, I.4.36, 558. Cudworth was consciously opposed to Scepticism and to the tolerant pluralism of the fourth-century Hellenes: cf. I.4.26, 434–433 and 446–447. The weakening of dogmatic absolutism, especially among the clergy, had not gone very far in his time. There is, however, much more positive attitude to Scepticism in Benjamin Whichcote's *Select Notions (Aphorisms)* I.7.

[26] Cf. Margaret L. Wiley, *The Subtle Knot* (London: Unwin, 1952; reprinted New York: Greenwood Press, 1968); *Creative Sceptics* (London: Unwin, 1966).

[27] I have attempted to suggest and illustrate some of them in a contribution, 'Apophatic-Kataphatic Tensions in Religious Thought from the Third to the Sixth Centuries A.D.', to a volume of essays to be published in honour of John O'Meara.

[28] J. Trouillard, 'Valeur critique de la mystique Plotinienne', *Revue Philosophique de Louvain* **59** (August 1961), 431–434. Trouillard has influenced my personal understanding of the *Via Negativa* greatly; my memorial tribute to him is in 'The Hidden and the Open in Hellenic Thought', *Eranos* **54** (1987), 101–106, [this volume, study V].

On Not Knowing Too Much About God

mysticism' could become manifest. Before that, it might mitigate dog-matic fanaticism by continually leading those who follow it on to a God beyond the dogmas, but it remained compatible with a rigid dogmatism because it took the kataphatic theology which it wrestled with and sought to transcend at its own valuation as the one exclusively true statement at the level of discourse and definition of what had been divinely revealed. The undermining and eventual overthrow of this sort of kataphatic absolutism, in so far as it has been undermined and overthrown, as for many of us it irrevocably has, in recent times, has been due not so much to the following of the Negative Way as to disciplines and ways of thinking which derive from that Hellenic tend-ency to continual critical questioning which found its clearest theoreti-cal formulations in ancient Scepticism. It is for this reason that in our present situation, when more and more even of those who retain a deep and strong religious faith feel that they know less and less about God, it has seemed to me important to distinguish the parts played by the Negative Way of the Neoplatonists and the ways of the Sceptics in leading towards a salutary and liberating ignorance in which faith rests on the Unknowable and is nourished by silence.

INDEX

Abammon: II 179
Abraham: XIV 121
Absolutism: VII 47–50, 52, 54, 56
Academy: V 89–90, 92–3, 104; IX 416;
 XII 31
 Old: IV 154; VII 80
Academics: VII 49, 58 n1; XV 141–2
 Academic, The: VII 58 n.1
Achilles: XIII 14
Ackrill, J.L.: V 97 n.17
Alcibiades: IV 70
Alcibiades, The: III 34; VI 175 n.25
Acropolis: IV 57
Adoniazousae: IV 53
Adonis: IV 52; VI 152
Aeschylus: IV 58; XII 33
Alcinous: IX 416
Alexander of Aphrodisias: IX 415
Alexandria: VIII 81; IX 428
Ambrose: VIII 82; XIV 119
Amelius: II 182, 185, 188
Ammianus: V 106; XV 129
Ammonius: IX 420; X 9
Ammonius Saccas: IX 429
Anaximander: V 87
Anchises: IV 54
Anebo: II 1n.2, 179
Antigone: IV 55
Antiochus of Ascalon: IX 415
Apeiron: VI 180
Aphrodite (Venus, Diana): IV 54, 56–7;
 XIV 130
Apokatastasis: V 113, 116
Apolline: VI 176, 181
Apollo: II 182; IV 57; V 82; VI 176,
 177
Aquinas, Thomas: II 185; VI 179; V
 102; VII 58n.5
Archimedes: VI 161n.5
Archons: XII 44
Armstrong, John: VI 159
Aristophanes: VI 152

Asherah: XIV 115
Arian(ism): III 36; VIII 95
Aristotelianism: IX 417
Aristotle: I 183; IV 61, 71; V 90, 92–3,
 97n17, 99, 109, 113; VI 154, 157,
 165; VII 48; IX 415–16; XI 397–8,
 400; XII 31n1, 32; XV 131
Aristoxenus: V 93
Arius: III 36; *see* Arian
Arnobius: VIII 80
Arsinoe, Queen: IV 52
Assyrian: II 1
Artemis: IV 57
Athanasius: VIII 84
Athanassiadi-Fowden, D.C.: XIII 5
Athena: I 186; II 183; XIII 14
Athens: I 186; IV 57, 59, 65; V 104; VI
 172; IX 420; XIV 109, 113,
 115–18, 122, 125, 128, 130; XV
 133
Atlantis: IV 80
Atticus: XI 399–400; XII 35–6; XIV
 130; XV 131
Augustine: II 185; III 31n.2; (Augustin)
 V 102; VI 174; VII 58n.5; VIII
 82–3; IX 430; XII 49, 51–2; XIII 5,
 10
Authupostata: VI 169n.17

Basil, Saint: XIII 8
Baynes, N.: IV 53
Beethoven, Ludwig: XII 42
Beggary: V 98
Blake, W.: IV 68n.11; VI 161n.5,
 164–5, 179
Bloch, E.: I 185
Blumenthal, H.J.: IV 80n.22
Boethus (of Sidon): V 114
Bonanate, U.: VI 154
Bray, Vicar of: XIII 13
Bréhier. E.: II 182; V 50; VI 171; XI
 401

British Museum: VI 151
Bruns, B.: VII 60n.17
Brown, P.: XII 49n.42, 50; XIV 106n.1
Browning, R.: II 184
Brunner, A.: IV 65n.8
Bubastis: II 185
Bultmann, R.: VII 59n.10
Burkert, W.: V 88
Buddhism: XIV 121
Byzantium: VIII 98

Calvary: XIV 125
Cambridge Platonists: XV 144
Cantwell-Smith, W.: VII 53
Carneades: XV 142
Carpocratians: IX 415
Celsus: IV 54, IX 417
Cézanne: XII 29
Chadwick, H.: IX 417; XIII 8
Chaldean: IV 81
  Oracles: II 180; VIII 77
Chartres: II 185
China: XV 121
Christ: XII 52; VIII 78, 97
  Way of: XIV 124
Christianity: I 185; V 82; VIII 76, 79, 88, 98; IX 427; XIII 1, 2, 3, 11; XIV 105, 106, 116, 117, 120-22, 126-8, 130; XV 129-31, 140
  Nicene: XIII 12
Christian(s): II 188; III 31; VIII 74-5, 80-83, 86-9, 91, 97, 99; IX 415, 417-18, 422, 424, 426; X 8-9; XIII 1-2, 4, 7-8, 12-15; XIV 114, 116-17, 122-4, 128-9; XV 129-33, 142
  Non-Gnostic: XII 48-9
  Platonist: V III
Chrysippus: XI 398-9
Church(es): IX 427; XIV 113, 118
  Donatist: XIV 119
  Great: XIV 118
  Greek Imperial: XIV 120
  Orthodox: IV 78
Cicero: VIII 99; XIII 10; XV 141, 143
Clement of Alexandria: VIII 85, 87, 89, 96; IX 425, 428, 430
Colonus: I 184; IV 55
Comedy (Old): VI 152
Conflagration: V 113, 116
Constantine: I 185; XIII 1, 2, 5, 11, 12; XIV 117, 119, 120

Constantinople: IV 53; XIV 124 (= New Rome)
Constantius: XIII 13
Cornford, F.M.: XII 33
Craftsman, The Divine: XI 399; XII 32, 33, 52
Creation: VII 53
Creator: VIII 91; IX 422
Croesus: V 85
Crouse, R.D.: X 8n.1
Corrigan, E.: IV 69n.12
Clark, S.: V 100
Croton: V 89
Cross (Christian): XII 52
Cusa, Nicholas of: III 31; XV 143
Cyprian, Saint: V 116

Dalhousie, University of: IX 429
Damascius: V 104; VI 175; XIII 6
Decapolis: VII 53
Delphi: IV 57
Demeter: IV 54
Demiurge: III 33-4; XIII 43-4
De Mysteriis: II 181
Dialogues: V 89, 99; VII 61n.23; X 10; XV 132, 135
Diana (of Ephesus): I 181
Dillon, J.: VIII 99; XI 399
Diogenes of Babylon: V 114
Dionysius: III 31; IV 57; V 91; VI 173-7; VII 55, 61n.19; VIII 92
Diotima: IV 69-70; V 98
Divine: I 186; II 181; IV 65; V 82
  Fire: V 113
  Intellect (Nous) (Intellection): I 185; IV 74; V 101; VI 156, 162, 165, 169 – or being: III 31
  Persons: VIII 94
  Reason: XII 32
Dodds, E.R.: II 180; IV 81; V 104, 112; VI 165; IX 429
Doric: VI 152
Dörrie, H.: V 94n.13; III 31; IX 418
Drake, H.A.: XIII 11
Dreaming Nature: VI 159, 160
Dualism: VIII 76; XII 29
  Cosmic: XII 29
Dunsany, Lord: V 82
Dyad: VI 180; XII 32, 40
  Indefinite: XII 31

Egypt: II 180

Einsiedeln: II 185; XIV 109
Eleusis: IV 54
Elgin Marbles: VI 151
Empedocles: IX 421
Empire: XIV 118, 121, 123
  Christian: XIV 107
  Pagan: XIV 107
  Eastern: XIV 107
  Western: XIV 107
  Roman: V 84; XIII 2, 11; XIV 117,
    121; XV 133
  Persian: XIII 11
Enchiridion (of Epictetus): I 186
England: XIII 1; XV 123
Enneads: III 32; VI 155, 160, 170; VIII
    75, 81; IX 420, 421; X 7; XI 397
  Sixth: VI 155
Entrepreneurial Spirit: V 98
Ephesus: XIII 11
Epicurean(ism): I 183; V 97; VI 160n.4;
    VIII 76, (ism) 79; IX 415, 426; XI
    398
Eranos: IV 49, 58; VI 178; XIV 107,
    114
Eriugena, Duns Scotus: III 35,
    (*Periphyseon*); X 11, 12; XV 143
Eros: IV 57; V 98, 103; XII 46
Eternal Recurrence: V 113, 115–17
Eucharist: 14
Eudemus of Rhodes: V 113
Eumenides: IV 58
Eunapius: II 186
Eunomius (the Anomoean): III 36; VIII
    94
Euripides: IV 57
Europe: XIV 107, 108, 121, 124, 130
Eusebius of Caesarea: VIII 81, 99; IX
    425; XV 131
Eustochius: VIII 81

Father: III 33; XII 44, 45, 48
Fall, The: VII 53
Fairyland (Elfland): V 81, 82
Festugiere, A.J.: I, 186, 187; II 185
Ficino: VI 170
Findlay, J.N.: V 92 & n.10; VIII 89
First Hypostasis: III 31
  Second: III 32
First Principle: I 186; VIII 92; *see* Nous
Forms: IV 66, 67; VI 148, 154; XII 32,
    46, 48
Fortin, E.L.: XIII n.8

Franz, Marie-Louise von: II 187n.24

Galen: VIII 85
Gallienus: XIII 4
Gallus: XIII 13
Gentile(s): VIII 76
Gersh, S. VII 61n.19
Gnostics: VI 154, 175; VIII 75, 76; IX
    418, 423; XII 41, 43, 45–7, 51; XV
    134
  or Marcionites: IX 423
  Christian: V 100; VIII 75
Gnosticism: VIII 76; IX 423; XII 29, 42
God (One): XIV 111, 114–16
  One True: XIV 116
  Word of: XIV 114; XV 132
  -Man, Jesus Christ: XIV 114
  Man: XV 130
Good (One): II 182; IV 66, 73, 75, 76,
    78, 80; V 93, 103, 111, 112; VI
    158, 163, 164, 167, 169, 170, 174,
    180, 181; VII 52; IX 424; XI 398,
    401, 403, 404; XII 37, 39, 40; XIV
    110; XV 136, 137, 138, 140; *see
    also* One (Good)
Gorgo: IV 53; VI 152
Gospels: XIV 119, 131
Gratian: XIII 2, 12
Great Divine Artist: VI 157
  Architect: VIII 91
  Year: V 113, 115
Greece: V 89; IX 419 (Classical); XIV
    105
Greeks: IV 58; V 83, 87, 106
Gregory of Nyssa: VIII 82, 94
Guthrie, W.K.C.: V 97n.17

Hades: VI 174
Hadot, P.: IV 73 & n.15, 80; V
    112n.32; VI 165, 173–5; VII 58n.4,
    60n.14; VIII 95; XIII 31, 32, 35;
    and I.: XV 132
Harder, R.: V 94; and Theiler; XI 401
Harnack: VII 62; X 12
Harran (Carrhae): XIV 121, 122
Harris, R. Baine: IV 50n.1
Heaven, Road to: V 81
Hebrews: XV 115
Hector: XIII 14
Hegel: VI 179
Helen (of Troy): IV 53
Helicon, *see* Olympus

Hell: V 81
Hellenes, Hellenism: I 180; V 83, 106, 107, 109, 110; VI 150; VII 74; X 8, 9; XIII 5, 13; XIV 117, 121, 122, 127, 129; XV 136
Henad(s): I 186; III 33; V 101; VII 53; XII 48
Helios-Mithras: XIII 6
Heraclitus: V 87
Hereford: IV 71
Herodotus: V 85, 106, 109; VII 49; XIII 9, 10
Hierocles: IX 416
Hippolytus: XI 403
Homer: IV 53; IX 420; XIII 15
Hylas: IV 52
Hypatia: XIII 11
Hyperboreans (Land of the): V 81
Hypostasis, First: III 31
  Second: III 32

Iamblichus: II 179; IV 78; VI 170, 180–81, 183–4, 186–8; VIII 94, 95; XIII 10; XIV 120
Ideal Numbers: XII 31
Incarnation: VII 56
India: I 181; IV 50; VII 56; VIII 78; XIV 114
Intellect: IV 74, 76; III 33; XV 140
  Divine, see Divine
Isis and Osiris: IX 420
Irenaeus: VIII 84; IX 423
Itineraries: XIV 105
Islam: IV 50; XV 130

Jaspers, B.: VII 59n.10
Jenkins, D.: V 112n.33
Jeremiah, Book of: XIV 115
Jerusalem: XIV 113, 114, 117, 124, 125
  New: 124
Jesus: VII 53; VIII 97; XIV 114
  Christ: XII 48
  of Nazareth: 118
Jews: VIII 78; XIII 5
Joachim: XI 398
Jonas, H.: V III
Jones, A.H.M.: XIII 5
Jovian: XIII 2, 8, 12; XIV 122
Judah: XIV 115
Judaism: VIII 74, 76; XV 130

Judgement, The: I 1; II passim; V 107, 108
Julian, Emperor: I 188; II 188; XIII 2, 5–8, 12–14; XIV 117, 119–20, 122, 128, 129
Jung: IV 49
Justin: VIII 85, 96; IX 430
  Pseudo: XI 404
Justinian: I 186

Kenney, J.: XIV 110
Keynes, G.: IV 69n.11
Kingdom, The: V 107, 108
Klimkeit, H.-J.: VI 181n.36

Lac d'Annecy: VI 152
Laws, The: II 181; V 92; XII 31
Lee, E.N.: VIII 91
Leighton, Sir Frederick (Lord): VI 151
Leo the Great, Saint: XIII 15
Lewis, C.S.: V 82
Liebeschuetz, J.H.W.G.: XII 50
Lloyd, A.C.: II 181, 183, 185; III 34n.12, 35; IV 80n.22
Logos: I 187; V 87, 111; VII 56; IX 418, 421; X II
  2nd Nous: VIII 94
  Son: VIII 94
  Unitary: XII 34, 35
Long, A.A.: V 84 & n.2; VII 58n.1
Longinus: II 188; VIII 81; IX 426

Macdonald, G.: V 82
Manchester, P.: V 107; VI 161n.5
Mani: XII 51
Manichees: XII 49, 51
Mann, U.: V 108n.30
Marcion: VIII 75
Marcus Aurelius: V 97
Margouliouth, H.M.: IV 71n.13
Marius Victorinus: VIII 82
Markus, R.A.: X 9
Maximus, Saint: XIII 6
Meijering, E.P.: VII 60n.18, 61; VIII 84; IX 422, 423; X 12n.12
Merlin, P.: II 182n.16
Metaphysics, The: V 109
Methodius of Olympus: XI 402
Middle Ages: IV 60
Middle Platonist(s): III 32; VI 158; VIII 94; IX 416; XI 399; XII 47, 49
Milan: XIII 13

Milesians: V 87
Moderatus (of Gades): XII 34–6
Molière: II 187
Moscow (Third Rome): XIV 124
Monotheism: I 184
Montaigne: VIII 98
Moses: VIII 78
Moule, C.F.D.: VII 54
Mother Maria (Lydia Gysi): V 98; III 36
Mount Carmel: XV 125
Murdoch, I.: IV 65n.8; VII 52
Murray, G.: VII 54, 60n.13

Narcissus: VI 179
Narnia: V 82
Nag Hammadi Library: VII 41
Naassenes: IX 415
Nature: VI 161, 168, 174
Negative Way (Via Negativa): XV 133, 135, 136, 141–5
Neoplatonist(ism): I 185; II 180–81, 184–5, 188; IV 76–8, 81; III 31, 33, 34; V 89–90, 95–6, 100–105, 115; VI 166, 168, 176, 177, 179; VII 51, 54, 55; IX 416, 417, 424, 430; X 10; XII 37, 49; XIII 5, 6, 10, 11; XIV 109, 111, 120, 127; XV 133, 134, 136, 138, 140, 145
  Hellenic: I 31; III 36; XV 138
  Christian: III 36
Neo-Neoplatonism: VII 47
Nestorius: XIII 11
Nicea, Council of: VIII 94; XI 404
Nicomachean Ethics: XI 398
Nilsson, M.P.: V 85
Nineham, D.: VII 59n.12
Nothing: VI 181
Nous: III 31, 33; X 11; XIV 113
Numenius: VIII 91, 92, 99; IX 416, 420, 425, 426, 429; XII 34, 36, 44, 48

Oedipus: IV 58, 59
Olympus (Parnassus): XV 125
One (Good): I 185–7; II 182; III 32; IV 74, 79; V 102; VI 162; VIII 90, 93, 96; XI 401; XII 32, 34, 40, 48; XIV 111, 116
  Ones: III 32
  Being: III 32
  God: XIV 111, 116
  True God: XIV 116

Page, D.L.: IV 57n.6
Pagel, E.: X 11n.8
Pan: IV 57; V 82
Panaetius: V 114
Parmenides, The: V 87, 92; III 31, 34, 35; VIII 93; XV 135
  Commentary on: III 32
Parousia: XII 48
Parthenon: IV 81
Pepin, J.: V 93n.11
Pegasus: XIII 13–15
People of God: VII 55
Persephone: IV 54
Persia: VIII 76, 78; XIII 7; XV 120
Peter, Saint: XIII 15
Phaedrus: V 90, 92
Philo of Alexandria: VIII 85, 87
Philosophy: XIV 112; XV 130
  Greek: III 31
Pisistratus: V 86
Places, E. des: II 187; IX 425
Plato: I 182, 183; IV 64–6, 69–71; V 88–9, 91–3, 97–100, 112, 114; VI 147–9, 151, 157; VII 48, 52; VIII 79, 80, 85, 87, 91; IX 416, 419, 421, 424, 426, 428, 430; X 7; XI 397, 399; XII 31, 32, 36, 42; XIV 128; XV 130, 132, 135
Platonism: II 182; IV 72, 74, 78; V 94, 104; VI 147, 154, 170–72, 179; VIII 78, 80–84; IX 417, 423; XII 37, 45; XIV 134; XV 132
  or Stoicism: VIII 75
  pre-Plotinian: VIII 82
Platonists: I 183; III 35; IV 49, 61, 64, 67, 70, 72, 75; V 99, 109, 111, 112, 115; VI 148, 157, 170, 171, 172; VII 47, 48; VIII 75, 79, 80, 88; IX 415, 423, 426; X 7
  Christian: III 36; see Christian
  Middle: see Middle Platonists
  Later: XII 31
pleroma (World of Light): XII 48
Plotinus: I 183–5; II 182–4, 186–7; III 50, 63, 67, 69, 73–9, 81; V 84, 91, 94, 95, 100, 101, 103, 104, 111, 114; VI 147, 149, 153, 154, 156–9, 162–4, 168, 170, 171, 173, 174, 177–9; VII 47, 51; VIII 75, 81–3, 85, 88, 90, 92, 94–7; IX 414, 416–18, 420–21, 423–5, 428–30; X 7–9, 11, 12; XI 388, 397–404;

(*Plotinus continued*) XII 37, 39, 40, 42, 44–8; XIII 3, 6, 10; XIV 111, 116n.9; XV 131, 133–5, 137–40, 143
Plutarch: VI 157; VIII 83, 90, 91; XII 35, 36
Polemo: IX 426
Polybius: V 106, 114; XV 113
Porphyry: II 179, 182, 183, 186, 187; III 31, 32; V 94, 95; VI 160; VII 58n.4; VIII 75; IX 416–18, 421, 424, 426; X 7; XII 34, 48; XIII 10
Posidonius: V 113
Praxinoa: IV 53; VI 152
Primal Light: IV 80
Press, G.A.: V 107n.28
Proclus: I 186; II 180, 183; III 32–5; IV 78, 80, 81; V 101, 112n.32; VI 148, 163, 170, 175, 180; VII 47, 52, 61n.19; VIII 82; IX 416n.8, 420; XII 30, 36; XIII 6
Psellus: II 186; IV 53
Pyrrho: XV 133, 142
Pyrrhonians: XV 141
Pyrrhonism: XV 133
    Neo-:XV 141
Pythagoras: V 88; VIII 78, 85, 87; IX 415, 421, 424, 426
Pythagoreanism: V 88; VIII 78, 81, 82, 92; IX 421; XII 35; XV 134
    Neo-: VIII 80
Pythagoreans: V 88, 93, 94, 100, 113; VIII 75, 88, 90; IX 421; XII 36
    Earlier: XII 40
    Brotherhood: V 88
    Old: V 89
    Table of Opposites: XII 31

Quakers: II 187
Quintessence: IV 62

Raine, K.: VI 165 & n.13
Raven, J.E.: V 113n.34
Ravindra, R.: IV 50n.1
Redeemer: XII 43
Renaissance: IV 60; VII 49; XV 134
Republic, The: IV 66
Resurrection: 59n.10
Ridler, A.: IV 71n.13
Rome: VIII 81; X 9; XI 403; XIV 126
    Old: XIV 124, 126
    New: *see* Constantinople
    Third (Moscow): XIV 124

Romes: XV 129
Roman Empire: VIII 74, 78, 84 *see also* Empire
Ross, W.P.: V 94n.12

Saffrey, H.D.: IV 80; V 101; VI 180n.35
    & Westerink, L.G.: II 181, 185
Sappho: IV 56, 57
Schwyzer, H.R.: V 95
Sceptic(ism): VIII 76, 98, 99; IX 430; XV 133, 134, 138, 141–3, 145
Sceptical, The: XV 133
Scholem, G.: XIV 114
Scriptures (Bible): XIV 114, 115
    Old Testament: XIV 115; XV 131
Second Hypostasis, *see* First Hypostasis
Seventh (Platonic) Letter (Letter VII): III 32, 34; V 90, 95, 97; XV 130
Seven Liberal Arts: VI 165
Sextus Empiricus: XV 141
Sheppard, A.D.R.: IV 80n.22; XII 40
Simplicius: I 186; XII 34
Smith, A.: II 181
Smith, John: IX 414, 415
Socrates: IV 70; V 91; IX 419; XIII 9
Solomon: XIII 9
Solon: V 85
Sophocles: I 184; IV 55, 59
Soul: I 185; IV 76; XV 140
Sperling, D.: XV 115n.8
Speusippus: V 100; VIII 93; IX 426
Spirit, The: VIII 88, 94; IX 423; XV 131
Stead, C.: VII 51
Stoic(ism): I 183; IV 60; V 97, 113, 116, 117, 157; VI 157, 158; IX 415; XI 398; XIII 3
    Middle: V 113
    Old: V 113
    Supreme: XV 133
Symmachus: XIII 8
Symposium, The: V 90, 97
Syrianus: IV 80; VIII 82; XII 30, 40
Szlezak, T.: V 90, & n.6, 91, & n.9, 95, 104

T'ang: II 185
Tardieu, M.: XV 121, 122
Taylor, A.E.: VI 157
Tertullian: VIII 79, 88, 89; IX 428n.11, 430; XV 109

Thales: V 87
Themistius: XIII 8; XV 143
Theocritus: IV 52, 53
Theodosius: II 11; XIII 1, 2; XIV 119; XV 123
Theophrastus: I 183; V 88
Theurgy: II 180, 184
Third Path: V 81
Thucydides: V 106, 109
Timaeus, The: III 33; V 112; VI 149, 156, 157, 159, 179; VII 61n.23; VIII 75; XI 399; XII 32–5, 37, 40, 46, 47, 50; XV 139
Titans: VI 175
Torah: XV 114
Traherne, Thomas: IV 71
Trinity: VII 53, 55; VIII 94; XIII 11
Trouillard, J.: II 181; V 101–5; VI 167; VII 51, 52 & n.8, 55; XII 41; XV 144
Troy: IV 53; XIII 13
Tyche: V 86

Ueda, S.: VI 181 n.36
Unbounded: IV 80
Unknowable: I 187; V 102
  God: VII 50, 56
  One: I 187; VII 52; XV 145
Unknown God: I 186

Upper Cosmos: IV 60, 63, 68

Valens: XIII 8, 12; XV 122
Valentinian: XIII 2, 12; XV 122
Vlastos, G.: XII 32n.2

Wallis, R.T.: XIII 9; XV 133n.10
Walsh, M. J.: XIII n.1
Waszink, J.H.: IX 418n.10, 423
Whittaker, J.: IV 67, n.10; VI 169n.17; IX 416n.4
Wiles, M.: III 36; VII 53
Wiseman, T.P.: V 107n.28
World of Forms: III 32; IV 73–6; VI 148, 156, 166, 169, 171; VIII 93; XII 32, 39
Wurm, K.: III 32

Xenocrates: IX 426
Xenophanes: XIII 9

Yahweh: XIV 115
Yang-Yin: IV 79; XII 30, 31
Yogas: II 188

Zen: VI 181n.36
Zeno: IX 416
Zoroaster: IX 418
Zurich: XV 109

DATE DUE

MAY 0 9 1996